The Future of Evidence-Based Policing

Evidence-based policing (EBP) has become a key perspective for practitioners and researchers concerned with the future of policing. This volume provides both a review of where evidence-based policing stands today and a consideration of emerging trends and ideas likely to be important in the future. It includes comparative and international contributions, as well as researcher and practitioner perspectives. While examining traditional evidence-based methods and approaches, the book also identifies barriers to the advancement of evidence-based policing and expands the vision of evidence-based policing by critically examining ethical and moral concerns and questions. The book's main focus is not on what has to happen in police agencies to advance EBP, but rather on an issue that has received far less attention – the science that is necessary to produce for EBP to be successfully integrated into policing.

David Weisburd is Distinguished Professor of Criminology, Law, and Society at George Mason University, and Walter E. Meyer Professor Emeritus of Law and Criminal Justice at the Hebrew University of Jerusalem.

Tal Jonathan-Zamir is an Associate Professor at the Institute of Criminology, Faculty of Law, the Hebrew University of Jerusalem.

Gali Perry is a Lecturer at the Institute of Criminology, Faculty of Law, the Hebrew University of Jerusalem.

Badi Hasisi is Full Professor and Chair of the Institute of Criminology, Faculty of Law, the Hebrew University of Jerusalem.

The Future of Evidence-Based Policing

Edited by

DAVID WEISBURD
George Mason University/The Hebrew University of Jerusalem

TAL JONATHAN-ZAMIR
The Hebrew University of Jerusalem

GALI PERRY
The Hebrew University of Jerusalem

BADI HASISI
The Hebrew University of Jerusalem

Shaftesbury Road, Cambridge CB2 8EA, United Kingdom

One Liberty Plaza, 20th Floor, New York, NY 10006, USA

477 Williamstown Road, Port Melbourne, VIC 3207, Australia

314–321, 3rd Floor, Plot 3, Splendor Forum, Jasola District Centre, New Delhi – 110025, India

103 Penang Road, #05–06/07, Visioncrest Commercial, Singapore 238467

Cambridge University Press is part of Cambridge University Press & Assessment, a department of the University of Cambridge.

We share the University's mission to contribute to society through the pursuit of education, learning and research at the highest international levels of excellence.

www.cambridge.org
Information on this title: www.cambridge.org/9781108840354
DOI: 10.1017/9781108885737

© Cambridge University Press & Assessment 2023

This publication is in copyright. Subject to statutory exception and to the provisions of relevant collective licensing agreements, no reproduction of any part may take place without the written permission of Cambridge University Press & Assessment.

First published 2023

A catalogue record for this publication is available from the British Library.

Library of Congress Cataloging-in-Publication Data
NAMES: Weisburd, David, editor. | Jonathan-Zamir, Tal, editor. | Perry, Gali, 1976– editor. | Hasisi, Badi, editor.
TITLE: The future of evidence-based policing / edited by David Weisburd, Tal Jonathan-Zamir, Gali Perry, Badi Hasisi.
DESCRIPTION: Cambridge ; New York, NY : Cambridge University Press, 2023. | Includes bibliographical references and index.
IDENTIFIERS: LCCN 2022051629 | ISBN 9781108840354 (hardback) | ISBN 9781108794558 (paperback) | ISBN 9781108885737 (ebook)
SUBJECTS: LCSH: Police. | Police administration.
CLASSIFICATION: LCC HV7921 .F888 2023 | DDC 353.3/6–dc23/eng/20230308
LC record available at https://lccn.loc.gov/2022051629

ISBN 978-1-108-84035-4 Hardback
ISBN 978-1-108-79455-8 Paperback

Cambridge University Press & Assessment has no responsibility for the persistence or accuracy of URLs for external or third-party internet websites referred to in this publication and does not guarantee that any content on such websites is, or will remain, accurate or appropriate.

Contents

List of Figures		*page* vii
List of Tables		viii
List of Contributors		ix
List of Editors		xii
1	The Future of Evidence-Based Policing: Introduction *David Weisburd, Tal Jonathan-Zamir, Gali Perry,* *and Badi Hasisi*	1
	PART I TAKING STOCK OF EVIDENCE-BASED POLICING	
2	Three Tiers for Evidence-Based Policing: Targeting "Minimalist" Policing with a Risk-Adjusted Disparity Index *Lawrence W. Sherman*	19
3	Re-inventing Policing: Using Science to Transform Policing *Peter Neyroud and David Weisburd*	44
4	A Way Ahead: Re-envisioning the Relationship between Evidence-Based Policing and the Police Craft *James J. Willis and Heather Toronjo*	64
	PART II THE EVIDENCE FOR EVIDENCE-BASED POLICING	
5	A Review of Systematic Reviews in Policing *Cody W. Telep and David Weisburd*	85
6	What Do We Know about Proactive Policing's Effects on Crime and Community?: Drawing Conclusions from a National Academies of Sciences, Engineering, and Medicine Report *David Weisburd, Anthony A. Braga, and Malay Majmundar*	107
7	Rethinking the Role of the Community in Proactive Policing *Charlotte Gill*	126

PART III INNOVATIONS IN TOOLS OF EVALUATION AND ASSESSMENT

8 The Role of Randomized Experiments in Developing the Evidence for Evidence-Based Policing   147
Lorraine Mazerolle, Elizabeth Eggins, Lorelei Hine, and Angela Higginson

9 The Potential Contribution of Subjective Causality to Policing Research: The Case of the Relationship between Procedural Justice and Police Legitimacy   170
Gali Perry, Tal Jonathan-Zamir, and James J. Willis

PART IV CHALLENGES TO THE IMPLEMENTATION OF EVIDENCE-BASED POLICING

10 Practitioners' Inclination to Rely on Experience: What Does This Mean for Evidence-Based Policing?   193
Tal Jonathan-Zamir and David Weisburd

11 Implementing Evidence-Based Policing: Findings from a Process Evaluation of the EMUN Reform in the Israel Police   211
Yael Litmanovitz, David Weisburd, and Badi Hasisi

12 Towards Implementing Evidence-Based Policing: Challenges in Latin America and Caribbean   235
Laura Jaitman

13 Evidence-Based Policing and the Law: The American Perspective   252
Rachel Harmon

PART V THE PRACTITIONER'S PERSPECTIVE

14 The Role of the "Super Evidence Cop" in Evidence-Based Policing: The Israeli Case   273
Simon Perry and Michael Wolfowicz

15 Looking Back on the Challenges to Evidence-Based Policing: A Chief's Perspective   292
Darrel Stephens

16 Support for Evidence-Based Policing at the National Level: More Help Than Harm?   315
James H. Burch, II

17 Conclusions: Police Science and the Future of Evidence-Based Policing   336
David Weisburd, Tal Jonathan-Zamir, Gali Perry, and Badi Hasisi

Index   359

Figures

2.1	Homicide victimization rate per 100,000 for the age group 16–24, England and Wales 2008–2018 (reprinted from Kumar et al., 2020, Figure 2)	page 25
7.1	Logic model for proactive policing and community outcomes (reproduced from Weisburd and Majmundar, 2018, Fig. 5.1, p. 180)	129
7.2	Illustration of the relationship between program, change lever, and outcome (adapted from Wilson, 2019)	137
7.3	Proposed simplified logic model for the role of community outcomes as change levers	138
8.1	Prisma	153
8.2	Types of design	155
8.3	Types of designs over time	156
11.1	Screenshots of the EMUN crime analysis computer system	217
12.1	Intentional homicide rates per 100,000 population, 1995–2018	237
12.2	Police personnel and homicide rates	242
12.3	(a) Citizen confidence in the police in LAC, 2018; (b) Perception of Proportion of police members involved in corruption in LAC, 2018	243
15.1	Directed patrol: A concept in community-specific, crime-specific, service-specific policing	296
15.2	Problem solving: Problem-oriented policing in Newport News	303

Tables

3.1	Changing to a science-based policing paradigm	page 56
5.1	Systematic reviews identified by Telep and Weisburd (2016)	87
5.2	Summary of newly identified reviews and main outcomes organized by year	92
5.3	Eligible studies and randomized experiments by review sorted by proportion of randomized experiments	93
5.4	Summary of community outcome findings from the reviews	95
6.1	Four approaches to proactive policing	110
6.2	Innovations adopted by departments, with and without formal policy, from the 2013 NPRP Survey (N = 76)	112
6.3	Prevalence of use of proactive policing strategies by percentage of agencies responding to the 2012 Future of Policing Survey (N = 200)	112
6.4	Crime outcomes of proactive policing strategies	113
6.5	Effects of police innovation on communities	117
8.1	Types of interventions by study design (N = 1,149)	161
8.2	Number of studies and RCTs by country	162

Contributors

Anthony A. Braga
Department of Criminology
School of Arts and Sciences
University of Pennsylvania

James H. Burch, II
National Policing Institute (Washington, D.C.)

Elizabeth Eggins
Menzies Health Institute
Griffith University

Charlotte Gill
Department of Criminology, Law and Society
George Mason University

Rachel Harmon
School of Law
University of Virginia

Badi Hasisi
Institute of Criminology
Faculty of Law
The Hebrew University of Jerusalem

Angela Higginson
School of Justice
Queensland University of Technology

Lorelei Hine
Australia's National Research Organization for Women's Safety (ANROWS)

Laura Jaitman
Centre for Economic Performance
London School of Economics

Tal Jonathan-Zamir
Institute of Criminology
Faculty of Law
The Hebrew University of Jerusalem

Yael Litmanovitz
Institute of Criminology
Faculty of Law
The Hebrew University of Jerusalem
Myers-JDC-Brookdale Research Institute

Malay Majmundar
National Academies of Sciences, Engineering, and Medicine

Lorraine Mazerolle
School of Social Science
Faculty of Humanities and Social Sciences
The University of Queensland

Peter Neyroud
Institute of Criminology
University of Cambridge

Gali Perry
Institute of Criminology
Faculty of Law
The Hebrew University of Jerusalem

Simon Perry
Institute of Criminology
Faculty of Law
The Hebrew University of Jerusalem

Lawrence W. Sherman
Metropolitan Police

Darrel Stephens
Policing, Security Technology and Private Security Research
 Policy Institute
College of Criminology and Criminal Justice
Florida State University

Cody W. Telep
School of Criminology and Criminal Justice
Arizona State University

Heather Toronjo
Schar School of Policy and Government
George Mason University

David Weisburd
Department of Criminology, Law and Society
George Mason University
Institute of Criminology
Faculty of Law
The Hebrew University of Jerusalem

James J. Willis
Department of Criminology, Law and Society
George Mason University

Michael Wolfowicz
Institute of Criminology
Faculty of Law
The Hebrew University of Jerusalem

Editors

David Weisburd is Distinguished Professor of Criminology, Law, and Society at George Mason University, and Walter E. Meyer Professor Emeritus of Law and Criminal Justice at the Hebrew University of Jerusalem. Professor Weisburd is well known for his research on policing and crime hot spots. He has received many international prizes for his work including the Stockholm Prize in Criminology (2010), the Sutherland (2014) and Vollmer Awards (2017) from the American Society of Criminology, the Israel Prize (2015), the Robert Peel Medal (2022), and the Rothschild Prize in the Social Sciences (2022). He was the Chair of the National Academy of Sciences Panel on Proactive Policing.

Tal Jonathan-Zamir is an Associate Professor at the Institute of Criminology, Faculty of Law, the Hebrew University of Jerusalem. Her work focuses on policing, particularly on police-community relations and evidence-based policing. She has investigated police legitimacy and procedural justice from the perspective of citizens, communities, police officers, and neutral observers, in diverse contexts such as routine encounters, security threats, protest events, and airport security. She has also examined the psychological mechanisms underlying police officers' orientation to evidence-based policing and, more recently – the effects of the COVID-19 pandemic on police-community relations in Israel. Tal is the recipient of the 2010–2011 Fulbright Visiting Scholar Program and the 2015 Early Career Award from the Division of Policing of the American Society of Criminology.

Gali Perry is a Lecturer at the Institute of Criminology, Faculty of Law, the Hebrew University of Jerusalem. Her research focuses on political violence and the policing of protest, political extremism, and terrorism. She has studied protesters' perceptions of and cooperation with the police, the effect of police militarization on public attitudes toward the police, developmental pathways to political extremism, lone-actor terrorism, and aviation security. Recently, she examined the effects of the COVID-19 pandemic on police and public relations. Gali is the recipient of the 2017 Golda Meir fellowship for early-career scholars and the 2019 Ellis and Alma Birk Prize in Law.

Badi Hasisi serves as Full Professor and Chair of the Institute of Criminology, Faculty of Law, the Hebrew University of Jerusalem. His work focuses on the interaction between the community and the criminal justice agencies, with specific emphasis on the particular problems faced by minority groups within the criminal justice system. He also specializes in response to violence, homeland security, and terrorism, evaluating innovations in the criminal justice system, and law and society. He received the 2018 best article prize from the Israeli Organization of Law and History and the Fattal Prize for Excellence in Legal Research and Criminology. Prof. Hasisi also serves as the chair of the Israeli Society of Criminology.

1

The Future of Evidence-Based Policing

Introduction

David Weisburd, Tal Jonathan-Zamir, Gali Perry, and Badi Hasisi

In 1998, at an "Ideas in Policing" lecture at the Police Foundation in Washington, DC, Lawrence Sherman "threw down the gauntlet" to police and researchers to join a movement toward "evidence-based policing" (EBP; see Sherman, 1998). Sherman was not the first scholar to suggest the importance of research evidence in policing, but he was the first to argue that policing should become part of the more general evidence-based policy movement that was gaining strong traction in medicine, education, and other areas of policy science. Sherman did not simply call for more or better use of research evidence in police practice; he called for an approach to policing that would bind academia and policing in a way that had not been done before: the police would not simply use evidence; evidence would become the key element of decision-making about organizational policy and practice (Sherman, 1998).

Sherman's call for EBP was followed by a broad interest in evidence-based policy in crime and justice. In part due to his essay about policing, there has been a growing recognition of the importance of evidence-based policy in reaching decisions about criminal justice programs and practices more generally (e.g., Blomberg et al., 2016; Bueermann, 2012; Cole et al., 2016; Lum & Koper, 2017; Pew Charitable Trusts, 2014; Sherman, 2013; Sherman et al., 2002; Wilson & Petersilia, 2010). Indeed, it is reasonable to say that the idea of evidence-based decision-making has become key not only to theory but also to practice.

In this book, we take stock of how the field of EBP developed since Sherman's seminal lecture, and where it is heading. We try to address specific impediments to EBP in terms of implementation, the research evidence that forms the basis for EBP, and the tools of evaluation and assessment that are used to develop this evidence (e.g., Lum & Koper, 2017; Lum et al., 2012; Weisburd & Neyroud, 2011). But in addition to questions that are often raised by policing scholars, such as "what is the present state of the evidence in EBP?" and "how can we get police agencies to implement EBP?," we also ask more fundamental questions such as does EBP mean that science will *contribute* to decision-making or will it *determine* decision-making? What is the role of practitioners' experience in EBP? What is the practitioner's perspective on EBP, and how does it differ from the perspectives of scientists? Twenty years after Lawrence Sherman's seminal address to the Police Foundation, and with the numerous theoretical and empirical papers that have been published since (e.g., Greene, 2014; Neyroud & Weisburd, 2014; Sherman, 2015; Sparrow, 2011; Willis & Mastrofski, 2014), it is time to look back and to consider the future of EBP. That is the purpose of our volume.

1.1 WHAT IS EVIDENCE-BASED POLICING?

EBP requires that decision-making in policing be strongly influenced by basic and applied research. For example, large-scale policing programs in this context would not be widely implemented without strong scientific evidence of the programs' success. In turn, programs that are implemented would be evaluated and assessed on a regular basis to ensure that they are meeting the goals of the organization. But EBP goes deeper than this because it suggests that science will become an integral part of the police mission, and the police will become advocates in the development of science in policing (Weisburd & Neyroud, 2011). This means that science would be relevant not just for defining whether programs or practices are effective, but also for aiding the police in identifying how they should be managed organizationally, how police officers should be chosen and trained, and how police agencies can encourage positive health outcomes for the police, just to name a few areas of importance that must be informed by science.

Unfortunately, when scholars and practitioners talk about EBP, they generally fall back upon what science tells us about the effectiveness of police practices. This is certainly an important area of focus and one of the key contributions of EBP to policing. And indeed, there have been major strides in the production of evidence about what works, as reflected by a recent review of the National Academy of Sciences, Engineering, and Medicine of proactive policing (Weisburd & Majmundar, 2018), and chapters in our volume that review the evidence base of police practices to reduce crime (see Chapters 5 and 6). There is also a growing body of evidence on outcomes relevant to policing beyond reducing crime, such as community satisfaction and police legitimacy (see Chapter 7). Nevertheless, we think it is a mistake to define EBP in narrow terms, relevant only to questions of "what works." EBP should cover every aspect of police organization and management. Decisions about management styles, for example, the number of police that are needed in a jurisdiction, the way they should be managed, the tools that they should be given, the tasks that they should focus upon, and more, should be informed by science. We believe that this is the essential idea of EBP: that evidence should become a key part of every aspect of police operations.

We are not arguing that EBP has not informed an array of questions and problems in policing. For example, there is a growing body of literature on how the police must change in management style, culture, and recruitment to be amenable to EBP (Lum & Koper, 2017; Sherman, 2013; Telep, 2016). A number of rigorous studies examine questions such as what are the most beneficial work schedules for police (Amendola et al., 2011) or how police investigations can be more effective (Roman et al., 2009; Wilson et al., 2010, 2011). But both advocates and critics of EBP have often focused on the question of "what works," and have left many other key questions that science should inform on the sidelines. The science of EBP in this context needs to expand much beyond its present focus. We return to this issue in more detail in our conclusions.

Similarly, debates over EBP often focus around the use of particular methods, such as experimental designs, to inform police practices. There is a widely held view among critics of EBP that its major contribution lies in the advocacy of rigorous experimental field trials, to the exclusion of other methods of gaining knowledge in science (Greene, 2014; Sparrow, 2011, 2016). We do not think there is doubt in science that well-implemented randomized trials provide the best method for isolating treatment or program impacts (see Boruch, 1975; Boruch et al., 2000; McCord, 2003; Weisburd, 2000, 2003; Weisburd & Hinkle, 2012). This is why in medicine, for example, new drug treatments must show results from experimental field trials before they can be approved for general use (Ruberg et al., 2019; Temple & Ellenberg, 2000).

But science includes an array of methods that are appropriate for answering different types of questions. Descriptive and observational research has great value in defining where problems lie, and in taking into account what is happening in the field (see Chapters 4 and 11). Qualitative methods can inform knowledge about the mechanisms of causal effects and help us to gain a more complete understanding of how problems develop and are understood (see Chapter 9). Survey research is key to informing our understanding of how citizens and the police view policing and its problems (see Chapters 7 and 10). There is not one method in science that is "right" for EBP. Indeed, EBP must have a large toolbox to deal with the broad array of questions in policing that it can inform, as is the case, for example, in evidence-based medicine (Audrey, 2011; Green & Britten, 1998) or evidence-based education (Kozleski, 2017; Odom et al., 2005). Making the debate over EBP about a particular method, for example, experimental field trials (Greene, 2014; Sparrow, 2011, 2016), is a distraction from the main contribution of EBP, which is to bring science to the broad array of policing challenges. In sum, we define EBP in broad terms, both in terms of the types of questions EBP seeks to answer and in terms of the research methods that are "right" for answering these questions.

1.2 EVIDENCE-BASED POLICING AND POLICE AGENCIES: TAKING "OWNERSHIP" OF SCIENCE

In our experience, a common criticism of EBP brought by practitioners is that it suggests the predominance of scientists over police practitioners (Lum & Koper, 2017; also see Chapters 4 and 10). In this vision of EBP, police agencies are "taken over" by scientists who make decisions with little reference to police craft, officers' professional experience, or other considerations such as the law, budget constraints, and local customs, norms, and priorities. This view of EBP is an anathema to police practitioners, and indeed to many police scholars who criticize the idea of EBP (Greene, 2014; Sparrow, 2011, 2016; Willis, 2013; Willis & Mastrofski, 2017, 2018; Willis & Toronjo, 2019). And their concerns are understandable. Scientists are in no position to run police agencies. The role of scientists is to develop a science of policing. Scientists are trained to produce knowledge, to develop theoretical paradigms, and to produce rigorous methods for gaining answers to questions. They are trained to theorize, investigate, and evaluate; they are not trained to run police agencies. The task of scientists is to produce knowledge and evidence about policing – to provide the science that can be used to make informed decisions in policing.

Does this mean that science is only advisory in EBP? In such a context, it is likely that the police will fall back to professional experience and intuition rather than utilize scientific knowledge. If science is only advisory, it will likely be relegated to a marginal place in policing. As Chapter 10 in our volume suggests, there is a natural predisposition to rely on experience and intuition in making decisions, not only in policing but in other fields. A series of studies of the police point to the difficulty of getting police to rely on science in making decisions, even though they are aware of and support the idea of EBP (Blaskovits et al., 2020; Fleming & Rhodes, 2018; Hunter et al., 2015; Jonathan-Zamir et al., 2019; Palmer, 2011; Telep & Lum, 2014; Telep & Winegar, 2015).

Scientists should not be running police agencies. At the same time, making science only "advisory" in policing will not provide the kind of reform that is required for EBP to take root in police agencies. For EBP to be fully integrated into policing, there will have to be a sea change in the culture of policing. Police must take "ownership" of science in policing (see Chapter 3; Weisburd & Neyroud, 2011, 2013). This means that they must be knowledgeable about what the science of policing requires. They must look at keeping up with scientific evidence in policing as a daily part of their job. They must participate in conferences and meetings where scientific evidence is presented and discussed, and they must encourage research in their agencies. Police must value science and accept the value of its normative framework. For example, police must value scientific evidence whether it supports their innovations or not.

One of us (Weisburd) once went to New York City to convince the then Police Commissioner to evaluate the COMPSTAT program that was widely credited by the media and the police as the key contributor to New York City's large crime decline in the 1990s and early 2000s (see review by Rosenfeld et al., 2005). After explaining to the Commissioner that the data being used are not rigorous enough to draw strong causal conclusions about the program's impacts on crime, the Commissioner responded by politely declining to support the research, saying: "You can only bring me bad news." This of course was true. There was wide support in the media and political circles for the role of COMPSTAT in reducing crime in NYC. But how would we respond to a leader of a major medical center saying he or she did not want to evaluate a new drug treatment that had gotten good press for the medical center because a rigorous study could show that the drug didn't work or was harmful? Imagine if the intervention was for breast cancer or a serious disease affecting children. We would simply say that this is wrong and dangerous.

One of the important contributions of the evidence-based policy movement is its recognition that sometimes "cures can harm" (McCord, 2003). A classic example in criminology is the Cambridge Summerville Youth Study (Cabot, 1940). The study initiated in the late 1930s was one of the first randomized experiments in any field in the United States.

It sought to examine whether a series of social, educational, and psychological interventions would aid high-risk youth in avoiding crime and, more generally, live successful lives. These interventions included counseling, tutoring, medical care, and group activities such as camps. There was a clear consensus then that the program would help the children involved, as there would be today.

This is one of the fallacies common in program development by practitioners. There is a strong assumption that the program will "do good" and certainly cannot do harm. But in a follow-up 30 years later, Joan McCord discovered that the treatment condition youth were more likely to be arrested, to have alcohol or drug abuse problems, and die on average two years earlier (McCord 1978, 1981, 1992). A variety of explanations were offered for the "backfire" effects of the program, including labeling of the children and the collective activities being "schools for crime" (Braga, 2016a; Gottfredson, 2010). But more generally, Joan McCord pointed out the importance of recognizing that "cures can harm."

We have no doubt that this is relevant to policing, where "cures" may include law enforcement activities such as stops or arrests, use of force in responding to citizens, or labeling of specific individuals or places as needing police attention. We are not arguing that this should lead us away from policing as a tool for improving communities, as some have recently argued ("defund the police"; see Chapter 2). But we think that in policing in particular we cannot assume that interventions will have positive impacts on the community. The view of the Commissioner in NYC we noted earlier is particularly troubling in a context where policing activities can indeed "do harm."

For EBP to be implemented in the real world of policing, police executives and police officers more broadly must come to value science and take "ownership" of science. In our volume, this point is made strongly, not simply in reference to scholars (Chapter 3) but also to police practitioners (Chapters 14 and 15) and policymakers (Chapter 16). Scientists do not take control of police organizations in EBP; they develop the science that underlies EBP.

An important trend in EBP today is the emergence of what some have called "pracademics" (Braga, 2016b; Huey & Mitchell, 2016; Willis, 2016). Pracademics are police officers who have training in science. Academic programs in policing around the world are now training substantial numbers of police officers in scientific methods and approaches. This is happening across the United States, in criminology programs such as those at George Mason University or the University of Cincinnati, and around the world, for example, at Cambridge University or the Hebrew University of Jerusalem. Cambridge University deserves special mention because of its ongoing master's program in Applied Criminology and Police Management (Police Executive Programme),[1] which has focused specifically on EBP, and has generated a large number of rigorous research studies, which are often published in the *Cambridge Journal of Evidence-Based Policing* published by Springer. Indeed, the journal is an outgrowth of the academic program. The police officers trained at Cambridge, who come from around the world, are becoming leaders for the advancement of EBP. The Hebrew University of Jerusalem also deserves specific mention because it has become the home for the Israel Police higher education program. Senior commanders in Israel are now gaining a BA led by the Institute of Criminology, and many of the most senior commanders are enrolled in an MA program in the Institute. Its results are yet to be seen, but the emphasis on EBP suggests that a generation of police executives who are being trained will be committed to the EBP idea.

This should not be underestimated, as a number of chapters in our volume emphasize the key role of police executives in successfully implementing EBP (Chapters 3, 11, 14, and 15), a point also made in Sherman's original proposal for EBP (see Sherman, 1998). Simon Perry and Michael Wolfowicz (Chapter 14) propose the idea of the "super evidence cop," arguing that a key indicator of success in implementing EBP programs is that the leader of a police agency have significant knowledge about police science and be committed to evidence-based practice.

1.3 THE IMPORTANCE OF ADVANCING THE SCIENCE OF EVIDENCE-BASED POLICING

In some sense, it would seem intuitive that EBP "should" be the dominant philosophy of policing. Speaking more generally about the importance of evidence-based policy, a report by the Pew Charitable Trusts describes the approach in a way that it seems self-evident:

Evidence-based policymaking uses the best available research and information on program results to guide decisions at all stages of the policy process and in each branch of government. It identifies what works, highlights gaps where evidence of program effectiveness is lacking, enables policymakers to use evidence in budget and policy decisions, and relies on systems to monitor implementation and measure key outcomes, using the information to continually improve program performance. (Pew Charitable Trust, 2014, p. 2)

[1] See: www.crim.cam.ac.uk/Courses/mst-courses/MStPolice

Why would governments not want to use the best available research and information to inform policies and practices? Shouldn't EBP be easy to integrate and implement for police agencies? In many papers that advocate evidence-based policy, there is much discussion of the benefits to the government and governmental agencies if they adopt the evidence-based approach (Boruch et al., 2010; Neyroud & Weisburd, 2014; Petrosino et al., 2001; Weisburd & Neyroud, 2013). This can give the impression that the adoption of EBP is a simple affair or that it has been adopted widely across police agencies over the last two decades. However, that is not the reality today. Despite the growing interest in research evidence in policing, there is still a good deal of disagreement as to what such an approach would require (e.g., Brown et al., 2018; Lumsden & Goode, 2018). And more generally, while evidence and science are in a much stronger position in policing than they were two decades ago, the call for EBP as a dominant paradigm for developing practices and programs in policing has not been realized (e.g., Sherman, 2015; Weisburd & Neyroud, 2011; see Chapter 3).

One reason for this is simply that in advancing EBP, scientists have often ignored the question of how police innovation can be institutionalized. This is part of a more general failure of scholars to be concerned not simply with developing police innovation, but with defining how such innovation can be broadly implemented in police agencies (see Chapter 5). Lum and Koper (2017) argue in regard to problem-oriented and community-oriented policing, for example:

Community policing and problem-oriented policing were likely viewed and developed as broader philosophies for policing, ones that should occupy the minds of every police officer and supervisor during his or her daily activities. Unfortunately, community and problem-oriented policing have not panned out in these ways because they were not institutionalized into the everyday systems of policing. (Lum & Koper, 2017, p. 151)

There is a large literature today on the barriers to the implementation of EBP. It details a wide range of issues, from the failures of implementation, as noted by Lum and Koper (2017), to the limitations of police training and education (Weisburd & Neyroud, 2011), to the natural proclivities of police to rely on professional experience (Jonathan-Zamir et al., 2019). In our volume, we touch on these issues in a number of chapters. But our main focus is not on what has to happen in police agencies to advance EBP, but rather on an issue that has received far less attention – the science that is necessary to produce for EBP to be successfully integrated into policing. We return to this theme in more detail in our conclusions, where we explore what our volume has taught us regarding the future of EBP.

1.4 ORGANIZATION OF THIS VOLUME

This volume includes five main parts. We begin by taking stock of EBP. Building on geographic "Tiers" recently used in the struggle against the COVID-19 pandemic, in Chapter 2 Sherman presents a recent view of EBP, in which he calls for a Tiered policing system: the extent to which intrusive policing measures are applied would match the level of serious, violent crime in the area. In Chapter 3, Neyroud and Weisburd provide a revised and updated version of their 2011 paper in which they have called for a new paradigm that changes the relationship between science and policing. Specifically, they add a new emphasis on moral and ethical considerations in research and practice that must, in their view, become an integral part of EBP. In the last chapter of this part (Chapter 4), Willis and Toronjo call for more attention in EBP to the choices that patrol officers make in their everyday encounters with the public and argue for the value of their rich experiences in generating useful knowledge. They also draw attention to the importance of going beyond questions of "what works" in EBP to normative and moral questions that characterize street-level discretion.

In the second part of the book, we recap the evidence that forms the basis for EBP. In Chapter 5, Telep and Weisburd update an earlier review of systematic reviews in policing (2004–2015), which now encompasses systematic reviews on 30 policing topics. They argue that while much knowledge is available today about the effectiveness of different policing approaches, scholars have paid little attention to questions about how evidence-based practices should be chosen and implemented in the field. To provide another view of the state of the evidence in EBP, in Chapter 6, Weisburd, Braga, and Majmundar summarize the findings of the National Academy of Sciences, Engineering, and Medicine report on proactive policing (Weisburd & Majmundar, 2018), which provides the most comprehensive and recent review to date of what proactive policing is and what it does. The report finds sufficient scientific evidence to support the adoption of many proactive policing practices. Successful strategies are often characterized by focusing police resources and expanding the tools of policing, and generally lead to successful outcomes without producing negative community reactions. In the final chapter of this part (Chapter 7), Gill reflects on the findings of the National Academy of

Sciences, Engineering, and Medicine report, and argues that contrary to what may appear as a disjuncture between crime control and community outcomes, community support and collaboration are essential to crime control and may moderate the success or failure of proactive, crime-control strategies.

Having reviewed the evidence base for EBP, the third part of the book discusses innovations in tools of evaluation and assessment. Drawing on the global policing database, in Chapter 8 Mazerolle, Eggins, Hine, and Higginson review the place of experiments in EBP. They identify that randomized controlled trials (RCTs) form only 12% of the evidence in policing but have had an enormous influence on policy. They also find that most of the evidence in policing concerns frontline policing practices, and that half of the RCTs in the world were carried out in the United States. In Chapter 9, Perry, Jonathan-Zamir, and Willis introduce the concept of "subjective causality" – a qualitative approach in which causality is determined through the subjective lens of the individual. Using qualitative interviews, they demonstrate the subjective, causal relationship that individuals make in their own minds between police-provided procedural justice and police legitimacy.

The fourth part of the book discusses different types of challenges to implementing EBP, many of which have not been given sufficient attention to date. In Chapter 10, Jonathan-Zamir and Weisburd draw attention to the "science-experience paradox" in policing: while police officers often support EBP, they tend to favor their experience and intuition when making decisions. Given the generality and psychological basis of the tendency to rely on experience, they argue that science should be "injected" into officers' experience, and that both science and experience should be treated as necessary components in successful policing. Taking advantage of a recent process evaluation of the EMUN reform in the Israel Police, in Chapter 11 Litmanovitz, Weisburd, and Hasisi identify three keys to the successful implementation of EBP in practice: the ability to analyze data and reflect on it, organizational flexibility, and local engagement with the reform. Lack of these three keys poses great challenge to the successful implementation of EBP.

Taking a comparative approach, in Chapter 12, Jaitman reviews and discusses some of the challenges to the implementation of EBP in Latin America and Caribbean. These include familiar challenges, such as the relationship between academia and practitioners, but also challenges that are more specific to the region, such as the instability of political institutions. In the final chapter of this part (Chapter 13), Harmon reviews some of the challenges to EBP posed by the law. Focusing on American law, she argues, for example, that the law influences which police practices are studied, and thus the practices that are likely to become supported by empirical evidence. More generally, Harmon reviews EBP within the context of the law and illuminates the interaction between the two.

All three chapters in the fifth and final part of the book were written by police practitioners (or pracademics) and policymakers, thus shifting our attention to the practitioners' perspective on EBP. In Chapter 14, Perry and Wolfowicz provide a description based on first-hand experience of two attempts to carry out a strategic reform in the Israel Police. The authors argue that the first failed while the second succeeded because the Commissioner who led the latter was a "super evidence cop," a concept the authors develop based on Sherman's (1998) notion of the "evidence cop." Based on his experience as chief in four different cities, in Chapter 15 Stephens provides a chief's perspective on the barriers to implementing EBP, the risks and rewards a police chief can expect, suggestions for broader adoption of EBP, and several important areas in policing in need of additional research. Again, based on much first-hand knowledge, in the final chapter of this part (Chapter 16), Burch, the President of the National Policing Institute, reviews the role that national organizations/entities have played in encouraging/discouraging the adoption of EBP in the United States. Burch identifies numerous challenges at this level to the implementation of EBP and proposes a Professional Policing Doctrine for moving forward in advancing EBP.

In the concluding chapter (Chapter 17), we reflect on what we have learned more generally from the contributions to this volume. We are particularly concerned with where EBP should be heading, and what is necessary to further advance the integration of EBP into policing. Based on our assessment of the field of EBP to date, as well as the discussions raised in the chapters of the volume, we argue that the future of EBP, as a meaningful paradigm with substantial influence on police policy and practice, lies in advancing the science of policing. In this sense, our focus differs from the emphasis that many scholars have put on what the police have to do to advance EBP, and points to the importance of improving the quality and quantity of the science that underlies EBP. Science is at the heart of EBP, and our volume places emphasis on the importance of advancing the science of policing in order to advance EBP.

References

Amendola, K. L., Weisburd, D., Hamilton, E. E., Jones, G., & Slipka, M. (2011). An experimental study of compressed work schedules in policing: Advantages and disadvantages of various shift lengths. *Journal of Experimental Criminology*, 7(4), 407–442.

Audrey, S. (2011). Qualitative research in evidence-based medicine: Improving decision-making and participation in randomized controlled trials of cancer treatments. *Palliative Medicine*, 25(8), 758–765.

Blaskovits, B., Bennell, C., Huey, L., Kalyal, H., Walker, T., & Javala, S. (2020). A Canadian replication of Telep and Lum's (2014) examination of police officers' receptivity to empirical research. *Policing and Society*, 30(3), 276–294. https://doi.org/10.1080/10439463.2018.1522315.

Blomberg, T. G., Brancale, J. M., Beaver, K. M., & Bales, W. D. (Eds.) (2016). *Advancing criminology and criminal justice policy*. Routledge.

Boruch, R. F. (1975). Coupling randomized experiments and approximations to experiments in social program evaluation. *Sociological Methods & Research*, 4(1), 31–53.

Boruch, R. F., Victor, T., & Cecil, J. S. (2000). Resolving ethical and legal problems in randomized experiments. *Crime & Delinquency*, 46(3), 330–353.

Boruch, R. F., Weisburd, D., & Berk, R. (2010). Place randomized trials. In A. R. Piquero & D. Weisburd (Eds.), *Handbook of quantitative criminology* (pp. 481–499). Springer.

Braga, A. A. (2016a). The continued importance of measuring potentially harmful impacts of crime prevention programs: The academy of experimental criminology 2014 Joan McCord lecture. *Journal of Experimental Criminology*, 12(1), 1–20.

Braga, A. A. (2016b). The value of 'pracademics' in enhancing crime analysis in police departments. *Policing: A Journal of Policy and Practice*, 10(3), 308–314.

Brown, J., Belur, J., Tompson, L., McDowall, A., Hunter, G., & May, T. (2018). Extending the remit of evidence-based policing. *International Journal of Police Science and Management*, 20(1), 38–51.

Bueermann, J. (2012). Being smart on crime with evidence-based policing. *NIJ Journal*, 269, 12–15.

Burch, J. H. (this volume). Support for evidence-based policing at the national level – More help than harm? In D. Weisburd, T. Jonathan, G. Perry, & B. Hasisi (Eds.), *The future of evidence-based policing*. Cambridge University Press.

Cabot, P. S. deQ. (1940). A long-term study of children: The Cambridge–Somerville Youth Study. *Child Development*, 11(2), 143–151.

Cole, G. F., Smith, C. E., & DeJong, C. (2016). *Criminal justice in America*. Nelson Education.

Fleming, J., & Rhodes, R. (2018). Can experience be evidence? Craft knowledge and evidence-based policing. *Policy & Politics*, 46(1), 3–26.

Gill, C. (this volume). Rethinking the role of the community in proactive policing. In D. Weisburd, T. Jonathan, G. Perry, & B. Hasisi (Eds.), *The future of evidence-based policing*. Cambridge University Press.

Gottfredson, D. C. (2010). Deviancy training: Understanding how preventive interventions harm. *Journal of Experimental Criminology*, 6(3), 229–243.

Greene, J. (2014). New directions in policing: Balancing prediction and meaning in police research. *Justice Quarterly, 31*(3), 193–228.
Green, J., & Britten, N. (1998). Qualitative research and evidence based medicine. *BMJ, 316*(7139), 1230–1232.
Harmon, R. (this volume). Evidence-based policing and the law: The American perspective. In D. Weisburd, T. Jonathan, G. Perry, & B. Hasisi (Eds.), *The future of evidence-based policing*. Cambridge University Press.
Huey, L., & Mitchell, R. J. (2016). Unearthing hidden keys: Why pracademics are an invaluable (if underutilized) resource in policing research. *Policing: A Journal of Policy and Practice, 10*(3), 300–307.
Hunter, G., Wigzell, A., May, T., & McSweeney, T. (2015). *An evaluation of the 'What Works Centre for Crime Reduction.' Year 1: Baseline*. Institute for Criminal Policy Research.
Jaitman, L. (this volume). Towards implementing evidence-based policing: Challenges in Latin America and Caribbean. In D. Weisburd, T. Jonathan, G. Perry, & B. Hasisi (Eds.), *The future of evidence-based policing*. Cambridge University Press.
Jonathan-Zamir, T., & Weisburd, D. (this volume). Practitioners' inclination to rely on experience: What does this mean for evidence-based policing? In D. Weisburd, T. Jonathan, G. Perry, & B. Hasisi (Eds.), *The future of evidence-based policing*. Cambridge University Press.
Jonathan-Zamir, T., Weisburd, D., Dayan, M., & Zisso, M. (2019). The proclivity to rely on professional experience and evidence-based policing: Findings from a survey of high-ranking officers in the Israel Police. *Criminal Justice and Behavior, 46*(10), 1456–1474.
Kozleski, E. B. (2017). The uses of qualitative research: Powerful methods to inform evidence-based practice in education. *Research and Practice for Persons with Severe Disabilities, 42*(1), 19–32.
Litmanovitz, Y., Weisburd, D., & Hasisi, B. (this volume). Implementing evidence-based policing: Findings from a process evaluation of the EMUN reform in the Israel Police. In D. Weisburd, T. Jonathan, G. Perry, & B. Hasisi (Eds.), *The future of evidence-based policing*. Cambridge University Press.
Lum, C., & Koper, C. S. (2017). *Evidence-based policing: Translating research into practice*. Oxford University Press.
Lum, C., Telep, C. W., Koper, C. S., & Grieco, J. (2012). Receptivity to research in policing. *Justice Research and Policy, 14*(1), 61–95.
Lumsden, K., & Goode, J. (2018). Policing research and the rise of the 'evidence-base': Police officer and staff understandings of research, its implementation, and 'what works.' *Sociology, 52*(4), 813–829.
Mazerolle, L., Eggins, E., Hine, L., & Higginson, A. (this volume). The role of randomized experiments in developing the evidence for evidence-based policing. In D. Weisburd, T. Jonathan, G. Perry, & B. Hasisi (Eds.), *The future of evidence-based policing*. Cambridge University Press.
McCord, J. (1978). A thirty-year follow-up of treatment effects. *American Psychologist, 33*(3), 284–289.
McCord, J. (1981). Consideration of some effects of a counseling program. In S. E. Martin, L. B. Sechrest, & R. Redner (Eds.), *New directions in the*

rehabilitation of criminal offenders (pp. 394–405). National Academy of Sciences.

McCord, J. (1992). The Cambridge–Somerville study: A pioneering longitudinal experimental study of delinquency prevention. In J. McCord & R. J. Tremblay (Eds.), *Preventing antisocial behavior: Interventions from birth through adolescence* (pp. 196–206). Guilford.

McCord, J. (2003). Cures that harm: Unanticipated outcomes of crime prevention programs. *The ANNALS of the American Academy of Political and Social Science, 587*(1), 16–30.

Neyroud, P., & Weisburd, D. (2014). Transforming the police through science: The challenge of ownership. *Policing: A Journal of Policy and Practice* 8(4), 287–293.

Neyroud, P., & Weisburd, D. (this volume). Re-inventing policing: Using science to transform policing. In D. Weisburd, T. Jonathan, G. Perry, & B. Hasisi (Eds.), *The future of evidence-based policing*. Cambridge University Press.

Odom, S. L., Brantlinger, E., Gersten, R., Horner, R. H., Thompson, B., & Harris, K. R. (2005). Research in special education: Scientific methods and evidence-based practices. *Exceptional Children, 71*(2), 137–148.

Palmer, I. (2011). Is the United Kingdom Police Service receptive to evidence-based policing? Testing attitudes towards experimentation [unpublished master's thesis]. University of Cambridge.

Perry, G., Jonathan-Zamir, T., & Willis, J. (this volume). The potential contribution of subjective causality to policing research: The case of the relationship between procedural justice and police legitimacy. In D. Weisburd, T. Jonathan, G. Perry, & B. Hasisi (Eds.), *The future of evidence-based policing*. Cambridge University Press.

Perry, S., & Wolfowicz, M. (this volume). The role of the "Super Evidence Cop" in evidence-based policing: The Israeli case. In D. Weisburd, T. Jonathan, G. Perry, & B. Hasisi (Eds.), *The future of evidence-based policing*. Cambridge University Press.

Petrosino, A., Boruch, R. F., Soydan, H., Duggan, L., & Sanchez-Meca, J. (2001). Meeting the challenges of evidence-based policy: The Campbell Collaboration. *The Annals of the American Academy of Political and Social Science, 578*(1), 14–34.

Pew Charitable Trusts. (2014). *Evidence-based policymaking: A guide for effective government*. MacArthur Foundation.

Roman, J. K., Reid, S. E., Chalfin, A. J., & Knight, C. R. (2009). The DNA field experiment: A randomized trial of the cost-effectiveness of using DNA to solve property crimes. *Journal of Experimental Criminology, 5*(4), 345–369.

Rosenfeld, R., Fornango, R., & Baumer, E. (2005). Did *Ceasefire, Compstat,* and *Exile* reduce homicide? *Criminology & Public Policy, 4*(3), 419–450. https://doi:10.1111/j.1745-9133.2005.00310.x.

Ruberg, S. J., Harrell Jr, F. E., Gamalo-Siebers, M., LaVange, L., Jack Lee, J., Price, K., & Peck, C. (2019). Inference and decision making for 21st-century drug development and approval. *The American Statistician, 73*(sup1), 319–327.

Sherman, L. W. (1998). *Evidence-based policing*. Police Foundation. www.policefoundation.org/wp-content/uploads/2015/06/Sherman-1998-Evidence-Based-Policing.pdf

Sherman, L. W. (2013). The rise of evidence-based policing: Targeting, testing, and tracking. *Crime and Justice*, 42(1), 377–451.

Sherman, L. W. (2015). A tipping point for "totally evidenced policing": Ten ideas for building an evidence-based police agency. *International Criminal Justice Review*, 25(1), 11–29.

Sherman, L. W. (this volume). Three tiers for evidence-based policing: Targeting "Minimalist" policing with a risk-adjusted disparity index. In D. Weisburd, T. Jonathan, G. Perry, & B. Hasisi (Eds.), *The future of evidence-based policing*. Cambridge University Press.

Sherman, L. W., MacKenzie, D. L., Farrington, D. P., & Welsh, B. C. (Eds.) (2002). *Evidence-based crime prevention*. Routledge.

Sparrow, M. K. (2011). *Governing science: New perspectives in policing*. Department of Justice, National Institute of Justice.

Sparrow, M. (2016). *Handcuffed: What holds policing back and the keys to reform*. Brooking Institution Press.

Stephens, D. (this volume). Looking back on the challenges to evidence-based policing: A chief's perspective. In D. Weisburd, T. Jonathan, G. Perry, & B. Hasisi (Eds.), *The future of evidence-based policing*. Cambridge University Press.

Telep, C. W. (2016). Expanding the scope of evidence-based policing. *Criminology and Public Policy*, 15, 243–252.

Telep, C. W., & Lum, C. (2014). The receptivity of officers to empirical research and evidence-based policing: An examination of survey data from three agencies. *Police Quarterly*, 17(4), 359–385.

Telep, C. W., & Weisburd, D. (this volume). A review of systematic reviews in policing. In D. Weisburd, T. Jonathan, G. Perry, & B. Hasisi (Eds.), *The future of evidence-based policing*. Cambridge University Press.

Telep, C. W., & Winegar, S. (2015). Police executive receptivity to research: A survey of chiefs and sheriffs in Oregon. *Policing: A Journal of Policy and Practice*, 10(3), 241–249.

Temple, R., & Ellenberg, S. S. (2000). Placebo-controlled trials and active-control trials in the evaluation of new treatments. Part 1: Ethical and scientific issues. *Annals of Internal Medicine*, 133(6), 455–463.

Weisburd, D. (2000). Randomized experiments in criminal justice policy: Prospects and problems. *Crime & Delinquency*, 46(2), 181–193.

Weisburd, D. (2003). Ethical practice and evaluation of interventions in crime and justice: The moral imperative for randomized trials. *Evaluation Review*, 27(3), 336–354.

Weisburd, D., Braga, A. A., & Majmundar, M. (this volume). What do we know about Proactive Policing's effects on Crime and Community?: Drawing conclusions from a National Academies of Sciences, Engineering, and Medicine Report. In D. Weisburd, T. Jonathan, G. Perry, & B. Hasisi (Eds.), *The future of evidence-based policing*. Cambridge University Press.

Weisburd, D., & Hinkle, J. C. (2012). The importance of randomized experiments in evaluating crime prevention. In B. C. Welsh & D. P. Farrington (Eds.), *The Oxford handbook on crime prevention* (pp. 446–465). Oxford University Press.

Weisburd, D., Jonathan-Zamir, T., Perry, G., & Hasisi, B. (this volume). Conclusions: Police science and the future of evidence-based policing. In D. Weisburd,

T. Jonathan, G. Perry, & B. Hasisi (Eds.), *The future of evidence-based policing*. Cambridge University Press.

Weisburd, D., & Majmundar, M. (Eds). (2018). *Proactive policing: Effects on crime and communities*. The National Academies Press.

Weisburd, D., & Neyroud, P. (2011). Police science: Toward a new paradigm. *New Perspectives in Policing*, January 2011, 1–23.

Weisburd, D., & Neyroud, P. (2013). Police science: Toward a new paradigm. *Australasian Policing, 5*(13), 15–20.

Willis, J. J. (2013). Improving police: What's craft got to do with it? *Ideas in American Policing, 16*, 1–13.

Willis, J. J. (2016). The romance of police pracademics. *Policing: A Journal of Policy and Practice, 10*(3), 315–321.

Willis, J. J., & Mastrofski, S. D. (2014). Pulling together: Integrating craft and science. *Policing: A Journal of Policy and Practice, 8*(4), 321–329.

Willis, J. J., & Mastrofski, S. D. (2017). Understanding the culture of craft: Lessons from two police agencies. *Journal of Crime and Justice, 40*(1), 84–100.

Willis, J. J., & Mastrofski, S. D. (2018). Improving policing by integrating craft and science: What can patrol officers teach us about good police work? *Policing and Society: An International Journal of Policy and Practice, 28*(1), 27–44.

Willis, J. J., & Toronjo, H. (2019). Translating police research into policy: Some implications of the national academies report on proactive policing for policymakers and researchers. *Police Practice and Research: An International Journal, 20*(6), 617–631.

Willis, J. J., & Toronjo, H. (this volume). A way ahead: Re-envisioning the relationship between evidence-based policing and the police craft. In D. Weisburd, T. Jonathan, G. Perry, & B. Hasisi (Eds.), *The future of evidence-based policing*. Cambridge University Press.

Wilson, D. B., McClure, D., & Weisburd, D. (2010). Does forensic DNA help to solve crime? The benefit of sophisticated answers to naive questions. *Journal of Contemporary Criminal Justice, 26*(4), 458–469.

Wilson, D. B., Weisburd, D., & McClure, D. (2011). Use of DNA testing in police investigative work for increasing offender identification, arrest, conviction and case clearance. *Campbell Systematic Reviews, 7*(1), 1–53.

Wilson, J. Q., & Petersilia, J. (Eds.) (2010). *Crime and public policy*. Oxford University Press.

PART I

TAKING STOCK OF EVIDENCE-BASED POLICING

2

Three Tiers for Evidence-Based Policing

Targeting "Minimalist" Policing with a Risk-Adjusted Disparity Index

Lawrence W. Sherman

The Year 2020 was a major milestone for democratic policing as we know it. Perhaps the strongest evidence for that claim comes from a Gallup (Crabtree, 2020) poll taken after global protests over the murdering of George Floyd by Minneapolis police: three out of four Americans said that they were opposed to police using their legal powers of stop and search. A broad, if ill-defined, campaign to "de-fund" the police became part of the US Presidential election; police stations were burned, police officers resigned or did less work, and protests blocked street traffic from New Delhi to Hong Kong to Lagos.

Meanwhile, violent crime spiked in many cities across the US, while murder rates of minority group members remained far higher than for whites in the UK. In New York alone, police reported a 41% increase in murders and 100% increase in shootings (Pavia, 2020; Watkins, 2020). Pandemic as well as protest (including more masks on criminals) may have changed police effectiveness at preventing violence. Whatever the reasons, the change was seismic.

Given that context, *what is the point of evidence-based policing?* Even a supporter of improving policing with the EBP framework (Sherman, 1998, 2013) might admit to profound despair over these fundamental challenges to democratic policing. Yet, there is a clear case that by 2021, evidence-based policing had become more important than ever. As this chapter suggests, the tools of science in targeting, testing, and tracking (Sherman, 2013) are well matched to the challenges policing now faces – challenges which otherwise may remain potentially disastrous for democracy and the rule of law.

A "pre-mortem" (Kahneman, 2011) of what might, in future years, cause democracies to replace or disrupt their current policing institutions should consider two possibilities. One is rising public perception of Western policing as *disproportionate* in the harm it *causes* relative to the harm it *prevents*, thus violating a 700-year-old mandate to limit full use of police powers in order to "keep the king's peace" (Judge, 2011). If a majority of Americans of all racial groups polled are opposed to police using their legal powers to stop and search (Crabtree, 2020) that reflects a profound challenge to police legitimacy.

The other potential cause of policing's demise is a perception that policing lacks adequate skills for ensuring the "*coupling*" of highest levels of police intrusions (including deadly force) to the tiny percentages of places, situations, and people in which most serious crime and harm are concentrated (Gladwell, 2019: 309–312; see also Weisburd, 2016, 2020; Weisburd et al., 2014). One cause of that problem is that most police, let alone most people, do not understand the extreme distribution of crime harm concentrations across offenders, victims, and places (Sherman, 2007), with most urban places having virtually no crime at all (Sherman et al., 1989; Weisburd, 2015). But since the advent of Cohen's (1985) concept of "net-widening," criminologists have been justifiably wary of interventions aimed at high-harm cases being applied more widely to lower harm targets.

As Gladwell (2019) suggested, it was the "uncoupling" of proactive traffic stops from elevated risks of crime that led to the suicide of an African-American woman named Sandra Bland after three days in a police lockup, where a state police officer had placed her in custody for a trivially minor offense (changing lanes without signaling) – in an area with no prior crime. In that example, the uncoupling of crime risk from a decision to justify depriving Bland of her liberty is what made the police decision shockingly *disproportionate*. As Gladwell (2019, p. 341) quotes from his interview with David Weisburd, after noting that Bland was stopped by police three miles from the nearest hot spot "Why are you stopping people in places where there's no crime? … That doesn't make sense to me."

The aim of this chapter is to show how evidence-based policing (EBP) can counter these two threats: (1) disproportionate use of force and intrusions such as stop & search and (2) intrusive policing uncoupled from risk. By striving to identify evidence of the *minimum* police presence and intrusion possible to prevent serious crime, evidence-based police can support the sustainability of democratic and legitimate policing. The core idea of *minimalist* policing, with the absolute bare minimum of policing needed to prevent harm (see Jacobs, 2021), can be applied systematically with the evidence-based policing framework of Targeting, Testing, and Tracking (Sherman, 2013). The chapter shows how this goal could be achieved with a public health strategy of creating graduated "Tiers" of increasing restriction on human liberty proportionate to the risk of death, as developed in the United Kingdom in late 2020.

The chapter proceeds as follows:

1) Reviewing the self-inflicted threats to policing world-wide from seemingly disproportionate force and uncoupling of intrusive policing from risk.
2) Assessing the nature of demand for police reform as a vision of more balanced, *better targeted*, but not necessarily *less*, policing, especially for people and places suffering highest rates of violent victimization.
3) Describing the UK's COVID-19 prevention "Tiers" of intrusive control as a metaphor to consider in coupling the levels of policing intensity to risk of harm.
4) Proposing similar Tiers of public safety to govern how much liberty can be restricted at varying levels of crime harm or mortality.
5) Proposing a risk-adjusted disparity (RAD) index for assessing evidence for "over-policing" and "under-policing" by racial groups.
6) Exploring methods of dialogue (Bottoms & Tankebe, 2012) between police and citizens for consultations about proactive policies for different "zones," people or situations, which could result in agreements to "stand down" certain police practices at lower levels of risk, with an evidence-based threshold at which they would be activated for public protection.
7) Re-stating the "Triple-T" framework of targeting, testing, and tracking as the basis for tiered policing.

2.1 A GLOBAL CRISIS OF POLICE LEGITIMACY

The year 2020 was unique in the history of democratic policing. Never before had a single police action in one country been so widely condemned around the world, so quickly, and with such generalizability of blame against police in all democratic nations, as the murdering of George Floyd. Coming on top of unprecedented restrictions on freedom of movement during the COVID19 lockdown, the suffocation of George Floyd by a Minneapolis police officer on May 25 led to the slogan "I can't breathe" being displayed in protests in New York, London, Paris (Allen and Burke, 2020), Sydney, and hundreds of other cities large and small.

That single police action in one city (Minneapolis) led to nightly anti-police protests in another city of the same country (Portland, OR), for virtually every day for at least four months (May 28 through September 28). These protests then sparked another unprecedented development, at least in the US: *pro-police demonstrators* coming from states far away, making counter-demonstrations against those protesting the police. Even Weimar Germany's street battles of the 1920s between Communists and Fascists were about political parties (Liang, 1969), but not about the police themselves.

The most distinctive feature of these protests was not their breadth, but their depth. The idea of "de-funding" police, or even an "end of policing,' as the title of a 2017 book put it (Vitale, 2017), was the deepest and most radical demand about modern policing since it took shape in the mid-nineteenth century – and perhaps since England's Justices of the Peace Act 1361 (Judge, 2011). New York City and Los Angeles responded rapidly to the demands to "de-fund" the police with budget cuts in the millions, while sustaining the police agencies themselves. A far deeper cut was promised by the City Council in Minneapolis, a remarkable birthplace of evidence-based policing (Sherman & Berk, 1984; Sherman, 1987; Sherman, et al., 1989; Sherman & Weisburd, 1995) under the leadership of the then-Police Chief Tony Bouza, a Spanish-born former NYPD chief widely hated by the many officers he suspended for excessive use of force, but dearly beloved by the Minneapolis general public. On June 7, 2020, a nine-member majority of the City Council announced that they would "end policing as we know it" and "De-Fund M.P.D." (Herndon 2020), in defiance of the Mayor who had been booed by protestors for refusing to "support the full abolition of the police department" (Mogelson, 2020). While these pledges were not fulfilled, merely hearing them made was a shock.

While the American narrative about 2020 understandably focused on George Floyd, the issues were hardly unique to Minnesota or the US. Similar protests over illegally disproportionate policing arose around the world that year, from France to Nigeria to Chile and beyond. The outrage directed at police in these countries can be distinguished from instances in China (including Hong Kong) and Belarus, in which the underlying issue was not police conduct but the absence of democracy itself. For present purposes, we try to confine this review to countries where the issue is about democratic policing rather than authoritarian government regimes.

That distinction, of course, is not always possible. In Nigeria, after years of disquiet over a particular police unit known for murdering citizens, the Special Anti-Robbery Squad, or "SARS" (Akinwotu, 2020a), protestors filled the streets to demand the abolition of SARS. This demand was "met" by the government, which quickly disbanded SARS and then proceeded to have other police shoot many protestors to death, as seen in video sent around the world (Akinwotu, 2020b). Protestors in Chile, Kenya, and other countries focused on local issues of excessive force, without reported reference to George Floyd or other policing in the US, but with ample anger aimed at governments as well. By early 2021, the distinction was further complicated by a right-wing attack on the US Capitol, in which police officers on duty to protect members of the Congress attacked by police officers off-duty from states across the US.

It is also worth noting that race or racism of the police was not the common denominator across the protests of all these (somewhat) democratic nations. The common denominator across the five continents was subject of this chapter – proportionate intrusions coupled to harm levels. While on November 28 cities across France had "anti-police brutality" riots about the beating of a black man who was not wearing an anti-COVID mask, the central issue was apparently a new law that prohibited identifying police officers on the internet, an issue in the white working class protests over fuel prices (Allen and Burke, 2020)). At the same time, overall public approval of the government in France rose in the aftermath of passing the same new security law. Thus France, as so many nations, ended the year with deep *divisions* over the legitimacy of policing, some based on race, but others (like Nigeria) based on political factions within racially homogeneous societies.

2.2 THE DEMAND FOR CHANGE: BETTER POLICING, NOT LESS

The US became even more divided about policing in 2020, even within the Democratic Party. By year end, some parts of the US saw first steps towards protestors' proposals to "de-fund" the police, largely by moving budgeted funds into other city departments (e.g., Durkan, 2020). Those moves in the so-called liberal cities apparently posed a major threat to the Democratic Party's victories in the US Presidential and House of Representatives elections, both of which were surprisingly slim. In the latter case, the loss of seats by the Democratic majority was blamed in part on the "de-funding" idea (Broadwater & Fandos, 2020): "Representative Abigail Spanberger, who narrowly escaped defeat...in a conservative-leaning district in Virginia that Democrats had also toiled to protect, chastised her progressive colleagues for embracing the "defund the police" movement."

The opposition to de-funding police was apparently not about a nuanced argument of refining the police mandate to off-load mental health and social service functions. More likely, it was a visceral response to the idea that police presence is not needed to deter crime, as suggested by Vitale (2017) – despite contrary evidence from police strikes and many other tests of that hypothesis (Sherman, 1992; 2013). The mere thought of such an "unthinkable" end of policing proved to be highly unpopular among both Democratic and Republican voters across the US (Crabtree, 2020).

The majoritarian demand for police reform in 2020 was for better policing, not less policing. Even in Minneapolis, where many Black and minority voters demanded abolition, others believed it would be dangerous for Black lives to do so. As Mogelson's (2020) in-depth interviews with friends and neighbors of George Floyd pointed out, many members of the Black community were opposed to de-funding the police. Several African-American friends of Floyd, when the reporter told them that the Council had pledged abolition, said they were shocked and opposed to the idea. As Mogelson summarized it, George Floyd's friends said that "violent, armed bad actors would inevitably dominate and exploit any environment free of law enforcement. They did not want to abolish the institution, just the mentality that it's us [police] against them [minorities]." In the months that followed, these residents' fears for their neighborhoods proved well founded. As police increasingly stayed home on sick leave or resigned, Minneapolis homicides rose by 50% and persons shot rose by 100% (Bailey, 2020). Legal and political disputes swirled while a degree of *de facto* "de-policing" rapidly developed.

Perhaps because of the strong underlying demand for police services – even by people furious at the police – the plan to "defund M.P.D." all but collapsed in Minneapolis within three months. It also collapsed because of the political science of American police reform, by which all power to create and destroy police agencies lies with the states, not cities (Sherman, 2020). Most widely acknowledged was the fact that no one had a clear plan for *replacing* the police with an institutional framework that would prove equally effective. In the short run, the challenge remained better policing with the existing police institutions.

Stop and Frisk as a Focus for Reform. One plan for better policing that it seems most Americans *do* want is especially relevant to issues of racial disparity in both policing and risk of victimization. That plan is to

Three Tiers for Evidence-Based Policing 25

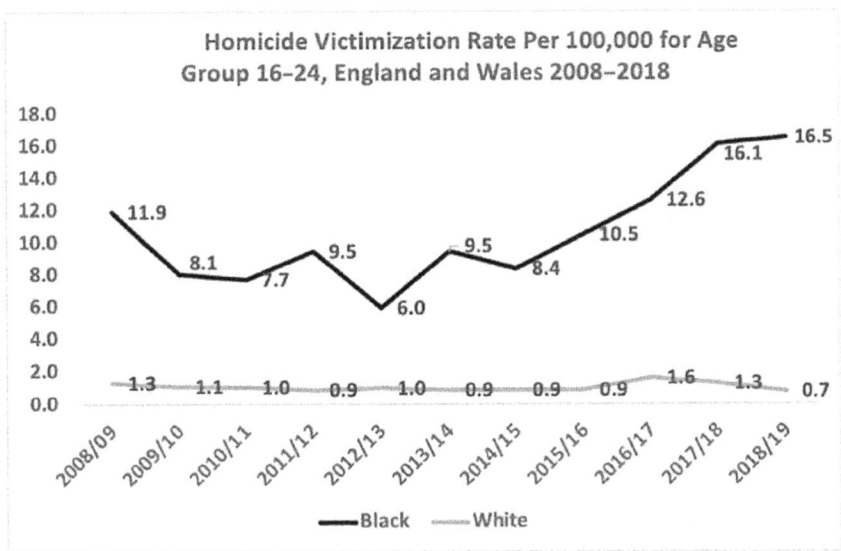

FIGURE 2.1 Homicide victimization rate per 100,000 for the age group 16–24, England and Wales 2008–2018
(reprinted from Kumar et al., 2020, Figure 2)

abolish the tool of stop, question, and frisk. According to a 2020 Gallup poll of 36,000 Americans, the majority of respondents want police to ban the use of "stop and frisk:"

Overall, 74% of Americans support the idea of ending stop-and-frisk policing altogether, with 58% saying they strongly support [ending it]. Though Black Americans are most likely to strongly or somewhat support ending stop and frisk at 93%, strong majorities of Hispanic (76%) and White Americans (70%) do as well. However, there is a much larger partisan divide; 94% of Democrats versus 44% of Republicans support ending the practice, with independents in between at 76%. (Crabtree, 2020)

Yet, this consensus could well "throw out the baby with the bath water." Far from promoting racial equality, banning stop and frisk altogether could increase racial inequality in crime rates, especially homicide. This inconvenient truth is supported by substantial evidence.

The evidence that Black people are far more likely to be murdered than whites is well established in both the US (Reiss &Roth, 1993; Centers for Disease Control, 2021) and the UK (Kumar et al., 2020). Not only are the murder victimization rates much higher for Blacks than whites, but as UK data show, those rates may be very responsive to policing. As Figure 2.1 shows, the risk of persons aged 16–24 being murdered per 100,000 in the UK was far higher for Blacks than whites at the beginning of the twenty-first century, but declined sharply until 2012. At that point, when major changes in police practice and funding occurred, the relative risk for Blacks to be murdered started rising. By the end of the second decade, murder victimizations of Black young people exceeded their level at the start of the first decade.

This evidence alone is insufficient to identify direct links between fewer stops and more Black lives lost. Yet, there is no doubt that stop and search frequency plummeted across London from 2012 through 2017 (Hopper, 2018), in tandem with a sharp upward trend in murders of young Blacks. Other factors besides fewer stops could explain the change, such as declining numbers of police officers employed across the UK. Yet, other countries offer stronger evidence for the life-saving benefits of stop and search, especially from the US.

The conclusion that stop and search can save lives is highly restricted to high-violence places. Virtually all of the evidence comes *not* from city-wide analyses, but rather from testing stop and search in highly targeted "hot spots" of violence. Some of that evidence was identified by a systematic review (Koper & Mayo-Wilson, 2012) about "hot spot" patrols that featured stop & frisk in areas of high gun violence. While the studies were quasi-experimental and weak in causal inference, they found consistent evidence that increases in proactive policing in high-risk areas (as described in Gladwell, 2019) reduced shooting injuries or deaths. The research includes studies in Kansas City (MO) (Sherman et al., 1995), two areas of Pittsburgh (Cohen & Ludwig, 2002), two areas of Indianapolis (McGarrell et al., 2002), several areas of St. Louis (Rosenfeld et al., 2014), as well as in separate tests in Bogota and Cali, Colombia. In St. Louis, the evidence suggests that increased patrols *without* proactive engagement (like stop & search) did not reduce shootings, while patrols *with* proactive encounters did (Rosenfeld et al., 2014).

The National Research Council of the US National Academy of Sciences (Weisburd & Majmunder, 2017) considered these and other studies in an extended discussion of how to interpret them. As the report concluded (p. 310) about "stop, question & frisk [SQF],"

CONCLUSION 4-9 Evaluations of focused uses of stop, question, and frisk (SQF) (combined with other self-initiated enforcement activities by officers), targeting places with violence or serious gun crimes and focusing on high-risk repeat offenders, consistently report short-term crime-reduction effects...

While there are correlational studies which claim to find no link between stop–search volume and overall crime, or even violent crime, the National Academies of Science (p. 311) report went on to note that:

Non-experimental analyses of SQF broadly applied across a jurisdiction show mixed findings. However, a separate body of controlled evaluation research (including randomized experiments) that examines the effectiveness of SQF and other self-initiated enforcement activities by officers in targeting places with serious gun crime problems and focusing on high risk repeat offenders consistently reports statistically significant short-term crime reductions.

The same National Academies report stressed the importance of SQF being *limited* and *proportionate* in its coupling to risk of high harm, and not un-coupled in a disproportionate way:

SQF indiscriminately focused across a jurisdiction or broken windows policing programs relying on a generalized approach to misdemeanor arrests ("zero tolerance") have not shown evidence of effectiveness. This caveat…should lead police executives to exercise caution in adopting generalized, aggressive enforcement tactics (p. 324)

Thus, the evidence on the value of SQF in preventing murder is highly important, but highly limited as to the kind of places that it works. If SQF is limited to the tiny fraction of all places in any city is consistently high risk, then it can save lives. While banning it in 95% of locations would make little difference, abandoning SQF in hot spots (or even reducing it) could allow murder rates to rise for people of all races. These facts are central to finding a balance between the risk of "over-policing" and "under-policing" (Brunson, 2020; Lum, 2021), as discussed below.

If we assume that "balanced" policing – with intrusiveness proportionate to the risks of violent injury or death – would be better policing, then we may need to accept different policing in different places depending on differences in risk. This is not a new idea, or even police practice. What is new is the extremity of contrast in policing levels required to match the recently discovered extremities of differences in risk of serious harm. Nor is this challenge limited to policing. Where high risks of harm can be identified in very specific places, all resources in government can be targeted selectively, with questions such as these:

- Which bridge will collapse first if not repaired?
- Which age groups should be vaccinated first against COVID?
- Which few places have the greatest risk of murder?

These are not just questions of *resource allocation*. They are also questions of *intrusions* on liberty, or about the apparent inequality of with-holding of services altogether from low-risk people or places. In all three examples, intrusive (or preferential) policies can be justified by a *balance* between harm prevented, and harm caused, by a decision to target a tested method.

If balanced policing can be based on proportionate intrusion and distribution, one model for developing it is England's 2020 Tiered system of COVID-19 prevention designed around risk of infection and death. While it is not clear whether a Tiered system is the ideal way to combat COVID, it is clear model of something else: tying legitimacy of intrusion to levels of risk of harm. That may be exactly what democratic policing needs to recover broader legitimacy.

2.3 PREVENTING COVID BY "TIERS" OF INTRUSIVE CONTROL: A METAPHOR OF PROPORTIONATE POLICING

The "Triple-T" of Evidence-Based Policing (Sherman, 2013) has had growing influence in policing across the UK (Jacobs, 2021), with the mnemonic clarity of using best evidence for *targeting* resources selectively to the greatest need, *testing* the effectiveness of police practices with rigorous field experiments, and *tracking* both police compliance with evidence-based policies and their relationship to outcomes such as crime harm. Yet, these core concepts are so broad in their potential application that we can learn more about policing when we see how they are applied in other areas of government – as a useful metaphor.

What use is a metaphor? One answer comes from renowned scientist who visited Athens airport, where he discovered that *"metaphoros."* is the Greek word for a luggage trolley. He was delighted because "metaphors *transport* [as a trolley does] a familiar concept from one sphere of experience to another, and we could scarcely begin to understand the world around us without them" (Gale, 2020: 279; emphasis added).

The aim of this section is to present a metaphor that shows how evidence-based policing could restructure the collateral harm of police practices to help reduce both racial inequality and harm crime. That aim requires explaining the UK's Tier system of COVID restrictions in 2020. That system can serve as a metaphor for the Tiered Policing system proposed below. The key dimension of similarity is that both systems justify their restrictions on civil liberties on the grounds of proportionate benefit in the prevention of harms, including death.

In an effort to minimize the economic disruption of limiting COVID infections through restrictions on social contact, the British government established three "Tiers" of restrictions on liberty in England in 2020. The extent of these restrictions was applied differentially, based on statistical evidence, to specific geographic areas. The version of these restrictions taking effect from December 2 (UK Government, 2020) were labeled

Tier 1: "Medium Alert" [Lowest]
Tier 2: "High Alert"
Tier 3: "Very High Alert" [Highest]

Each of these Tiers was to be based on complex algorithms and decision processes. These were to be determined not only with a daily supply of new data, but on frequent changes about *which* data were more important in deciding the level of intrusiveness, and thus which tier an area should be in. For example, the rate of reproduction of the Coronavirus ("R") had a great weight, but so did the death count, as well as hospital beds available. If the beds approached maximum capacity, however, the hospital factor could be given a higher weighting.

The implied goal of the Tiered system was to try to balance the principles of fairness and risk. Even though the first three Tiers were later followed by a 4th (and proposed 5th) Tier, the principle remained consistent: matching (or "coupling") restrictions to liberty with risks of serious harm. The principle of fairness was that no one should suffer more intrusion on their liberties than was *proportionate* to their community's level of risk of harm – or the average level in their general area. Some unfairness, of course, inevitably came from aggregating people of all ages (with widely varying risk levels) and towns across large districts, which also varied widely in death rates and infection rates. At the same time, the extent of economic damage from closing businesses was lower from this *targeted* system than it would have been (and later was) under a *universal* system, thus minimizing the harm of the cure.

What is important about the system was its attempt to gain clarity about who could (and could not) do what, where. That was intended to provide clarity for police, merchants, and citizens, after a period in which a complex set of rules had previously applied to everyone in England – with substantial confusion about some rules and their interpretation. The need for clarity became even greater with a move from one system to three, distributed differentially across the landscape. For example, as of December 2, 2020, the people in

> *Tier 1 areas* would have to wear facemasks indoors in shops, except when they went to pubs or restaurants to eat – where they could eat with people who were not members of their households, unlike people in
>
> *Tier 2 areas* who were not allowed to eat in restaurants at all, unless they were alone or with members of their household, while in
>
> *Tier 3 areas* the restaurants and pubs were to be closed down and locked up, with no one allowed to buy anything but take-away from the front door.

By using precision *targeting*, the Tier system was designed to reduce the costs of false positives, by which commerce would have been forbidden unnecessarily in low-risk areas. The mathematics predicted that a Tier system would minimize the reduction of economic production and income without increasing deaths or harm from COVID.

Targeting vs. Testing. What legitimized this system in the view of the Cabinet was evidence-based *targeting* with daily micro-geographic data about infections and death risks. But in the eyes of its Parliamentary majority of legislators who were not in the governing Cabinet, a lack of explicit *testing* of the components of the intrusions made the intrusions illegitimate. Restrictions on multi-household dining at Tiers 2 and 3, for example, caused major economic damage to the restaurant industry. Yet, the evidence to show that the restrictions would save lives was not presented with the proposal. Members of Parliament who were not in the Cabinet then demanded that a full "cost-effectiveness" analysis of the evidence for the restrictions be provided. The government was largely unable to provide direct evidence because there had been no such tests, i.e., field experiments, comparing infections linked to restaurants with and without the ban on multiple households.

Tracking? What the Members of Parliament did not raise was the extent to which compliance with these rules would be tracked. The issue had already surfaced with high-level officials breaking the rules, but widespread tracking of ordinary people was virtually impossible. It relied largely on good will and belief in the efficacy of the policies. Thus, the need for *testing* was pressed by challenges for both *targeting* and *tracking* (Sherman, 2013).

Indirect evidence from case studies (such as all of Wales) did provide some testing, after Welsh infections dropped within weeks of a Tier 3 style lockdown. But the imperfections of an impromptu innovation on this scale are not the point. Rather, the question is whether the goal of clarity is still better served by clearly *coupling* intrusiveness to levels of risk that are *proportionate* to the intrusion.

More precisely, our question is how this idea would work in policing against serious violence – and reducing intrusion levels against minor offenses?

2.4 POLICING SERIOUS VIOLENCE BY TIERS

Tiered policing against serious violence could be developed from evidence-based analysis of risk across medium-sized areas, combined with public consultation of local elected and governmental officials. A three-level system of risk could reflect the logic of the COVID prevention Tiers in England. Resource constraints would be more prominent in a police system than in a COVID system, given the far lower numbers of deaths from violence than deaths from COVID (over 155,000 COVID deaths in one year versus ~700 murders across England). With less harm at stake, the targeting of violence by Tiers could be far more limited at Tier 2, with Tier 3 designations an extremely rare occurrence nation-wide – even though most murders might occur in Tier 3.

Taking harm, resources, and other demands into account, Tiered Policing *could* be structured as follows, but with other versions of this schematic clearly possible:

> *Tier 1*: Low Risk of Serious Violence. No restrictions on civil liberties, minimal policing for violence prevention or full enforcement, *stop & search by police of both vehicles and pedestrians generally prohibited or greatly restricted.*
>
> *Tier 2*: Medium Risk of Serious Violence. No special powers to search, but some use of targeted violence-prevention policing in geographic areas or with potential victims or offenders. *Stop and search generally prohibited without specific intelligence.*
>
> *Tier 3*: High Risk of Serious Violence. Extra resources assigned to target areas, with all powers of stop & search under standard rules of evidence used to *substantially increase stop and search to reduce serious violence.*

What would this system change? At the very least, it could reduce the numbers of stop & search encounters of innocent people (especially minority group members) that have caused so much anger at police, especially by members of minority groups (see Weisburd & Majmundar, 2018). At the same time, it would increase the use of stop & search where it is needed most, and where it could create the biggest effect in reducing racial disparity in homicide victimization.

Many would say that there is already "no policing without tiers." They might even say that something like the system described above already exists. Yet, it is clear that many, if not most, stop–search encounters take place in areas that are Tier 1 or 2 (under this proposed system); see Gladwell's (2019, p. 310) discussion, for example, of North Carolina traffic stops. More precise evidence is found in Dorset, UK (Sherman & Kumar, 2021).

Nonetheless, as demands on UK police services have risen, a wide range of triage tools have been developed for the purpose of allocating more resources to more serious matters, and fewer resources to less serious business. Pursuing organized criminals, chasing wanted cars identified on motorways by cameras (Sidhu et al., 2017), checking on sex offenders released from prison (Jackman, 2015) – these and other tasks are already performed in the UK by sorting (triaging) targets into Tiers. There are also criteria for deciding when to send multiple officers, extra armaments, or (in the UK) even whether to send officers with firearms to a scene.

2.5 TIERS, TRANSPARENCY, AND TARGETING

One key difference between current police tiers and a more formal "Tiered Policing" system for preventing homicide is *transparency*. The idea of declaring precisely *where* the danger of murder is elevated would make policing as transparent – and perhaps as subject to debate – as England's COVID Prevention Tiers. But debate can be a valuable means of creating legitimacy for a controversial practice. If police agencies adopted evidence-based targeting, they could declare that top-Tier locations were selected solely on the basis of statistical evidence of risk – not by race of local residents, or by intuition, or by untestable intelligence. These locations could be large or small, depending on resources and population density. Whatever the design, it can be fully explained to the public.

The key issue for areas will be how large or small they should be, and whether that decision should be generalized or particularized. If the 34,753 LSOAs (Lower-Layer Super Output Areas, comparable to US Census Tracts) in England & Wales were the generalized unit of analysis, there could be debates about crime clusters that sit across the boundary between two or three LSOAs. The counter-proposal could then be to particularize that hot spot based on where the crime is concentrated, rather than where the standard boundaries are drawn. This is not an issue for this chapter to resolve, but one for it to identify. Police leaders at the level of entire forces, district or city council areas, or police precincts could all be empowered to make those decisions in consultation with local citizens – subject to review by superior officers or regulators. The entire process could remain highly transparent.

The same transparency could apply to people as well as areas that could serve to limit the targeting of individuals even within violence hot spots, and further limit false-positive searches. In a recent analysis, Campana and Giovanetti (2020) were able to predict future violence by individuals in Liverpool with substantial accuracy, without using any demographic information on those individuals. The sole predictors in the model were prior offences of the potentially targetable individuals (from all people with recent prior arrests), as well as offences of their co-offenders, with a focus on knife-crime offenders and their degrees of separation from co-offenders with no knife-crime charges (yet). Thus, even without a conviction for a knife offence, police could have reliable statistical evidence of which people are more at risk of carrying weapons illegally. Rather than imposing stop & search activity on just anyone or everyone found in a violence hot spot, a Tiered system of notice to individuals could be limited to those most dangerous persons, based solely on their prior crime history.

A further benefit of transparency is that it is an antidote to potential false negatives, as well as false positives. If a street segment or other area is *not* listed as a "Tier 3" area for violence prevention, but a murder subsequently does occur there, the residents could ask local police for a review of the data in order to qualify that area for future (and more stop–searches). They might also, looking backwards to the Tiering decision before the murder, add further intelligence which could be incorporated, in a systematic way, in the decision to list a location as Tier 3 (or not). Parents of children murdered in such areas in London have already demanded increases in stop & search frequency (Gadher & Lamb, 2020).

Conversely, identification by police of a place as a Tier 3 area might be a shock to local residents or leaders. They may be galvanized to meet with police to understand the evidence for such a designation. They might challenge the data, or take issue with how Tier 3 powers are being applied. But there would be no doubt that due diligence had been undertaken by police in deciding to use stop–search powers in an area.

Most important, the transparent presentation of any system would allow a dialogue about racial disparity in policing, framed in a completely different way: seeking a balance between "over-policing" and "under-policing." That balance is about how much liberty must – or should – be lost in exchange for how much reduction in harm can be gained. There is no "right' answer to that question. But there is a wealth of evidence-based policing and Triple-T decision frameworks that can support the discussion – including a new proposal of an index for Risk-Adjusted Disparity for *tracking* police intrusions by race, age, gender, or any category.

2.6 TRACKING "OVER-" AND "UNDER-POLICING": A RISK-ADJUSTED DISPARITY (RAD) INDEX

For a meaningful dialogue about intrusions on liberty, a Tiered system for targeting intrusive policing can begin with a different way to calculate a *balance* between over-policing and under-policing – at least for the *small number of Top-Tier areas*. The key task is to specify the "line" that intrusive policing, relative to risk of criminal victimization, would be "under" or "over." If that line is conceptualized as a measure of both proportionality of risk to intrusion and equal protection across races, it can be measured objectively across thousands of cases. That statistical concept of "the line" would offer more evidence-based and balanced criteria than investigations of specific tragedies emerging from "system failures" (Sherman, 2018). Such tragedies become infamous because they are atypical, rather than representative of everyday practice.

The application of a Risk-Adjusted Disparity Index in any location can consist of six steps.

Step 1. *Target the Tier 3 Areas* within specific and measurable boundaries, on the general principles discussed above.

Step 2. *Track Violent Crimes* by Victim Race in each Tier 3 Area for any specific time period. This does not need to depend upon the census data for residents by race; it can rely solely on the self-identified race or ethnicity supplied by crime victims to police at the time of each crime or incident report (despite some limitations on accuracy of those data). The race of crime victims also serves to provide a "benchmark" or denominator that is influenced more by the characteristics of the street population at risk of being stopped than by a decennial count of the local resident population, meeting a standard that a National Academy of Sciences report has recommended in the US (Skogan & Frydl, 2004, pp. 321–322).

Step 3. *Track the Imposition of Stops* by Race of Persons Stopped. These reports, if generated consistently by officers conducting stop–searches or vehicle stops, can also rely on the self-identified race or ethnicity supplied by crime victims to police at the time of each crime or incident report (despite some limitations on accuracy of those data as well). Here again, it does not matter whether the persons stopped are residents or visitors from other areas of the city, country, or world. Their presence on the street provides an estimate of the level of treatment by police in relation to the crimes suffered by people of their own race, in a context by which most serious violent crime is intra-racial. With high rates of victim–offender overlap for serious violent crimes (Sandall et al., 2018; Hiltz et al., 2020), there is a reasonable case for any deterrence of weapons-carrying to help prevent injuries to the persons that police stop.

Step 4. *Compute Ratio of Police Stops to Violent Victimizations* for each racial group. These ratios are not the measure of proportionality of stops to crime risk. They are simply the building blocks for the calculation of the RAD Index. If the ratio of stops is 77 stops per 100 violent crimes against white people versus 770 stops per 100 violent crimes against non-white people that is a striking difference. But it can also be stated more precisely, and with greater value for comparisons.

Step 5. *Compute Ratio of Ratios* for Risk-Adjusted Disparity Index. In the example above, a ratio of 770 stops per 100 violent crimes against non-whites would be divided by the ratio of 77 stops per 100 violent crimes against non-whites. The result would be 770/77 = 10 to 1. That result would show, in effect, that holding constant the risk of crimes against non-whites, they are still ten times more likely to be searched by police than whites. This would seem to indicate a greater level of intrusiveness against non-whites than whites. The indication would be much clearer than relying on raw numbers alone, by which (for example) the whites could have had 770 stops against 1,000 violent crimes, yielding equal raw numbers of stops by race but concealing the unequal ratio of ratios.

Step 6. *Discuss Imbalanced Ratios* of "Balanced Policing." There may well be local or short-term circumstances that could allow a community to consider even heavily imbalanced ratios. A recent spike in murders of young black men in gang conflict, for example, might explain or even justify a large imbalance. Better yet, however, in that example police could consult with a community and deliver a planned imbalance, for the sole purpose of reducing inequality in murders of young Black men. Otherwise, the data could be used to radically overhaul stop search practices throughout an area or across an entire police force.

This process is not purely hypothetical. With the support of the Dorset (UK) Police, Cambridge criminologists (Sherman and Kumar, 2021) analyzed the RAD Index for all 173 of the 452 LSOAs that had any serious violent crimes against both whites and non-whites. They computed the RAD Index for the entire police force area, for which the population-based rate of stops was 20 times higher for Black Britons than for whites. With the RAD Index, this ratio fell to 6.6 to 1. But even with the RAD formula, the racial disparity was still higher than many thought desirable. That analysis then led to developing a series of options for lowering both the RAD Index and the inequality by race in the rates of violent crime victimizations, which have been substantially higher for non-whites. Those options are described in Sherman and Kumar, 2021.

The key point for any police agency is that the equity in policing remains a separate issue from whether police are doing enough to reduce violent crime. There is a crucial tension between doing enough to fight a crime problem and maintaining equity by race in the process. The line between under-policing an ethnic or racial group and over-policing it is centered, in effect, on whether stop and searches within groups are *equally* proportionate to their level of risk of violent crimes across ethnicities. The greater the risk, the more intrusion by SQF would be justified. Yet, even if a RAD Index of 1:1 is achieved, a persistent finding of non-whites suffering homicide rates five times higher than whites would still constitute a major problem of equal protection (Sherman and Kumar, 2021). What the RAD Index provides is a means of getting to the point of assessing whether equity in intrusions can be established, and *then* asking whether that equity can also produce equal risks of serious victimization.

What the RAD Index – as a ratio of the two race-specific ratios of stops to crimes – adds to the concept is therefore important but limited. It does not answer the question of whether there is "enough" policing given the level of risk. What it measures is whether there is an *equal* application of SQF to people in the two ethnic categories, based on their respective risks of victimization by serious violence. It is only by using the comparison across ethnicities that we can define "over" or "under" the same intrusiveness-to-risk ratio experienced by the other group. While the idea of "how much policing is "enough" for any community is essentially a subjective or ethical one, the question of whether two groups have *equal* application of SQF based on risks of violent crime can now have a highly objective answer.

One possible response to a RAD Index analysis, then, would be to *greatly increase stops of both Whites and Non-Whites in high-violence areas*. If tracking that decision showed substantial reductions in violence, that would be consistent with prior research. It could also legitimate the idea of more stop–search in a few hot spots, while reducing them in most other locations. The combination of reduced false positives outside violence hot spots with reduced false negatives inside hot spots might just bring praise for police actions, or at least reduce the level of anger at police over issues of race.

That is, in effect, what some minority group leaders in London have said, while campaigning for *more* stop & search, such as the Times reported in late 2020: "Richard Taylor, whose 10-year-old son, Damilola, was stabbed to death in Peckham, south London, two decades ago on Friday, said the use of stop and search should be increased, as long as it is used in a 'humane' way" (Gadher & Lamb, 2020).

Parents like Taylor, and other community leaders, could ask to see the data on stops, searches, and knives seized from suspects, by race, with trends over several years. If police can develop the data systems to help share these decisions, there could be an increase in public trust in policing. The RAD index could also change the focus of SQF discussions from "how many" to "how," which is the focus of Richard Taylor's concern about "humane" policing. Communities care not only about whether police use the tool with equal *frequency*. They care about whether police conduct stops with equal *courtesy*. More broadly, police leaders care about whether the manner of delivery can better follow principles of procedural justice: explanations, listening, respect and other dimensions that can be tracked with coding of body-worn video records of SQF encounters (Nawaz & Tankebe, 2018). These codings can also produce tracking data for each area, and compare the treatment during SQFs of white and non-white subjects. With a limited number of Top Tier areas in which to focus all this tracking and analysis, it is far more feasible to achieve than trying to do the same across an entire police force area – most of which has no violent crime, most years.

One way any of this proposal is likely to happen is with the help of better platforms for dialogue between police and the public.

2.7 TALKING THROUGH TIERS

Just as the English national government needed to consult with local governments about COVID Tiers, each police force (from Minneapolis to Paris) would be well advised to consult about the use of intrusive policing. That would apply to all kinds of intrusion, not just stop & search.

CCTV, traffic enforcement, and focused deterrence are all examples of decisions for consultation with local communities. Given the evidence that precisely targeted SQF save lives, however, it is a prime example of what can be better delivered with a system of Tiered Policing supported by legitimacy. That legitimacy would apply to both police and the public.

The proposed methods of improving police legitimacy include a notable emphasis on community dialogue (Bottoms & Tankebe, 2012) between police and citizens. While the specifics of such dialogue have not been proposed or tested, a focus on classifying each local area into one or three Tiers would provide a concrete focus for discussion. Whether the discussions occur in local government Councils, community centers or police stations, they would all have a common data dashboard for evidence-based policing.

Since 2019, for example, legal tools such as a Knife Crime Protective Order have been developed in England to give police special powers with such persons. The implementation of KCPOs would raise the issue of how best to identify such persons: reactively, through recent cases, or proactively (as well) by ongoing digital analysis of the kind pioneered with Merseyside Police. Should police warn those with orders that they will be stopped whenever they are sighted? Should stops be combined with other 'focused deterrence' measures like door knocks and arrest for all minor infringements? These and other questions could be answered in a proposal that could be announced to the public with a 60-day period for written comments or even voice-mail messages – all before police implemented a new set of practices.

Crucial to the dialogue, however, is the question of whether policing "works." As long as a theme of protest is that policing does not prevent crime, the dialogue can yield little more than two groups talking past each other. As Tankebe (2013; Tankebe et al., 2016) has found on several continents, police legitimacy depends not only on trust in police to be *fair*, it also depends on trust in them to be effective.

Thus, another way to introduce evidence-based changes concerning racial equity in crime and policing is to propose controlled experiments with the changes. The crossover design used by Barnes et al. (2020) provides a particularly democratic model, in which all small areas get equal amounts of policing and intrusiveness, but on different days that were randomly assigned. If the "trial" results are then presented to local communities before a final decision is made, evidence of effectiveness (if that is the finding) could shore up public trust and confidence in the innovations being tested. Moreover, a crossover design need not be prolonged. A 90-day trial in even 15–25 hot spots can provide a statistically powerful test.

And how would the results be presented: in a church basement? In a district council chamber? Or in a hybrid model, with up to 10,000 people watching on Zoom? The COVID era has increased the possibilities for police dialogue with the public – even to the point of showing PowerPoint slides of research evidence on Zoom screens.

2.8 CONCLUSION

If democratic policing in the digital age can invent new platforms for fostering dialogue, it will help to strengthen democracy itself. It can also strengthen the use of evidence to make policing decisions in consultation with communities. But we must walk before we run. First we need good principles and conceptual tools, of the kind outlined in this chapter. Then we can communicate broadly about how the tools work, how to use them, and what results they may show in any given community.

After two decades of evidence-based policing, we have learned many facts. What our future depends on, however, may be two principles: *proportionality* of intrusion to risk and a very limited use of high intrusion by *coupling* it to very high risk. The idea of an equally applied "carpet" of policing spread evenly across a vast area is inconsistent with the evidence of crime concentrated in high spikes across that area (Weinborn et al., 2017). The evidence must become better known, so the debates can be as informed as they are compassionate.

If democratic policing can use better evidence to hold back intrusive policing wherever and whenever it is disproportionate to the harm prevented, then democratic policing will have a secure future. George Floyd died when four officers responded to a call about an allegedly counterfeit $20 bill; in the aftermath of that death, many wanted policing itself to die. Now is the time for democratic policing to develop systems to prevent such disproportionately harmful intrusions by policing. Systematic coupling – and limitation – of proactive policing to places and people of high risk of high harm is a good hypothesis to test. If it works, democratic policing may adapt and thrive for another two centuries. More important, it may help the rule of law itself to survive, as well as democracy, with equal protection for all.

References

Akinwotu, E. (2020a). Nigeria to disband Sars police unit accused of killings and brutality. *The Guardian*. www.theguardian.com/world/2020/oct/11/nigeria-to-disband-sars-police-unit-accused-of-killings-and-brutality

Akinwotu, E. (2020b). Nigeria cracks down on 'end Sars' protesters, alleging terrorism; Authorities suspend accounts of supporters and fine media for 'exaggerated reporting'. *The Guardian*. www.theguardian.com/world/2020/nov/13/nigeria-cracks-down-on-end-sars-protesters-alleging-terrorism

Allen, P., & Burke, D. (2020). Paris riots: Protesters launch fireworks during 'anti-police brutality' demonstrations. *Mirror*. www.mirror.co.uk/news/world-news/paris-riots-protesters-launch-fireworks-23085085

Bailey, H. (2020, November 13). Minneapolis violence surges as police officers leave department in droves. *Washington Post*. www.washingtonpost.com/national/minneapolis-police-shortage-violence-floyd/2020/11/12/642f741a-1a1d-11eb-befb-8864259bd2d8_story.html

Barnes, G. C., Williams, S., Sherman, L. W., Parmar, J., House, P., &Brown, S. A. (2020). Sweet spots of residual deterrence: A randomized crossover experiment in minimalist police patrol. https://osf.io/preprints/socarxiv/kwf98/

Bottoms, A., &Tankebe, J. (2012). Beyond procedural justice: A dialogic approach to legitimacy in criminal justice. *The Journal of Criminal Law and Criminology*, *102*, 119–170.

Broadwater, L., & Fandos, N. (2020). Amid tears and anger, House democrats promise 'Deep Dive' on election losses. *New York Times*. www.nytimes.com/2020/11/05/us/house-democrats-election-losses.html?action=click&module=RelatedLinks&pgtype=Article

Brunson, R. K. (2020). Protests focus on over-policing. But under-policing is also deadly. *Washington Post*. www.washingtonpost.com/outlook/underpolicing-cities-violent-crime/2020/06/12/b5d1fd26-ac0c-11ea-9063-e69bd6520940_story.html

Campana, P., & Giovanetti. (2020). Predicting violence in Merseyside: A network-based approach using no demographic information. *Cambridge Journal of Evidence-Based Policing*, *4* (3), 89–102.

Centers for Disease Control. (2021). *Data Finder – Health, United States – Products*. Retrieved February 28, 2021, from www.cdc.gov.

Cohen, S. (1985). *Visions of social control: Crime, punishment and classification*. Basil Blackwell.

Cohen, J., & Ludwig, J. (2002). Policing crime guns. In J. Ludwig, & P. Cook (Eds.), *Evaluating gun policy: Effects on crime and violence*. (pp. 217–239) Brookings Institution.

Crabtree, S. (2020). Most Americans Say Policing Needs 'Major Changes'. *Gallup News*. https://news.gallup.com/poll/315962/americans-say-policing-needs-major-changes.aspx

Durkan, J. A. (2020). *Executive Order 2020–10: Reimagining Policing and Community Safety in Seattle*. https://durkan.seattle.gov/wp-content/uploads/sites/9/2020/10/Executive-Order-2020-10-Reimagining-Policing-and-Community-Safety-in-Seattle.pdf

Gadher, D., & Lamb, C. (2020). Cressida Dick: Black boys 'nine times more likely to be murdered'. The increased use of stop and search is disproportionately affecting black people but the Met chief says it is saving young lives. *The Times*. www.thetimes.co.uk/edition/news/cressida-dick-black-boys-nine-times-more-likely-to-be-murdered-cv6ts7qmm

Gale, E. (2020). *The species that changed itself: How prosperity reshaped humanity.* Allen Lane.
Gladwell, M. (2019). *Talking to strangers.* Allen Lane.
Herndon, A. W. (2020) How a Pledge to Dismantle the Minneapolis Police Collapsed. *New York Times* 27 September.
Hiltz, N., Bland, M., & Barnes, G. C. (2020). Victim-offender overlap in violent crime: Targeting crime harm in a Canadian suburb. *Cambridge Journal of Evidence-Based Policing*, 217–239, 1–11.
Hopper, S. (2018). *Predicting discovery of weapons during stop-and-search encounters in London: Implications for proportionate use of a controversial tactic.* [Unpublished thesis]. University of Cambridge.
Jackman, R. (2015). *Measuring harm in a cohort of sex offenders in Norfolk.* [Unpublished thesis]. University of Cambridge.
Jacobs, J. (2021). The radical idea to reduce crime by policing less, not more: Evidence-based policing aims to make policing more fair, by treating it like medicine running controlled trials to see which interventions work, and which don't. *Wired.* www.wired.co.uk/article/evidence-based-policing
Judge, I. (2011). *Summary Justice in and Out of Court* [Annual Harris Lecture]. The Police Foundation.
Kahneman, D. (2011). *Thinking, fast and slow.* Macmillan.
Koper, C. S., & Mayo-Wilson, E. (2012). Police strategies to reduce illegal possession and carrying of firearms: Effects on gun crimes. *Campbell Systematic Review, 8*(1), 1–53.
Kumar, S., Sherman, L. W., & Strang, H. (2020). Racial disparities in homicide victimisation rates: How to improve transparency by the Office of National Statistics in England and Wales. *Cambridge Journal of Evidence-Based Policing*, 4(3), 178–186.
Liang, H. H. (1969). The Berlin police and the Weimar Republic. *Journal of Contemporary History*, 4(4), 157–172.
Lum, C. (2021). Perspectives on policing. *Annual Review of Criminology*, 4, 19–25.
McGarrell, E. F., Chermak, S. M., & Weiss, A. (2002). Reducing gun violence: Evaluation of the Indianapolis Police Department's Directed Patrol Project. *US Department of Justice Office of Justice Programs.*
Mogelson, L. (2020). The heart of the uprising in Minneapolis. *The New Yorker.*
Nawaz, A., & Tankebe, J. (2018). Tracking procedural justice in stop and search encounters: Coding evidence from body-worn video cameras. *Cambridge Journal of Evidence-Based Policing*, 2(3–4), 139–163.
Pavia, W. (2020). Murders in New York at highest level for a decade. *The Times.* www.thetimes.co.uk/article/murders-in-new-york-at-highest-level-for-a-decade-3bvvrsns9
Reiss, A. J., & Roth, J. (Eds.) (1993). *Understanding and controlling violence*, 1. National Academies Press.
Rosenfeld, R., Deckard, M. J., & Blackburn, E. (2014). The effects of directed patrol and self-initiated enforcement on firearm violence: A randomized controlled study of hot spot policing. *Criminology*, 52(3), 428–449.

Sandall, D., Angel, C. M., & White, J. (2018). 'Victim-offenders': A third category in police targeting of harm reduction. *Cambridge Journal of Evidence-Based Policing*, 2(3), 95–110.

Sherman, L. W. (1987). *Repeat Calls to Police in Minneapolis*. Office of Justice Programs. www.ojp.gov/ncjrs/virtual-library/abstracts/repeat-calls-police-minneapolis

Sherman, L. W. (1992). Attacking crime: Police and crime control. In N. Morris & M. Tonry, (Eds.), *Modern policing: Crime and justice, 15*, (pp. 159–230). University of Chicago Press.

Sherman, L. W. (1998). Evidence-based policing. *Police Foundation*. www.policefoundation.org/wp-content/uploads/2015/06/Sherman-1998-Evidence-Based-Policing.pdf

Sherman, L. W. (2007). The power few: Experimental criminology and the reduction of harm. *Journal of Experimental Criminology*, 3(4), 299–321.

Sherman, L. W. (2013). The rise of evidence-based policing: Targeting, testing, and tracking. *Crime and justice*, 42(1), 377–451.

Sherman, L. W. (2018). Reducing fatal police shootings as system crashes: Research, theory, and practice. *Annual Review of Criminology*, 1, 421–449.

Sherman, L. W. (2020). Avoidable deaths in police encounters with citizens: Immediate priorities. *The ANNALS of the American Academy of Political and Social Science*, 687(1), 216–226.

Sherman, L. W., & Berk, R. A. (1984). The specific deterrent effects of arrest for domestic assault. *American Sociological Review*, 49(2), 261–272.

Sherman, L. W., Gartin, P. R., & Buerger, M. E. (1989). Hot spots of predatory crime: Routine activities and the criminology of place. *Criminology*, 27(1), 27–56.

Sherman, L. W., & Kumar, S. (2021). Equal protection by race with stop and frisk: A Risk-Adjusted Disparity (RAD) index for balanced policing. *Cambridge Journal of Evidence-Based Policing*, 5, 1–19.

Sherman, L. W., Shaw, J. W., & Rogan, D. P. (1995). The Kansas City Gun Experiment. US Department of Justice, Office of Justice Programs, National Institute of Justice.

Sherman, L. W., & Weisburd, D. (1995). General deterrent effects of police patrol in crime "hot spots": A randomized, controlled trial. *Justice Quarterly*, 12(4), 625–648.

Sidhu, B., Barnes, G. C., & Sherman, L. W. (2017). Tracking police responses to "hot" vehicle alerts: Automatic number plate recognition and the Cambridge crime harm index. *Cambridge Journal of Evidence-Based Policing*, 1(4), 211–224.

Skogan, W., & Frydl, K. (Eds.) (2004). *Fairness and Effectiveness in Policing: The Evidence*. Report of the Committee to Review Research on Police Policy and Practices. National Academies Press.

Tankebe, J. (2013). Viewing things differently: The dimensions of public perceptions of police legitimacy. *Criminology*, 51(1), 103–135.

Tankebe, J., Reisig, M. D., & Wang, X. (2016). A multidimensional model of police legitimacy: A cross-cultural assessment. *Law and Human Behavior*, 40(1), 11–22.

UK Government. (2020). Local Restriction Tiers: What You Need to Know. Gov. www.gov.uk/guidance/local-restriction-tiers-what-you-need-to-know, downloaded December 1, 2020.

Vitale, A.S. (2017). *The end of policing*. Verso.

Watkins, A. (2020). Violent year in New York and across U.S. as pandemic fuels crime spike. *New York Times*.

Weinborn, C., Ariel, B., Sherman, L., & O'Dwyer, E. (2017). Hotspots vs. harmspots: Shifting the focus from counts to harm in the criminology of place. *Applied Geography, 86*, 226–244.

Weisburd, D. (2015). The law of crime concentration and the criminology of place. *Criminology, 53*(2), 133–157.

Weisburd, D. (2016). Does hot spots policing inevitably lead to unfair and abusive police practices, or can we maximize both fairness and effectiveness in the new proactive policing? University of Chicago Legal Forum, 661–689.

Weisburd, D. (2020). Review of *Talking to Strangers*, by Malcolm Gladwell. *Cambridge Journal of Evidence-Based Policing*, 4(3–4).

Weisburd, D., Groff, E. R., & Yang, S. M. (2014). Understanding and controlling hot spots of crime: The importance of formal and informal social controls. *Prevention Science, 15*(1), 31–43.

Weisburd, D., & Majmundar (Eds.) (2018). *Proactive Policing: Effects on Crime and Communities*. Committee on Proactive Policing: Effects on Crime, Communities, and Civil Liberties, Committee on Law and Justice. National Research Council.

3

Re-inventing Policing

Using Science to Transform Policing

Peter Neyroud and David Weisburd

In our 2011, as members of the Harvard Executive Session on Policing and Public Safety, we contributed a paper on "Police Science: Towards a New Paradigm." In it we envisaged that the application of science to all aspects of policing, the organization as well as its intended outcomes, would be crucial to reform and transformation (Weisburd & Neyroud, 2011). We argued that sustainable transformation of policing could not be achieved by pursuing solely either technical improvements (to the science of evaluation of outcomes) or institutional improvements (to the rules and internal and external regulation of the organization), but necessarily required both (Mastrofski & Uchida, 1993).

The paper has become one of the most cited papers in the debates over the role of science and evidence in policing. From first publication, it has attracted a lively debate. It has been argued (e.g., Sparrow, 2011; Fielding et al., 2019) that we advocated exclusively experimental methods and provided too narrow a focus on crime and disorder outcomes. We suggest that this has been a wilful misreading of our advocacy of police science as a broad field of knowledge, drawing on the best research available to address questions of importance and urgency for policing. Right from Sherman's original definition of evidence-based policing (EBP) it was described as the "best available research on the outcomes of police work to implement guidelines and evaluate agencies, units, and officers" (1998, p. 3). While this definition might seem to imply a focus on crime, harm, and disorder, Sherman's subsequent development of the "Triple T" model explicitly embraced the whole institutional framework and was not confined to the evaluation of operational strategies and interventions, nor exclusively to the advocacy of experimental methods (Sherman, 2013).

Re-inventing Policing: Using Science to Transform Policing 45

Where both Weisburd and Neyroud (2011) and Sherman (1998, 2013) converge is on the need for the science of policing to be applied and for those in the field of policing to be engaged in its production, dissemination, and deployment into policy and practices.

This paper will follow that lead and focus on the application of science to the whole organization. As such it presents an updating and restating of our 2011 proposal on police science (Weisburd & Neyroud, 2011) and should be read in conjunction with that paper. We will conclude, however, that our earlier model failed to emphasize specific issues in science and policing that have emerged as particularly important over the last few years – they fall not under the rubric of scientific methods, but rather within the domain of moral and ethical dimensions of the scientific model.

3.1 POLICING AND SCIENCE

Over the last three decades, the police have innovated at a rapid pace, developing new practices and policies that have reformed and changed the policing industry (Weisburd & Braga, 2019). The police, who were once considered conservative and resistant to change, have become a model for criminal justice systems experimentation and innovation. The police have pioneered the development of new relationships between criminal justice and the public in community policing. They have crafted new strategies of crime control, introducing problem-oriented policing, hot spots policing, pulling levers policing, and a host of other new strategic innovations, including the introduction of new technologies such as DNA testing and Body-Worn Cameras. The police also have experimented with new management methods in programs such as Compstat, EMUN, and "Copstat" (Sherman et al., 2014; Weisburd et al., 2003; Weisburd et al., 2020) and have integrated the new technologies into crime prevention and control through innovative crime analysis approaches such as intelligence-led policing (Ratcliffe, 2008) and with new methods of describing data such as computerized crime mapping.

In their efforts to innovate and change over the last two decades, the police have often enlisted the help of academics and researchers. In the development of Compstat in New York City, for example, academic research not only helped to define why new approaches were necessary (Bratton, 1998; Bratton & Knobler, 1998), but police scholars like George Kelling were enlisted to help identify and refine promising police practices. In the more recent EMUN program in Israel, academics became a key part of the development and assessment of innovative efforts to institutionalize problem-oriented policing (Weisburd et al., 2020). Hot spots policing has its origins in basic academic research and has been the subject of systematic scientific evaluation (Braga et al., 2019; Braga & Weisburd, 2010). Police–researcher partnerships have been a prominent feature of the policing landscape over the last two decades, and it is no longer surprising to see researchers in police agencies.

Yet, despite progress, there remains a fundamental disconnect between science and policing. By "science" we include the broadest array of methods and technologies that police have confronted and which have been used to study, evaluate, critique, and understand policing over the last half-century. This includes advances in forensics, such as DNA testing, digital fingerprinting, and other technologies meant to improve detection and identification; the development of algorithmic systems; lastly, also social science, which often has been neglected by the police, but has begun to play an increasingly important role over the last few decades both in terms of advancing crime analysis and in evaluating and assessing traditional police practices and new innovations in police strategies. By science, we also mean the advancement of the use of scientific models of inquiry such as problem-oriented policing. Despite the advances made in the use of science in policing and in the leadership and management of policing, science has yet to move to center stage in most police agencies and in most jurisdictions.

While the number and scope of evaluation studies have expanded (Neyroud, 2017), most police practices are still not systematically evaluated. We still know too little about what works and under what conditions in policing (National Research Council [NRC], 2004; Weisburd & Eck, 2004; Weisburd & Majmundar, 2018; Telep & Weisburd, this volume). The evidence-based model for developing practices and policies has not been widely adopted by police agencies. Strategies developed in police agencies are generally implemented with little reference to research evidence (Weisburd &Neyroud, 2011). The adoption of police innovation has tended not to have a strong relationship with science. Most police agencies still have limited interest in using scientific methods to evaluate programs and practices. Surveys examining the adoption of evidence-based approaches have suggested a relatively low level of adoption across European police forces (Nägel & Vera, 2020). Even police practitioners who are committed to using scientific evidence recognize that the present state of practice makes a sophisticated use of science difficult in many police agencies (Jaschke et al., 2007; Neyroud, 2008).

Often, the introduction of research develops serendipitously from a "bright idea" of police practitioners or researchers rather than through systematic development of knowledge about practice. There is often little baseline data from which to define an innovation, and the outcomes that are examined are usually restricted to official data measured over very short periods. Most studies of innovations are based on simplistic methodologies, focus on process rather than design, and often fail to address key issues around transferability or, equally crucial, sustainability (Willis & Mastrofski, 2011). Based on an assessment of whether the idea worked, innovative police leaders try to diffuse the idea more widely in their agencies, and across agencies, without adequately having researched what the real effect was. Despite some notable exemplars, even in many innovative police agencies, innovation is more a symbolic activity than a real scientific activity.

While there are many examples of good practice, most police agencies do not see science as critical to their everyday operations. Yet, can one imagine medicine today without the large infrastructure of research that stands behind medical practices and public health policies? While some of the debates about our scientific knowledge in handling the COVID pandemic have illustrated that the science is far from providing clear and simple answers, the debates have generally been bounded by science from a range of disciplines. As such "Science" is valued both by medical practitioners and by ordinary citizens. In policing there is a problem with the "credibility of social science research" (Shepherd, 2004). The police do not see social science as essential to the work of police agencies. A perfect illustration of this can be found in the content of most core police education and training (Neyroud, 2011). There is little concern with either scientific evidence or evidence-based policing (Telep & Lum, 2014). In turn, police science is often ignored even when the evidence is unambiguous. Take for example the continued application of programs like Drug Abuse Resistance Education (D.A.R.E.) that have been shown to be ineffective but continue to be supported and implemented by police agencies (Clayton et al., 1996; Rosenbaum, 2007; Rosenbaum et al., 1994).

It is not just the application of social science that has missed its mark in policing. The National Academy of Sciences report on forensics expressed significant concern regarding the identification and application of science in areas such as fingerprint identification and forensic odontology (NRC, 2009). There is a strong relationship between the weaknesses of applying the scientific method to forensics and a lack of acceptance of social science in policing. The police have long been interested in how new technologies can be harnessed to advance police work. Yet, they have seldom sought to evaluate how these new technologies affect policing, and whether and how they make the police more effective. The Urban Institute study of DNA effectiveness (Roman et al., 2009) and more recently, the extensive research on Body-Worn Cameras (Ariel et al., 2018: Lum et al., 2020) provide both important exceptions and a glimpse of the real potential for science to support police reform.

One consequence of the lack of value of science in much of the policing industry is that there is little advocacy of such science in government. Medical research in the United States received more than 41.6 billion a year in government funding (National Institutes of Health, 2020) and in the United Kingdom, more than £746 million ($954.5 million) (Department for Business, Energy and Industrial Strategy, 2018). However, the National Institute of Justice (NIJ), the primary US funder of research in criminal justice, had a total budget of only $43.5 million in fiscal year 2020 and a budget for research and evaluation (in which its policing division is located) of only $15.6 million. The primary funder of crime research in the United Kingdom, the Home Office, has a budget for research of only £1.5 million ($2 million) (Home Office, 2020). Although there is evidence that police associations such as the International Association of Chiefs of Police (IACP) and major city chiefs in the USA and the National Police Chiefs Council in the UK have objected to cuts in research budgets in the past, we do not think that such efforts have been consistent or sustained.

We started by focusing on the responsibility of policing to step up its use and ownership of science. However, we also think that the academic support for policing has, for the most part, failed to meet the needs of policing. To focus only on the police when noting the disturbing absence of a large infrastructure for science in policing neglects the failure of academic police scholars to make themselves relevant to the everyday world of the police. Much academic research has been divorced from the dynamics of policing. The police operate in a reality in which decisions must be made quickly, and issues of finance and efficiency can be as important as effectiveness. But academic policing research generally ignores these aspects of the police world, often delivering results long after they have relevance, and many times focusing on issues that police managers have little interest in and little ability to respond to.

Real issues in policing often have little salience in the halls of universities. In medicine, clinical involvement is seen as an important part of the research enterprise, and clinical professors are well integrated into medical science. In policing, academics would be unlikely to advance in universities if they nested themselves in police agencies to address specific problems such as burglary or car theft, and it is rare for clinicians to have an active research role in universities. Recent calls for academics to disengage from policing following the death of George Floyd will only damage the prospects for research impact on policing still further. As it is, the everyday problems of policing have little status in the universities. In return, in general, the police have tended until quite recently not to insist on graduate and post-graduate educational and professional standards, or at least have been discouraged from doing so by police unions and other interested political forces, and this has distanced the police even further from academia (Baechler, 2019; Paterson, 2011).

3.2 THE CHALLENGE OF DEVELOPING NEW INSTITUTIONS FOR POLICE SCIENCE

One area where collaboration between police and academics is greater is crime analysis, which has become an integral part of police agencies (Weisburd, 2008). In the UK in particular, a number of partnerships have been developed between universities and the police as illustrated by the National Intelligence Model (Grieve et al., 2008). But it is important to note that in most police agencies there are still problems achieving integration between crime analysis and the everyday world of policing, and still less involvement between scientific work in universities and the work of crime analysis in policing (HMIC, 2014).

Compare this with laboratories in major university hospitals where the skills of scientists are not only cutting-edge but are also integrated into a larger world of science. Major university hospitals expect their scientific staff to be conducting research that is published in the best scientific journals and disseminated widely. They encourage them to look for new "discoveries" in their clinical work, and to follow standards set by national scientific bodies.

It might be argued that police do not have the resources to develop science of this type in their agencies. Of course, one reason for this is that police do not place a high priority on science, and thus there is little support for funding for police science on the part of government. It might be argued as well that this challenge is being overcome in policing with the development of police–researcher partnerships. Such partnerships have played a role in raising the profile of science in police agencies and in bringing new technologies and skills, especially in crime analysis. In the US, the roots of police–researcher partnerships go back to the 1970s with the relationship of the Kansas City Police Department, Mo., to the Midwest Research Institute. The New York City Police Department (NYPD) also had an early collaboration with the Vera Institute of Justice. The Vera Institute–NYPD collaboration can be seen as a model not only because of the serious research that was conducted but also because the police invested in this partnership over a long period by providing the Vera Institute with a yearly grant for technical assistance (Bloom & Currie, 2001). More recently in Israel, Roni Alsheich, who served as General Director of the Israel Police, allocated monies for evaluations of programs, and for a high-level advisory committee of scientists to give advice on police innovation. In this case, as with many other efforts to advance Science in Policing, the investment in science did not extend beyond the innovative "evidence cop's" tenure (Sherman, 1998; See Perry and Wolfowicz, this volume).

The Vera Institute and Israeli models are unusual; partnerships are more commonly a product of funding by state or federal agencies. The 1990s saw an explosion of such funding opportunities, and the research partnership model became a common part of the policing landscape. The origins of these partnerships supported by government can be found in the early 1990s when the then Director James Stewart of NIJ funded a series of collaborations in which police agencies and researchers both received funding to enhance research on the police (Garner & Visher, 2003).

The partnership model was further reinforced with the U.S. Crime Bill of 1994 and the creation of the Office of Community Oriented Policing Services in 1994. Following upon earlier successes, the federal government now began to fund an array of different types of partnerships between police and scholars, paving the way for the acceptance of research in police agencies and recognition of the importance of policing as a focus of academic study. It became common to visit police agencies and see criminologists "in the building."

In the United Kingdom, partnerships between the police and researchers also began to have influence in the everyday world of policing. Ken Pease's ground-breaking Home Office research on repeat victimization in Kirkholt and Manchester showed how scientific evidence could change police practices, in this case by recognizing that a recent victim is very likely to be victimized again (Pease, 1991). The diploma/masters in applied criminology at Cambridge, which included practice-based research, was required for senior law enforcement managers for a period in the late 1990s, but was then unilaterally discontinued by the police, as yet another wave of changes was introduced to senior leadership development.

Throughout this period, the science of police research remained a province of the universities and not police agencies. By this we mean that the questions asked generally had their origins in the questions of researchers, and not necessarily in the needs of the policing industry. The ownership of such research was not in the agencies that were the sites for its development, but in the academic institutions and among the academic researchers that sponsored them. The perception of many police is that the real beneficiaries of research programs are the researchers and not the police. And why they would not they feel this way, considering that the research findings are often disseminated long after the sites have lost interest in the questions asked and usually after new administrators that have little contact with the original research are in office?

Finally, a deeper and more fundamental reason for the disconnect between police science and police practitioners lies in the fundamentals of police education and training. As we have suggested above, science is normally not central to police education and training. Neither CEPOL's survey (Hanak & Hofinger, 2005) nor Janet Chan and colleagues' seminal study of student officer training (Chan et al., 2003) nor the Review of Police Leadership and Training in the UK (Neyroud, 2011) showed much evidence of a professional and evidence-based approach to learning. Although it may be critical for police officers to have a good working knowledge of the law, that this is to the exclusion of a good working knowledge of the theory and evidence for its effective practice strikes us as a major factor in the failure of science to establish itself in policing. Moreover, the limited progress of police to create accredited standards for education prior to joining the force and throughout the careers of police officers has reinforced the realities of policing as a "blue collar job" (Reiner, 2000) rather than a profession supported by a credible corpus of knowledge. This, in turn, has further distanced police from the importance and relevance of police science.

3.3 TOWARD OUR NEW PARADIGM: POLICE OWNERSHIP OF POLICE SCIENCE

For police science to succeed the way science has in other professions, it must move from the outside to the center of policing. Scientific research must become a natural and organic part of the police mission. Science must become a natural part of police education, and police education must become based in science (Neyroud, 2011). Science in policing must answer questions that are critical to the police function, in a timely fashion and it must address problems that are at the core of policing and address the everyday realities that police face. In this context "evidence-based policing" must become a central tenet of police management and organization (Lum & Koper, 2017).

For that to happen, the policing profession must take ownership of police science. To take ownership the police will have to take science seriously and accept that they cannot continue to justify their activities on the basis of simplistic statistics, often presented in ways that bias findings to whatever is advantageous to police. Evidence-based practice is becoming a key component of public institutions in medicine, education, and government (Sanderson, 2002; Slavin, 2002). In this regard, education provides a particularly instructive example for the policing industry. Education, like policing, operates in a world of decentralized and independent agencies. And before the turn of the twenty-first century, large education programs were seldom subjected to evaluation, and there was little federal investment in high-quality experimental field trials (Cook, 2001). However, in fiscal year 2009, just seven years after the establishment of the Institute of Education Sciences in the US Department of Education, the federal budget for high-quality research reached $167 million, with a fiscal year 2010 request for $224.2 million (US Department of Education, 2020). Evidence-based science has grown exponentially in education.

One missing component of police science today is large public, government-supported, research institutes that can play the leadership role in advancing research about police practices. In the 1970s, the government and foundations in the US developed institutions such as the Police Foundation, the Police Executive Research Forum, and the research arm of the International Association of Chiefs of Police. But, whatever the many successes of these institutes in the development of police science, they cannot take on the central role of government entities such as the National Institutes of Health or the Institute of Education Sciences. There is clearly a need for a large government agency that would play a central role in police science. Such an agency could also provide the much-needed guidance as to standards for police agencies, license and accredit police practice, require continuous professional development, and perhaps most importantly hold agencies that continue to use ineffective or harmful practices accountable.

We are, personally, only too aware of the fragility of new agencies in this sphere. The National Police Improvement Agency (NPIA) in the UK had been following this approach, underpinned by an ambitious "science strategy" which had strong police ownership. The NPIA did not survive the incoming Coalition government's austerity drive in 2011. The College of Policing, setup following the first author's report (Neyroud, 2011) recommending the creation of a professional body for policing, has had some successes in building a "What Works" center but with very reduced resource and implementation capacity.

For police science to succeed it must also be a "blue chip" science. Universities must become an important part of police infrastructure. It is instructive to remember that hospitals were not always integrated with major university centers. Indeed, in the early nineteenth century, the integration of universities and hospitals was a major innovation. Tenon (1788) pioneered this innovation by pointing out that hospitals were like butcheries and that medical training and research needed to be brought into the medical centers. Note that innovators did not remove medical research from the hospital, but rather sought to bring the "universities into the hospitals" (Bonner, 2000). In this same sense, we must bring the universities into police centers. Again, there are important examples of such programs already developing. In Providence, R.I. (with John Jay College of Criminal Justice) and Alexandria, Va. (with George Mason University), new partnerships between police and researchers developed that built on the university medical center model and that have been initiated by the partners rather than federal funding agencies. In the UK, regional research partnerships have brought clusters of police agencies and police forces together (Crawford, 2020).

Such partnerships remain dependent on short-term funding rather than a more permanent restructuring of the police–university relationship. We think more generally that there should be "clinical professors" of policing, and even of police specialities like burglary or homicide investigations. There should as well be "practitioner-scientists" who are supported by and located in police agencies. But this would mean that the universities would have to value police practice and reward scholars for advancing such practice, and police agencies would have to accord greater recognition to science and reward police officers involved in science. The emergence of the national societies of Evidence-based policing in the UK, US, Canada, and Australasia has been one important development, signalling an appetite for police science from within the profession. Similarly, the emergence of the Division of Policing at the American

Society of Criminology, together with smaller but important groups within the British and European Societies, provide a network of policing scholars committed to making an impact with research.

Another change that will likely have to occur if the paradigm we are advocating is to succeed is that training of police and police researchers will need to take place, at least in part, at university policing centers. In medicine, practitioners and researchers are trained in the same university teaching hospitals. Shepherd argued that a major impediment to the development of crime science is the fact that practitioners have little understanding of science, and scientists little understanding of practice (Shepherd, 2001; see also Feucht & Innes, 2009). He advocated for a major change in education for police and police researchers and the introduction of a university hospital model for policing. We think this proposal has much merit and would play a major role in putting police research in police agencies so that it is connected to the real world of policing. Of course, there are significant impediments to such a model. Many police agencies still only require a high school degree for employment. Even though there has been a call for decades for a bachelor's requirement in policing both by scholars and police executives (Carte & Carte, 1973; Carter & Sapp, 1990; Roberg & Bonn, 2004), the resistance of police unions in the US and the Police Federation and some Police and Crime Commissioners in the UK will make it difficult to implement this change generally anytime soon. Again, we think it short-sighted on the part of unions to resist a college education requirement or a degree basis to the training qualification, both because the new realities of policing demand greater education and because the relatively higher salaries of young police officers make their educational requirements inconsistent with those in other professions.

Finally, there is no question that the measures of success of police agencies will have to be changed if police science is to be accorded a high priority within the police. Today, there is limited pressure on police executives to show that their policies and practices are evidence-based. Compstat represents one of the few major management innovations in policing that succeeded even in part in putting outcomes, and especially crime outcomes, at the center of evaluation of performance in policing. More recently, there has also been the development of Crime Harm Indices as a measure of value-added impact (Sherman et al., 2016), and the EMUN program in Israel (Weisburd et al., 2020). The shift we are suggesting would place science as a key component of such evaluation.

Instead of being incidental to change and development in policing, we envisage science at the heart of a progressive approach to policing. From the very beginning, recruits to the organization would be inducted and trained within a scientific framework. Although knowledge of the law is a critical component of effective policing, our recruits would understand the evidential base not only of legislation but also of the most effective strategies to harness the law for the betterment of society. They would learn that, as professional police officers, there would be a constant expectation that they would contribute to the expansion of knowledge through their own research and field experimentation, an expectation strongly reinforced by an informed and committed leadership that understands that knowledge drives improvement in policing, just as it provides better medicine, teaching, and forensic provision. Throughout their careers, our officers would be constantly exposed to the challenge of excellent teaching from police universities, at which the very best of their number would hold posts as clinical professors. The constant cycle of learning and improvement would be supported by the commitment of a significant percentage of the organization's budget, in the firm and committed belief that excellence is a product of knowledge and constant, systematic challenge, and research. Our vision of the changes from the current to our new paradigm can be summarized in Table 3.1.

3.4 POLICE SCIENCE, POLICE REFORM, AND THE ETHICAL TRANSFORMATION OF THE POLICE

Since we wrote our original paper on this topic in 2011, the calls for reform of policing have become more pressing and the demands for change have increased to "de-funding," "abolition," and transformation (Vitale, 2017; Yglesias, 2020). During the Global COVID-19 pandemic, police found themselves as the principal agent of public enforcement of restrictions on personal liberty. The death of George Floyd threw a stark focus on the disproportionate impact of police enforcement operations and police use of force. The event acted as a catalyst for calls for change to which police chiefs were largely unable to respond with science. A response which simply referenced stop and search or use of force would, in any case, have been inadequate. While there are serious flaws in the arguments of some of the proponents of defunding and abolition such as Vitale (Yglesias, 2020), merely relying on the reform of tactics, the publication of statistics and the prosecution of officers presented a reactive rather than transformative response.

TABLE 3.1 *Changing to a science-based policing paradigm*

	Old paradigm	Science-based policing
Education and training	Based around legal knowledge and work-based learning.	Founded in science, linking scientific knowledge with practice and continual professional development.
Leadership	Leaders see science as useful when it supports initiatives, but an inconvenient truth when it does not.	Leaders both value science and see it as a crucial part of their own, their staff, and their agencies' development and essential to the agencies' efficiency, effectiveness, and legitimacy with the public.
Academic–police relationship	Separate and distinct institutional and professional structures.	University police schools combine both teaching and research, with strong institutional links and personnel exchange with local police agencies.
Development of practice	Practice develops by individual initiatives and political mandates.	Practitioners and agencies are committed to constant and systematic research and evaluation of practice.
Investment in research	A limited national and local or individual commitment to evaluating specific initiatives.	A committed percentage of police spending is devoted to research, evaluation, and the development of the science and research base which is framed within a national (and possibly international) strategy to build the knowledge base over the medium to long term.
Ethical framework for decision-making and prioritization	Ethical codes and decision models developed but not tested.	Ethical codes and decision models developed, tested, and embedded in leadership and management doctrine.

In Sherman's original conception of EBP, the most important emphasis was not on the process of research, but rather on its application. He stated that "just doing research is not enough and that proactive efforts are required to push accumulated research evidence into practice through national and community guidelines" (Sherman, 1998, p. 1). Sherman made a strong connection to the organizational theories of continuous improvement. He argued that in contrast to traditional departmental custom and practice, EBP could provide a means to reform policing because it "challenges those [traditional] principles of decision making and creates systematic feedback to provide continuous quality improvement in the achievement of police objectives" (Sherman, 1998, p. 6).

And here we think we missed a key ingredient to the Science in Policing perspective. The issue is not focused on technical measures for increasing effectiveness in policing, or even for improving relationships between the police and the public. Rather it is about the ethical and moral dimension of police service (Neyroud, 2019). In this context, we think that it is critical to add another category to Table 3.1. The Ethical and Moral Context of Policing. To date that has been defined primarily by political echelons or the courts. But science also has something key to say about what the ethical questions surrounding what the police should do, and how they should do it. Coming back to the example of medicine, medical ethics is a key component of evidence-based medical science. We think that it is time for the police to look to develop a model of policing ethics and moral responsibility akin to the large-scale concern for this issue in medicine. If this had been part of the scientific model of policing, the police today and police scholars would be in a much stronger position to respond to challenges surrounding the policing task. Many of the most important challenges to policing today relate to the lack of moral boundaries in policing in relationship to use of force, arrests, and other law enforcement activities. These concerns are not about police effectiveness but about fairness, discrimination, and more generally the moral boundaries of police conduct. To that end we have added an additional element to our original table to incorporate ethical codes and decision-making and frame them within our model of police science.

How would this moral dimension influence science in policing? For one, it would add an additional level of discussion to police strategies. Hot spots policing for example, has been advanced in evidence-based policing primarily because of its crime prevention benefits (Weisburd and Majmundar, 2018). But another key issue is whether it increases or decreases police surveillance of disadvantaged and minority communities? Does it increase freedom in society because of its reduction in crime, or decrease freedom because of its intensive policing activities at particular places? Such questions must be addressed both in terms of the ethical dilemmas that are raised, as well as with scientific data. For example, there is little evidence that hot spots policing impacts upon citizen perceptions of the police (Weisburd, 2016). Moreover, by focusing on hot spots, police surveillance is applied to only very specific streets in communities (Weisburd, 2016). In traditional large area or community-based approaches, police surveillance is applied in such areas. In this context, hot spots policing may reduce police intrusion in the lives of communities. In applying this new element of our new paradigm into an operational context Sherman (2013) argues that policing must focus more generally on the harm caused by the "power few" most harmful offenders and the harm caused to the most vulnerable victims (Sherman, 2013). This aligns with a science-based and a human rights compliant approach by encouraging police to adopt a proportionate use of police powers.

Ethical and moral judgements are integral to the application of science in the public sphere. Good science is not simply about what works, but also about how we learn about what works. Good science is not simply about what we do, but the ethical and moral dimensions of what we do. And finally, science includes supervision over the ways in which we learn about successes or failures in the field. Institutional review boards are as much a part of science in universities as the scientific method. For Science in Policing to be truly scientific, police will have to take ownership of the ethical and moral dimensions of police science. This is something we left out of our 2011 paper, but which we think is key if policing is to prosper in the coming decades.

3.5 CONCLUSION: POLICE SCIENCE AND POLICE TRANSFORMATION

We judge that some of the most important broader, transformative, institutional aspects of the original conception of EBP, and police science have been obscured by a technical debate over the relative validity of different research methods (Sherman, 2013; Hope, 2017). Much of the criticism of evidence-based policing has centered on the primacy placed on randomized trials. Recognizing the value of randomized trials does not negate other forms of research. Indeed, in many of areas of policing randomized trials may not only be difficult to carry out but also may not answer some of the key questions needed to advance policing.

In our proposals set out in this chapter, we have continued to emphasize the importance of the ownership of police science by the profession of policing. In our view, the transformation of policing requires an evidence and science informed leadership prepared to challenge practice and policies, using science as the gold thread to support that process. Treasured tactics borrowed strategies and "good practice" must all be subjected to the hard light of scientific inquiry, in which assumptions are objectively tested and the balance of harms the police protect us from and harms caused by policing interventions are measured and, therefore, capable of being managed and subjected to democratic oversight.

But we have emphasized in our rethinking of Science in Policing the importance of adding to the mix the key importance of ethics and moral judgements as part of the scientific enterprise. The police version of the Hippocratic oath – "first, do no harm" – is that police in a democratic society should only intervene to the extent that the harm they are seeking to prevent is far greater than the unintended harms that their interventions cause, and that they should use the best science to target their interventions, to test the impacts and track the outcomes (Sherman, 2013). Ownership of police science also, therefore, requires police leaders to own the ethical obligation to use science to transform the people that they recruit and develop, the processes upon which policing depends and the technology that supports it, within a governance framework (see Lum & Koper, 2017) that should also reinforce and respect police science as a key part of oversight.

References

Ariel, B., Sutherland, A., Henstock, D., Young, J., & Sosinski, G. (2018). The Deterrence Spectrum: Explaining Why Police Body-Worn Cameras 'Work' or 'Backfire' in Aggressive Police–Public Encounters. *Policing: A Journal of Policy and Practice, 12*(1), 6–26. https://doi.org/10.1093/police/paw051

Baechler, S. (2019). Do We Need to Know Each Other? Bridging the Gap between the University and the Professional Field. *Policing: A Journal of Policy and Practice, 13*(1), 102–114. https://doi.org/10.1093/police/pax091

Bloom, A., & Currie, D. (2001). *A Short History of Vera's Work on Policing.* Vera Institute of Justice.

Bonner, T. N. (2000). *Becoming a Physician: Medical Education in Britain, France, Germany, and the United States, 1750–1945.* Johns Hopkins University Press.

Braga, A. A., Turchan, B., Papachristos, A. V., & Hureau, D. M. (2019). Hot Spots Policing of Small Geographic Areas Effects on Crime. *Campbell Systematic Reviews, 15*(3), 1–88. https://doi.org/10.1002/cl2.1046

Braga, A., & Weisburd, D. (2010). *Policing Problem Places: Crime Hot Spots and Effective Prevention.* Oxford University Press.

Bratton, W. (1998). Crime is Down in New York City: Blame the Police. In N. Dennis (Ed.), *Zero Tolerance: Policing a Free Society* (2nd ed). IEA Health and Welfare Unit.

Bratton, W. J., & Knobler, P. (1998). *Turnaround: How America's Top Cop Reversed the Crime Epidemic*. Random House.

Carte, G. E., & Carte, E. H. (1973). *Police Reform in the United States: The Era of August Vollmer, 1905 1932*. University of California Press.

Carter, D. L., & Sapp, A. D. (1990). The Evolution of Higher Education in Law Enforcement: Preliminary Findings from a National Study. *Journal of Criminal Justice Education, 1*(1), 59–85.

Chan, J., Devery, C., & Doran, S. (2003). *Fair Cop: Learning the Art of Policing*. University of Toronto.

Clayton, R. R., Cattarello, A. M., & Johnstone, B. M. (1996). The Effectiveness of Drug Abuse Resistance Education (Project DARE): 5-Year Follow-Up Results. *Preventive Medicine, 25*(3), 307–318.

Cook, T. D. (2001). Sciencephobia: Why Education Researchers Reject Randomized Experiments. *Education Next, 1*(3), 63–68.

Crawford, A. (2020). Societal Impact as 'Rituals of Verification' and The Co-Production of Knowledge, *The British Journal of Criminology, 60*(3), 493–518. https://doi.org/10.1093/bjc/azz076

Department for Business, Energy and Industrial Strategy. (2018). The Allocation of Funding for Research and Innovation. *Gov*. https://assets.publishing.service.gov.uk/government/uploads/system/uploads/attachment_data/file/731507/research-innovation-funding-allocation-2017-2021.pdf

Feucht, T. E., & Innes, C. (2009). Creating Research Evidence: Work to Enhance the Capacity of Justice Agencies for Generating Evidence [Unpublished manuscript].

Fielding, N., Bullock, K., & Holdaway, S. (2019). *Critical Reflections on Evidence-based Policing*. Routledge.

Garner, J., & Visher, C. A. (2003). The Production of Criminological Experiments. *Evaluation Review, 27*(3), 316–335.

Grieve, J., MacVean, A., Harfield, C., & Phillips, D. (Eds.) (2008). *Handbook of Intelligent Policing: Consilience, Crime Control, and Community Safety*. Oxford University Press.

Hanak, G., & Hofinger, V. (2005). *Police Science and Research in the European Union*. CEPOL.

Her Majesty's Inspectorate of Constabulary. (2014). *Crime Recording: Making the Victim Count*. www.justiceinspectorates.gov.uk/hmicfrs/wp-content/uploads/crime-recording-making-the-victim-count.pdf

Home Office. (2020). *Annual Reports and Accounts 2019–20*. Home Office. https://assets.publishing.service.gov.uk/government/uploads/system/uploads/attachment_data/file/902593/HO_Annual_Report_and_Accounts_2019-20_FINAL.pdf

Hope, T. (Ed.) (2017). *Perspectives on Crime Reduction*. Routledge.

Jaschke, H. G., Bjørgo, T., Del Barrio Romero, F., Kwanten, C., Mawby, R. I., & Pagon, M. (2007). *European Approach to Police Science*. CEPOL.

Lum, C. M., & Koper, C. S. (2017). *Evidence-based Policing: Translating Research into Practice*. Oxford University Press.

Lum, C., Koper, C., Wilson, D.B., Stoltz, M., Goodier, M., Eggins, E., Higginson, A., & Mazerolle, L. (2020). Body Worn Camera on Police Officer and Citizen Behavior: A Systematic Review. *Campbell Systematic Reviews, 16*(3), 1–40.

Mastrofski, S. D., & Uchida, C. D. (1993). Transforming the Police. *Journal of Research in Crime and Delinquency*, 30(3), 330–358. https://doi.org/10.1177/0022427893030003005

Nägel, C., & Vera, A. (2020). Police Science as an Emerging Scientific Discipline. *International Journal of Police Science & Management*, 22(3), 242–252. 1461355720917413.

National Institutes of Health. (2020). *Appropriations Language*, FY 2020 (H.R. 1865 PDF). Office of Budget, Department of Health and Human Services, National Institutes of Health.

National Research Council. (2004). Effectiveness of Police Activity in Reducing Crime, Disorder and Fear. *Fairness and Effectiveness in Policing: The Evidence*, 217–251.

National Research Council. (2009). *Strengthening Forensic Science in the United States: A Path Forward*. National Academies Press.

Neyroud, P. (2008). Past, Present and Future Performance: Lessons and Prospects for the Measurement of Police Performance. *Policing: A Journal of Policy and Practice*, 2(3), 340–348.

Neyroud, P. (2011). Professional Policing in Times of Change. *Policing: A Journal of Policy and Practice*, 5(4), 285–286. https://doi.org/10.1093/police/paro51

Neyroud, P. (2017). Policing with Science: A New Evidence-based Professionalism for Policing. *European Police Science and Research Bulletin, Special Issue* 2, 39–44.

Neyroud, P. (2019). Ethical Leadership in Policing: Towards a New Evidence-Based, Ethical Professionalism? In *Police Leadership* (pp. 3–22). Palgrave Macmillan, Cham.

Paterson, C. (2011). Adding Value? A Review of the International Literature on the Role of Higher Education in Police Training and Education. *Police Practice and Research*, 12(4), 286–297. https://doi.org/10.1080/15614263.2011.563969

Pease, K. (1991). The Kirkholt Project: Preventing Burglary on a British Public Housing Estate. *Security Journal*, 2(2), 73–77.

Perry, S., & Wolfowitz, M. (this volume). The Role of the "Super Evidence Cop" in Evidence-Based Policing: The Israeli Case. In D. Weisburd, T. Jonathan, G. Perry & B. Hasisi, (Eds.), *The Future of Evidence-Based Policing*. Cambridge University Press.

Ratcliffe, J. (2008). *Intelligence-Led Policing*. Routledge.

Reiner, R. (2000). *The Politics of the Police*. Oxford University Press.

Roberg, R., & Bonn, S. (2004). Higher Education and Policing: Where Are We Now? *Policing: An International Journal of Police Strategies & Management*.

Roman, J. K., Reid, S. E., Chalfin, A. J., & Knight, C. R. (2009). The DNA Field Experiment: A Randomized Trial of the Cost-effectiveness of Using DNA to Solve Property Crimes. *Journal of Experimental Criminology*, 5(4), 345.

Rosenbaum, D. P. (2007). Just Say No to D.A.R.E. *Criminology and Public Policy*, 6(4), 815–824.

Rosenbaum, D. P., Flewelling, R. L., Bailey, S. L., Ringwalt, C. L., & Wilkinson, D. L. (1994). Cops in the Classroom: A Longitudinal Evaluation of Drug Abuse Resistance Education (DARE). *Journal of Research in Crime and Delinquency*, 31(1), 3–31.

Sanderson, I. (2002). Evaluation, Policy Learning and Evidence-based Policy Making. *Public Administration, 80*(1), 1–22.

Shepherd, J. P. (2001). Emergency Medicine and Police Collaboration to Prevent Community Violence. *Annals of Emergency Medicine, 38*(4), 430–437.

Shepherd, J. P. (2004). A Scientific Approach to Policing. *Police Review, 9*, 15.

Sherman, L. W. (1998). *Evidence-Based Policing*. Police Foundation. www.policefoundation.org/wp-content/uploads/2015/06/Sherman-1998-Evidence-Based-Policing.pdf

Sherman, L. W. (2013). The Rise of Evidence-Based Policing: Targeting, Testing, and Tracking. *Crime and Justice, 42*(2013), 1–75. https://doi.org/10.1086/670819

Sherman, L. W., Neyroud, P. W. & Neyroud, E. C. (2016) The Cambridge Crime Harm Index: Measuring Total Harm from Crime based on Sentencing Guidelines. *Policing, a Journal of Policy and Practice, 10*(3),171–183.

Sherman, L. W., Williams, S., Ariel, B., Strang, L. R., Wain, N., Slothower, M., & Norton, A. (2014). An Integrated Theory of Hot Spots Patrol Strategy: Implementing Prevention by Scaling Up and Feeding Back. *Journal of Contemporary Criminal Justice, 30*(2), 95–122. https://doi.org/10.1177/1043986214525082

Slavin, R. E. (2002). Evidence-Based Education Policies: Transforming Educational Practice and Research. *Educational Researcher, 31*(7), 15–21.

Sparrow, M. (2011). *Governing Science*. National Institute of Justice.

Telep, C. W., & Lum, C. (2014). The Receptivity of Officers to Empirical Research and Evidence-Based Policing: An Examination of Survey Data from Three Agencies. *Police Quarterly, 17*(4), 359–385.

Telep, C. W., & Weisburd, D. (this volume). A Review of Systematic Reviews in Policing. In D.Weisburd, T.Jonathan, G.Perry, & B.Hasisi (Eds.), *The Future of Evidence-Based Policing*. Cambridge University Press.

Tenon, J. (1788). *Journal d'Observations sur les Principaux Hôpitaux et sur Quelques Prisons d'Angleterre*. Paris.

U.S. Department of Education. (2020). *Fiscal Year 2020 Budget Summary. Section II F. Institute of Education Sciences*. U.S. Department of Education. www2.ed.gov/about/overview/budget/budget20/summary/20summary.pdf

Vitale, A. S. (2017). *The End of Policing*. Verso Books.

Weisburd, D. (2008). Place-Based Policing. *Ideas in American Policing, 9*, 1–16. Police Foundation.

Weisburd, D. (2016). Does Hot Spots Policing Inevitably Lead to Unfair and Abusive Police Practices, or Can We Maximize Both Fairness and Effectiveness in the New Proactive Policing? *The University of Chicago Legal Forum, 2016*(16), 661.

Weisburd, D., & Braga, A. A. (Eds.) (2019). *Police Innovation: Contrasting Perspectives*. Cambridge University Press.

Weisburd, D., & Eck, J. E. (2004). What Can Police Do to Reduce Crime, Disorder, and Fear? *The ANNALS of the American Academy of Political and Social Science, 593*(1), 42–65.

Weisburd, D., Hasisi, B., Litmanovitz, Y., Carmel, T., & Tshuva, S. (2020). Institutionalizing Problem-Oriented Policing: An Evaluation of the EMUN Reform in Israel. *Criminology & Public Policy, 19*(3), 941–964.

Weisburd, D., & Majmundar. K. M. (Eds.) (2018). *Proactive Policing: Effects on Crime and Communities.* The National Academies Press.

Weisburd, D., Mastrofski, S., Mcnally, A., Greenspan, R., & Willis, J. (2003). Reforming to Preserve: COMPSTAT and Strategic Problem Solving in American Policing. *Criminology & Public Policy,* 2(3), 421–456. https://doi.org/10.1111/j.1745-9133.2003.tb00006.x

Weisburd, D., & Neyroud, P. (2011). *Police Science: Towards a New Paradigm.* New Perspectives in Policing. Department of Justice, National Institute of Justice.

Willis, J. J., & Mastrofski, S. D. (2011). Innovations in Policing: Meanings, Structures, and Processes. *Annual Review of Law and Social Science,* 7, 309–334.

Yglesias, M. (2020). The End of Policing Left Me Convinced We Still Need Policing. *Vox.* www.vox.com/2020/6/18/21293784/alex-vitale-end-of-policing-review

4

A Way Ahead

Re-envisioning the Relationship between Evidence-Based Policing and the Police Craft

James J. Willis and Heather Toronjo

> It's not what the vision is, it's what the vision does
> —Peter Senge

Americans abhor the status quo. When Alexis de Tocqueville journeyed to the United States in 1831 he observed the "perpetual change" that went on in this country, where "no natural boundary seems to be set to the efforts of man; and what is not yet done is only what he has not yet attempted to do" (1835/1990, p. 425). Since Americans first formed full-time professional police agencies around the time of de Tocqueville's visit, they have strived to improve them. Currently, one of the most powerful reforms is evidence-based policing (EBP). EBP's origins can be traced back to the domestic violence experiments of the 1980s (Sherman, 1992), but EBP rose to prominence in the late 1990s when Lawrence Sherman articulated many of its core elements in an influential Police Foundation essay (1998). Inspired by the medical model's goal of applying the systematic use of rigorous scientific evidence to clinical practice, Sherman envisioned a similar approach to discerning what works best for police agencies in preventing crime.

Just as the medical model espoused the virtues of randomized controlled trials, so too did Sherman, who wrote about the need for experimental research in policing and has, along with others, continued to do so (Sherman, 1998, 2013; Weisburd, 2010). Over the last two decades, this initial conception of EBP has evolved, with its followers now encouraging a broader definition, including a willingness to support methods other than experimental designs, and to conduct research on a wider range of outcomes than crime reduction and prevention. These outcomes include better police training, increasing officer wellness, and improving use-of-force policies (Sherman, 2013; Telep, 2016; Lum & Koper, 2017). It is too soon to know how much this widening of EBP's scope will affect its development as a reform, but it is fair to say that EBP remains largely rooted in a program evaluation paradigm focused on reducing or preventing crime (Thacher, 2018).

The visibility of several templates for systematically judging the strength of the statistical evidence available, and for facilitating its translation into policy and practice, reveals the prominence of high quality experimental and quasi-experimental evaluations within EBP, particularly in regard to crime prevention (Weisburd & Majmundar, 2018). For example, the U.S. federal government provides a web-based clearinghouse that rates the effectiveness of crime programs and practices on a straightforward scale. There is also the Evidence-Based Matrix, from the Center for Evidence-Based Crime Policy at George Mason University, which categorizes the effects of over 130 rigorous policing evaluations on crime and disorder in a simple visual format for making evidence readily accessible to practitioners.[1]

The EBP movement is committed to elevating the role of science in police decision making (Neyroud & Weisburd, 2014) and to transforming policing into a more "legitimate and respected profession" (Brown et al., 2018, p. 40). Still, similar to past reforms (Weisburd & Braga, 2019), EBP has its critics. Some challenge the special status of randomized controlled trials as a means for understanding the police (Greene, 2014; Moore, 2006; Sampson, 2010; Sparrow, 2016), or examine the limitations of the evidence they produce for informing actual policy in a complex and causally uncertain world. Sampson et al. (2013, p. 1) note the difficulty with "straightforward exportation of causal effects to policy recommendations," observing that any link between causal evidence and policy recommendation requires careful attention to issues around mechanisms and causal pathways, effect heterogeneity, and contextualization. For example, the Minneapolis Domestic Violence Experiment and its subsequent follow-ups found significant variations across cities regarding the effectiveness of arrest, including backfire effects, and demonstrated how contingent results complicate the ability of casual effect studies to make policy recommendations (Sherman, 1992). Other scholars object to the epistemological assumptions that elevate causal explanations over scientific approaches for interpreting human action and generating meaning (Flyvbjerg, 2001; Greene, 2014, 2019; Thacher, 2001, 2006, 2018).

[1] https://crimesolutions.ojp.gov/; https://cebcp.org/evidence-based-policing/the-matrix/

The purpose of our essay is not to revisit these debates (see Brown et al., 2018; Lumsden & Goode, 2018), but to present an intellectual framework for improving street-level police work that may prove useful to EBP's development. In this chapter, we suggest the following: we encourage EBP to broaden its focus from evaluating the outcomes of police programs or strategies toward assessing the tactical choices that experience has taught practitioners are most relevant in their everyday encounters with the public. In doing so, EBP stands to benefit from practitioners' rich and varied experiences, and from considering how to make science more relevant to the complicated situational realities of policing on the front lines (Ratcliffe et al., 2019; Thacher, 2008). We further encourage EBP to cultivate research that can generate knowledge on the essential normative or moral questions that characterize street-level discretion. Albert Reiss (1971: p. 121) once noted that, as a profession, policing required officers to make decisions affecting the "fate of people" that were not just technical but involved making "moral judgments." As such, patrol officers will not only benefit from knowing more about which operational tactics to adopt or to avoid, but also from knowing how to make principled decisions about doing "the right thing" (Mastrofski, 2018; Thacher, 2001; Willis & Toronjo, 2019). To make our argument, we build on existing scholarship (see Bayley & Bittner, 1984; Mastrofski, 1996; Thacher, 2001, 2008), and on some of our own empirical research using a case study, to better understand the police craft at the level of police encounters with the public. This helps illustrate some of the distinctive contributions craft can make to science (and vice versa) in order to enhance overall police performance (Willis & Mastrofski, 2017, 2018).

4.1 EBP'S AMBIVALENCE TOWARD CRAFT

The recent publication of a report from the National Academies of Sciences, Engineering, and Medicine is yet another indicator of the growing importance of EBP within the field of police research (and the specific program evaluation agenda with which it is most commonly associated) (Weisburd & Majmundar, 2018). The report, *Proactive Policing: Effects on Crime and Communities*, assesses the scientific evidence on different proactive policing strategies or programs, such as community policing and hot spots policing, in relation to crime and disorder, racial disparities, trust, and other community outcomes. The report's focus on a wider variety of outcomes than just crime demonstrates how EBP, as it matures, is expanding its scope (Greene 2019). Though valuable, the report's reliance on findings produced primarily through experimental and quasi-experimental program evaluation studies presents a narrow and incomplete vision for police reform. On the one hand, this research agenda provides important knowledge about the utility of different policing interventions to those police administrators who must make strategic decisions about what programs to implement in their own agencies. But on the other, the report pays scant attention to understanding the situated judgments that street-level police officers make in their everyday encounters with the public and their reasons behind them (Thacher, 2008). In fact, the report deliberately excludes patrol officers' direct needs and interests from its ambit (Weisburd & Majmundar, 2018). Some might argue that EBP is already embracing a wider range of topics and methods, highlighting, for example, the practitioner-led research projects conducted through the Police Executive Program at Cambridge University. We find this encouraging, but generating interpretive knowledge through case studies and assessing the micro-dynamics of police–civilian encounters still appear to be less central to EBP's identity than causal knowledge and programmatic evaluations at the strategic level. Indeed, the Committee's approach stands in stark contrast to a theory of policing that defines good police work in terms of how well individual patrol officers respond to "the particular circumstances they are called upon to handle" (Mastrofski, 1988, p. 65). Police work encompasses a wide range of problems, most of which do not involve responding to crime or enforcing the law. Donald Black calls these "human troubles," which include responding to auto accidents, mediating disputes, and handling "youthful disturbances of adult peace" (Black, 1971, p. 1090).

One of the leading proponents of this nonprogrammatic view of policing is Egon Bittner who defined police as having the unique capacity to use force, if necessary, in all those events where "something-that-ought-not-to-be-happening-and-about-which-somebody-had-better-do-something-now" (Bittner, 1990, p. 249). How well police officers respond to the particularities of these varied situations is the craft of policing, or an officer's ability to draw on what hands-on experience that has been "intuitively processed" (Bayley & Bittner, 1984, p. 35) has taught about "making good arrests, deescalating crises, investigating crimes, using coercion and language effectively, abiding by the law and protecting individual rights, developing knowledge of the community, and imparting a sense of fairness to one's actions" (Mastrofski, 1988, p. 65). Elsewhere, Egon Bittner referred to the police craft as "workmanship" and identified aspects of street-level patrol work highly valued by practitioners as the "resources of knowledge, skill, and judgment to meet and master the unexpected within one's sphere of competence" (Bittner, 1983, p. 3). At its best, craft establishes standards of excellence for police performance that far surpass those of law and bureaucracy. Those master craftspeople recognized by their peers as "cool, poised, inventive, careful, active, and nonviolent" are capable of handling complex situations judiciously and with uncanny skill and insight (Bayley & Bitter, 1984, p. 51).

EBP seems ambivalent about the police craft, initially treating it with suspicion before somewhat softening its stance (Brown et al., 2018: p. 43). It might be that proponents of EBP are beginning to recognize craft as "necessary" for "successful policing," but it is unclear to what extent this represents a decisive shift toward incorporating experienced-based learning into EBP approaches, and to what extent the balance between science and craft represents an equal and mutually rewarding partnership (Jonathan-Zamir & Weisburd, this volume; Willis, 2013). Unlike science, EBP has characterized craft as unsystematic and heavily shaped by "local custom, opinions, theories, and subjective impressions" (Sherman, 1998, p. 6), or "whims, hunches, feeling, and best guesses" (Lum, 2009, p. 3). Moreover, similar to other professions, EBP has emphasized the police craft's inferiority to science in making accurate predictions, noting how evidence-based algorithms consistently out-perform the judgments of experienced clinicians (Sherman, 2013). EBP has also tended to associate craft with those elements of police work that have been largely discredited as outmoded or antithetical to progressive policing (Lum et al., 2012). In this narrative, craft's more skillful, creative, and nuanced practices are easily forgotten or ignored.

Perhaps EBP's ambivalence toward craft is revealed most clearly by its lament that craft is a barrier or even a "smothering paradigm" to receptivity to science (Sherman, 2015). Studies consistently show that while police officers generally recognize the virtues of scientific research, they assign a much greater role to experience in their daily decision-making (Lum et al., 2012; Telep & Lum, 2014). This "proclivity" of the police to rely on experience is similar to other fields (e.g., medicine and psychology), and it is deeply rooted in "various emotional needs and cognitive biases and heuristics" to which all of us are subject (Jonathan-Zamir et al., 2019, p. 4). These criticisms notwithstanding, EBP does not advocate that science "replace the wisdom and experience of police professionals" (Lum & Koper, 2017, p. 17), but blend evidence into policing (Sherman, 2015). However, even with the recognition that craft and science should co-exist, EBP has had much more to say about the benefits of science than the distinct contributions craft can make to this relationship (Willis, 2013). What might EBP gain by taking craft's contributions to good police work more seriously?

4.2 WHAT CAN CRAFT CONTRIBUTE TO EBP?

When it comes to the craft of street-level police decision making, EBP has drawn a sharp distinction between System II thinking, which is deliberative, systematic, and grounded in analysis and evidence, and System I, which is rapid, intuitive, and based on practical experience (Sherman, 2013, p. 416; Sherman, 2015). EBP has highlighted the flaws of System I thinking, including its susceptibility to a range of cognitive errors (Mears & Bacon, 2009, p. 143), but while some street-level decision-making is intuitive, street-level observations of the police suggest a decision-making process that can also closely resemble System II approaches, and is a much richer source of decision-making creativity and effectiveness than EBP admits (Mastrofski, 2018; Muir, 1977).

Often described as 'common sense' by police officers, System I thinking is similar to the naturalistic decision-making model (NDM) (Alpert & Rojek, 2011). Focused on how experts make decisions in real-world settings under "difficult conditions such as limited time, uncertainty, high stakes, vague goals, and unstable conditions" (Klein, 2008, pp. 456–7), NDM suggests that skilled practitioners are like chess masters. Over many years playing different opponents, chess masters are able to recognize similarities across the many scenarios they have learned, and they draw on this "repertoire of patterns" to make good decisions (Kahneman & Klein, 2009, p. 515). Some have suggested that experienced patrol officers, like chess players, bring these repertoires to bear on some situations that share common features in order to identify plausible resolutions (Thacher, 2008).

Bent Flyvbjerg illustrates this type of "virtuosity" in performance by referencing an experiment conducted on a group of paramedics in the United States (2001, p. 10). Six persons, five of whom were trainees and one who was an experienced paramedic in life-saving techniques, were video-taped administering cardiopulmonary resuscitation (CPR) to victims of heart failure. These videos were then shown to three groups (students being trained in CPR, paramedics with practical experience, and instructors in life-saving techniques). Members of these groups were then asked, "Which of the six persons would you choose to resuscitate you, if you were the victim of such an accident?" Compared to the other groups, the group of experienced paramedics were far more likely to choose the one experienced paramedic in the video, with instructors having the poorest results. Flyvbjerg's point is that "proficient performers" achieve this status through "intimate experience from different situations" and pay careful attention to situational complexities, rather than robotically applying generalized decision-making rules (2001, p. 17). The Flyvbjerg example highlights the hands-on skills and learning processes that contribute to skillful performance, and yet to this point EBP, especially in the form of field experiments, has not turned much of its scientific gaze toward the decision processes of street-level policing.

In our research on police craft, we used a video clip to learn what 38 patrol officers in a single police agency considered to be good police work. We showed patrol officers the video clip of a neighbor dispute and asked them to assess the performance of the two officers depicted in the clip (Willis & Mastrofski, 2017, 2018). We chose this clip because it showed police handling a disorderly situation that is typical of the mundane, but challenging, problems that police confront regularly. The clip depicted two patrol officers responding to an actual dispute between two neighbors in an apartment building in New York City sometime in the 1970s. A complainant was upset that the woman living in the adjacent apartment, who may or may not have been mentally ill, had been pounding on her door with a flat iron (an iron heated on a stove and used to press clothes) and physically threatening her. When questioned, the woman with the flat iron said she was frustrated by the complainant slamming her door. The officers were puzzled that this should be the cause of so much hostility, but they did not explore this in any detail with the second neighbor. They advised her that she should get a summons, but that she was not allowed to take the law into her own hands and retaliate by damaging the complainant's door. When she remained calmly defiant, and even made multiple threats to assault the complainant, they warned her that, if that happened, then she would be arrested. The officers then departed, disposing of the flat iron through a trash chute. The encounter lasted about seven minutes.

We stopped the clip during the encounter when the second neighbor admitted to using the flat iron, and we asked the officer, "What would a highly skilled officer be doing at this point in the situation?" At the end of the clip when the outcome was clear, we asked respondents to judge the success of the officers' overall performance and to suggest an approach that would have been better (recognizing this was informed by the benefit of hindsight).

One of our key findings was the importance our respondents assigned to the process of problem identification. This is a key dimension of police performance, but it has received little attention from EBP, which focuses more on treatments than how best to assess a situation and clarify the state of a given problem. About half of interviewees remarked on this performance aspect, with most expressing dissatisfaction that the officers in the clip had expended far too little investigative efforts in trying to understand the issue between the two neighbors. For example, one officer said:

They could have talked to the second neighbor more to get more background. They still don't know what the problem is. They could try to break it down and see what the underlying issues are. Why is she so mad at her? What is the noise? Where is it coming from? Through the wall? From out in the hallway?

Identifying *what* and *how* to ask about a specific problem takes considerable skill, and yet much remains unknown about this diagnostic process, raising interesting possibilities for how science could contribute to this knowledge gap. Given that the potential success of any "treatment," necessarily depends on the accuracy of the diagnosis, EBP could mobilize police expertise to learn about how officers identify relevant cues or harbingers, what questions they might ask to elicit additional cues, and what subtleties of observation they could use to interpret what they learn (Bonner, 2016). Individual officers vary in the richness of their decision-making processes and their ability to make judgments, and so policing would stand to gain much from EBP devoting more attention to identifying the elements of different diagnostic protocols that could be then scientifically tested. At the very least, this might improve those whose diagnostic skills are under-developed, or who are novices (Mastrofski, 2018).

In addition to the challenges of problem identification, our interviewees also identified maintaining safety and order at the scene as a critical aspect of police performance, as well as the ability to understand and apply the law to specific situations. EBP might consider how it could contribute to helping police perform better in these areas, perhaps by testing different tactical choices for reducing the possibility of on-scene violence and disorder (e.g., low-key verbal techniques) (Bayley, 1986), or by assessing various training or educational methods for enhancing officers' capacity to interpret and apply the law to different types of situations, including misdemeanor disputes. Earlier studies have highlighted how police officers may struggle with understanding and applying legal requirements, such as in search and seizure cases (Gould & Mastrofski, 2004). Similarly, there was confusion among respondents in our study about whether this was a criminal or civil matter, and whether the law permitted an on-scene arrest. This helps highlight the need to consider and test strategies to help improve this aspect of everyday police work.

In sum, the rhetorical approach of EBP, similar to evidence-based medicine, is to try and convince practitioners to embrace science based on the "logic of its reasons" (Van De Ven & Shomaker, 2002, p. 89). But effective persuasion also depends on the ability to connect with the beliefs and experiences of an intended audience. Patrol officers often feel estranged from the concerns and interests of upper-level managers and scientific researchers, so it is vital their views are represented and not misunderstood, and their practice priorities taken seriously (Ratcliffe et al., 2019). According to a recent National Institute of Justice study, the most successful model for research knowledge translation involves an interactive process based on "partnerships and bi-directional communication between researchers and practitioners" (Park, 2018, p. 19).

EBP can further benefit from tapping into the *creativity* of the stock of 'ordinary' knowledge among patrol officers (Lindblom & Cohen, 1979, p. 12). As the popular adage states, "necessity is the mother of invention," and EBP could probably do more to consult with officers to understand some of the best options for achieving a desirable objective. As Mark Moore writes:

One doesn't have to be romantic to imagine that frequently those who have the most direct experience of a problem will have ideas about how to deal with it that are both different and sometimes plausibly more effective than experts who have studied it with their particular disciplinary biases. (1995, p. 310)

As we have noted elsewhere, systematically tapping into these "possibilities of practice" would provide opportunities for science to test the best that craft has to offer and not just a narrow range of options educed by scholars (Thacher, 2008, p. 48; Willis & Mastrofski, 2018).

In the video of our neighbor dispute, our respondents identified a wide range of possible responses, often in combination with one another, for holding the second woman accountable for damaging her neighbor's door and issuing threats and for trying to reduce the risk of the problem reoccurring in the future. These included warning and threatening arrest, trying to counsel and persuade her, negotiating and encouraging self-control, and mediating or conciliating between the parties (either separately or together). EBP could help patrol officers identify those options that are most likely to be effective and test them in relation to a range of relevant outcomes, including citizen satisfaction and problem solving. The most promising interventions suggested by craft and tested by science could then lead to the development of decision-making protocols whose guidance would be contingent upon the particular situation.

Skeptics might argue that the social world is simply too complicated for EBP to make reliable predictions about the distal outcomes of a given policing decision (Thacher, 2018). In his critique of the National Academies report on proactive policing, David Thacher notes how the heterogeneity of practices combined under the umbrella of a single intervention (such as hot spots or broken windows policing) and the complex relationship between a given intervention and the larger organizational context within which it is embedded, makes it hard to understand exactly what the treatment is and thus interpret a program's causal effects, especially in the long term (Thacher, 2018, pp. 6–7).

These are challenging issues, but at the same time, not using science to help identify the likely consequences of street-level choices seems less satisfactory. Scientific research might not be able to offer definitive decision rules that can account for the complexities of every situation, but knowing the likely consequences of an approach derived from scientific knowledge and police expertise would seem to be an improvement over simply tolerating different police practices based on experience with no understanding of their effects.

In sum, observing what officers do on the street and speaking to them directly about what craft has taught them is a way for EBP to identify what skills or tactics officers consider to be particularly helpful in their daily work and subjecting them to rigorous examination to learn to what extent they produce desirable outcomes. An added benefit is that taking police officers' concerns seriously by talking and listening to them directly could increase officers' willingness to adopt evidence-based practices. It is also possible that mobilizing craft expertise could lead to officers framing their own questions and even conducting their own research. There are some encouraging precedents for this. Hans Toch conducted one of the most well-known problem-solving efforts in the Oakland Police Department in the 1970s. Here, the department's crime analysis unit recognized that only a very small number of police officers were responsible for a large share of the department's violence. Toch interviewed the officers involved and those civilians who were chronic assaulters. Based on these interviews and various other data collection techniques, a small group of officers designed and conducted a four-month evaluation of a violence reduction program that eventually included the entire department (Toch, 1980).

4.3 CRAFT, EBP, AND ADVANCING IMPORTANT PUBLIC VALUES

Identifying and evaluating the priorities of street-level decision making is certainly worthwhile for helping improve policing, but this approach still has its limitations. Good choices also depend on police officers being able to make good moral judgments (Muir, 1977; Mastrofski, 2018). EBP and police themselves have generally been reluctant to engage directly with the unavoidable moral dimensions of police work (Thacher, 2001). As Bayley and Bittner note, "Police have always tried to appear exclusively as technical agents of law rather than instruments of public morality" (1984, p. 59). Normative questions about what "ought to be done" lie at the core of how police officers use their discretion, and they are also a major reason for why civilians query the actions of the police as right or wrong, or simply unjust. How might EBP contribute to identifying what important values seem to matter in a given situation, to helping improve police officers' moral understanding, and to nurturing their moral development?

As others have suggested, we think that using case studies of the police craft that allow for a close study of the "nuances of police practice and thinking" within the actual context in which they occur could be a useful starting point (Thacher, 2001, p. 400). Such a case-based approach makes use of craft expertise to help identify and clarify the specific values that are implicated by a police officer's decisions. Earlier scholarship has suggested the possibilities of this approach (Bayley & Bittner, 1984; Kelling, 1999; Mastrofski, 1996; Thacher, 2001), but there are few empirical examples assessing its feasibility at the micro-level of police–civilian encounters. Although we did not specifically ask officers about their moral choices, our case study process was an opportunity for us to explore normative questions about what it means to do the right thing, or how to avoid doing the wrong thing – to analyze and reflect on the values that officers' responses implicated, and to consider one possibility for how EBP might engage more fully with the complex "normative structures" of various police practices (Thacher, 2018, p. 14).

One of the benefits of a case study approach is that it helps identify and clarify the relevant values underlying different police officers' choices in a particular situation, values that are often not obvious and "perceived only dimly, if at all" (Thacher, 2006, p. 1641). In telling us what a good officer should be trying to do in the video clip of our neighbor dispute, our interviewees evoked several important public values, including lawfulness (whether and how the criminal law applied), and parsimony, or the obligation to minimize unwarranted intrusions of state power. For space reasons, we will focus on the latter.

In a democratic society, one of the central issues regarding the exercise of state power is the tension between protecting individual liberties and society's need for the preservation of peace and social order. In our neighbor dispute, a small number of officers advocated for an on-scene arrest, while others suggested a range of less restrictive alternatives. The deprivation of a person's liberty represents a significant exercise of state coercion and raises important legal and moral issues about whether this is the right or wrong thing to do. These issues are undoubtedly complex, but a key benefit of the case study approach is that it provides a strategy for bringing these issues to light, so they can at least be subjected to critical analysis rather than simply left unexamined. What constitutes a proper exercise of police authority might not be so conspicuous in the abstract, but by suggesting responses that involved higher or lower levels of infringement on individual liberty, police officers helped expose their value judgments to closer analysis within the specific context in which they arose. In the absence of such efforts to identify and clarify relevant values, officers are left with little guidance on the moral implications of their actions, making it difficult to hold them accountable for this crucial aspect of their performance.

Our case study gave us an opportunity to explore more systematically some criteria for assessing the moral quality of their actions. One key criterion for evaluating the appropriate use of state power in this particular dispute is whether or not there was sufficient legal justification for a misdemeanor arrest. As a general principle, the law requires an officer to gather and consider the evidence in deciding whether to make an arrest, and it was not clear-cut, at least to some of our officers, that there were sufficient legal grounds for an arrest under these circumstances. In the clip, even though the two officers did not observe the second woman hit her neighbor's door, she confessed to doing so, and she also made threats in the officer's presence. In addition, she presented the officers with physical evidence of the flat iron she used to damage her neighbor. An additional legal consideration was whether there were sufficient grounds for the involuntary commitment of the second neighbor for mental health reasons.

Even if officers were legally entitled to make an arrest, this did not mean it was morally appropriate. The law is broadly written and overreaches, and so there are undoubtedly many situations where its application is unnecessary or excessive (Klockars, 1985). Officers therefore rely on other normative considerations in deciding how to exert their authority to meet police goals, including the value of just deserts. As agents of the criminal justice system, police officers "inevitably ascribe a measure of blame" to people for their actions based on the seriousness of the offense and the suspect's prior record (Thacher, 2001, p. 393). The majority of our officers were disposed toward leniency, preferring to resolve the situation informally. It seems reasonable to assume based on our interviews, that whatever the legal requirements, at least some felt the offense was too minor (a misdemeanor not committed in the officer's presence) to justify the kind of serious infringement of a person's liberty that arrest entails (Harmon, 2016).

In addition to the seriousness of the offense, the judgment of an offender's culpability from a just deserts perspective can also depend on an assessment of their prior criminal record (Von Hirsch, 1976). We noted above that many of our interviewees were dissatisfied that the officers in the clip failed to do more problem diagnosis, including finding out whether the dispute was an isolated encounter or a more frequent pattern of behavior. Presumably, were the officers in the clip to have learned that there had been several complaints against the second woman, or that she had a prior criminal record, they would have considered her more blameworthy. As a result, some might have been less disposed toward leniency. While first offenders might deserve a break, repeat offenders can be considered more culpable for continuing to engage in wrongdoing and therefore more deserving of a harsher sanction in the form of an arrest. To further complicate how to determine whether an arrest is the right decision in this situation, the offender's possible mental health problems might have led some officers to consider her to be less culpable for her behavior and worthier of assistance than punishment in the form of an arrest.

In determining the appropriate scope of police authority in the neighbor dispute, it would undoubtedly be useful for officers to have a clearer sense of the likely outcomes of their actions. Is arrest or mediation more or less likely to mitigate future harm? But given the conflicting ends or values that police must consider when making decisions, this instrumental knowledge is unable to provide a fixed or precise guide to action (Thacher, 2001).

What we have tried to show here is that using video clips can be a practical means for officers to identify relevant values that otherwise might have been overlooked. This can then be a basis for discussing their implications (legal considerations, just deserts, etc.), and an opportunity for officers to engage in a deliberative process with others to help reflect on their own existing moral convictions. It is possible that this opportunity to discuss and reflect on the values implicated by their choices "destabilizes" some officers' views about how to handle these kinds of disputes and results in "ethical growth" (Thacher, 2006, pp. 1637, 1657).

Whether or not the use of a case study approach to promote clarification, criticism, and reflection, among officers about the major values worth accomplishing improves moral understanding, and whether it can contribute to officers' moral development over time, could be tested. If moral choices are largely dictated by System I or intuitive thinking (Haidt, 2001), then finding ways to subject them to a process of more conscious deliberation would be consistent with EBP's commitment to advancing more rigorous decision-making in police work. Fortunately, there is some evidence to suggest that meaningful dialogue and thoughtful reflection between officers can improve normative outcomes. For example, a key element of the violence reduction study in Oakland was the creation of a Peer Review Panel composed of experienced officers. Its purpose was to stimulate officers to consider their own contributions to violence incidents and to help them come up with alternative strategies for coping with incidents that resulted in violence (Toch, 1980, p. 60). Similarly, learning-oriented reviews for use-of-force cases may contribute to normative improvement by bringing to light "tacit knowledge and assumptions," so that these can be debated openly (Thacher, 2020, p. 762). Researchers can play an essential role in this process by using the tools of social science to help identify police officers' implicit moral commitments that may be ambiguous, or have become taken-for-granted, and help re-sensitize them to their relevance through the processes described above.

4.4 CONCLUSION

In this essay, we have suggested that as EBP develops it would benefit from learning more about what craft teaches officers to do in response to the many problems they encounter on the street. This would allow researchers to identify and test the priorities of actual police practice, such as how best to diagnose a problem, including the creative possibilities that have developed over years in response to myriad police experiences. In addition to these technical aspects of police work, EBP could engage more directly with the meanings officers assign to their actions and the values these meanings implicate. Using case studies to empirically uncover this interpretive knowledge, could help officers clarify the meaning and implications of these values and deepen their appreciation for the moral complexities of police work. Ideally, this approach would then help strengthen their capacity for making principled judgments. Designing and testing different approaches for normative improvement, such as developing and evaluating a training program designed to improve not just practical but moral outcomes, would be time well spent given the difficult moral judgments that suffuse police discretion. In advancing his vision for better policing, Egon Bittner insisted that any real advancement in the overall quality of street-level police work depended on people beginning "to give a damn whether it is done well" (Bittner, 1983, p. 7). What we have tried to sketch here is one approach to confronting this challenge.

References

Alpert, G., & Rojek, J. (2011). Frontline police officer assessments of risks and decision making during encounters with offenders. *CEPS Briefing Paper, 5*, 1–6.

Bayley, D. H. (1986). The tactical choices of police patrol officers. *Journal of Criminal Justice, 14*(4), 329–348.

Bayley, D. H., & Bittner E. (1984). Learning the skills of policing. *Law and Contemporary Problems, 47*, 35–59.

Bittner, E. (1983). Legality and workmanship: Introduction to Control in the police organization. In M. Punch (Ed.), *Control in the police organization* (pp. 1–11). MIT Press.

Bittner, E. (1990). *Aspects of police work*. Northeastern University Press.

Black, D. (1971). The social organization of arrest. *Stanford Law Review, 23*, 1087–1111.

Bonner, H. S. (2016). The decision process: Police officers' search for information in dispute encounters. *Policing and Society, 28*(1), 90–113. https://doi.org/10.1080/10439463.2016.1147040

Brown, J., Belur, J., Tompson, L., McDowall, A., Hunter, G., & May, T. (2018). Extending the remit of evidence-based policing. *International Journal of Police Science and Management, 20*(1), 38–51.

Flyvbjerg, B. (2001). *Making social science matter: Why social science inquiry fails and how it can succeed again*. Cambridge University Press.

Gould, J. B., & Mastrofski, S. D. (2004). Suspect searches: Assessing police behavior under the US Constitution. *Criminology and Public Policy, 3*(3), 315–62.

Greene, J. R. (2014). New directions in policing: Balancing prediction and meaning in research. *Justice Quarterly, 31*(2), 193–228.

Greene, J.R. (2019). Critic: Which evidence? What knowledge? Broadening information about their police and their interventions. In D. Weisburd & A. A. Braga (Eds.), *Police innovation: Contrasting perspectives* (pp. 457–484). Second edition. Cambridge University Press.

Haidt, J. (2001). The emotional dog and its rational tail: A social intuitionist approach to moral judgment. *Psychological Review, 108*(4), 814–834.
Harmon, R. (2016). Why arrest?. *Michigan Law Review, 113*(3), 307–64.
Jonathan-Zamir, T., &Weisburd, D. (this volume). Practitioners' inclination to rely on experience: What does this mean for evidence-based policing? In D. Weisburd, T. Jonathan, G. Perry & B. Hasisi, (Eds.), *The Future of Evidence-Based Policing*. Cambridge University Press.
Jonathan- Zamir, T., Weisburd, D., Dayan, M., & Zisso, M. (2019). The proclivity to rely on professional experience and evidence-based policing: Findings from a survey of high-ranking officers in the Israel police. *Criminal Justice and Behavior, 46*(10), 1456–147. https://doi.org/10.1177/0093854819842903
Kahneman, D., & Klein, G. (2009). Conditions for intuitive expertise. *American Psychologist, 64*(6), 515–526.
Kelling, G. L. (1999). *Broken windows and police discretion*. U.S. Department of Justice.
Klein, G. (2008). Naturalistic decision making. *Human Factors, 50*, 456–60.
Klockars, C. (1985). *The idea of police*. Sage Publications.
Lindblom, C. E., & Cohen, D. K. (1979). *Usable knowledge: Social science and social problem solving*. Yale University Press.
Lum, C. (2009). *Translating police research into practice*. Police Foundation.
Lum, C., & Koper, C. (2017). *Evidence-based policing: Translating research into practice*. Oxford University Press.
Lum, C., Telep, C. W., Koper, C., & Grieco, J. (2012). Receptivity to research in policing. *Justice Research and Policy, 14*(1), 61–95.
Lumsden, K., & Goode, J. (2018). Policing research and the rise of the 'evidence-base': Police officer and staff understandings of research, its implementation, and 'what works.' *Sociology, 52*(4), 813–829.
Mastrofski, S. D. (1988). Community policing as reform. In J. R. Greene & S. D. Mastrofski (Eds.), *Community policing: Rhetoric or reality?* (pp. 47–67). Praeger.
Mastrofski, S. D. (1996). Measuring police performance in public encounters. In L. T. Hoover (Ed.), *Quantifying quality in policing* (pp. 207–241). Police Executive Research Forum.
Mastrofski, S. D. (2018). *Do the right thing: Evaluating street-level policing* [Inaugural Mastrofski Lecture]. George Mason University.
Mears, D. P., & Bacon, S. (2009). Improving criminal justice through better decision making: Lessons from the medical system. *Journal of Criminal Justice, 37*(2), 142–154.
Moore, M. H. (1995). Learning while doing: Linking knowledge to policy in the development of community policing and violence prevention in the United States. In P. O. Wikstrom, R. V. Clarke & J. McCord (Eds.), *Integrating crime prevention strategies: Propensity and opportunity* (pp. 301–33). The National Council for Crime Prevention.
Moore, M. H. (2006). Critic: improving police through expertise, experience, and experiments. In D. Weisburd & A. A. Braga (Eds.), *Police innovation: Contrasting perspectives* (pp. 322–338). Cambridge University Press.
Muir, W. K. (1977). *Police: Streetcorner politicians*. University of Chicago Press.

Neyroud, P., & Weisburd, D. (2014). Transforming the police through science: The challenge of ownership. *Policing: A Journal of Policy and Practice*, 8, 287–293.

Park, Y. (2018). How research is translated to policy and practice in the criminal justice system. *nij.ojp.gov*. https://nij.ojp.gov/topics/articles/how-research-translated-policy-and-practice-criminal-justice-system

Ratcliffe, J. H., Taylor, R. B., &Fisher, R. (2019). Conflicts and congruencies between predictive policing and the patrol officer's craft. *Policing and Society*, 1–17. https://doi.org/10.1080/10439463.2019.1577844

Reiss, A. J. (1971). *The police and the public*. Yale University Press.

Sampson, R. J. (2010). Gold standard myths: Observations on the experimental turn in quantitative criminology. *Journal of Quantitative Criminology*, 26(4), 489–500.

Sampson, R. J., Winship, C., & Knight, C. (2013). Translating causal claims: Principles and strategies for policy-relevant criminology. *Criminology and Public Policy*, 12, 587.

Sherman, L. (1992). *Policing domestic violence: Experiments and dilemmas*. Free Press.

Sherman, L. (1998). *Evidence-based policing*. The Police Foundation.

Sherman, L. (2013). The rise of evidence-based policing: targeting, testing, and tracking. *Crime and Justice*, 42(1), 377–451.

Sherman, L. (2015). A tipping point for 'totally evidenced policing:' Ten ideas for building an evidence-based police agency. *International Criminal Justice Review*, 25(1), 11–29.

Sparrow, M. (2016). *Handcuffed: what holds policing back and the keys to reform*. Brooking Institution Press.

Telep, C. W. (2016). Expanding the scope of evidence-based policing. *Criminology and Public Policy*, 15, 243–252.

Telep, C. W., &Lum, C. (2014). The receptivity of officers to empirical research and evidence-based policing: An examination of survey data from three agencies. *Police Quarterly*, 17(4), 359–385.

Thacher, D. (2001). Policing is not a treatment: Alternatives to the medical model of police research. *Journal of Research in Crime and Delinquency*, 38(4), 387–415.

Thacher, D. (2006). The normative case study. *American Journal of Sociology*, 111(6), 1631–76.

Thacher, D. (2008). Research for the front lines. *Policing and Society: An International Journal of Policy and Practice*, 18(1), 46–59.

Thacher, D. (2018). The aspiration of scientific policing. *Law and Social Inquiry*, 44(1), 273–297. https://doi.org/10.1111/lsi.12367

Thacher, D. (2020). The learning model of use of force reviews. *Law and Social Inquiry*, 45(3), 755–786.

Toch, H. (1980). Mobilizing police expertise. *The ANNALS of the American Academy of Political and Social Science*, 452(1), 53–62.

Tocqueville, A. D. (1835/1990). *Democracy in America*. Vintage Classics. Random House.

Van de Ven, A. H. & Shomaker, M. S. (2002). Commentary: The rhetoric of evidence-based medicine. *Health Care Management Review*, 27(3), 89–91.

Von Hirsch, A. (1976). *Doing Justice: The Choice of Punishments* (No. 31685). www.ojp.gov/ncjrs/virtual-library/abstracts/doing-justice-choice-punishments

Weisburd, D. (2010). Justifying the use of non-experimental methods and disqualifying the use of randomized controlled trials: challenging folklore in evaluation research in crime and justice. *Journal of Experimental Criminology*, 6(2), 209–227.

Weisburd, D., & Braga, A. A. (Eds.) (2019). *Police innovation: Contrasting perspectives*. Second edition. Cambridge University Press.

Weisburd, D., & Majmundar, M. K. (Eds.) (2018). *Proactive policing: Effects on crime and communities*. National Academies Press.

Willis, J. J. (2013). *Improving police: What's craft got to do with it?* Police Foundation.

Willis, J. J., &Mastrofski, S. D. (2017). Understanding the culture of craft: Lessons from two police agencies. *Journal of Crime and Justice*, 40(1), 84–100.

Willis, J. J., &Mastrofski, S. D. (2018). Improving policing by integrating craft and science: What can patrol officers teach us about good police work? *Policing and Society: An International Journal of Policy and Practice*, 28(1), 27–44.

Willis, J. J., & Toronjo, H. (2019). Translating police research into policy: Some implications of the national academies report on proactive policing for policymakers and researchers. *Police Practice and Research: An International Journal*, 20(6), 617–31.

PART II

THE EVIDENCE FOR EVIDENCE-BASED POLICING

5

A Review of Systematic Reviews in Policing

Cody W. Telep and David Weisburd

Systematic reviews in policing have become an increasingly common way for researchers to synthesize the state of research on programs, practices, and policies. Such reviews utilize comprehensive and transparent search strategies to identify and summarize the evidence base for a particular topic and can include quantitative summaries with meta-analyses (Weisburd et al., 2017). These reviews provide rigorous assessments of the state of scientific knowledge about policing strategies. Such knowledge is essential for the development of evidence-based policing.

This chapter reviews findings and conclusions from systematic reviews on policing, building on and updating from our prior work. We previously found a rapid growth of reviews from 2004 to 2015 in our examination of 17 policing reviews (Telep & Weisburd, 2016). Our updated systematic search has located completed updates to five of these reviews, as well as new reviews on 13 policing topics. The chapter focuses on lessons learned from these reviews about effective strategies in policing to reduce crime and disorder, build trust and maximize fairness, and address officer stress and health. These multiple outcomes suggest the breadth of policing systematic reviews to date and in particular the growth of reviews in recent years on topics other than crime control. While our review suggests a rapid growth of rigorous research in policing, it also points to a failure of existing research to provide practitioners and policymakers with specific information about what works for what types of problems. Such information is critical if systematic reviews are to become widely used in evidence-based policing in the field. We argue in concluding that scholars have succeeded in providing a "first generation" of studies that tell us whether general policing approaches (such as hot spots policing and problem-oriented policing) are effective, but a much larger evidence-base is needed for a "second generation" of systematic reviews that would provide specific guidance about choosing and implementing evidence-based policing practices in the field (see Weisburd et al., 2017; Weisburd & Telep, 2014).

In the sections that follow, we first highlight the usefulness of systematic reviews as a tool for evidence-based policing before turning to a review of the findings from our first review of systematic reviews (Telep & Weisburd, 2016). We then describe our methods and findings from the current synthesis of reviews, highlighting newly found systematic reviews and their coverage areas and conclusions, as well as changes in the number of eligible studies and number of randomized experiments included in existing reviews. Before concluding, we discuss the state of systematic reviews in policing for evidence-based policing.

5.1 SYSTEMATIC REVIEW AS A TOOL FOR EVIDENCE-BASED POLICING

Beginning in the 1970s, the traditional methods used in reviews of research evidence began to be seriously criticized (see Petrosino et al., 2001 for a review). One criticism focused on the general lack of explicitness of reviews.[1] Most suffered from a lack of detail about how the reviewer conducted the search for studies. Information was often missing about why certain studies were included while others were excluded from the review. A second criticism focused on the methods used. Most of the reviewers did not attempt to control for problems that could potentially bias their review toward one conclusion rather than another. Another criticism was the failure to deal with potential biases that could compromise the results of a review. For example, some reviewers examining what works relied on easy-to-obtain journal articles as the only source of reports of evaluations. An advantage of journal articles over other documents is that they have usually passed a rigorous peer review process. Unfortunately, research suggests that relying on journal articles can bias the results toward concluding that interventions are more effective than they really are (see Rothstein et al., 2005; Wilson, 2009).

Systematic reviews have become a key tool for evidence-based policing because they overcome many of these criticisms. Systematic reviews use

---

[1] See Weisburd, Farrington, and Gill (2016) for a more detailed discussion of these concerns.

TABLE 5.1 *Systematic reviews identified by Telep and Weisburd (2016)*

Review	Authors and year	Updates?
Drug Abuse Resistance Education	West & O'Neal, (2004)	Yes (2015, 2017)
Interventions to reduce traffic accidents	Blais & Dupont, (2005)	No
Drug law enforcement	Mazerolle et al., (2007)	Yes (2020)
Problem-oriented policing (POP)	Weisburd et al., (2008)	Yes (2020)
Second responders for domestic violence	Davis et al., (2008)	No
Police patrol for drunken driving	Goss et al., (2008)	No
Micro displacement	Bowers et al., (2011)	No
DNA for police investigations	Wilson et al., (2011)	No
Stress management programs	Patterson et al., (2012)	No
Focused deterrence (i.e., pulling levers)	Braga & Weisburd, (2012)	Yes (2019)
Hot spots	Braga et al., (2012)	Yes (2019)
Gun carrying	Koper & Mayo-Wilson, (2012)	No
Interrogation techniques	Meissner et al., (2012)	No
Interventions to increase legitimacy	Mazerolle et al., (2013)	In progress
Community policing	Gill et al., (2014)	In progress
Macro displacement	Telep et al., (2014)	In progress
Policing disorder	Braga et al., (2015)	No (2019 report)

(and transparently describe) rigorous methods for locating, appraising, and synthesizing evidence from previous evaluation studies (see Farrington & Petrosino, 2000; Farrington et al., 2011; Littell et al., 2008). They contain methods and results sections, and are reported with the same level of detail that characterizes high-quality reports of original research. In sum, systematic reviews provide an evidence base that is rigorous and transparent for establishing what works in policing.

5.2 A FIRST REVIEW OF SYSTEMATIC REVIEWS

In our prior review (Telep & Weisburd, 2016), we summarized 17 completed systematic reviews of policing practices, covering the period 2004–2015. A list of these reviews appears in Table 5.1 with a column indicating whether our searches for this chapter located an update to the original review. While these reviews covered a range of policing topics, they focused largely on crime and disorder-related outcomes with a smaller number of reviews focused at least in part on fairness and police legitimacy and officer health. About half of these reviews currently have a published update or an in-progress update, and we discuss below the large growth in the policing evidence base, which has led to recent reviews drawing from a much larger pool of eligible studies.

Our earlier "review of reviews" found that a number of policing strategies can be effective in reducing crime, including hot spots policing, focused deterrence strategies, and problem-oriented policing (POP) and that these geographically focused strategies infrequently lead to significant crime displacement. The review found promising evidence for legitimacy-building strategies, including incorporating procedural justice into interventions, community policing, and information gathering interrogation strategies. It also concluded that not all strategies are effective. The evidence for both second responder programs for family violence and Drug Abuse Resistance Education (DARE) suggests that these interventions are not effective or are even harmful. Almost every systematic review examined concluded by noting a need for more rigorous primary studies.

5.3 METHODS

To update these findings, we used a multi-faceted search strategy to identify new systematic reviews published since 2015. We began by reviewing the Campbell Collaboration Crime and Justice Group database. Campbell has been the main publisher of systematic reviews in policing and has a standardized process for registering and completing reviews. Wiley now publishes these reviews in an open access journal called *Campbell Systematic Reviews*. We reviewed all completed reviews, as well as approved protocols and registered titles to assess what reviews are in progress. Given that some policing topics have overlap with medicine, we also searched the Cochrane Collaboration database using the keywords "police" and "policing."

We recognize though that systematic reviews may not necessarily be registered with Campbell. We also searched four additional sources for other potential reviews. We searched PROSPERO, a University of York database funded by the UK National Institute for Health Research as a prospective register of systematic reviews. We also used "police" and "policing" as keywords. We also searched three commonly used academic databases, Criminal Justice Abstracts, the National Criminal Justice Reference Service, and Google Scholar. Given the larger number of hits here, we searched for "police" or "policing" and "systematic review." For Criminal Justice Abstracts and Google Scholar, we reviewed the first 1,000 most relevant results.[2] We conducted initial searches in May 2019 and updated our searches in July 2020.

To be included in our review of systematic reviews, a published systematic review had to meet three main criteria. First, the police had to be the main focus of the review. This is the most obvious criteria, but one that can be complicated to assess in practice, given the number of multi-agency partnerships in criminal justice, but we required that police be heavily involved in the review topic area. Second, the review had to have high methodological standards for eligible studies, which generally meant including only experimental and quasi-experimental studies. Third, we only included reviews that involved some sort of strategy, practice, or intervention. We excluded purely descriptive or observational reviews.

5.4 FINDINGS

Our searches of the Campbell Collaboration databases located two new published reviews on police-led diversion (Wilson et al., 2018) and body-worn cameras (BWCs; Lum et al., 2020), as well as updates of three previously published reviews on hot spots policing (Braga et al., 2019a), focused deterrence (Braga et al., 2019b), and problem-oriented policing (Hinkle et al., 2020). The Braga, Welsh, and Schnell (2019) disorder policing review that previously had only been published in article form is also now published through Campbell.[3] Additionally, Telep and Weisburd (2016) excluded a systematic review on restorative justice (Strang et al., 2013) because it was covered by other chapters in that volume, but is included here since police led most of the restorative justice conferences

---

[2] There were over 20,000 results identified, which would have demanded more resources than available for our work. However, given that these databases are sorted by relevance it seems unlikely that the results lower than this threshold would have provided eligible reviews.

[3] We also considered additional Campbell reviews that had some relevance to policing, but ultimately we decided were not sufficiently focused on policing. These included reviews on juvenile curfew policies (Wilson et al., 2016), and youth gang violence prevention (Higginson et al., 2015).

in the eligible studies. We also located an update on the street-law drug enforcement review published by the Australian Institute of Criminology (Mazerolle et al., 2020a). Searches of the Cochrane Collaboration database identified a review of psychosocial interventions for the prevention of psychological disorder in police by Peñalba and colleagues (2008). This research was inadvertently excluded in our earlier review.

Our Campbell searches also showed a number of in-progress reviews, an issue we discuss more below. The Telep et al. (2014) macro displacement review and Gill et al. (2014) community policing reviews are technically still in-progress because they do not have a final Campbell report, but have been published in article form. Some reviews are also in the process of being updated, but may not have materials published yet through Campbell. For example, discussions with the lead author revealed that the Global Policing Database (GPD; Higginson et al., 2014; Chapter 8 this volume) is currently being used to update the legitimacy in policing review.

Other in-progress reviews at this point only have a published title or protocol. Campbell recently approved some of these protocols, while others have been online for five years or more, which raises question about whether the authors will ultimately complete the review. We identified seven approved titles or protocols for which we could not yet find a published review. These reviews cover multi-agency programs with police to reduce radicalization (Mazerolle et al., 2020b), police programs to reduce violent extremism (Mazerolle et al., 2020c)[4], training interventions to improve democratic policing of protests (Litmanovitz & Montgomery, 2016), third party policing (Mazerolle et al., 2016), police patrol presence (Telep et al., 2016), mandatory arrest for domestic violence (Ariel & Sherman, 2012), and traffic safety (Mohan et al., 2020).

Our searches of articles from online databases also identified a number of other systematic reviews. Indeed, the majority of newly identified reviews in this chapter came from non-Campbell Collaboration reviews published in peer-reviewed outlets. These include more up-to-date reviews of DARE (Caputi & McLellan 2017; Flynn et al. 2015). The other newly identified reviews were on topic areas not covered in Telep and Weisburd (2016). These cover a wide range of policing topics from the effectiveness of police programs to use automated external

---

[4] This review was published in September 2020, after our searches were completed, but included just one eligible study (Mazerolle et al. 2020d).

defibrillators (AED; Husain & Eisenberg, 2013) to de-escalation training (Engel et al., 2020) to intervention programs for posttraumatic stress disorder (PTSD; Haugen et al., 2012) and anxiety (Lees et al., 2019). In all, we identified 17 total reviews[5] through Campbell, Cochrane, Google Scholar, and other online databases, although in some cases, there were multiple reviews on a single topic. These reviews cover 13 total topics. We located four recent reviews of the effects of Crisis Intervention Team (CIT) programs (Dewa et al., 2018; Kane et al., 2018; Peterson & Densley, 2018; Taheri, 2016) designed to provide officers extra training on interactions with people experiencing a mental health crisis.[6] We summarize the topics covered in these reviews in Table 5.2.[7]

5.5 RESULTS OF THE REVIEWS

Before looking at the substantive conclusions from each review, we first examined the number of studies and rigor of these studies. While randomized controlled trials (RCTs) are not the only useful methodology for generating evidence about program effectiveness, we can be more confident in the ability of experiments to establish causal relationships between an intervention and desired outcomes. While a systematic review with more experiments is not automatically better (particularly if the experiments have implementation issues), we suggest that reviews that have few or no randomized experiments raise questions about the validity of conclusions drawn from narrative or meta-analytic reviews. We present the number of eligible studies and number of randomized experiments for each review, including reviews identified by Telep and Weisburd (2016) in Table 5.3.

---

[5] The Belur et al. (2020) and McGinley et al. (2020) papers both come from the same review and so while we include 18 references in Table 5.2, they represent 17 distinct reviews.
[6] Interestingly, we found multiple citations in the literature to a 2014 Campbell Collaboration review of CIT by Marotta and colleagues, but we could not locate a title, protocol, or review through Campbell's website.
[7] We also excluded a number of articles that used the terminology "systematic review" in reference to a policing topic, but that did not focus on a particular intervention, program, or practice. For example, a review by Stanley and colleagues (2016) of suicidal thoughts by police and other first responders did not focus on suicide prevention, while a review of obesity in policing (DaSilva et al., 2014) described the extent of obesity in the profession rather than responses to it. We also excluded a review of in-service training (Huey, 2018) that met our other criteria, but due to issues with the eligible studies, there was no attempt to synthesize findings.

TABLE 5.2 *Summary of newly identified reviews and main outcomes organized by year*

Review	Authors and year	Main outcomes
Psychosocial interventions	Peñalba et al., (2008)	Psychological measures; Physiological measures
Posttraumatic stress disorder (PTSD) treatment	Haugen et al., (2012)	PTSD symptoms
Restorative justice	Strang et al., (2013)	Offender rearrest/reconviction; Victim satisfaction
Automated external defibrillator (AED) programs	Husain & Eisenberg (2013)	Survival rates
Police force size	Lee et al. (2016)	Overall crime
School resource officers (SROs)	Fisher & Hennessy (2016); Petrosino et al. (2012)	Exclusionary discipline
Crisis intervention team (CIT)	Taheri (2016); Kane et al. (2018); Peterson & Densley (2018); Dewa et al. (2018)	Officer attitudes; Officer behavior (arrests, case processing)
Co-responder models	Puntis et al. (2018)	Officer arrests, use of hospitalization; Client satisfaction
Diversion for youth	Wilson et al. (2018)	Delinquent behavior
Anxiety and fatigue interventions	Lees et al. (2019)	Anxiety and fatigue symptoms
Body-worn cameras (BWCs)	Lum et al. (2020)	Officer & citizen behavior; Officer & citizen attitudes
De-escalation training	Engel et al. (2020)	Knowledge/attitudes; Self-reported behavior
Academy training	Belur et al. (2020); McGinley et al. (2020)	Knowledge/learning

Overall, both the number of eligible studies and the proportion of these studies that are RCTs vary considerably across the 30 review topics. In total, 708 studies were included across reviews, about 22% of which were randomized experiments. This represents a more than doubling in the total number of studies covered by reviews in Telep and Weisburd (2016), reinforcing the view that there has been a growth in both systematic reviews and primary studies in policing. This is also a small increase from the proportion of experiments we

TABLE 5.3 *Eligible studies and randomized experiments by review sorted by proportion of randomized experiments*

Review	Eligible studies	Experiments	%
Psychosocial interventions	10	10	100
Restorative justice	10	10	100
Stress management	12	9	75.0
Interrogation techniques	17	12	70.6
Police-initiated diversion	19	13	68.4
BWCs	30	20	66.7
Anxiety and fatigue	7	4	57.1
Second responders	10	5	50.0
Hot spots (updated)	65	27	41.5
Policing disorder	28	9	32.1
Problem-oriented policing (updated)	34	9	26.5
PTSD	18	4	22.2
DNA for police investigations	5	1	20.0
DARE (updated)	12	2	16.7
Legitimacy	30	4	13.3
Academy training (quantitative)	54	7	13.0
Drug law enforcement (updated)	26	3	11.5
Micro displacement	44	5	11.4
AED	10	1	10.0
Community policing	25	1	4.0
Police patrol for drunken driving	32	1	3.1
Police force size	62	0	0
Macro displacement	33	0	0
Traffic accident prevention	33	0	0
Co-responder model	26	0	0
Focused deterrence strategies (updated)	24	0	0
CIT	21	0	0
SROs	7	0	0
Gun carrying	4	0	0
De-escalation (policing studies)	0	0	N/A
TOTAL	708	157	22.2

Note: Duplicates within topic areas removed (e.g., studies appearing in multiple CIT reviews), but duplicates across reviews (e.g., studies in both hot spots and POP reviews) not removed

found in the earlier paper (Telep & Weisburd, 2016; 19.2%), though quasi-experimental studies are still far more common than randomized trials. For eight topic areas, half or more of the eligible studies were randomized experiments, while for nine other topics areas, there were no RCTs included in the review.

To examine the overall conclusions of our eligible systematic review, we divided them into two general types based on outcome, recognizing that some reviews focus on multiple outcome measures. We can broadly categorize reviews into those focused on the impact of police on the community (i.e., external outcomes) and those that focus on the impact of programs on police officers (i.e., internal outcomes). Within these two main categories, we can further categorize community-focused reviews based on whether they emphasize crime and disorder outcomes, legitimacy and fairness outcomes, or citizen health and well-being outcomes. Within officer-focused reviews, we can divide between those focused on officer health and wellness and those looking at officer knowledge or attitudinal change resulting from training. Given the wide variability in the reviews and the fact that a number of our newer reviews do not include meta-analyses, we focus below on a narrative synthesis of what we know about the effectiveness of interventions involving the police.

In Table 5.4, we first organize the community-focused reviews by main outcome and organize them broadly from reviews showing greater evidence of effectiveness to those demonstrating programs that are less impactful. We then include a review of outcomes for studies focused on officers. We do not have the space here to review findings from each review in detail, but we do think it is useful to synthesize what we know about policing interventions. We previously (Telep & Weisburd, 2016) categorized reviews based on what works? what's promising? and what seems to have little or no effect? We also add a category here for reviews that suggest more research is needed to draw strong conclusions.

5.6 WHAT WORKS?

Our conclusions about the reviews covered in Telep and Weisburd (2016) remain unchanged, even though several were updated. We still have the most confidence about the effectiveness of focused, proactive crime control strategies. These include updated reviews on hot spots policing, focused deterrence strategies, and problem-oriented policing. We add restorative justice to the "what works?" category as conferences are effective in reducing recidivism and improving victim satisfaction.

5.7 WHAT'S PROMISING?

We continue to view a number of legitimacy-building strategies, including community policing, as promising for enhancing community trust.

TABLE 5.4 *Summary of community outcome findings from the reviews*

Review	Conclusions
Crime, disorder, and recidivism	
Hot spots	Small but significant impact on crime and disorder; POP strategies associated with larger effects
Focused deterrence strategies	Moderate impact on reducing violence, gang-focused approaches more effective than drug market initiatives
Problem-oriented policing	Associated with a significant reduction in crime; effect size heterogeneity, but consistent evidence POP reduces crime
Restorative justice	Conferences associated with fewer offender arrests, convictions for two-years after; victims satisfied
Policing disorder	"Broken windows" policing effective; community problem solving works better than aggressive order maintenance
Gun carrying	Directed patrol generally effective in reducing gun crime
DNA for police investigations	Appears effective in helping clear cases/identify suspects
Drug law enforcement	Targeted approaches more effective than unfocused approaches, benefits of partnerships
Micro displacement	Displacement not inevitable, diffusion of crime control benefits more likely
Macro displacement	
Police-initiated diversion for youth	Modest reduction in future delinquency for low-risk youth compared to traditional processing
Police patrol for drunk driving	Associated with reduced crashes/injuries but poor studies
Programs to reduce accidents	Increased patrols generally reduce accidents/fatalities
Police force size	Increasing force size has small, non-significant impact on crime
Second responders	No significant impact on reducing domestic violence
Legitimacy and fairness	
Interrogation techniques	Information-gathering techniques better than accusatory in acquiring true confessions
Interventions to increase legitimacy	Efforts to enhance procedural justice generally help build legitimacy, variability in strategies
Community policing	Small impact on crime, greater positive impact on citizen satisfaction and legitimacy
Body-worn cameras	Mixed findings on officer behavior (force and arrest), tend to reduce citizen complaints
SROs	Impact on exclusionary discipline mixed, but suggestive of association with more suspensions/expulsions

(continued)

TABLE 5.4 (*continued*)

Review	Conclusions
Citizen health and well-being	
Co-responder models	Associated with reduction in use of police detention and psychiatric hospitalization for service users
AED programs	Time to defibrillation decreased and survival from heart attacks increased
CIT	Mixed impact on arrest and case processing, overall weak studies with lack of follow-up
DARE	No significant impact on drug, alcohol, or tobacco use; no studies found of new keepin' It REAL DARE

Summary of officer-level outcomes from the reviews

Review	Conclusions
Officer health and well-being	
Psychosocial interventions	Some potential benefits in terms of psychological and physical health, but small n studies
Anxiety and fatigue interventions	Stress management programs focused on resiliency and coping show promise for managing anxiety; only one fatigue intervention (mindfulness) shows promising results
PTSD treatment	Psychosocial treatment reduces PTSD, but only small number of rigorous studies
Stress management	No effects on psychological, physiological, or behavioral outcomes
Officer training knowledge and attitudes	
CIT training	Officers generally feel more prepared after training, but potential selection bias issues
Academy training	Mixed effects of specialized training on knowledge and attitudes, limited impact of training on officer attitudes towards the profession
De-escalation training	No studies in policing, interventions in other fields associated with improved knowledge, confidence, and attitudes

We know this is an area where the evidence base is quickly growing (see Nagin & Telep, 2020), and so expect an increase in eligible studies in the updated legitimacy in policing review. We also view body-worn cameras as a promising tool for reducing citizen complaints. Evidence here has been more consistently positive than for other outcomes. We also view police-led diversion programs as promising for reducing subsequent delinquency. While there is limited rigorous research on police using AEDs, such efforts seem promising for saving lives. Additionally, co-responder models where mental health clinicians respond with police are promising for improving outcomes for clients, though this approach has been evaluated primarily in non-US contexts.

5.8 WHAT SEEMS TO HAVE LITTLE OR NO EFFECT?

DARE remains ineffective, even with updated efforts to improve the DARE curriculum. We also add increasing police force size and the use of school resource officers (SROs) to this category. While findings for both are somewhat mixed, for force size, it seems that what additional police officers are used for and how agencies deploy their manpower is more important for reducing crime than simply examining the number of officers (though we recognize the challenges in assessing this relationship; see Chalfin & McCrary, 2018). There is little evidence that SROs help reduce school crime, and instead greater evidence that they lead to more students being disciplined by the school or through the criminal justice system.

5.9 WHAT DO WE NEED TO KNOW MORE ABOUT?

There are also a number of areas where existing reviews supply insufficient information to draw strong conclusions. In particular, we emphasize the need for better research on training. There is no rigorous research on de-escalation training, mixed findings and no randomized trials on CIT training, and mixed findings and limited research on academy training. There is more rigorous research on interventions to improve officer mental health, but studies tend to be small scale, and so it is difficult to reach any conclusions about the best programs for officers on psychosocial issues, PTSD, and anxiety. Finally, research is more mixed for BWCs when it comes to officer and citizen behavior. There is a larger body of rigorous research here than on officer wellness or training, suggesting the effectiveness of BWCs for outcomes like reducing officer force may be context-specific.

5.10 DISCUSSION

Our review of systematic reviews suggests that they have contributed significantly to the development of the evidence base for evidence-based policing. We have reviews that now cover a broad array of strategies, and those reviews often provide compelling scientific evidence that policing strategies can reduce crime or improve citizen outcomes. In this sense, we have been successful at developing research studies that give us general insights about the effectiveness of different policing approaches. Nonetheless, we think our review points to the importance of developing systematic reviews that would provide much more detailed and practical guidance for evidence-based policing.

When we focus in particular on police efforts to reduce crime, our findings tell a positive story, but they are based on what might be called "first-generation studies" (Weisburd et al., 2017). They provide rigorous evidence that the police can prevent crime. Nevertheless, they generally do not provide specific guidance regarding what types of programs are effective, for which populations, and in which types of settings (Gottfredson et al., 2015). This is what we term "second-generation studies" (Weisburd & Telep, 2014) or what has been referred to elsewhere as "next generation" studies (Gottfredson et al., 2015). Our conception of first vs. second generation is similar to ideas of Type 1 and Type 2 translation raised by Spoth and colleagues (2013). Type 1 translation focuses on applying basic research to intervention development, while Type 2 research "investigates the complex processes and mechanisms through which tested and proven interventions are integrated into practice and policy on a large scale and in a sustainable way, across targeted populations and settings" (Spoth et al., 2013, p. 321). Similarly, we view "first-generation studies" and reviews as helping us answer the question "does it work?" when it comes to policing practices and interventions. But "second-generation studies" and reviews are needed to address "how does it work?" and the ways evidence-based strategies can be implemented in particular contexts to address specific problems (see Telep, 2018).

An example of this can be found in the hot spots policing review (Braga, et al., 2019a), which has more studies, and more randomized experiments, than any other review we examined. The review provides rigorous evidence that hot spots policing is effective, but it provides little guidance beyond that conclusion. In meta-analysis, the primary quantitative tool of systematic review, systematic reviewers have started to conduct moderator analyses to identify the impacts of specific types of interventions, or settings on program outcomes. Braga et al. (2019a) examine, for example, whether POP has larger impacts on crime hot spots than generalized patrol approaches. They find a significantly larger impact for POP, suggesting that police agencies will gain stronger crime prevention outcomes with this approach. But the police in the field need much more specific guidance than this.

Police commanders faced with specific types of crime problems want to know what types of approaches are most effective for controlling these specific problems. The Braga et al. review was notable for conducting moderator analyses for alternative strategies. Most of the reviews we examined provided only a very general conclusion on effectiveness. For systematic reviews to become a more useful tool for evidence-based policing, a second generation of studies is needed that would provide much more specific guidance to police in the field. Moreover, we found little evidence regarding the relative costs and benefits of different types of hot spots policing. In some cases, this is because the police are often reallocating resources for innovative strategies rather than adding new resources. Irrespective, systematic reviews in policing must begin to estimate the costs of strategies applied, and compare that cost to benefits if they are to become fully relevant to police managers who need to decide on how their policing resources can be most effectively distributed.

We think that there is evidence that policing research is moving, if slowly, to the type of second generation of studies we are suggesting, at least in terms of the size of the evidence base that is available for drawing conclusions. This is illustrated in particular by the large growth in the number of eligible studies for reviews that have been updated. For example, the original hot spots policing review (Braga, 2007) had just seven eligible studies. This increased to 19 with the 2012 update (Braga et al., 2012). The latest update (Braga et al., 2019a) includes 65 eligible studies. The focused deterrence review update also more than doubled the number of eligible studies going from 10 in 2012 (Braga & Weisburd, 2012) to 24 in 2019 (Braga et al., 2019b). The POP review had more than three times as many studies in the recent update (Hinkle et al., 2020), increasing from 10 to 34 eligible studies.

Another way in which systematic reviews must move to a second generation of studies to become a useful tool in the field concerns the coverage of outcomes addressed. Our initial review in 2016 showed that systematic reviews of policing focused almost entirely on crime and disorder outcomes. Crime and disorder remains the primary focus of the 30 review topics described here, but half of the reviews also focus on other non-crime outcomes. This seems important in the current context for policing, particularly in the United States, where a main concern for the public and policymakers has been on police fairness and use of force (Telep, 2016). Systematic reviews cannot be a central tool for evidence-based policing if they do not examine the broad array of outcomes the police must address.

The President's Task Force Report on 21st Century Policing (2015), which was established by President Obama to identify the key elements that should concern policing in the United States, laid out six key pillars, or concerns, for policing. Assessing the systematic review evidence in terms of these six pillars (building trust and legitimacy, policy and oversight, technology and social media, community policing and crime reduction, training and education, officer safety and wellness) illustrates the extent to which the scope of outcomes in systematic reviews needs to be broadened (see Lum et al., 2016).

There are reviews covering much of Pillar 1 on legitimacy and fairness, as well as Pillar 4 on community policing and crime reduction. For Pillar 3 on technology and social media, there is good coverage on body-worn cameras, but no reviews on the effectiveness of other police technologies. Pillar 6 on officer health and wellness now has multiple reviews, but they all suffer from a lack of large-scale, rigorous studies, and so there is limited guidance on how to best address officer stress and mental health concerns. Pillar 2 on policy and oversight is not well covered by existing reviews, particularly strategies to reduce use of force outside of BWCs. Finally, there are a few reviews focused on education and training, the subject of Pillar 5, but overall a lack of primary studies and reviews here make drawing any conclusions about effectiveness challenging. While the Task Force report is but one source of key outcomes for policing, the gaps that remain in understanding the effectiveness of prominent police reform efforts suggest that there is room for additional future reviews.

Another area that needs development to get to the kind of second generation of studies we are suggesting relates not to the research itself, but rather to the approaches that systematic reviewers use to assess policing interventions. In our earlier review (Telep & Weisburd, 2016), we raised concerns about the challenge of using standard effect size conventions for assessing the impact of crime control strategies, particularly for the large number of reviews that are focused on geographic areas, where a "small" effect could be quite influential. Wilson (2022) has recently proposed an alternative to Cohen's d that is more appropriate for place-based data and more easily interpretable as a relative percent decline in crime in the intervention area compared to the control. Hinkle et al. (2020) were the first to use Wilson's (2022) approach in a published Campbell review, and their findings demonstrated how conventional effect size calculations can make effects seem overly modest. The mean effect for all studies using Cohen's d was 0.183, which is considered a small effect. However, using Wilson's (2022) relative incident rate ratio, the mean effect of 0.291 when exponentiated translated to a 33.8% reduction in crime in intervention sites relative to controls. In an updated review of the impacts of hot spots policing, Braga and Weisburd (2022) also find that the observed effect size doubles using Wilson's approach. These outcomes suggest that second-generation studies also need to develop methods appropriate for interpreting and understanding the impacts of policing strategies. Such methods have strong impacts on what we tell practitioners about what works, and in the long-run impact whether programs will be adopted in the field.

5.11 CONCLUSIONS

Our updated review of systematic reviews in policing suggests a growth in both the size of the policing evidence base and the scope and coverage of reviews. This is good news for evidence-based policing, as more reviews means better answers to questions of what works (and what is less effective). Still, for a number of reviews, the main conclusion is that more research is needed. Most importantly, the reviews often do not provide specific guidance on the specific types of strategies that police should use for addressing specific types of problems. We have termed such guidance as second-generation studies. We see evidence in our update of our 2016 review that systematic reviews of policing practices are moving toward second-generation studies, not only in terms of the number of studies and reviews available, but also in the types of outcomes examined, and in the tools that are used to summarize evidence in the area of policing. There is much reason to be optimistic about the relevance of systematic reviews for evidence-based policing, but there is much work to be done.

References

Ariel, B., & Sherman, L. W. (2012). Protocol: Mandatory arrest for misdemeanor domestic violence effects on repeat offending. *Campbell Systematic Reviews*, 8(1), 1–30.

Belur, J., Agnew-Pauley, W., McGinley, B., & Tompson, L. (2020). A systematic review of police recruit training programmes. *Policing: A Journal of Policy and Practice*, 14(1), 76–90.

Blais, E., & Dupont, B. (2005). Assessing the capability of intensive police programmes to prevent severe road accidents. *British Journal of Criminology*, 45(6), 914–937.

Bowers, K., Johnson, S., Guerette, R. T., Summers, L., & Poynton, S. (2011). Spatial displacement and diffusion of benefits among geographically focused policing interventions. *Campbell Systematic Reviews*, 7(1), 1–144.

Braga, A. A. (2007). The effects of hot spots policing on crime. *Campbell Systematic Reviews*, 3(1), 1–36.

Braga, A. A., Papachristos, A. V., & Hureau, D. M. (2012). Hot spots policing effects on crime. *Campbell Systematic Reviews*, 8(1), 1–96.

Braga, A. A., Turchan, B., Papachristos, A. V., & Hureau, D. M. (2019a). Hot spots policing of small geographic areas effects on crime. *Campbell Systematic Reviews*, 15(3), e1046.

Braga, A. A., & Weisburd, D. L. (2012). The effects of "pulling levers" focused deterrence strategies on crime. *Campbell Systematic Reviews*, 8(1), 1–90.

Braga, A. A., &Weisburd, D. L. (2022). Does hot spots policing have meaningful impacts on crime? Findings from an alternative approach to estimating effect sizes from place-based program evaluations. *Journal of Quantitative Criminology*, 38(1), 1–22.

Braga, A. A., Weisburd, D., & Turchan, B. (2019b). Focused deterrence strategies effects on crime: A systematic review. *Campbell Systematic Reviews*, 15(3), e1051.

Braga, A. A., Welsh, B. C., & Schnell, C. (2015). Can policing disorder reduce crime? A systematic review and meta-analysis. *Journal of Research in Crime and Delinquency*, 52(4), 567–588.

Braga, A. A., Welsh, B. C., & Schnell, C. (2019). Disorder policing to reduce crime: A systematic review. *Campbell Systematic Reviews*, 15(3), 1–38.

Caputi, T. L., & McLellan, A. T. (2017). Truth and D.A.R.E.: Is D.A.R.E.'s new Keepin' it REAL curriculum suitable for American nationwide implementation? *Drugs: Education, Prevention and Policy*, 24(1), 49–57.

Chalfin, A., & McCrary, J. (2018). Are U.S. cities underpoliced? Theory and evidence. *Review of Economics and Statistics*, 100(1), 167–186.

Da Silva, F. C., Hernandez, S. S. S., Gonçalves, E., Arancibia, B. A. V., Castro, T. L. D. S., & Da Silva, R. (2014). Anthropometric indicators of obesity in policemen: A systematic review of observational studies. *International Journal of Occupational Medicine and Environmental Health*, 27(6), 891–901.

Davis, R. C., Weisburd, D., & Taylor, B. (2008). Effects of second responder programs on repeat incidents of family abuse. *Campbell Systematic Reviews*, 4(1), 1–38.

Dewa, C. S., Loong, D., Trujillo, A., & Bonato, S. (2018). Evidence for the effectiveness of police-based pre-booking diversion programs in decriminalizing mental illness: A systematic literature review. *Plos One*, 13(6), 1–14. https://doi.org/10.1371/journal.pone.0199368

Engel, R. S., McManus, H. D., & Herold, T. D. (2020). Does de-escalation training work? A systematic review and call for evidence in police use-of-force reform. *Criminology & Public Policy*, 19(3), 721–759.

Farrington, D. P., & Petrosino, A. (2000). Systematic reviews of criminological interventions: The Campbell Collaboration Crime and Justice Group. *International Annals of Criminology*, 38(1–2), 49–66.

Farrington, D. P., Weisburd, D., & Gill C. E. (2011). The Campbell Collaboration Crime and Justice Group: A decade of progress. In C. J. Smith, S. X. Zhang & R. Barberet (Eds.), *Routledge handbook of international criminology* (pp. 53–63). Routledge.

Fisher, B. W., & Hennessy, E. A. (2016). School resource officers and exclusionary discipline in US high schools: A systematic review and meta-analysis. *Adolescent Research Review, 1*(3), 217-233.

Flynn, A. B., Falco, M., & Hocini, S. (2015). Independent evaluation of middle school-based drug prevention curricula: a systematic review. *JAMA Pediatrics, 169*(11), 1046-1052.

Gill, C. E., Weisburd, D., Telep, C. W., Bennett, T., & Vitter, Z. (2014). Community-oriented policing to reduce crime, disorder, and fear and increase legitimacy and citizen satisfaction in neighborhoods. *Journal of Experimental Criminology, 10*(4), 399-428.

Goss, C. W, Van Bramer, L. D, Gliner, J. A, Porter, T. R, Roberts, I. G, & DiGuiseppi, C. (2008). Increased police patrols for preventing alcohol-impaired driving. *Cochrane Database of Systematic Review*, (4), DOI: 10.1002/14651858.CD005242.pub2.

Gottfredson, D. C., Cook, T. D., Gardner, F. E., Gorman-Smith, D., Howe, G. W., Sandler, I. N., & Zafft, K. M. (2015). Standards of evidence for efficacy, effectiveness, and scale-up research in prevention science: Next generation. *Prevention Science, 16*(7), 893-926.

Haugen, P. T., Evces, M., & Weiss, D. S. (2012). Treating posttraumatic stress disorder in first responders: A systematic review. *Clinical Psychology Review, 32*(5), 370-380.

Higginson, A., Benier, K., Shenderovich, Y., Bedford, L., Mazerolle, L., & Murray, J. (2015). Preventive interventions to reduce youth involvement in gangs and gang crime in low-and middle-income countries: A systematic review. *Campbell Systematic Reviews, 11*(1), 1-176.

Higginson, A., Eggins, E., Mazerolle, L., & Stanko, E. (2014). The Global Policing Database [Database and Protocol]. www.gpd.uq.edu.au/

Hinkle, J. C., Weisburd, D., Telep, C. W., & Petersen, K. (2020). Problem-oriented policing for reducing crime and disorder: An updated systematic review and meta-analysis. *Campbell Systematic Reviews, 16*(2), 1-86.

Huey, L. (2018). *What do we know about in-service police training? Results of a failed systematic review*. University of Western Ontario.

Husain, S., & Eisenberg, M. (2013). Police AED programs: a systematic review and meta-analysis. *Resuscitation, 84*(9), 1184-1191.

Kane, E., Evans, E., & Shokraneh, F. (2018). Effectiveness of current policing-related mental health interventions: A systematic review. *Criminal Behaviour and Mental Health, 28*(2), 108-119.

Koper, C. S., & Mayo-Wilson, E. (2012). Police strategies to reduce illegal possession and carrying of firearms: Effects on gun crime. *Campbell Systematic Reviews, 8*(1), 1-53.

Lee, Y., Eck, J. E., & Corsaro, N. (2016). Conclusions from the history of research into the effects of police force size on crime – 1968 through 2013: A historical systematic review. *Journal of Experimental Criminology, 12*(3), 431-451.

Lees, T., Elliott, J. L., Gunning, S., Newton, P. J., Rai, T., & Lal, S. (2019). A systematic review of the current evidence regarding interventions for anxiety, PTSD, sleepiness and fatigue in the law enforcement workplace. *Industrial Health, 57*(6), 655-667.

Litmanovitz, Y., & Montgomery, P. (2016). Protocol: Police training interventions to improve the democratic policing of protests. *Campbell Systematic Reviews, 12*(1), 1–39.

Littell, J. H., Corcoran, J., & Pillai, V. (2008). *Systematic review and meta-analysis.* Oxford University Press.

Lum, C., Koper, C. S., Gill, C., Hibdon, J., Telep, C., & Robinson, L. (2016). *An evidence-assessment of the recommendations of the President's Task Force on 21st Century Policing: Implementation and research priorities.* International Association of Chiefs of Police.

Lum, C., Koper, C. S., Wilson, D. B., Stoltz, M., Goodier, M., Eggins, E., Higginson, A., & Mazerolle, L. (2020). Research on body-worn cameras: What we know, what we need to know. *Campbell Systematic Review, 16*(3), 93–118.

Mazerolle, L., Bennett, S., Davis, J., Sargeant, E., & Manning, M. (2013). Legitimacy in policing: A systematic review. *Campbell Systematic Reviews, 9*(1), 1–147.

Mazerolle, L., Cherney, A., Eggins, E., Higginson, A., Hine, L., & Belton, E. (2020d). Police programs that seek to increase community connectedness for reducing violent extremism behaviour, attitudes and beliefs. *Campbell Systematic Reviews, 16*(1), e1111.

Mazerolle, L., Cherney, A., Eggins, E., Higginson, A., Hine, L., & Belton, E. (2020b). Protocol: Multiagency programmes with police as a partner for reducing radicalisation to violence. *Campbell Systematic Reviews, 16*(1), e1110.

Mazerolle, L., Cherney, A., Eggins, E., Higginson, A., Hine, L., & Belton, E. (2020c). Protocol: Police programs that seek to increase community connectedness for reducing violent extremism behaviour, attitudes and beliefs. *Campbell Systematic Reviews,* e1076.

Mazerolle, L., Eggins, E., &Higginson, A. (2016). Protocol: Third party policing for reducing crime and disorder: A systematic review. *Campbell Systematic Reviews, 12*(1), 1–77.

Mazerolle, L., Eggins, E., &Higginson, A. (2020a). Street-level drug law enforcement: An updated systematic review. *Trends & Issues in Crime and Criminal Justice,* 599 16(1), 1–20.

Mazerolle, L., Eggins, E., Hine, L., & Higginson, A. (this volume). The Role of Randomized Experiments in Developing the Evidence for Evidence-Based Policing. In D. Weisburd, T. Jonathan, G. Perry & B. Hasisi, (Eds.), *The Future of Evidence-Based Policing.* Cambridge University Press.

Mazerolle, L., Soole, D. W., & Rombouts, S. (2007). Street-level drug law enforcement: A meta-analytic review. *Campbell Systematic Reviews, 3*(1), 1–47.

McGinley, B., Agnew-Pauley, W., Tompson, L., & Belur, J. (2020). Police recruit training programmes: A systematic map of research literature. *Policing: A Journal of Policy and Practice, 14*(1), 52–75.

Meissner, C. A., Redlich, A. D. Bhatt, S., & Brandon, S. (2012). Interview and interrogation methods and their effects on true and false confessions. *Campbell Systematic Reviews, 8*(1),1–53.

Mohan, D., Tiwari, G., Varghese, M., Bhalla, K., John, D., Saran, A., & White, H. (2020). Protocol: Effectiveness of road safety interventions: An evidence and gap map. *Campbell Systematic Reviews, 16*(1), 1–20.

Nagin, D. S., & Telep, C. W. (2020). Procedural justice and legal compliance: A revisionist perspective. *Criminology & Public Policy, 19*(3), 761–786.

Patterson, G. T., Chung, I. W., & Swan, P. G. (2012). The effects of stress management interventions among police officers and recruits. *Campbell Systematic Reviews, 8*(1), 1–54.

Peñalba, V., McGuire, H., & Leite, J. R. (2008). Psychosocial interventions for prevention of psychological disorders in law enforcement officers. *Cochrane Database of Systematic Reviews*, (3). DOI: 10.1002/14651858.CD005601.pub2

Peterson, J., & Densley, J. (2018). Is Crisis Intervention Team (CIT) training evidence-based practice? A systematic review. *Journal of Crime and Justice, 41*(5), 521–534.

Petrosino, A., Boruch, R. F., Soydan, H., Duggan, L., & Sanchez-Meca, J. (2001). Meeting the challenges of evidence-based policy: The Campbell Collaboration. *The ANNALS of the American Academy of Political and Social Science, 578*(1), 14–34.

Petrosino, A., Guckenburg, S., & Fronius, T. (2012). Policing schools" strategies: A review of the evaluation evidence. *Journal of Multidisciplinary Evaluation, 8*(17), 80–101.

President's Task Force on 21st Century Policing. (2015). *Final report of the President's Task Force on 21st Century Policing*. Office of Community Oriented Policing Services, U.S. Department of Justice.

Puntis, S., Perfect, D., Kirubarajan, A., Bolton, S., Davies, F., Hayes, A., Harriss, E., & Molodynski, A. (2018). A systematic review of co-responder models of police mental health 'street' triage. *BMC Psychiatry, 18*(1), 256.

Rothstein, H. R., Sutton, A. J., & Borenstein, M. (Eds.) (2005). *Publication bias in meta-analysis: Prevention, assessment and adjustments*. Wiley.

Spoth, R., Rohrbach, L. A., Greenberg, M., Leaf, P., Brown, C. H., Fagan, A., Catalano, R. F., Pentz, M. A., Sloboda, Z., & Hawkins, J. D. (2013). Addressing core challenges for the next generation of type 2 translation research and systems: The translation science to population impact (TSci Impact) framework. *Prevention Science, 14*(4), 319–351.

Stanley, I. H., Hom, M. A., & Joiner, T. E. (2016). A systematic review of suicidal thoughts and behaviors among police officers, firefighters, EMTs, and paramedics. *Clinical Psychology Review, 44*(1), 25–44.

Strang, H., Sherman, L. W., Mayo-Wilson, E., Woods, D., & Ariel, B. (2013). Restorative justice conferencing (RJC) using face-to-face meetings of offenders and victims: Effects on offender recidivism and victim satisfaction. A systematic review. *Campbell Systematic Reviews, 9*(1), 1–59.

Taheri, S. A. (2016). Do crisis intervention teams reduce arrests and improve officer safety? A systematic review and meta-analysis. *Criminal Justice Policy Review, 27*(1), 76–96.

Telep, C. W. (2016). Expanding the scope of evidence-based policing. *Criminology and Public Policy, 15*(1), 243–252.

Telep, C. W. (2018). Not just what works, but how it works: Mechanisms and context in the effectiveness of place-based policing. In D. Weisburd & J. E. Eck (Eds.), *Unraveling the crime-place connection: New directions in theory and practice. Advances in Criminological Theory*, vol. 22 (pp. 237–259). Routledge.

Telep, C. W., & Weisburd, D. (2016). Policing. In D. P. Farrington, D. Weisburd, & C. E. Gill (Eds.), *What works in crime prevention and rehabilitation: Lessons from systematic reviews* (pp. 137–168). Springer.

Telep, C. W., Weisburd, D., Gill, C. E., Teichman, D., & Vitter, Z. (2014). Displacement of crime and diffusion of crime control benefits in large-scale geographic areas: A systematic review. *Journal of Experimental Criminology, 10*(4), 515–548.

Telep, C. W., Weisburd, D., Wire, S., & Farrington, D. (2016). Protocol: Increased police patrol presence effects on crime and disorder. *Campbell Systematic Reviews, 12*(1), 1–35.

Weisburd, D., Farrington, D. P., & Gill, C. (2016). Introduction: What works in crime prevention? In D. Weisburd, D. P. Farrington, & C. Gill (Eds.), *What works in crime prevention and rehabilitation* (pp. 1–13). Springer.

Weisburd, D., Farrington, D. P., & Gill, C. (2017). What works in crime prevention and rehabilitation: An assessment of systematic reviews. *Criminology & Public Policy, 16*(2), 415–449.

Weisburd, D., & Telep, C. W. (2014). Hot spots policing: What we know and what we need to know. *Journal of Contemporary Criminal Justice, 30*(2), 200–220.

Weisburd, D., Telep, C. W., Hinkle, J. C., & Eck, J. E. (2008). Effects of problem-oriented policing on crime and disorder. *Campbell Systematic Reviews, 4*(1), 1–87.

West, S. L., & O'Neal, K. K. (2004). Project DARE outcome effectiveness revisited. *American Journal of Public Health, 94*(6), 1027–1029.

Wilson, D. B. (2009). Missing a critical piece of the pie: simple document search strategies inadequate for systematic reviews. *Journal of Experimental Criminology, 5*(4), 429–440.

Wilson, D. (2022). The relative incident rate ratio effect size for count-based impact evaluations: When an odds ratio is not an odds ratio. *Journal of Quantitative Criminology, 38*(2), 323–341.

Wilson, D. B., Brennan, I., & Olaghere, A. (2018). Police-initiated diversion for youth to prevent future delinquent behavior: a systematic review. *Campbell Systematic Reviews, 14*(1), 1–88.

Wilson, D. B., Gill, C., Olaghere, A., & McClure, D. (2016). Juvenile curfew effects on criminal behavior and victimization: a systematic review. *Campbell Systematic Reviews, 12*(1), 1–97.

Wilson, D. B., Weisburd, D., & McClure, D. (2011). Use of DNA testing in police investigative work for increasing offender identification, arrest, conviction and case clearance. *Campbell Systematic Reviews, 7*(1), 1–53.

6

What Do We Know about Proactive Policing's Effects on Crime and Community?

Drawing Conclusions from a National Academies of Sciences, Engineering, and Medicine Report

David Weisburd, Anthony A. Braga,
and Malay Majmundar

One of the key questions in evidence-based policing is how the evidence of effectiveness should be summarized. The systematic review approach uses rigorous methods for locating, appraising, and synthesizing evidence from previous evaluation studies (see Farrington & Petrosino, 2000; Farrington et al., 2011; Littell et al., 2008). While systematic reviews have played an important role in advancing evidence-based policing, they are sometimes criticized precisely because they rely on quantification, producing average effects across studies that often differ in substantive ways and in the specific outcomes that are examined (see Allen, 2020; Eysenck, 1994; Noble, 2006; Pratt, 2010; Vrieze, 2018). A review method that addresses this concern, and also capitalizes on the experience of experts is the narrative review approach. The narrative review draws upon the expertise of the reviewers to assess and evaluate the research literature, and generally draws more qualitative assessments of what the research tells us. At the same time, narrative reviews are sometimes criticized because of their potential to allow reviewer bias into the review process (Farrington & Jolliffe, 2017; Petrosino & Lavenberg, 2007). More generally, we would argue that both review approaches can add significantly to the development of evidence-based policing.

In this chapter, we focus on a narrative review conducted by the National Academies of Sciences, Engineering, and Medicine (NAS) Committee on Proactive Policing. Like other NAS reviews, the Committee was made up of well-recognized experts from a variety of fields, including criminology, law, psychology, statistics, economics, and sociology, as well as senior police practitioners.[1] The study was supported by the Laura and John Arnold Foundation and the National Institute of Justice and was begun in 2015, and the final report was published in 2018 (Weisburd & Majmundar, 2018; see also Weisburd et al., 2019). We note at the outset that the Committee reviewed research evidence from around the world, but it focused its discussions on the implications of the report for American policing.

The Committee met six times over three years, and developed a "consensus report" of their findings. The importance of a consensus report is that each of the experts on the Committee must agree to the conclusions reached. This is a distinct advantage of NAS narrative reviews, because when there is consensus it suggests broad professional support for the overall conclusions that are stated. The report was also reviewed by a panel of leading experts from a variety of fields,[2] and the NAS itself, which also led to revisions approved by the Committee.

In this chapter, we summarize the findings of the NAS report regarding the impacts of proactive policing on crime and communities. We begin below with a description of how proactive policing was defined

---

[1] The committee included: David Weisburd *(Chair)*, George Mason University; Hassan Aden, The Aden Group; Anthony A. Braga, Northeastern University; Jim Bueermann, Police Foundation, Washington, DC; Philip J. Cook, Duke University; Phillip Goff, John Jay College of Criminal Justice; Rachel A. Harmon, University of Virginia Law School; Amelia Haviland, Heinz College, Carnegie Mellon University; Cynthia Lum, George Mason University; Charles Manski, Northwestern University; Stephen Mastrofski, George Mason University; Tracey Meares, Yale Law School; Daniel Nagin, Heinz College, Carnegie Mellon University; Emily Owens, University of California-Irvine; Steven Raphael, University of California-Berkeley; Jerry Ratcliffe, Temple University; Tom Tyler, Yale Law School. The study director for the NAS was Malay Majmundar.

[2] Reviewers included: Robert D. Crutchfield, Department of Sociology, University of Washington; John F. Dovidio, Department of Psychology, Yale University; Lorraine Mazerolle, School of Social Science, The University of Queensland; John V. Pepper, Department of Economics, University of Virginia; Ruth D. Peterson, emerita, Department of Sociology, The Ohio State University; Donald W. Pfaff, Laboratory of Neurobiology and Behavior, The Rockefeller University; Sue Rahr, Executive Director, Criminal Justice Training Commission, Burien, WA; Nancy M. Reid, Department of Statistical Sciences, University of Toronto; Jennifer Richeson, Department of Psychology, Yale University; Robert J. Sampson, Department of Sociology, Harvard University; Lawrence W. Sherman, Cambridge Police Executive Programme, Institute of Criminology, University of Cambridge and Department of Criminology and Criminal Justice, University of Maryland; Wesley G. Skogan, Institute for Policy Research, Northwestern University; Christopher Slobogin, School of Law, Vanderbilt University; Darrel W. Stephens, Executive Director, Major Cities Chiefs Association; David R. Williams, Department of Social and Behavioral Sciences, T. H. Chan School of Public Health, Harvard University.

in the report, and a summary of the wide-scale use of proactive policing approaches in American police agencies. We then turn first to the evidence on crime control, and then to the evidence on community outcomes. In concluding, we provide our own view on the implications of the report for proactive policing in the future.

6.1 WHAT IS PROACTIVE POLICING?

The Committee used the term "proactive policing" to refer to "all policing strategies that have as one of their goals the prevention or reduction of crime and disorder and that are not reactive in terms of focusing primarily on uncovering ongoing crime or on investigating or responding to crimes once they have occurred" (Weisburd & Majmundar, 2018, p. 30). Proactivity includes an emphasis on prevention and mobilizes resources based on police initiative and not necessarily on citizen requests for assistance. This approach can be contrasted with the "standard model of policing" first described in an earlier report of the NAS in 2004 (Skogan & Frydl, 2004; see also Weisburd & Eck, 2004). This standard model relies generally on a "one-size-fits-all" application of reactive strategies to suppress crime and continues to be the dominant form of police practices in the United States. The standard model is based on the assumption that generic strategies for crime reduction can be applied throughout a jurisdiction regardless of the level of crime, the nature of crime, or other variations. Strategies such as increasing the size of police agencies, random patrol across all parts of the community, rapid response to calls for service, generally applied follow-up investigations, and generally applied intensive enforcement and arrest policies are all examples of this standard model of policing.

Proactive policing is distinguished from the everyday decisions of police officers to be proactive in specific situations and instead refers to a strategic decision by police agencies to use proactive police responses in a programmatic way to reduce crime. The Committee identified four broad approaches to crime prevention that summarize the directions that proactive policing has taken over the past few decades: place-based approaches, problem-solving approaches, person-focused approaches, and community-based approaches. Table 6.1 describes the logic model for each approach as well as specific strategies associated with that logic model, the primary objectives of the approach, and the key ways that those objectives are accomplished.

TABLE 6.1 *Four approaches to proactive policing*[a]

	Place-based approach	Problem-solving approach	Person-focused approach	Community-based approach
Logic model for crime prevention	Capitalize on the evidence for the concentration of crime at micro-geographic places	Use a problem-oriented approach, which seeks to identify problems as patterns across crime events and then identify the causes of those problems. Draw upon solutions tailored to the problem causes, with attention to assessment	Capitalize on the strong concentration of crime among a small proportion of the criminal population	Capitalize on the resources of communities to identify and control crime
Policing strategies	Hot spots policing; predictive policing.	Problem-oriented policing; third-party policing; proactive partnering	Focused deterrence; repeat offender programs; stop, question, and frisk	Community-oriented policing; procedural justice policing; broken windows policing
Primary objective	Prevent crime in micro-geographic places	Solve recurring problems to prevent future crime	Prevent and deter specific crimes by targeting known offenders	Enhance collective efficacy and community collaboration with police
Key ways to accomplish objective	Identification of crime hot spots and application of focused strategies	Scan and analyze crime problems, identify solutions and assess them (SARA model)	Identification of known high-rate offenders and application of strategies to these specific offenders	Develop approaches that engage the community, or that change the way police interact with citizens

[a]Reprinted from the NAS report (Weisburd &Majmundar, 2018)

The place-based approach seeks to focus policing resources more efficiently and effectively by capitalizing on the concentration of crime incidents at certain locations, or micro-geographic places, within a department's entire jurisdiction (Braga & Weisburd, 2010; Weisburd 2008, 2015). Policing strategies that take a place-based approach include hot spots policing and predictive policing. The problem-solving approach seeks to take a scientific approach to diagnosing the problems that underlie a pattern of crime incidents (Braga, 2008; Goldstein, 1979). After identifying the causes of these problems, it attempts to tailor solutions to the problems by addressing their causes, thereby preventing (or reducing) future crime. Strategies that take this approach include problem-oriented policing and third party policing. The third approach focuses on deterring crime by capitalizing on the insight that a small proportion of the crime-committing population commits a disproportionate share of the crimes (Pate et al., 1976; Wolfgang et al., 1972). Strategies that employ this person-focused approach include focused deterrence; repeat offender programs; and stop, question, and frisk (SQF). The fourth approach, which the Committee called the community-based approach, focuses on involving the community in defining the key problems of policing and on fostering the community's role (as understood by a strategy's logic model) in maintaining order and public safety (Skogan, 1992, 2006; Tyler, 2004). Strategies that take a community-based approach include community-oriented policing, procedural justice policing, and broken windows policing.

The Committee assessed to what extent these four proactive policing approaches had spread across the landscape of American policing relying on two national surveys. The first, the National Police Research Platform survey (Mastrofski & Fridell, Forthcoming), used a diverse national sample of approximately 100 municipal police and sheriff's agencies, of which the majority are agencies that have between 100 and 3,000 sworn officers (see Table 6.2). The second conducted by PERF was the Future of Policing survey in 2012 (Police Executive Research Forum). The survey instrument was distributed to 500 police departments across the country, and nearly 200 police departments responded (see Table 6.3).

These data tell us that many of the proactive policing approaches are not isolated programs used by a select group of agencies but rather a set of strategies that have been diffused widely across the landscape of American policing. Indeed, most of the proactive strategies were adopted in one form or another by a majority of American police agencies.

TABLE 6.2 *Innovations adopted by departments, with and without formal policy, from the 2013 NPRP Survey (N = 76)*[a]

	Departments adopting with formal policy	Departments adopting without formal policy	Total departments adopting (either with or without formal policy)
Broken windows policing	59.2% (N = 45)	19.7% (N = 15)	78.9% (N = 60)
Problem-oriented policing	68.4% (N = 52)	13.2% (N = 10)	81.6% (N = 62)
Procedural justice policing	81.6% (N = 62)	7.9% (N = 6)	89.5% (N = 68)
Hot spots policing	75.0% (N = 57)	15.8% (N = 12)	90.8% (N = 69)
Community-oriented policing	90.8% (N = 69)	6.6% (N = 5)	97.4% (N = 74)

[a] Reprinted from the NAS report (Weisburd & Majmundar, 2018)
Source: Adapted from Mastrofski & Fridell (forthcoming, p. 2).
Note: The NPRP survey asks departments if they are engaged in "community policing." The survey's use of "community policing" is equivalent to the committee's articulation of Table 6.3.

TABLE 6.3 *Prevalence of use of proactive policing strategies by percentage of agencies responding to the 2012 Future of Policing Survey (N = 200)*[a]

Strategy	Current Use (%)
Community-oriented policing	93.7
Problem-oriented policing	88.9
Hot spots policing	79.9
Directed police patrols/focused deterrence	92.1
Targeting known offenders	79.3
Predictive policing	38.2

[a] Reprinted from the NAS report (Weisburd &Majmundar, 2018)

6.2 WHICH PROACTIVE POLICING PROGRAMS ARE EFFECTIVE IN REDUCING CRIME?

We summarize the conclusions of the Committee regarding the crime control effectiveness of proactive policing programs in Table 6.4. We detail the specific program or strategy in Table 6.4, as well as our assessment

TABLE 6.4 *Crime outcomes of proactive policing strategies*

Program or strategy	Primary mechanism for prevention	Do studies show crime prevention benefits?	Strength of the evidence
Hot Spots Policing	Increase in Focus	Yes	Strong: A large number of strong experimental and quasi-experimental studies.
Predictive Policing	Increase in Focus	No	Weak: Evidence Base is Small
Focused Deterrence	Increase in Focus and Expansion of Tools	Yes	Medium: A number of strong quasi-experimental studies
Stop–question–frisk (type I) Example: High-volume *Terry* stops throughout jurisdiction	Deterrence	Mixed	Medium: No RCTs
Stop–question–frisk (type II) Example: High-volume *Terry* stops in violent-crime hot spots	Deterrence	Yes	Strong: But studies are confounded with hot spots policing.
Third Party Policing	Increase in Focus and Expansion of Tools	Yes	Medium: A small number of strong experimental and quasi-experimental studies.
Problem-Oriented Policing	Increase in Focus and Expansion of Tools	Yes	Medium: A small number of strong experimental and quasi-experimental studies.
Broken Windows Policing – Type I ("zero tolerance" unfocused)	Neither an Increase in Focus or Expansion of Tools	No	Medium: A small number of rigorous studies. No RCTs.

(continued)

TABLE 6.4 (*continued*)

Program or strategy	Primary mechanism for prevention	Do studies show crime prevention benefits?	Strength of the evidence
Broken Windows – Type II (focused) disorder policing)	Increase in Focus	Yes	Strong: However, evaluations to date do not allow identification of whether impact is due to collective efficacy or deterrence.
Community Policing	Expansion of Tools	No	Weak: Broad category, not well defined
Procedural Justice Policing	Expansion of Tools	Mixed	Weak: Evaluated interventions typically include tactics from other strategies, so effect of procedural justice component is not determinable

of the main mechanism for crime control outcomes of the program. We focus here in particular whether the innovation was based on greater focus in policing, or expanding the tool box of policing. These are two key elements of innovations in policing noted by Weisburd and Eck (2004) and the 2004 NAS report on policing (Skogan & Frydl, 2004). As we note in our conclusions, we think that this distinction provides an important perspective on the underlying drivers of crime prevention effectiveness. We also summarize whether the Committee identified crime prevention benefits for a program. Such conclusions were drawn only when the evidence base was seen as strong based upon in-depth critiques of studies' methods and conclusions (see "strength of evidence" in Table 6.4).

As is apparent from Table 6.3, the programs or strategies that emphasize focus as the key element of proactive policing are most likely to evidence crime prevention benefits. Hot spots policing, for example, first proposed by Sherman & Weisburd (1995), has now been found to have strong crime prevention benefits across a large number of studies (Braga et al., 2019; Braga & Weisburd, 2020). Many of these studies are randomized field experiments, and accordingly allow us to draw strong causal conclusions about the effectiveness of hot spots policing. In turn, the evidence base suggests that focusing on hot spots does not just move crime "around the corner" (see Weisburd et al., 2004). Indeed, the evidence to date suggests that hot spots policing is more likely to lead to a "diffusion of crime control benefits" to areas nearby, than displacement of crime. We do not have enough studies of predictive policing to draw conclusions about its impacts.

When police strategies focus on high-risk people, they are also likely to yield crime prevention benefits. The strongest example of this is found in the case of "focused deterrence policing" (Braga et al., 2018), where police focus on very high-rate violent crime offenders. While there were no randomized field trials in this area at the time of the report, the NAS Committee concluded that the quasi-experimental studies were persuasive, and that focused deterrence policing has strong impacts on crime.[3] SQF strategies that were focused on crime hot spots were also found to have crime prevention impacts. However, the evidence base for stop, question, and frisk broadly spread across a jurisdiction is mixed, leading the committee to argue that it is not an evidence-based approach.

The NAS report suggests that simply expanding the tool box of policing will not necessarily lead to crime prevention benefits. What appears to be key is a focus on developing tools specifically for crime control (see below). Following this neither community policing nor procedural justice policing were found to reduce crime. Importantly, neither originally focused on crime prevention. Community policing was developed to improve the relationship between the police and communities (Skogan, 2019), and procedural justice policing sought to improve police legitimacy (Tyler, 2004). At the same time, we note that a recent experimental field trial in three cities found that intensive training in procedural justice for officers who focus on crime hot spots will have crime prevention benefits (as compared to hot spots with officers that did not received such training, see Weisburd et al., 2022). This study suggests that applying procedural justice in the context of a focused crime prevention approach may yield benefits that have not been observed in more generally focused procedural justice interventions. More research on this is needed.

---

[3] There is now one randomized trial in this area. Hamilton, Rosenfeld, & Levin (2018) evaluated an individual offender-focused deterrence program centered on reducing subsequent recidivism by high-risk probationers and parolees in St. Louis (MO). The randomized experiment found that the parolees and probationers who did attend the focused deterrence notification meeting were less likely to recidivate relative to those who did not attend the meeting.

In turn, a recent randomized trial of a community policing intervention emphasizing collective efficacy in Brooklyn Park, Minnesota, found that the intervention increased crime reporting and thus made it difficult to observe crime prevention outcomes. When adjusting for the increased reporting, non-significant effects on crime became statistically significant (Weisburd et al. 2019), suggesting that assessments of community policing may be biased due to impacts of the intervention on reporting of crime. While the existing evidence overall supports a conclusion that community policing does not have meaningful crime prevention outcomes, this study raises measurement questions that need to be addressed in order to attain valid estimates of community policings's impacts upon crime.

Problem-oriented policing, which expands the tool box of policing with an emphasis on crime control, was found to have consistent crime prevention outcomes – though the number of rigorous studies available is small. Similarly, though again based on a small number of studies, third party policing, which also relies on the problem-solving model was noted as effective by the NAS committee.

As we noted earlier, broken windows policing often relies on traditional law enforcement tools, such as crackdowns or arrests. When applied with focus at specific places and when it embraces community problem-solving strategies to change underlying place dynamics, broken windows policing can yield positive impacts on crime outcomes (Braga et al., 2015). When unfocused it does not lead to crime control benefits.

We think the overall evidence on proactive policing leads to an optimistic view of what the police can do to prevent crime. The assumptions prevalent in the 1990s that the police could not prevent crime (Bayley, 1994; Gottfredson & Hirschi, 1990) are simply wrong. There is much the police can do to successfully prevent crime. Not every proactive policing strategy has shown prevention success, but a series of strategies have. The main lessons we draw from the report are that increasing the focus of police practices and expanding crime prevention tools (focusing on crime control) of the police can lead to crime prevention benefits.

6.3 COMMUNITY REACTION TO PROACTIVE POLICING

While evidence-based policing is often developed in reference to crime control, community reaction must also be a key outcome of evidence-based policing studies. Accordingly, we draw on the NAS Committee report on proactive policing, to summarize the impacts of different strategies and programs on outcomes such as evaluations of the police, police legitimacy, and fear of crime. Table 6.5 notes whether the

TABLE 6.5 *Effects of police innovation on communities*

Police program or strategy	Is it primarily focused on crime control?	Does it have positive community outcomes?	Does it have negative community outcomes?	What is the strength of the evidence?
Hot spots policing	Yes	No	No	A small number of rigorous studies
Predictive policing	Yes	–	–	No Studies
Focused deterrence	Yes	–	–	No Studies
Stop, question, and frisk	Yes	No	Yes – when measured at the individual level. No – when measured at the area level	Studies are mostly correlational, with few rigorous causal analyses.
Third-party policing	Yes	–	–	Little information on community outcomes
Problem-oriented policing	Yes	Yes	No	A small number of rigorous studies
Broken windows policing	Yes	No	SQFs and similar aggressive tactics have been found to lead to negative outcomes for individuals	A small number of rigorous studies.
Community policing	No	Yes	No	A number of strong quasi-experimental and a few experimental studies.
Procedural justice policing	No	No	No	A limited number of studies available to date.

117

strategy or program was primarily focused on crime control, whether it has positive community outcomes, or negative community outcomes, and describes briefly the strength of the evidence the NAS Committee reviewed.

Since citizen involvement in policing is a core element of community policing (Skogan, 2019), it is not surprising that we know most about citizen reaction to these types of programs. Community policing strategies that entail direct involvement of citizens and police, such as police community stations or community meetings, improve citizen attitudes toward the police. In turn, they also have been found to reduce fear of crime among individuals and decrease individual concern about crime in neighborhoods (Brown & Wycoff, 1987; Pate & Skogan, 1985; Wycoff & Skogan, 1986). Interestingly, the evidence base is mixed on whether community policing increases cooperation between the police and the public. This is important because it may explain the lack of crime prevention outcomes for community policing programs that are implemented primarily to engage the public and improve police citizen relationships.

While community policing has been found to impact positively on communities, other strategies that have looked to impact communities have not been shown to be effective. Advocates of procedural justice policing argue that this approach will change the way citizens view the police, and that police behavior towards citizens that they have contact with will affect the broader community's evaluations of the police (Tyler & Meares, 2019). This is an important hypothesis to examine, but one that has not been confirmed in research to date. Some studies do suggest that treating citizens in procedurally just ways will lead to more positive evaluations of police legitimacy among those who have contact with the police (Mazerolle et al., 2013; Sahin et al., 2017), but others do not (e.g., see MacQueen & Bradford, 2015). In turn, the recent three-city randomized trial of procedural justice policing noted earlier found that people who live in the procedural justice condition hot spots were significantly less likely to see the police as harassing or using unnecessary violence (Weisburd, et al., 2022). At the same time, that study found no impact on police legitimacy. Despite the support this approach has gained (e.g., see President's Task Force on 21st Century Policing, 2015), much more rigorous research is needed to support its claims.

Broken windows policing has failed to produce the kind of changes in communities that its originators suggested. The broken windows policing model relies on a developmental sequence that begins with police responding to disorder, but leads in the long run to lower levels of fear in the community and heightened collective efficacy. These changes in the community, which enhance informal social controls, are expected to reduce crime more generally. However, there is simply little evidence that broken windows policing reduces fear of crime, and even less that it increases collective efficacy (see Weisburd et al., 2015).

Most of the effective crime control strategies that were identified by the National Academy of Sciences committee have little impact on community attitudes. Hot spots policing, for example, has not been found to lead to negative community reactions. This in itself is important because of a growing narrative among scholars and the public that these types of effective policing approaches lead to negative outcomes in the community (e.g., see Rosenbaum, 2019). At the same time, it is noteworthy that most of these effective strategies in terms of crime control show little evidence of improving citizen attitudes toward the police or improving cooperation with the police. This is true in the case of hot spots policing, third party policing, and focused deterrence policing, all of which have robust impacts upon crime. If police leaders look to effective crime control to enhance community evaluations of the police, the existing evidence does not support this approach. In turn, there is qualitative and descriptive evidence that SQFs have negative impacts on attitudes of those who are stopped, and especially upon young people (who also have been found to suffer negative health impacts from SQFs). A small group of studies report that there are not negative area wide impacts of proactive SQF interventions.

The case of problem-oriented policing suggests that police may gain the most benefits both in terms of crime and in terms of improving their standing in the community by combining community policing with innovations that have shown strong crime prevention benefits. The NAS committee noted, "(s)tudies show consistent small-to-moderate, positive impacts of problem-solving interventions on short-term community satisfaction with the police" (Weisburd &Majmundar, 2018, p. 228). This dual impact seems to be due to the strong reliance of problem-oriented policing on collaborative community problem solving.

6.4 CONCLUSIONS

Our review of the findings of the NAS report on proactive policing leads us to two broad conclusions regarding future proactive policing programs. The first is that crime control effectiveness of proactive policing lies in the ability of police to create greater focus in their activities. To the extent that the focusing and targeting of police activities are increased, there is a greater likelihood of proactive policing having successful impacts on crime (see Sherman, 2013). This was the case, for example, with hot spots policing which focuses on high crime places, and focused deterrence which identifies high-rate offenders.

The second conclusion is that increasing the diversity of approaches used in policing strategies can enhance crime prevention effectiveness when they are focused on crime control. The standard model of policing relies primarily on law enforcement. To the extent that police strategies expand the tools of crime prevention focusing specifically on prevention (and not other goals), and fit those strategies to the problems they seek to solve, they are also likely to have stronger impacts. This is best illustrated in the case of problem-oriented policing where solutions are developed to problems that are directly linked to the nature of the problems encountered.

But crime control is not the only relevant outcome for proactive policing programs, and for evidence-based policing more generally. Recent events in the United States and around the world have reinforced the importance of community evaluations of the police. In the mind of many police executives, their effectiveness in reducing crime should be enough for them to gain the trust and support of the public. Police often believe crime control effectiveness will lead to improved perceptions of law enforcement. What surprises most police executives is that public evaluations of police do not seem to be consistent with their improvements in fighting crime (Weisburd & Jonathan, 2020). In the NAS report, strategies that were found to be effective in reducing crime, such as hot spot policing, had little or no impact on community evaluations of the police. These findings are consistent with a growing body of research that suggests that citizen evaluations of the police are more connected to the way the police interact with the public than to the effectiveness of policing on crime (Hinds & Murphy, 2007; Reisig et al., 2012; Tyler & Meares, 2019).[4] Community surveys almost always show that police legitimacy – often defined as trust in the police – is more closely related to evaluations

---

[4] At the same time, it is important to note that crime control is related to citizen evaluations of the police, among a number of factors other than procedural justice (e.g., see Bottoms & Tankebe, 2012; Tankebe, 2013; Tankebe et al., 2016). While the way police interact with citizens appears to be much more important than crime control effectiveness for understanding police legitimacy, we suspect that persistently high levels of crime will reduce police legitimacy in the eyes of citizens who want safe public spaces.

of "procedural justice," that is, the fairness of the processes by which the police exercise their authority, than to assessments of police effectiveness in fighting crime (Sunshine & Tyler, 2003; Tyler et al., 2014).

Proactive policing programs that focused on community collaboration, such as community policing, were found to improve citizen evaluations of the police in the NAS report. But they were not effective, in themselves, in reducing crime. This suggests that there are two goals the police must pursue simultaneously, using different strategies. It is a mistake to assume that by being effective in fighting crime the police inevitably will win the hearts and minds of the public, or that by working closely with the community crime will naturally drop. Both are important, worthy goals for police in democratic societies, but, in contrast to popular arguments, the research suggests that they are not directly connected.

Our review of the findings of the NAS report on proactive policing suggests that police need to consider carefully how different proactive policing strategies can be combined to produce both crime control and positive community outcomes. Problem-oriented policing provides a good example in this regard. As we noted above, problem-oriented policing often includes a community engagement component. In this sense, problem-oriented policing includes key elements of community policing. In turn, problem-oriented policing stands alone among effective crime prevention strategies that also seem to have positive community outcomes. We think that this provides a promising model for other strategies we reviewed that showed strong crime prevention effectiveness. Infusing such programs as hot spots policing, third party policing, and focused deterrence with community policing components may allow the police to successfully prevent crime and increase community support for the police simultaneously.

References

Allen, M. (2020). Understanding the practice, application, and limitations of meta-analysis. *American Behavioral Scientist, 64*(1), 74–96.

Bayley, D. H. (1994). *Police for the future.* Oxford University Press.

Bottoms, A., & Tankebe, J. (2012). Beyond procedural justice: A dialogic approach to legitimacy in criminal justice. *Journal of Criminal Law & Criminology, 102*(1), 119–170.

Braga, A. A. (2008). *Problem oriented policing and crime prevention* (2nd ed.). Criminal Justice Press.

Braga, A. A., Turchan, B., Papachristos, A. V., & Hureau, D. M. (2019). Hot spots policing of small geographic areas effects on crime. *Campbell Systematic Reviews, 15*(3), 1–88.

Braga, A., & Weisburd, D. (2010). *Policing problem places: Crime hot spots and effective prevention*. Oxford University Press.

Braga, A. A., &Weisburd, D. (2020). Does hot spots policing have meaningful impacts on crime? Findings from an alternative approach to estimating effect sizes from place-based program evaluations. *Journal of Quantitative Criminology*, 1–22. https://doi.org/10.1007/s10940-020-09481-7

Braga, A. A., Weisburd, D., & Turchan, B. (2018). Focused deterrence strategies and crime control: An updated systematic review and meta-analysis of the empirical evidence. *Criminology & Public Policy, 17*(1), 205–250.

Braga, A. A., Welsh, B. C., &Schnell, C. (2015). Can policing disorder reduce crime? A systematic review and meta-analysis. *Journal of Research in Crime and Delinquency, 52*(4), 567–588.

Brown, L. P., & Wycoff, M. A. (1987). Policing Houston: Reducing fear and improving service. *Crime & Delinquency, 33*(1), 71–89.

Eysenck, H. J. (1994). Meta-analysis and its problems. *British Medical Journal, 309*, 789–792.

Farrington, D. P., & Jolliffe, D. (2017). Special issue on systematic reviews in criminology. *Aggression and Violent Behavior, 33*, 1–3.

Farrington, D.P., & Petrosino, A. (2000). Systematic reviews of criminological interventions: The Campbell Collaboration crime and justice group. *International Annals of Criminology, 38*, 49–66.

Farrington, D. P., Weisburd, D., &Gill, C. E. (2011). The Campbell Collaboration Crime and Justice Group: A decade of progress. In C. J. Smith, S. X. Zhang & R. Barberet (Eds.), *Routledge handbook of international criminology* (pp. 53–63). Routledge.

Goldstein, H. (1979). Improving policing: A problem oriented approach. *Crime and Delinquency, 25*(2), 235–258.

Gottfredson, M. R., & Hirschi, T. (1990). *A general theory of crime*. Stanford University Press.

Hamilton, B., Rosenfeld, R., &Levin, A. (2018). Opting out of treatment: Self-selection bias in a randomized controlled study of a focused deterrence notification meeting. *Journal of Experimental Criminology, 17*(1), 1–17.

Hinds, L., & Murphy, K. (2007). Public satisfaction with police: Using procedural justice to improve police legitimacy. *Australian and New Zealand Journal of Criminology, 40*(4), 27–43.

Littell, J. H., Corcoran, J., & Pillai, V. (2008). *Systematic reviews and meta-analysis*. Oxford University Press.

MacQueen, S., & Bradford, B. (2015). Enhancing public trust and police legitimacy during road traffic encounters: Results from a randomized controlled trial in Scotland. *Journal of Experimental Criminology, 11*(3), 419–443.

Mastrofski, S. D., & Fridell, L. (Forthcoming). *Police departments' adoption of innovative practice*. National Police Research Platform. http://static1.1.sqspcdn.com/static/f/733761/26580910/1443907094233/Department+Characteristics+Survey.pdf?token=1xxue9jmC71p%2BeA7gpKCf2WEf7U%3D

Mazerolle, L., Antrobus, E., Bennett, S., & Tyler, T. R. (2013). Shaping citizen perceptions of police legitimacy: A randomized field trial of procedural justice. *Criminology, 51*(1), 33–63.

Noble Jr, J. H. (2006). Meta-analysis: Methods, strengths, weaknesses, and political uses. *Journal of Laboratory and Clinical Medicine*, 147(1), 7–20. https://doi.org/10.1016/j.lab.2005.08.006. PMID: 16443000.
Pate, A., Bowers, R., & Parks, R. (1976). *Three approaches to criminal apprehension in Kansas City: An evaluation report*. Police Foundation.
Pate, T., & Skogan, W. (1985). *Coordinated community policing: The Newark experience*. Technical Report. Police Foundation.
Petrosino, A., & Lavenberg, J. (2007). Systematic reviews and meta-analyses: Best evidence on what works for criminal justice decision makers. *Western Criminology Review*, 8(1), 1–15.
Police Executive Research Forum. (2014). *Future trends in policing*. Department of Justice, Office of Community Oriented Policing Services.
Pratt, T. C. (2010). Meta-analysis in criminal justice and criminology: What it is, when it's useful, and what to watch out for. *Journal of Criminal Justice Education*, 21, 152–168.
President's Task Force on 21st Century Policing. (2015). *Final report of the President's task force on 21st century policing*. Office of Community Oriented Policing Services.
Reisig, M. D., Tankebe, J., & Meško, G. (2012). Procedural justice, police legitimacy, and public cooperation with the police among young Slovene adults. *Journal of Criminal Justice & Security*, 14(2), 147–164.
Rosenbaum, D. P. (2019). The limits of hot spots policing. In D. Weisburd & A. A. Braga (Eds.), *Police innovation: Contrasting perspectives* (pp. 314–344). Cambridge University Press.
Sahin, N., Braga, A. A., Apel, R., & Brunson, R. K. (2017). The impact of procedurally-just policing on citizen perceptions of police during traffic stops: The Adana randomized controlled trial. *Journal of Quantitative Criminology*, 33(4), 701–726.
Sherman, L. W. (2013). The rise of evidence-based policing: Targeting, testing and tracking. *Crime and Justice*, 42, 377–451. https://doi.org/10.1086/670819.
Sherman, L., & Weisburd, D. (1995). General deterrent effects of police patrol in crime 'hot spots': A randomized study. *Justice Quarterly*, 12(4), 625–648.
Skogan, W. G. (1992). *Impact of policing on social disorder: Summary of findings*. Department of Justice, Office of Justice Programs.
Skogan, W. G. (2006). *Police and community in Chicago: A tale of three cities*. Oxford University Press.
Skogan, W. G. (2019). Community policing. In D. Weisburd & A. A. Braga (Eds.), *Police innovation: Contrasting perspectives* (pp. 27–44). Cambridge University Press.
Skogan, W., & Frydl, K. (2004). *Fairness and effectiveness in policing: The evidence*. The National Academies Press.
Sunshine, J., & Tyler, T. R. (2003). The role of procedural justice and legitimacy in shaping public support for policing. *Law & Society Review*, 37(3), 513–548.
Tankebe, J. (2013). Viewing things differently: The dimensions of public perceptions of police legitimacy. *Criminology*, 51(1), 103–135.

Tankebe, J., Reisig, M. D., & Wang, X. (2016). A multidimensional model of police legitimacy: A cross-cultural assessment. *Law and Human Behavior*, 40(1), 11.

Tyler, T. R. (2004). Enhancing police legitimacy. *The ANNALS of the American Academy of Political and Social Science*, 593(1), 84–99.

Tyler, T. R., Fagan, J., & Geller, A. (2014). Street stops and police legitimacy: Teachable moments in young urban men's legal socialization. *Journal of Empirical Legal Studies*, 11(4), 751–785.

Tyler, T. R., & Meares, T. L. (2019). Procedural justice policing. In D. Weisburd & A. A. Braga (Eds.), *Police innovation: Contrasting perspectives* (pp. 71–94). Cambridge University Press.

Vrieze, J. (2018). *Meta-analyses were supposed to end scientific debates. Often, they only cause more controversy*. www.science.org/content/article/meta-analyses-were-supposed-end-scientific-debates-often-they-only-cause-more

Weisburd, D. (2008). *Place-based policing. Ideas in American Policing*. Police Foundation.

Weisburd, D. (2015). The law of crime concentration and the criminology of place. *Criminology*, 53(2), 133–157.

Weisburd, D., & Eck, J. E. (2004). What can police do to reduce crime, disorder, and fear? *The ANNALS of the American Academy of Political and Social Science*, 593(1), 42–65.

Weisburd, D., & Gill, C. (2020). Rethinking the conclusion that community policing does not reduce crime: Experimental evidence of crime reporting inflation. *Translational Criminology*, Spring, 4–6.

Weisburd, D., Gill, C., Wooditch, A., Barritt, W., & Murphy, J. (2020). Building collective action at crime hot spots: Findings from a randomized field experiment. *Journal of Experimental Criminology*, 17(2), 161–191. https://doi.org/10.1007/s11292-019-09401-1.

Weisburd, D., Hinkle, J. C., Braga, A. A., & Wooditch, A. (2015). Understanding the mechanisms underlying broken windows policing: The need for evaluation evidence. *Journal of Research in Crime & Delinquency*, 52(4), 589–608.

Weisburd, D., & Johnathan-Zamir, T. (2020). Fighting crime and gaining public support are two distinct goals for police. *The Hill*. https://thehill.com/opinion/criminal-justice/505593-fighting-crime-and-gaining-public-support-are-two-distinct-goals-for

Weisburd, D., & Majmundar, D. K. (Eds.) (2018). *Proactive policing: Effects on crime and communities*. The National Academies Press.

Weisburd, D., Majmundar, M. K., Aden, H., Braga, A., Bueermann, J., Cook, P. J., Goff, A. P., Harmon, R. A., Haviland, A., Lum, C., Manski, C., Mastrofski, S., Meares, T., Nagin, D., Owens, E., Raphael, S., Ratcliffe, J., & Tyler, T. (2019). Proactive policing: A summary of the report of the National Academies of Sciences, Engineering, and Medicine. *Asian Journal of Criminology*, 14(2), 145–177.

Weisburd, D., Telep, C., Fogg, H., Zastrow, T., Braga, A., & Turchen, B. (2022). Reforming the police through procedural justice training: A multi-city randomized trial at crime hot spots. *Proceedings of the National Academy of Sciences* 119(14), 1–6.

Weisburd, D., Wyckoff, L. A., Ready, J., Eck, J. E., Hinkle, J. C., & Gajewski, F. (2004). *Does crime just move around the corner? A study of displacement and diffusion in Jersey City, NJ.* US Department of Justice National Institute of Justice.

Wolfgang, M. E., Figlio, R. M., & Sellin, T. (1972). *Delinquency in a birth cohort.* University of Chicago Press.

Wycoff, M., & Skogan, W. (1986). Storefront police offices: The Houston field test. In D. Rosenbaum (Ed.), *Community crime prevention: Does it work?* Sage Publications.

7

Rethinking the Role of the Community in Proactive Policing

Charlotte Gill

7.1 RETHINKING THE ROLE OF THE COMMUNITY IN PROACTIVE POLICING

Proactive policing, which includes approaches such as hot spots policing, problem-oriented policing, and community-oriented policing, emerged as a response to a "crisis of confidence" in American policing that began in the 1960s and 1970s. That era was marked by civil unrest, rising crime, and a feeling that nothing worked to prevent crime and improve public safety. In the late 2010s, a similar crisis was emerging following the high-profile killings of predominantly Black and African-American men at the hands of police and the resulting protests against police misconduct and use of force. This recent crisis led to increased scrutiny of proactive policing. Is it applied fairly and equitably? Does it contribute to excessive use of force? And to what extent can police use proactive strategies to heal and rebuild fractured relationships with the communities they serve? The National Academy of Sciences, Engineering, and Medicine convened a Committee on Proactive Policing: Effects on Crime, Communities, and Civil Liberties to examine these questions (Weisburd & Majmundar, 2018).[1]

The report of the committee (hereafter described as the "NAS report"), published in 2018, defines proactive policing as follows:

[A]ll policing strategies that have as one of their goals the **prevention or reduction of crime and disorder** and that are not reactive in terms of focusing primarily on uncovering ongoing crime or on investigating or responding to crimes once they have occurred. (Weisburd & Majmundar, 2018, p. 30, emphasis added)

---

[1] The committee was funded by the National Institute of Justice and the Laura and John Arnold Foundation.

Consistent with its definition of proactive policing, the NAS report is primarily concerned with outlining the evidence for the *crime prevention* effectiveness of four broad categories of police strategies: place-based, problem-solving, person-focused, and community-based policing. The report acknowledges that all four types of approach at least have collateral consequences on community outcomes. However, strategies in the community-based category – which focuses on community involvement in identifying problems and maintaining order – are the only approaches that seek to achieve crime prevention indirectly rather than directly, through enhanced collective efficacy and community collaboration with the police (Weisburd & Majmundar, 2018, pp. 43–44).

The report concludes that while there is strong evidence that proactive place-based, problem-solving, and person-focused policing strategies reduce crime, there is minimal evidence for the crime control effectiveness of community-based proactive policing (CBPP). However, CBPP has clear benefits for community perceptions of police such as increased satisfaction and evaluations of legitimacy. At the same time, the effects of the other approaches on community perceptions are mixed. Overall, the report authors conclude that crime control and community support are both important goals for police, but they are separate goals and operate via separate logic models. On the other hand, they also acknowledge that some approaches that rely on both focused problem-solving and community involvement are highly effective precisely because of the collaborative element (see Weisburd et al., this volume). Conversely, other strategies are effective at reducing crime but may negatively affect the community. Thus, the relationship between proactive policing and community perceptions, orientations, and behavior is complex.

In this chapter, I argue that the future of evidence-based, proactive policing depends on better understanding the nature of the relationship between the police and the community. While I agree with the statement by Weisburd, Braga, and Majmundar in this volume that "[i]t is a mistake to assume that by being effective in fighting crime the police inevitably will win the hearts and minds of the public, or that by working closely with the community crime will naturally drop," I contend that researchers and practitioners alike need to look beyond community perceptions, orientations, and behavior as solely outcomes of policing approaches. I propose that community support and collaboration are inherent to proactivity and may ultimately moderate the success or failure of proactive policing strategies. As I write this chapter against the backdrop of the murder of George Floyd and subsequent Black Lives

Matter protests around the world in 2020, and the U.S. Capitol insurrection in early 2021, it strikes me that the role of community goes beyond simply a set of outcomes – it is the foundation or mandate for any successful policing approach and thus essential to the future development of evidence-based policing.

This chapter begins with a review of research on the relationship between proactive policing and community outcomes identified in the NAS report. I then argue that the lack of empirical support for the relationship between proactive policing, community support, and crime prevention may stem from two important limitations: existing research does not focus on the processes or mechanisms by which this relationship may operate and follow-up periods are insufficient to identify long-term processes (as the NAS report also acknowledges). I conclude this chapter with suggestions for future research and theory development to better unpack this complex relationship and translate the lessons learned into effective police practice.

7.2 THE IMPACT OF PROACTIVE POLICING ON COMMUNITY OUTCOMES

Chapters 5 and 6 of the NAS report specifically assess the relationship between proactive policing and community outcomes. The report defines community outcomes in three ways (Weisburd & Majmundar, 2018, p. 179):

1. Community members' evaluations of the police (e.g., satisfaction with police services).
2. Community members' orientation toward the police as an institution (e.g., perceptions of police legitimacy).
3. Community members' behavior toward the police and the community itself (e.g., willingness to participate in crime prevention efforts; i.e., collective efficacy).

Figure 7.1 shows the logic model illustrating the relationship between proactive policing and community outcomes proposed in the NAS report. Police department policies oriented toward proactive efforts affect street-level police activity, which in turn impacts community evaluations, orientation, and subsequent behavior. The logic model is also cyclical, in that community behavior, orientation, and perceptions can shape police officers' activities and departmental decision-making. Of the four categories of proactive policing, only community-based strategies are assumed

Rethinking the Role of the Community in Proactive Policing 129

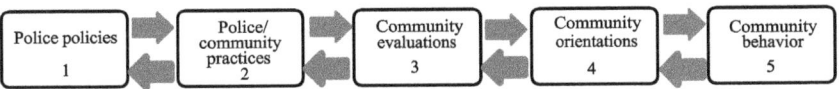

FIGURE 7.1 Logic model for proactive policing and community outcomes (reproduced from Weisburd and Majmundar, 2018, Fig. 5.1, p. 180)

to have a direct effect on community outcomes, in the sense that these strategies are usually deployed specifically to influence community evaluations, orientation, and behavior. Place-based, problem-solving, and person-focused strategies are assumed to affect these outcomes as a secondary or collateral consequence of their crime prevention effects (Weisburd & Majmundar, 2018, p. 178).

The NAS report includes community-oriented policing, procedural justice policing, and broken windows policing within the community-based proactive strategies category. The majority of research on community outcomes applies to the first two approaches. The report finds that community-oriented policing improves community members' satisfaction with police and has modest positive effects on their perceptions of legitimacy (Weisburd & Majmundar, 2018; see also Gill et al., 2014). However, less is known about the specific mechanisms by which procedurally just policing influences perceptions of legitimacy (see also Nagin & Telep, 2017), and there is limited evidence for community outcomes of broken windows policing or for the influence of any of the community-based strategies on actual changes in community behavior.

The nature of the indirect relationship between proactive strategies to reduce crime and community outcomes is less clear. In part, this is likely due to the substantial diversity of tactics and approaches that are categorized as proactive place-based, problem-solving, or person-focused policing, which creates a "black box" problem in many evaluations. The NAS report found that problem-solving approaches were most likely to have positive effects on community members' satisfaction with police, although these effects were small (Weisburd & Majmundar, 2018). This is not surprising given that, while problem-oriented policing does not require community collaboration, community-oriented policing and problem-solving tend to go hand-in-hand. Indeed, problem-solving is one element of the U.S. Department of Justice Office of Community Oriented Policing Services' three-part definition of community-oriented policing (Office of Community Oriented Policing Services, 2014).

Place-based policing had no effect, positive or negative, on short-term community outcomes. Some scholars have suggested that more aggressive place-based tactics, such as crackdowns and sweeps at hot spots, could lead to unfavorable community perceptions of the police (e.g., Kochel, 2011), but this has not been borne out in empirical research (Kochel & Weisburd, 2017). Research on the impact of these approaches on fear of crime is also mixed: Hinkle and Weisburd (2008) found that they increase fear, but Weisburd and colleagues (2011) found the opposite. The research on community impacts of person-focused strategies is extremely limited, but the report found some evidence that stop, question, and frisk tactics, focused deterrence programs, and traffic enforcement may result in less favorable orientations toward police (i.e., perceptions of police legitimacy) for those who experience them. The report did not identify any conclusive research on the long-term effects of proactive place-based, problem-solving, or person-focused policing strategies on community orientation or behavior.

The NAS report suggests that the lack of a clear, consistent relationship between proactive policing and community outcomes stems from a corresponding lack of a theoretical connection between the two in prior research. Indeed, the committee was unable to find much research at all documenting the long-term effects of proactive policing on community orientations toward the police and subsequent behavior. This finding aligns with the committee's definition of proactive policing, which focuses on crime prevention, not community outcomes, as the overarching goal of these strategies. At the same time, they found a lack of evidence for the crime prevention effectiveness of proactive policing strategies that have the explicit goal of improving community outcomes, such as community-oriented policing (see Gill et al., 2014; Skogan & Frydl, 2004; Weisburd & Eck, 2004; Weisburd & Majmundar, 2018). This supports the contention of Weisburd and colleagues in this volume that proactive policing strategies affect crime and community outcomes via different processes (see also Weisburd & Jonathan-Zamir, 2020).

Weisburd and colleagues are likely correct that proactive policing affects crime and community *outcomes* in different ways. The historical context for the development of proactive approaches like community-oriented policing and problem-oriented policing helps to explain the distinction between these processes. Community-oriented policing emerged during a period of civil unrest in the United States, driven largely by the civil rights and anti-war protests of the 1960s and 1970s, which highlighted the public's dissatisfaction with traditional reactive, enforcement-heavy policing, and undermined police legitimacy (President's Commission on Law Enforcement and Administration of Justice, 1967;

Weisburd & Eck, 2004). Community-oriented policing offered an alternative that de-emphasized the crime fighting role of the police and aimed to reconnect police with the communities they served and prioritize community needs (Reiss, 1971; Scheider et al., 2009; Skogan & Frydl, 2004; Skolnick & Bayley, 1988). To that end, community policing as originally envisaged was fundamentally concerned with broadening the police role *beyond* law enforcement and crime control (Kelling & Moore, 1988; Mastrofski et al., 1995; Skogan & Frydl, 2004; Tuffin et al., 2006). It is not surprising, then, that community-oriented policing improves community outcomes but has no impact on crime.

On the other hand, while community-oriented policing developed as a response to the crisis of police legitimacy, problem-oriented policing responded to the crisis of police effectiveness (Sherman et al., 1997). Rising crime rates in the 1970s through the early 1990s in the United States, coupled with a general consensus that "nothing worked" in criminal justice policy and practice (Martinson, 1974) and specific studies undermining the effectiveness of traditional policing practices like preventive patrol and rapid response to 911 calls (Kelling et al., 1974; Spelman & Brown, 1984; see also Weisburd & Braga, 2006), led scholars to argue that the police were ineffective at crime prevention (Bayley, 1994; Goldstein, 1990; Gottfredson & Hirschi, 1990). While problem-oriented policing is closely connected with community-oriented policing (Office of Community Oriented Policing Services, 2014; see also Cordner, 1999), it is primarily concerned with identifying the "root causes" of crime so that strategies can be put in place to address them, ultimately preventing crime (Eck & Spelman, 1987; Goldstein, 1979, 1990). Broken windows policing follows a similar logic, with a focus on physical and social disorder as specific "root causes" (e.g., Braga et al., 2015). It follows that these strategies could effectively reduce crime regardless of their impact on community outcomes.

7.3 COMMUNITY AND THE FUTURE OF PROACTIVE POLICING

While the research supports two separate logic models for community and crime *outcomes*, I argue that thinking about community perceptions, orientations, and behaviors only as outcomes of proactive policing overlooks the important role these factors may play in mediating the overall effectiveness of these strategies. In thinking about crime impacts and community impacts as separate processes, researchers have overlooked opportunities to consider the complex interplay between the two. The

NAS report argues that improving police–community relations should be an important goal for police departments regardless of the effectiveness of their strategies (Weisburd & Majmundar, 2018, p. 177; see also Lum & Nagin, 2017), but I contend that the goals of community relations and crime prevention cannot be divorced from each other. Community is inherent to proactivity, and thus has important implications for how we think about the crime prevention effectiveness of proactive policing. At a fundamental level, the community provides the mandate for proactive policing strategies, and furthermore improved police–community collaboration may strengthen their crime control effectiveness. Thus, the future of proactive, evidence-based policing depends heavily on how we think about the role of the community. While the nature of this relationship has not been fully explored, in the following sections, I discuss some of the research that supports these statements.

7.3.1 The Community Mandate for Proactive Policing

The community is the foundation of social institutions (Sherman, 1997) and provides the mandate for policing, so the future of evidence-based, proactive policing strategies depends on the community's support and perception of the police as legitimate. This goes beyond simply thinking about community perceptions as secondary outcomes of proactive policing programs. Rather than being separate, linear processes, community support and police effectiveness may build on each other in an iterative, incremental process over long periods of time. For example, can community support be maintained if the police are not effective at keeping the community safe? And to what extent are communities willing to tolerate practices that oppress their members at the expense of strong crime prevention gains?

The idea that the police need the support of the community to be effective ties into the literature on legitimacy and democratic policing. The community is more than a source of information and support for police agencies, and in a democratic society it is not sufficient for police to simply maintain order within the bounds of the law (Greene, 2000; Meares, 2013). The police are expected to be for and of the people – an idea that harks back to Robert Peel – and their core role is to uphold the civil and constitutional rights of the community, allowing people to exercise their freedoms safely and equitably (Bayley, 1994; Manning, 2010; Mastrofski, 1999; Moore, 1992; Rahr & Rice, 2015; Shilston, 2015). Furthermore, the majority of people who interact with the police do so in non-crime settings. Thus, democratic policing requires a delicate balance between ensuring public safety, while maintaining the trust of the community (Lum & Nagin, 2017).

Kelling and Moore (1988) argued that what they call the "community problem solving era" (1970s–80s), which gave rise to many of the proactive policing strategies discussed in the NAS report, ushered in a renewed emphasis on community legitimacy as the foundation for police work, given the emphasis on community involvement in problem-solving strategies. While community-oriented and democratic policing are not synonymous, community-oriented policing is central to policing in a democracy and shares many of the same elements, such as expectations around the 'co-production' of public safety (Bayley, 2005; Shilston, 2015; Skolnick & Bayley, 1988). Proactive strategies like problem-oriented policing can therefore be viewed as tactics to accomplish the overall goal of establishing community trust and legitimacy (Kelling & Moore, 1988; see also Scheider et al., 2009).

The connection between community legitimacy and police effectiveness is encapsulated in Tyler's seminal work on the process-based model of policing, commonly known as procedural justice (e.g., Tyler, 2004). According to this model, the support of the community is crucial to the effectiveness of the police at maintaining order. The police rely on the community to obey the law most of the time (so that police resources are not overwhelmed); report crime; and collaborate in problem-solving. This support comes from community members' judgments of police legitimacy – people comply, cooperate, and collaborate with the police because they see the police as entitled to their support. Related to the idea of democratic policing, this compliance and collaboration cannot be forced or based solely in deterrence (i.e., fear of the consequences of non-compliance). It has to be voluntary and rooted in community members' feelings of obligation toward the police. Thus, it cannot be achieved if the community feels that the police are untrustworthy or not entitled to their help; in other words, if they do not perceive that they are treated in a procedurally just manner by the police. Again, this indicates the extent to which the community provides the mandate for all police activities and the inextricable link between community support/involvement and crime prevention effectiveness (see also Sunshine & Tyler, 2003).

While Tyler's process-based model has been criticized in part for the lack of evidence for community-wide impacts of procedurally just policing (as opposed to changes in individual perceptions as a result of encounters with the police; Nagin & Telep, 2017), there is some evidence that procedurally just policing is associated with trust in police (Nix et al., 2015) and lower crime rates in neighborhoods (Higginson & Mazerolle, 2014). The study by Nix and colleagues (2015) also suggests a relationship between collective efficacy and trust in the police, which aligns with other studies that have found a relationship between social cohesion, willingness to intervene, and proactive policing strategies (Kochel & Gau, 2019; Kochel & Weisburd, 2019). However, the relationship between community-oriented policing, proactive policing efforts that focus primarily on crime prevention, trust and confidence in the police, and collective efficacy has not been fully unpacked (Gill et al., 2014).

7.3.2 Community Collaboration and Crime Prevention Effectiveness

One reason why the complex relationship between proactive policing and community perceptions has not been fully explored is the typically short timeframe of research and evaluation studies. Furthermore, innovative interventions developed through grant-funded researcher–practitioner partnerships are often not sustained (or further evaluated) after the funding ends (e.g., Gill & Gross Shader, 2020). This limits our ability to fully examine whether policing strategies that successfully improve community perceptions also lead to crime control gains in the long term, and how both police strategies and community involvement might lead to sustained neighborhood change. As Gill et al. (2014) suggest, in entrenched hot spots of crime within neighborhoods where residents have a long history of distrusting the police, it could take years or even decades before community members' perceptions of the police improve to the point that they recognize the benefits of proactive policing approaches and/or are willing to collaborate with the police to prevent crime. As a result, short-term research studies may conclude that there is no relationship between crime prevention and community building strategies.

However, as Weisburd and colleagues acknowledge in this volume, the success of crime prevention strategies like problem-oriented policing may depend on the extent to which they are combined with community-oriented policing strategies. In that case, rather than treating community-oriented policing, problem-oriented policing, broken windows policing, hot spots policing, procedural justice policing, and so on simply as an assortment of discrete tools in the police department's toolkit, future research needs to examine in a nuanced way how these strategies work together and build upon one another over time. Perhaps there is an ideal sequencing of proactive efforts, first to build community support through procedural justice-based and community-oriented efforts, followed by collaborative crime prevention efforts like problem-oriented policing. Alternatively, successful police-led crime prevention efforts may help to build community satisfaction and trust in the long term, paving the way for future collaborative efforts. Or, as Scheider and colleagues (2009) suggest, perhaps community-oriented policing should be viewed not as a strategy in itself, but as a backdrop against which all other proactive, evidence-based policing strategies are implemented. At present we do not have sufficient research to assess whether any of these propositions are true, but they all illustrate the possibility of non-linear, reciprocal relationships between community perceptions and crime prevention effects.

At a theoretical level, the origins of strategies like problem-oriented and broken windows policing lend some support to the idea that community is inherent to proactivity. Like community-oriented policing, these approaches were founded on the idea that police should draw directly upon community resources and work in partnership with neighborhood residents, rather than being police-centric strategies that only passively impact the community. Herman Goldstein's original conceptualization of POP explicitly called for the police to draw on community expertise in problem-solving. He stated that "A community must police itself. The police can, at best, only assist in that task" (Goldstein, 1990, p. 21). While a specific problem-solving effort cannot be expected to establish long-term community relations or police effectiveness, a long-term commitment to community collaboration – when it is necessary to address each specific problem that arises – should *eventually* strengthen police–community relations. Goldstein recognized that "the effectiveness of the police depends on community involvement" (1990, p. 26).

Similarly, broken windows policing has become synonymous with aggressive, zero-tolerance strategies that risk alienating community members, but the original expression of broken windows theory was very different. Kelling and Wilson (1982) advocated for order maintenance as part of their argument that community members' feelings of safety are more important than actual crime statistics. Defending the theory years later in Politico Magazine, Kelling argued that police departments often miss the point of the theory, which is prevention, and that the role of the police is to maintain order in collaboration with the community rather than impose it on them (Kelling, 2015). Furthermore, evidence from a recent meta-analysis of broken windows (or 'disorder') policing shows that collaborative efforts are more effective than zero-tolerance approaches (Braga et al., 2015).

Scheider and colleagues (2009) suggest that these proactive approaches (as well as traditional policing strategies) are most effective when they are integrated into a department-wide community policing framework. Similar to Goldstein's argument, this recognizes that the effectiveness of specific proactive strategies that were "intentionally designed with a more narrow focus or to solve a specific problem" (Scheider et al., 2009, p. 701) is founded on the extent to which they align with the broader organizational recognition that the community provides the mandate for everything the agency does. Thus, the true "community-oriented" police department is oriented at the organizational level toward leadership approaches, performance management structures, and strategic planning that reflect community values, and at the street level emphasizes effective proactive strategies that draw upon community expertise to solve problems and promote community safety.

7.4 FUTURE DIRECTIONS: COMMUNITY AS A "CHANGE LEVER"

If unpacking the complex relationship between community and crime prevention is key to the future of proactive policing, we will need to expand on existing research approaches to better understand it. The interconnectedness of community involvement and perceptions with crime prevention suggests a more complex logic model than the ones proposed in the NAS report. One way that future research could re-examine the role of community is by thinking of community factors as "**change levers**" (Wilson, 2019) that mediate the longer-term outcome of crime prevention. While the evidence reviewed in the NAS report suggests that policing strategies intended primarily to improve community perceptions do not impact crime and vice versa, I have argued above for a more nuanced model that does not view crime and community outcomes as distinct causal pathways. At present, we have not adequately tested whether programs that seek to reduce crime *via* community collaboration are effective – crime prevention is not an explicit goal of most community-oriented policing programs, and many programs that have crime reduction as their primary goal have not engaged community members in a systematic or meaningful way. In both cases, studies have not been able to follow up over the long timeframes that are likely needed for substantial changes in community orientations or solutions to entrenched crime problems to take hold. However, as I discussed above, there is some evidence that problem-oriented policing and broken windows policing are more effective when they involve such collaboration.

Rethinking the Role of the Community in Proactive Policing 137

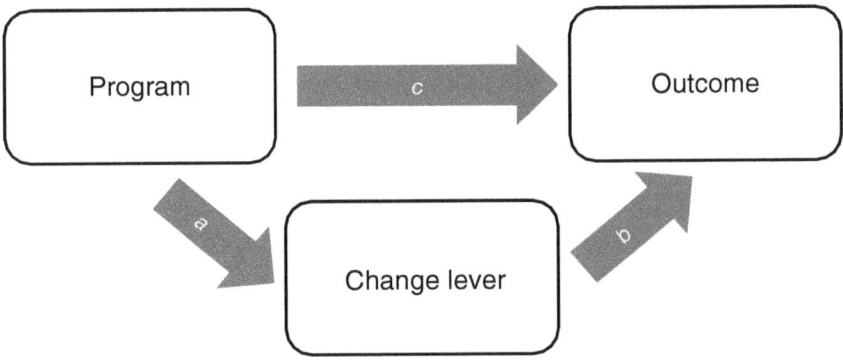

FIGURE 7.2 Illustration of the relationship between program, change lever, and outcome (adapted from Wilson, 2019)

Wilson (2019), in the context of juvenile delinquency prevention programs, argues that studying change levers offers a more meaningful way to examine the pattern of evidence for the effectiveness of programs than trying to understand the impact of specific elements of each program, which can be highly variable. Change levers are mediating factors in the causal chain (Figure 7.2): the relationship between the program and the change lever (*a*) and between the change lever and the outcome (*b*) must account for some of the direct relationship between the program and outcome (*c*). Applying this idea to proactive policing, we could center the role of the community as a "change lever" that mediates the relationship between proactive strategies and crime prevention, rather than categorizing proactive strategies as hot spots policing, community-oriented policing, problem-oriented policing, and various other approaches that have different outcomes (see Figure 7.3). This is based on the ideas described above – that the community provides the mandate for proactive policing and increased collaboration might lead to more favorable crime prevention outcomes in the long term. As I have noted, it is possible that this process could take decades, or that proactive strategies still successfully reduce crime regardless of community collaboration but community involvement changes the *magnitude* of that effect. These are questions that have not been explored in existing research.

Thus, my call for the future development of proactive policing as it relates to the community is for a renewed focus on basic research in addition to (or as part of) continued program evaluations of proactive policing strategies. While developing logic models and causal frameworks has traditionally been the domain of quantitative research, the

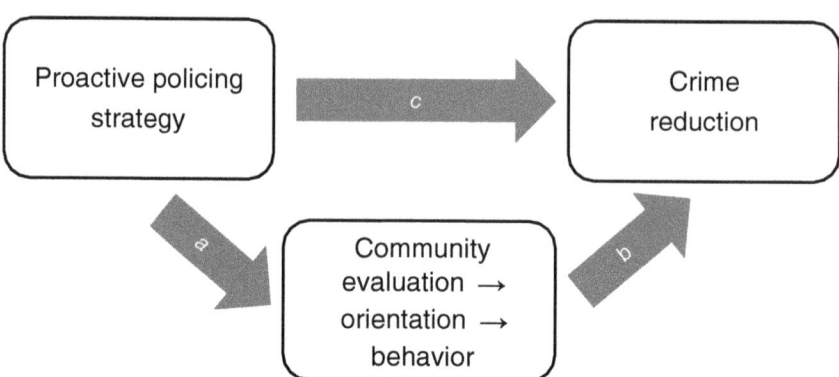

FIGURE 7.3 Proposed simplified logic model for the role of community outcomes as change levers

complexity of understanding community priorities and aligning them with evidence-based policing strategies also lends itself to qualitative inquiry. *Participatory action research* (PAR), which can involve both quantitative and qualitative methods, involves researchers and community members – including, in this context, police officers and leaders – engaging in critical, self-reflective inquiry together in order to better "understand and improve upon the practices in which they participate and the situations in which they find themselves" (Baum et al., 2006, p. 854; see also Kidd & Kral, 2005; McTaggart, 1991; Whyte, 1989). Examples of the use of the PAR framework in public health research (e.g., Baum et al., 2006) show a natural alignment with problem-oriented policing approaches: PAR typically involves collaborative processes like community planning, identifying, and prioritizing problems, and shared responsibility for implementation. Crucially, in the current climate of strained police–community relations, PAR is intended to break down barriers between research participants and place community members on an equal footing with researchers and other institutional representatives like the police. This could allow for stronger and more authentic representation of the community's experiences of proactive policing (including differential expectations, priorities, and impacts across different sections of the community), which has so far received limited attention in the research literature (for an exception, see Kochel, 2011).

Process tracing is another qualitative framework that could be employed to make sense of how community evaluations, orientations, and behaviors affect crime prevention outcomes. This method, more often used in political science and public health research, seeks to systematically identify causal relationships through case studies that follow a sequence of events over time (Collier, 2011). Briefly, process tracing involves subjecting "diagnostic evidence" – any piece of information that might help to establish the relationship between dependent and independent variables – to a series of four tests considered necessary and sufficient for establishing causal inference. Collier (2011) likens the methodology to a Sherlock Holmes mystery, in which the reader develops hypotheses based on clues in the story that ultimately lead to figuring out "whodunit." In the context of proactive policing, case studies of initiatives that were successful and unsuccessful at reducing crime could be examined in the same way to develop an understanding of the nature and extent of community involvement and how this may have contributed to the outcome. Process tracing could also be used in addition to or in tandem with a *subjective causality* approach as described by Perry, Jonathan-Zamir, and Willis in Chapter 9 of this volume. In that approach, causal relationships are identified according to the perceptions of individuals involved.

A benefit of process tracing and subjective causality approaches over traditional quantitative methods for identifying change levers, such as structural equation modeling, is that they can help us get inside the "black box" of causation, telling us not only that one concept is related to something else (which is not always consistent across studies), but *why*, and in what order. Returning to Wilson's (2019) argument, this could help both researchers and police agencies identify the most effective processes for engaging the community in successful crime prevention, improving the likelihood that best practices can be replicated across settings. In turn, this knowledge about which community factors are important and why can be translated into practice. For example, measures of community evaluations, orientations, and/or behavior could be incorporated into officer performance evaluations and strategic leadership decision-making to incentivize police officers and leaders to engage in activities and policy development that emphasize community participation and could ultimately lead to successful crime prevention (Lum & Nagin, 2017).

7.5 CONCLUSION

In this chapter, I have argued that community perceptions are not simply secondary outcomes or collateral consequences of crime prevention-focused proactive policing strategies. The community is foundational to the legitimacy and effectiveness of the police. Therefore, proactive policing is not simply about the development of strategies to prevent crime.

It is important to acknowledge that my arguments are speculative and based on limited information: we clearly need a great deal more research to fully articulate the causal relationships between proactive policing, community factors, and crime prevention. However, I hope to have made the point that it is crucial to view police effectiveness through a community lens. Thinking more about the community "change levers" that can shape, or be shaped by, police activity may influence the future development and success of proactive policing. The events of 2020–2021 illustrate that, despite increasing evidence for the success of proactive policing, there remains a fundamental disconnect between the police and many communities, both in the United States and worldwide, which undermines the community mandate for policing. Amid calls to defund – divert public resources back to community-based services, mental health treatment, and education (e.g., Lopez, 2020; Weichselbaum & Lewis, 2020) – and even abolish the police, it is more important than ever to actively engage the community to understand the key values, orientations, and needs that shape their willingness to support and collaborate with the police, while recognizing the importance and challenge of maintaining equity across different groups with varying and potentially competing interests (Thacher, 2001).

References

Baum, F., MacDougall, C., & Smith, D. (2006). Participatory action research. *Journal of Epidemiology & Community Health, 60*(10), 854–857. https://doi.org/10.1136/jech.2004.028662

Bayley, D. H. (1994). *Police for the future.* Oxford University Press.

Bayley, D. H. (2005). Police reform as foreign policy. *Australian & New Zealand Journal of Criminology, 38*(2), 206–215. https://doi.org/10.1375/acri.38.2.206

Braga, A. A., Welsh, B. C., & Schnell, C. (2015). Can policing disorder reduce crime? A systematic review and meta-analysis. *Journal of Research in Crime & Delinquency, 52*(4), 567–588. https://doi.org/10.1177/0022427815576576

Collier, D. (2011). Understanding process tracing. *PS: Political Science & Politics, 44*(4), 823–830. https://doi.org/10.1017/S1049096511001429

Cordner, G. W. (1999). Elements of community policing. In L. K. Gaines & G. W. Cordner (Eds.), *Policing perspectives: An anthology* (pp. 137–149). Roxbury.

Eck, J. E., & Spelman, W. (1987). *Problem-solving: Problem-oriented policing in Newport News.* Police Executive Research Forum. www.ncjrs.gov/pdffiles1/Digitization/111964NCJRS.pdf

Gill, C., & Gross Shader, C. (2020). Building a "Beautiful Safe Place for Youth:" The story of an effective community-research-practice partnership in Rainier Beach, Seattle. In R. J. Stokes & C. Gill (Eds.), *Innovations in community-based crime prevention: Case studies and lessons learned.* Springer.

Gill, C., Weisburd, D., Telep, C. W., Vitter, Z., & Bennett, T. (2014). Community-oriented policing to reduce crime, disorder and fear and increase satisfaction and legitimacy among citizens: A systematic review. *Journal of Experimental Criminology, 10*(4), 399–428. https://doi.org/10.1007/s11292-014-9210-y

Goldstein, H. (1979). Improving policing: A problem-oriented approach. *Crime & Delinquency, 25*(2), 236–258. https://doi.org/10.1177/001112877902500207

Goldstein, H. (1990). *Problem-oriented policing*. McGraw-Hill.

Gottfredson, M., & Hirschi, T. (1990). *A general theory of crime*. Stanford University Press.

Greene, J. R. (2000). Community policing in America: Changing the nature, structure, and function of the police. In Horney, Julie (Ed.), *Criminal justice 2000: Policies, processes, and decisions of the criminal justice system* (pp. 299–370). U.S. Department of Justice, Office of Justice Programs, National Institute of Justice.

Higginson, A., & Mazerolle, L. (2014). Legitimacy policing of places: The impact on crime and disorder. *Journal of Experimental Criminology, 10*(4), 429–457. https://doi.org/10.1007/s11292-014-9215-6

Hinkle, J. C., & Weisburd, D. (2008). The irony of broken windows policing: A micro-place study of the relationship between disorder, focused police crackdowns and fear of crime. *Journal of Criminal Justice, 36*(6), 503–512. https://doi.org/10.1016/j.jcrimjus.2008.09.010

Kelling, G. L. (2015). Don't blame my 'broken windows' theory for poor policing [magazine]. *Politico Magazine.* www.politico.com/magazine/story/2015/08/broken-windows-theory-poor-policing-ferguson-kelling-121268.html

Kelling, G. L., & Moore, M. H. (1988). From political to reform to community: The evolving strategy of police. In J. R. Greene & S. D. Mastrofski (Eds.), *Community policing: Rhetoric or reality* (pp. 3–26). Praeger.

Kelling, G. L., Pate, A. M., Dieckman, D., & Brown, C. E. (1974). *The Kansas City Preventive Patrol Experiment: A summary report.* Police Foundation. www.policefoundation.org/projects/the-kansas-city-preventive-patrol-experiment/

Kelling, G. L., & Wilson, J. Q. (1982). Broken windows: The police and neighborhood safety. *Atlantic Monthly, 249*(3), 1–9.

Kidd, S. A., & Kral, M. J. (2005). Practicing participatory action research. *Journal of Counseling Psychology, 52*(2), 187–195. https://doi.org/10.1037/0022-0167.52.2.187

Kochel, T. R. (2011). Constructing hot spots policing: Unexamined consequences for disadvantaged populations and for police legitimacy. *Criminal Justice Policy Review, 22*(3), 350–374. https://doi.org/10.1177/0887403410376233

Kochel, T. R., & Gau, J. M. (2019). Examining police presence, tactics, and engagement as facilitators of informal social control in high-crime areas. *Justice Quarterly, 38*(2), 301–321. https://doi.org/10.1080/07418825.2019.1632917

Kochel, T. R., & Weisburd, D. (2017). Assessing community consequences of implementing hot spots policing in residential areas: Findings from a randomized field trial. *Journal of Experimental Criminology, 13*(2), 143–170. https://doi.org/10.1007/s11292-017-9283-5

Kochel, T. R., & Weisburd, D. (2019). The impact of hot spots policing on collective efficacy: Findings from a randomized field trial. *Justice Quarterly, 36*(5), 900–928. https://doi.org/10.1080/07418825.2018.1465579

Lopez, C. E. (2020, June7). *Opinion: Defund the police? Here's what that really means.* www.washingtonpost.com/opinions/2020/06/07/defund-police-hereswhat-that-really-means/

Lum, C., &Nagin, D. S. (2017). Reinventing American policing. *Crime and Justice, 46*(1), 339–393. https://doi.org/10.1086/688462

Manning, P. K. (2010). *Democratic policing in a changing world.* Routledge.

Martinson, R. (1974). What works? – Questions and answers about prison reform. *The Public Interest, 35,* 22–54.

Mastrofski, S. D. (1999). *Policing for people* (Ideas in American Policing). Police Foundation. www.policefoundation.org/wp-content/uploads/2015/06/Mastrofski-1999-Policing-For-People.pdf

Mastrofski, S. D., Worden, R. E., & Snipes, J. B. (1995). Law enforcement in a time of community policing. *Criminology, 33*(4), 539–563. https://doi.org/10.1111/j.1745-9125.1995.tb01189.x

McTaggart, R. (1991). Principles for participatory action research. *Adult Education Quarterly, 41*(3), 168–187. https://doi.org/10.1177/0001848191041003003

Meares, T. L. (2013). The good cop: Knowing the difference between lawful or effective policing and rightful policing – and why it matters. *William & Mary Law Review, 54*(6), 1865–1856.

Moore, M. H. (1992). Problem-solving and community policing. *Crime and Justice, 15,* 99–158. https://doi.org/10.1086/449194

Nagin, D. S., &Telep, C. W. (2017). Procedural justice and legal compliance. *Annual Review of Law and Social Science, 13,* 5–28. https://doi.org/10.1146/annurev-lawsocsci-110316-113310

Nix, J., Wolfe, S. E., Rojek, J., & Kaminski, R. J. (2015). Trust in the police: The influence of procedural justice and perceived collective efficacy. *Crime & Delinquency, 61*(4), 610–640. https://doi.org/10.1177/0011128714530548

Office of Community Oriented Policing Services. (2014). *Community policing-defined.* U.S. Department of Justice, Office of Community Oriented Policing Services. https://cops.usdoj.gov/pdf/vets-to-cops/e030917193-cp-defined.pdf

Perry, G., Jonathan-Zamir, T., & Willis, J. (this volume). The Potential Contribution of Subjective Causality to Policing Research: The Case of the Relationship between Procedural Justice and Police Legitimacy. In D. Weisburd, T. Jonathan, G. Perry & B. Hasisi, (Eds.), *The Future of Evidence-Based Policing.* Cambridge University Press.

President's Commission on Law Enforcement and Administration of Justice. (1967). *The challenge of crime in a free society.* United States Government Printing Office.

Rahr, S., & Rice, S. K. (2015). *From warriors to guardians: Recommitting American police culture to democratic ideals (NCJ 248654).* U.S. Department of Justice, Office of Justice Programs, National Institute of Justice. www.ncjrs.gov/pdffiles1/nij/248654.pdf

Reiss, A. J. (1971). *The police and the public.* Yale University Press.

Scheider, M. C., Chapman, R., & Schapiro, A. (2009). Towards the unification of policing innovations under community policing. *Policing: An International Journal of Police Strategies & Management*, 32(4), 694–718. https://doi.org/10.1108/13639510911000777

Sherman, L. W. (1997). Communities and crime prevention. In L. W. Sherman, D. C. Gottfredson, D. L. MacKenzie, J. E. Eck, P. Reuter, & S. D. Bushway (Eds.), *Preventing crime: What works, what doesn't, what's promising*. United States Department of Justice, National Institute of Justice.

Sherman, L. W., Gottfredson, D. C., MacKenzie, D. L., Eck, J. E., Reuter, P., & Bushway, S. (1997). *Preventing crime: What works, what doesn't, what's promising*. U.S. Department of Justice, Office of Justice Programs, National Institute of Justice. https://doi.org/678910

Shilston, T. (2015). Democratic policing, community policing and the fallacy of conflation in international police development missions. *International Journal of Police Science& Management*, 17(4), 207–215. https://doi.org/10.1177/1461355715618331

Skogan, W. G., & Frydl, K. (Eds.) (2004). *Fairness and effectiveness in policing: The evidence*. National Academies Press.

Skolnick, J. H., & Bayley, D. H. (1988). *Community policing: Issues and practices around the world*. U.S. Department of Justice, Office of Justice Programs, National Institute of Justice.

Spelman, W., & Brown, D. K. (1984). *Calling the police: Citizen reporting of serious crime*. Police Executive Research Forum.

Sunshine, J., & Tyler, T. R. (2003). The role of procedural justice and legitimacy in shaping public support for policing. *Law & Society Review*, 37(3), 513–548. https://doi.org/10.1111/1540-5893.3703002

Thacher, D. (2001). Equity and community policing: A new view of community partnerships. *Criminal Justice Ethics*, 20(1), 3–16. https://doi.org/10.1080/0731129X.2001.9992093

Tuffin, R., Morris, J., & Poole, A. (2006). *An Evaluation of the Impact of the National Reassurance Policing Programme* (HORS 296). Home Office Research, Development and Statistics Directorate.

Tyler, T. R. (2004). Enhancing police legitimacy. *The ANNALS of the American Academy of Political and Social Science*, 593(1), 84–99. https://doi.org/10.1177/0002716203262627

Weichselbaum, S., & Lewis, N. (2020, June 9). *Support for defunding the police department is growing. Here's why it's not a silver bullet*. The Marshall Project. www.themarshallproject.org/2020/06/09/support-for-defunding-the-police-department-is-growing-here-s-why-it-s-not-a-silver-bullet

Weisburd, D., & Braga, A. A. (Eds.) (2006). *Police innovation: Contrasting perspectives*. Cambridge University Press.

Weisburd, D., Braga, A.A., & Majmundar, M. (this volume). What do we know about Proactive Policing's effects on Crime and Community?: Drawing conclusions from a National Academies of Sciences, Engineering, and Medicine Report. In D. Weisburd, T. Jonathan, G. Perry & B. Hasisi, (Eds.), *The Future of Evidence-Based Policing*. Cambridge University Press.

Weisburd, D., & Eck, J. E. (2004). What can police do to reduce crime, disorder, and fear? *The ANNALS of the American Academy of Political and Social Science, 593*(1), 42–65. https://doi.org/10.1177/0002716203262548

Weisburd, D., Hinkle, J. C., Famega, C., & Ready, J. (2011). The possible "backfire" effects of hot spots policing: An experimental assessment of impacts on legitimacy, fear and collective efficacy. *Journal of Experimental Criminology, 7*(4), 297–320. https://doi.org/10.1007/s11292-011-9130-z

Weisburd, D., & Jonathan-Zamir, T. (2020, July 6). *Fighting crime and gaining public support are two distinct goals for police*. The Hill. https://thehill.com/opinion/criminal-justice/505593-fighting-crime-and-gaining-public-support-are-two-distinct-goals-for

Weisburd, D., & Majmundar, M. K. (Eds.) (2018). *Proactive policing: Effects on crime and communities*. National Academies Press.

Whyte, W. F. (1989). Advancing scientific knowledge through participatory action research. *Sociological Forum, 4*(3), 367–385. https://doi.org/10.1007/BF01115015

Wilson, D. B. (2019). *Developing a theory of effective juvenile delinquency programming through an examination of change-levers rather than program types: Preliminary evidence from a large juvenile delinquency meta-analysis* [PDF slides]. www.bocsar.nsw.gov.au/Documents/2019_Conference/0213_0930_ARCJ19_C4.05_K101_David_Wilson.pdf

PART III

INNOVATIONS IN TOOLS OF EVALUATION AND ASSESSMENT

8

The Role of Randomized Experiments in Developing the Evidence for Evidence-Based Policing

Lorraine Mazerolle, Elizabeth Eggins, Lorelei Hine, and Angela Higginson

An important debate around the Evidence-Based Policing movement is determining what constitutes "evidence" and what does not. Sherman's original rendition of evidence-based policing (Sherman, 1998) argued for a strong foundation of scientific evidence to guide proactive efforts to underpin policing practices. Sherman (1998) based these arguments on the medical model which prioritized randomized control trials (RCT) as the primary source of research "evidence". Over the years this definition of what constitutes scientific evidence has led to considerable debate. Practitioners often value their experiences as evidence, rewarding knowledge of the standard operating procedure and "hunches" in investigations over the input from academics (Lum & Koper, 2017). Policy-makers draw on political interpretation and social norms to influence their interpretation and acceptance of research (Head, 2008). Academics are similarly divided regarding what evidence is and how it influences policy and practice. Lum and colleagues (2006), for example, prioritize systematic reviews and experimental studies in shaping policy and practice responses to crime problems (Lum & Kennedy, 2012). Laycock (2012), on the other hand, argues that there is great value in adopting a broad concept of what constitutes evidence, drawing from a wide range of methodological approaches to understand what works in policing.

Numerous initiatives over the last decade have sought to gather together the scientific evidence on policing – with "evidence" defined in different ways – to make information about policing practices readily and openly available to researchers, policy-makers and practitioners.

At least six open access websites offer evidence on policing practices, each compiling the research evidence with different search methods, different scoping of outcome measures and different evidence inclusion criteria. For example, the Campbell Collaboration[1], the Evidence-Based Policing Matrix[2], Crime Solutions[3], the Crime Reduction Toolkit[4], the Center for Problem-Oriented Policing[5] and the Global Policing Database (GPD)[6] all provide policy-makers and practitioners with easy access to different types of research evidence about policing practices. Collectively these websites offer police comprehensive information about what is known about the effectiveness of police practices and tread a fine line between satisfying the desire for the highest-quality scientific "evidence", yet at the same time providing systematic access to a substantial breadth of policing research generated across the world.

We begin this chapter with an historical examination of the role of randomized experiments in developing the scientific evidence for evidence-based policing. We then use the GPD to show the trends in the use of randomized experimental studies in policing. We identify the types of programmes more likely to be evaluated using randomized experiments and conclude with a discussion of the significance of experiments in shaping the global evidence base in policing.

8.1 EXPERIMENTATION IN POLICING

Anthony Braga and colleagues (2014), in their study of randomized experiments in policing, track the maturing of the experimental policing movement since the 1970s. They argue that, by the turn of the century, there was sufficient critical mass in human and social capital to "…shift scientific paradigms in mainstream criminology towards increased experimentation" (Braga et al., 2014, p. 22). In this section, we explore the key milestones and turning points that have characterized this process of maturing in the use of experiments in policing, providing the background needed to understand the current status of experimental evidence in policing.

---

[1] www.campbellcollaboration.org
[2] http://cebcp.org/evidence-based-policing/the-matrix/
[3] www.crimesolutions.gov
[4] http://whatworks.college.police.uk/toolkit/Pages/Toolkit.aspx
[5] www.popcenter.org
[6] www.gpd.uq.edu.au

The story of police experimentation really begins with the Police Foundation in the early 1970s. The Foundation was established by a grant from the Ford Foundation as a non-profit, non-partisan and independent research hub that sought to advance policing through innovation and science. Over the last fifty years a parade of highly respected police practitioner leaders (including James Q Wilson, Patrick V Murphy, Hubert Williams and Jim Bueermann) and police scientists (including Lawrence Sherman, George Kelling and David Weisburd) have served in a variety of different capacities for the Police Foundation, conducting some of the most influential experiments in the field of policing.

One of the most widely cited experiments undertaken by the Police Foundation is the 1970 Kansas City Preventive Patrol Experiment. Led by George Kelling and his colleagues Pate, Dieckman and Brown (Kelling et al., 1974), the experiment found that random patrol had very little impact on crime and community perceptions of safety, challenging the prevailing wisdom at the time that assumed preventive patrols were effective at deterring crime. The Kansas City experiment set the scene for a number of subsequent Police Foundation experiments that were fundamental for shaping new thinking in police policy and practice across the world. For example, the Newark Foot Patrol Experiment – specifically the matched pairing of foot patrol beats – found that fair engagement between police and community residents reduced fear of crime (Kelling et al., 1981). The experiences and results from the Newark Foot Patrol Experiment were significant in shaping the highly influential Broken Windows thesis, proposed by Police Foundation Chair James Q Wilson and foundation-based scientist George Kelling. The original Broken Windows paper published in the Atlantic Monthly (Kelling & Wilson, 1982) is identified as one of the most cited and popular articles ever published in The Atlantic Monthly in its 163-year history.

By the mid-1980s, the preventive value of police started to receive renewed attention leading to a second wave of policing experiments that have again shaped and defined policy and practice across the globe. In 1988, Lawrence Sherman and David Weisburd received funding from the National Institute of Justice to conduct the Minneapolis Hot Spots Experiment to test whether or not directed patrols in high crime places could reduce crime (Sherman and Weisburd, 1995). Sherman and Weisburd (1995) used what had been recently discovered about the consistent patterns of crime clustering in very small micro places (Sherman et al., 1989; Pierce et al., 1988) to conceptualize crime hotspots as the experimental units of analysis. With random allocation of 110 crime hotspots (55 receiving, on average, twice as much observed patrol presence as the 55 control hotspots), they discovered that substantial increases in police patrol presence could lead to reductions in crime and disorder in crime hotspots (Sherman & Weisburd, 1995). This experiment was the starting point for the widespread adoption of directed patrol policies targeted at crime hotspots across the world (National Academies of Sciences, Engineering, and Medicine, 2018).

Braga and colleagues (2014) study of networks of police scholars examines the people who have shaped the use of experimentation in policing. Their social network analysis shows that Weisburd and Sherman, both mentored by Albert J. Reiss, Jr. when they were doctoral students in sociology at Yale University, "form two highly central nodes that have proliferated nearly the entire social network of experiments in policing undertaken up until 2011" (Braga et al., 2014, p. 17). The impact of the experimental work of Sherman and Weisburd is significant and most recently acknowledged in them ranking numbers 1 and 2 as the world's most influential scholars in criminology (Austin, 2021). For two experimental criminologists and police scholars to occupy those positions of influence is indicative of the role of field experimentation in shaping public policy, scholarly thinking and policing practice.

Beyond the influence of individual policing experiments, systematic reviews of the research evidence are highly reliant on a healthy supply chain of experiments in policing. The establishment of the Campbell Collaboration in 2000 (Farrington & Petrosino, 2001) with the Crime and Justice Group as a foundation coordinating group, subsequently set up a policy appetite and demand for high-quality evaluations of policing practices. At the time of writing, 26 systematic reviews in policing have been undertaken under the auspices of the Campbell Collaboration, collectively generating more than 3,635 citations. The policy impacts of these Campbell policing reviews are extensive. For example, the Braga and colleagues (2007, 2019) review of hotspots policing has been a key driver behind reforms in policing strategies across the world. In Trinidad and Tobago, the Braga (2007) review was the foundation for a decision to implement hotspots patrols to tackle a serious escalation in gun-related homicide. Commissioner Williams of Trinidad and Tobago started the national roll out of hotspots patrols in 2014 following promising results from a randomized controlled trial undertaken locally. The new approach to policing patrols has shown a significant impact on the level of gun-related homicide (Sherman et al., 2014). In Colombia, the Braga review (2007) led to discussions with police in Medellin and Bogota, resulting in RCTs on hotspots policing in both cities (Collazos et al., 2020; Blattman et al., 2018).

Despite the clear influence of experimentation in policing over the last fifty years, randomized field trials that test policing practices comprise just a small fraction of the research evidence in policing (Garner & Visher, 2003). Braga and colleagues (2014) systematic search of policing experiments find a total of just 63 policing experiments ever undertaken from 1970 to 2011, with the pace of experimentation starting to increase in the mid- to late 1980s and then proliferating during the 1990s. Interestingly, 75% of all of the policing experiments identified in the 2011 search were conducted in the United States. Neyroud (2017) in his search of policing experiments conducted up to and including 2017 finds a total of 122 randomized controlled trials in policing. What both the Braga et al. (2014) and Neyroud (2017) studies suggest is that police experimentation is highly influential yet a relatively rare method for shaping the policing evidence base. In the sections that follow we take a systematic approach to updating these prior policing experiment searches and exploring the number, scope and influence of experimentation in policing in shaping the global evidence base.

8.2 THE GLOBAL POLICING DATABASE

To better understand and quantify the role of experimentation in policing, we draw from the Global Policing Database (GPD). The GPD is a web-based exhaustive repository of intervention research relating to police and policing practices. The GPD is designed to capture all high-quality published and unpublished impact evaluations of interventions relating to police and policing conducted since 1950. Using systematic search and review techniques, the GPD compiles all experimental and quasi-experimental evaluations into one searchable location. It places no limits on outcome measure(s) and includes any policing intervention approach with no restrictions on the type of policing techniques or the language documents are published in. The GPD aims to be updated at least biennially, facilitating an up-to-date body of work from which practitioners, policy-makers, academics and those interested in policing can derive knowledge and evidence. The goal of the GPD repository is to encourage the translation of research into evidence-based practices, thereby cultivating a global approach to policing practice.

In the GPD, evidence is captured through a series of comprehensive systematic searches for documents that are about police and policing. Indeed, 293,616 unique records from 1950 to 2018 constitute the corpus of studies that are captured in the GPD search prior to systematic screening for evaluation studies. Of the documents screened to date, a total of 3,586 documents are identified as impact evaluation studies using evaluation methods that meet our criteria (Higginson et al., 2015), representing 2.2% of the N = 165,525 documents that were screened at title and abstract screening stage, 6% of the N = 59,927 documents that were screened at stage 1 full-text screening stage and 23.4% of the N = 15,339 documents that were screened at stage 2 full-text screening stage. A summary of the systematic screening stages of the GPD process is summarized in Figure 8.1.

8.3 TYPES OF EVALUATION DESIGNS

The protocol for the GPD describes the types of evaluation designs that are eligible for inclusion in the GPD corpus. These are designs that contain a quantitative impact evaluation of policing interventions that, at a minimum, include a valid comparison group. The GPD includes studies where the comparison group receives no intervention, "business-as-usual" policing or an alternative type of intervention[7]. At the time of writing there is a caveat with reporting on the status of the contents of the GPD because our first- and second-stage screening of documents identified in the systematic search are prioritized in two specific ways: first, by date, with the most recent records being screened first before moving backwards in time and second, by the specific search terms that have been used by researchers utilizing the GPD for specific systematic reviews. Final eligibility screening – the most time and training intensive

---

[7] The list of research designs included in the GPD is as follows: systematic reviews with or without meta-analyses; cross-over designs; cost–benefit analyses; regression discontinuity designs; cost–benefit analyses; regression discontinuity designs; designs using multivariate controls (e.g. multiple regression); matched control group designs with or without pre-intervention baseline measures (propensity or statistically matched); unmatched control group designs with pre–post-intervention measures which allow for difference-in-difference analysis; unmatched control group designs without pre-intervention measures where the control group has face validity; short interrupted time-series designs with control group (less than 25 pre- and 25 post-intervention observations); long interrupted time-series designs with or without a control group (≥25 pre- and post-intervention observations; raw unadjusted correlational designs where the variation in the level of the intervention is compared to the variation in the level of the outcome.

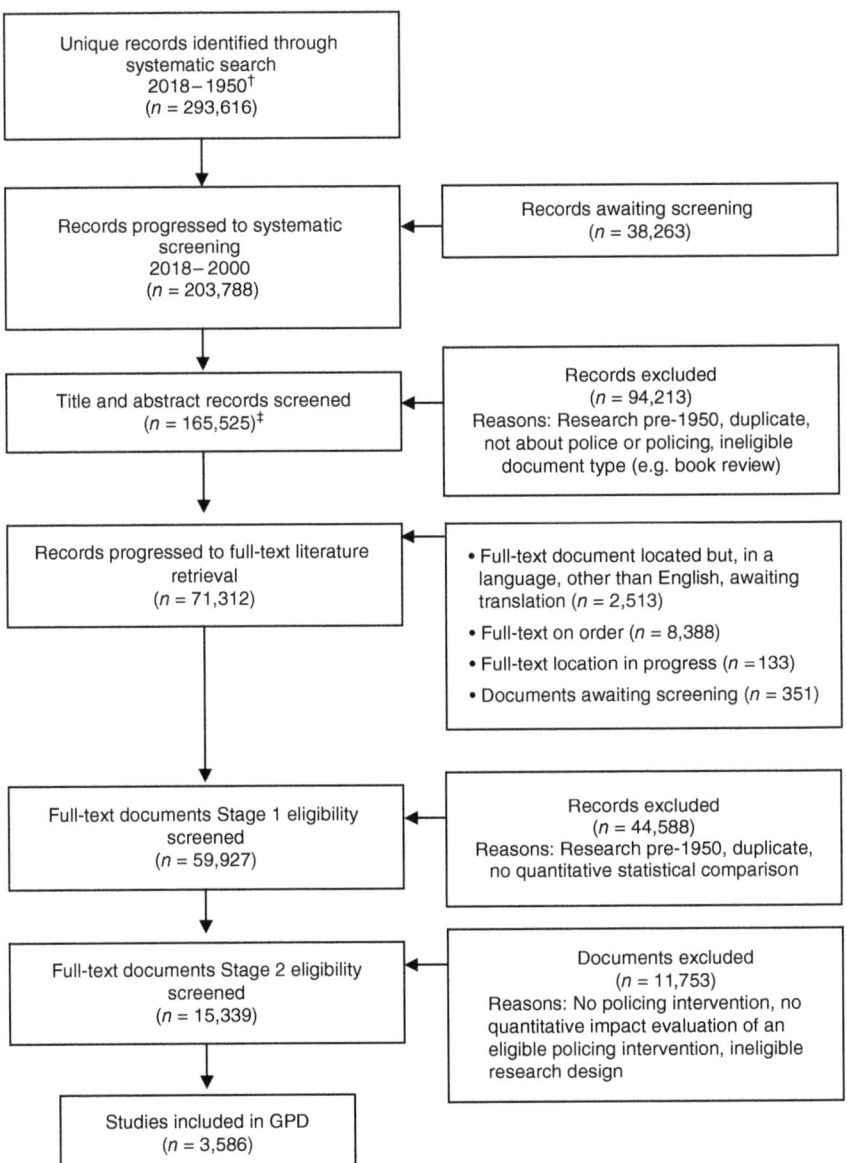

FIGURE 8.1 Prisma

†Search period 1 January 1950–31 December 2018. Number represents N raw search results which have had duplicates and clearly ineligible document types removed (e.g., book reviews, tables of contents). Estimate only, as data cleaning for <2000 still in progress.

‡Represents 2018–2000 (≈81.23% of all records between 2000 and 2018 and 56.37% of 1950–2018 identified by systematic search)

component of the GPD compilation – has been targeted to documents that expedite specific systematic reviews. As such, the current corpus of eligible evaluations in the GPD are slightly skewed towards specific topics that have been the subject of GPD-related research grants and contracts.

At the time of writing, the GPD has been used to produce eight Campbell Collaboration reviews, including Body Worn Cameras (Lum et al., 2020) and police programmes to increase community connectedness (Mazerolle et al., 2020a); updates of three Campbell reviews, including problem-oriented policing (POP) (Hinkle et al., 2020), legitimacy policing (Mazerolle et al., 2018a) and street level drug law enforcement (Mazerolle et al., 2020b); three in-progress Campbell Collaboration reviews, including Third Party Policing (Mazerolle et al., 2016), multiagency interventions with police as a partner for preventing radicalization to violence review (Mazerolle et al., 2020c); and community-oriented policing to reduce crime, disorder and fear and improve legitimacy and satisfaction with police (Gill et al., 2017); and three non-Campbell Collaboration reviews, including police techniques for investigating serious violent crime (Higginson et al., 2017), criminal justice responses to Child Exploitation Material (CEM) offending (Eggins et al., 2020a); and the impact of supplier arrests and seizures on drug crime, drug use, drug price, drug purity and drug harm outcomes (Eggins et al., 2020b). Research teams have also used the GPD to conduct six rapid reviews on a variety of policing topics, including police partnerships with agencies to tackle mental health problems (Eggins et al., 2020c), child sex offender risk management (Eggins, et al., 2020d), organizational approaches to road policing (Mazerolle et al., 2019a), best practices in policing alcohol impaired driving (Mazerolle et al., 2019b), police training (Bennett & Newman, 2018) and criminal justice responses to domestic violence, including a review of policing domestic violence (Mazerolle et al., 2018b, 2019c). All of these review topics have skewed the distribution of screened records in the GPD which influences, to some degree, the data presented in this paper in terms of the trends by year and by policing practice. Figure 8.2 provides a pie chart illustrating the breakdown of screened and eligible studies in the GPD by RCT, systematic review and quasi-experimental design.

As this chart shows, the majority of the studies in the GPD (of the 3,586) are quasi-experimental designs (82%), with RCTs comprising only 12% (N = 431) of all documents systematically processed to date according to the GPD protocol. Six per cent of the studies in the GPD are systematic reviews with or without meta-analysis, presenting a high

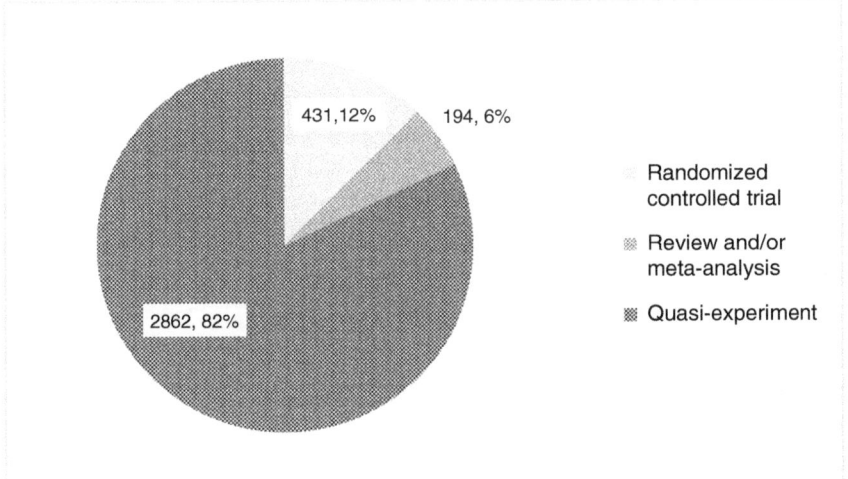

FIGURE 8.2 Types of design
Note: Includes data 2004–2018 only. N = 3487

quality of synthesized material. The GPD excludes single group designs with pre- and post-intervention measures as these designs are highly subject to bias and threats to internal validity.

Compared to the earlier searches by Braga and colleagues (2014) and Neyroud (2017), the number of experiments in policing identified in the GPD is far greater than what had previously been uncovered. In our GPD systematic search for policing evidence, we identify 431 policing experiments across the world (at the time of writing). This is a nearly sixfold increase on the number of policing experiments located by Braga et al. (2014) and two and a half times increase over what was found by Neyroud (2017). Importantly, this increase in located policing experiments are not just from the years post the searches by Braga and colleagues (2014) and Neyroud (2017). Rather, our revisiting of the years 2000 to the present time has located previously undiscovered policing experiments using the GPD search methods. We explore the nature of these newly located experiments further in the sections below.

When we examine the trends in police experimentation over time, our analysis of the GPD data confirms Braga and colleagues (2014) earlier finding that experimentation had waves of increasing popularity in the 1980s and then again in the 1990s. Figure 8.3 illustrates the type of designs the GPD systematic search has identified over time. Over the 15-year period from 2004 to 2018 there is a slight upward trend in

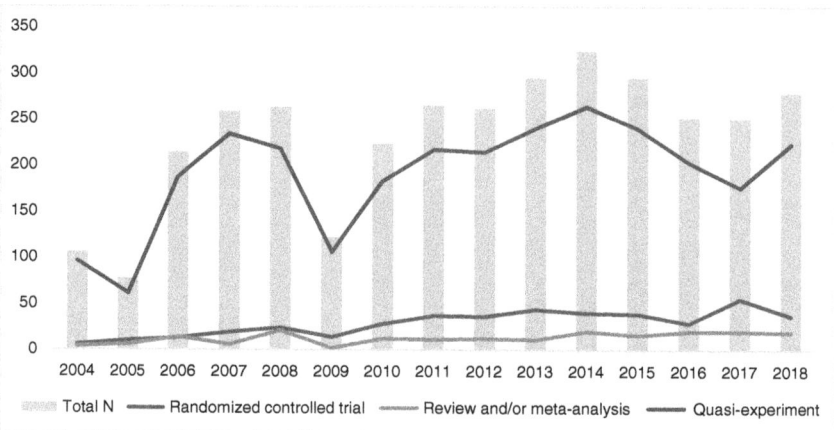

FIGURE 8.3 Types of designs over time*
*Note: Includes data 2004–2018 only. N = 3487

the quantity of studies identified by the GPD systematic search. The only exception is a down-turn in 2009, which is presumably the effects of the global financial crisis on funding for research. The quantities of studies which use an RCT or are systematic reviews, with or without meta-anlysis, show a steady upward trajectory. This indicates that these designs, specifically RCTs, are gaining traction amongst researchers and becoming more common in shaping the body of knowledge relating to police and policing practitices.

The increase in systematic reviews, albeit small, is perhaps in response to the creation of the Campbell Collaboration in 2000 and the funding to support a cluster of reviews by the UK National Policing Improvement Agency (now part of the UK College of Policing) in 2008 (Wilson et al., 2020). Figure 8.3 also shows a general upward trend in studies using a quasi-experimental design, with some year-to-year fluctuations. But what is of primary interest to this paper, Figure 8.3 shows the number of RCTs per year have increased each and every year since the turn of the century: the calendar year 2005 shows just 6 new RCTs in policing published, in 2010, there were 28 studies published, then in 2013 there were 44 policing RCTs just in that calendar year and then in 2017 there were 55 which is an 817% increase in the number of policing RCTs produced from 2005 to 2017.

There are a range of reasons why we see this extraordinary increase in the number of RCTs in policing. First, the efforts of the field RCT pioneers in policing, led by Sherman and Weisburd, demonstrated that field experimentation in policing could be done to a high level of scientific rigor. This laid the foundations for an increase in the confidence of RCTs to be fair tests of policing practices. Second, the highly influential Maryland Report (Sherman et al., 1997) captured the imagination of policy advocates, most prominently Jon Baron and Jerry Lee, who invested heavily in the establishment of centres of experimental excellence both at the University of Pennsylvania and then later at Cambridge University under the leadership of Lawrence Sherman. Jerry Lee in particular was instrumental in pushing the global need for RCTs to inform criminal justice policy and practice. He went on to become a major sponsor of the Stockholm Prize in Criminology that awarded the prize based on strong scientific methods in the discovery and use of evidence to shape global crime and justice policy and practice. Third, the establishment of the Campbell Collaboration in 2000 (Farrington & Petrosino, 2001) created an unprecedented demand for RCTs in particular and high-quality evaluations of crime and justice practices, including policing practices. Fourth, funding agencies, such as the National Institute of Justice in the United States, the Australian Research Council and the UK Economic and Social Research Council began funding RCTs at a rate not previously seen at the end of the twentieth century. Telep and his colleagues (2015) offer some insights around the increase in funding experimentation. Using data from official records of grant awards made by the US National Institute of Justice between fiscal years 2001 and 2013, they categorized awards based on study design (including RCT design). They identified 99 grant awards for experiments where support for the use of experimental designs increased during their 13-year study period, dwarfing the funding support for the use of experimental designs providing during the 1990s (Telep et al., 2015).

The GPD repository of policing evidence also challenges the earlier thinking that the vast majority of experiments had been proliferated by "the salient few" (Braga et al., 2014). Of the 431 experiments in the GPD, just 37 of these experiments (8.6%) have been undertaken by scholars listed as lead experimental policing scholars in the Braga et al. (2014) study (see Table 2, page 13[8]). This suggests that there are likely a much larger number of scholars throughout the world who are producing police experiments that have previously gone unnoticed in prior audits of policing experiments. The emergence and escalating pace over the last

---

[8] These scholars include Sherman, Strang, Davis, Weisburd, Pate, Mazerolle, Angel, Taylor, Braga, Dunford and McCold (see Table 2, page 13).

twenty years of systematic reviews in policing will bring to light many of these previously hidden experiments and high-quality quasi experiments in policing. Our discovery of a treasure trove of policing experimentation is a boost to capacity of researchers to conduct many more systematic reviews of policing practice and thereby increase the role of scientific evidence in shaping policy and practice.

8.4 CATEGORIES OF POLICE AND POLICING STUDIES

The GPD can be used to examine the range of different topics of police experimentation. To be included in the GPD, each document must contain an impact evaluation of a policing intervention. Policing interventions are defined in the GPD as some kind of a strategy, programme, technique, approach, activity, campaign, training, directive or funding/ organizational change that involves police in some way (other agencies or organizations can be involved). Police involvement is broadly defined as police initiation, development or leadership; or police as recipients of the intervention; or the intervention is related, focused or targeted to police practices; or that there is delivery or implementation of the intervention by police. To gain a better understanding of the type of interventions being implemented and tested, the GPD developed categories for the policing interventions. These cover five broad areas which distinguishes the intervention based on the role of police in the intervention.

The first category examines *policing practices with police as implementers*. These interventions examine policing practices, such as hotspot policing (the targeting of activities and resources to the areas where crime is most concentrated), problem-oriented policing (POP; the identification and analysis of a specific crime problem to develop a targeted response) and order maintenance policing (the management of minor offences and neighbourhood disorder, in line with broken windows theory, to reduce community level crime). An example that falls into this category is Braga and Bond's (2008) experiment that evaluated the effects of policing disorder in Lowell, Massachusetts is categorized as a study where the police are the implementers of the intervention. In this study, the officers implemented a general policing disorder strategy finding that the strongest crime prevention gains were generated by situational prevention strategies.

The policing practices category also includes **police as intervention partners**, where the police seek to co-produce crime control by working with citizens, other public sectors or private industry. Some of the interventions that are in this category include third-party policing (where police persuade or coerce third parties, such as businesses or other government agencies, to partner with police and activate their legal levers to assist in crime control) and community policing (where police seek to partner with citizens to promote crime control within communities, such as neighbourhood watch). For example, Mazerolle and her colleagues (2017) evaluated, under randomized field trial conditions, the deterrent effects of a police–school partnership, called the Ability School Engagement Program (ASEP). The partnership with schools sought to co-produce truancy reduction by actively engaging parents and their truanting children in a group conference dialogue that was designed to increase parental and child awareness of the truancy laws (and the consequences of non-compliance), and thereby foster students' willingness to attend school. The authors found that the police–school partnership intervention increased parental awareness of prosecution likelihood, which moderated students' self-reported willingness to attend school (Mazerolle et al., 2017).

The second category of studies in the GPD are **investigative techniques** which includes interrogation and forensic evidence gathering. Woody et al. (2014), for example, compared the effects of explicit and implicit false-evidence ploys on mock jurors' verdicts, sentencing recommendations and perceptions of police interrogation. They explored how false-evidence ploys (FEPs) in police interrogations were viewed by jurors, comparing implicit FEP, where police interrogators ask the suspects about potential evidence without making a claim of possessing the evidence, and explicit FEP, which involve direct claims from by interrogators about false evidence. Their experiment involved 255 college students randomly assigned to one of three conditions: implicit FEP, explicit FEP or control with results indicating that jurors do not discriminate between the FEP methods, therefore causing implications in how police use such methods in suspect interrogations (Woody et al., 2014).

The third category contains studies examining *police organizational structure, department sizes and human resource policies*. An example in the GPD of a study in this category is by Ater et al. (2014) who examined how the organizational structure of law enforcement agencies affected police activity and crime. They published their results in the *Journal of Public Economics*, examining the consequences of an organizational reform in Israel that transferred the responsibility for housing arrestees from the police to the prison authority. Their evaluation framework capitalized on a staggered rollout of the reform in different regions of the country, showing how organizational change led to an increase of 11% in a number of arrests and to a decrease of 4% in a number of reported crimes.

The fourth category covers interventions which *test police tools, techniques and technologies*. This category of studies includes Body Worn Cameras, Tasers, forensic techniques (such as collection and processing), line-up practices and investigative interview protocols. For example, in an RCT by Sousa et al. (2010), they present findings from a randomized field-training experiment designed to study the impact TASERs on police officers' use-of-force decisions. In this study, officers were randomly assigned to either a treatment group (with TASERs) or a control group (without TASERs) to assess the extent that officers armed with the TASER use it as an alternative to other types of less-lethal force, finding that officers with TASERs are less likely to deploy pepper spray and the baton in response to aggressive physical resistance.

The fifth category includes *legislative, regulatory or policy reforms or changes affecting police*. The GPD includes a range of studies from different countries around the world that fall into this category yet none, for obvious reasons, use RCTs to evaluate legislative reform. For example, in a study by Heide et al. (2012) on police custody regulations, they analysed 3,674 medical records on fitness for custody, taken from two large German towns (Halle and Bremen). They found that the introduction of new police custody regulations in Halle had a significant influence on the medical decision on fitness for custody.

Table 8.1 presents the different intervention categories by study design coded only for a sub-set of N = 1,149 documents that have been used in reviews we have conducted so far (see earlier for the list of different review topics that have driven the focus of screening within the GPD). As Table 8.1 shows, from this selective sample of stage 2 screened and eligible documents in the GPD, we find 181 RCTs (16%, which is a slightly higher per cent than for the whole of the GPD), 63 systematic reviews (5.5%) and 905 quasi-experiments in policing (78.8%, which is slightly less than for the whole GPD), for a total of 1,149 studies that have been Stage 2 screened and uploaded to the GPD website[9].

What we find from this analysis is that policing practices comprise the largest category of policing studies using RCTs (N = 67), with 60 RCTs in policing that relate to investigative techniques, including interrogation

---

[9] We note that there are many more studies in the GPD at various stages of processing. As such, this represents a somewhat biased sample of GPD cases that are weighted to the systematic searches we have conducted so far using the GPD.

TABLE 8.1 *Types of interventions by study design (N = 1,149)* *

Broad intervention category	RCT	Review	Quasi-experiment	Total
Policing practices	67	44	378	489
Investigative techniques (interrogation and evidence gathering)	60	6	92	158
Police organizations, staffing and training	39	8	335	382
Police technologies, equipment and safety	12	2	54	68
Legislative, regulatory or policy reforms or changes	3	3	46	52
Total by evaluation design*	181 (16%)	63 (5.5%)	905 (78.5%)	1,149

Note: This includes a sample of all S2 eligible that are drawn from reviews and extractions we have conducted. The distribution of categories may change as more reviews are completed.

and different forms of evidence gathering, and 39 RCTs in police organizational reform and training. Table 8.1 also shows a total of 63 systematic reviews in policing (at least in this Stage 2 of GPD screening), most of which (N = 44) being about policing practices, such as hotspots policing, problem-oriented policing, pulling levers and community policing. This sample of studies also contain 905 quasi-experimental studies, with N = 378 being about policing practices and 335 being about police organizational reform, staffing and training.

The fact that the GPD reveals that the majority of policing experiments have added to the evidence base in the category of policing practices – as opposed to policing tools or technologies, or organizational reforms or HR practices, or legislative reforms, or investigative techniques – speaks volumes about the topic focus for policing researchers and funding agencies. It suggests that funding agencies are highly willing to fund researchers to better understand what policing practices (like POP, hotspots policing, co-responder models, community policing, pulling levers) actually work to reduce crime and disorder. Given that policing practices comprise a significant portion of the dollar value attached to the deployment of police at the frontline, a strong evidence base in policing practices is an important foundation for future rationalization and focus on the way scarce policing resources is deployed.

TABLE 8.2 *Number of studies and RCTs by country**

Ranking	Country	Total N	RCT N
1.	United States	1822	216
2.	Multiple countries	248	13
3.	United Kingdom	241	43
4.	Australia	190	36
5.	Country not reported	158	41
6.	Canada	128	19
7.	Sweden	63	10
8.	The Netherlands	47	8
9.	India	42	5
10.	Norway	32	5
11.	Italy	29	2
12.	South Korea	28	0
13.	Turkey	26	1
14.	Mexico	24	0
15.	Brazil/China	23	1^a
16.	Israel/Spain/Taiwan	22	4^b
17.	Germany	20	5
18.	France/New Zealand/Nigeria	16	7^c
19.	Slovenia	14	0
20.	Switzerland	13	1
21.	Japan	12	1
22.	Russia	11	0
23.	Belgium/South Africa	10	1^d
24.	Finland	9	0
25.	Thailand	8	2
26.	Chile/Denmark/Ghana	7	2^e
27.	Pakistan	6	0
28.	Argentina/Colombia/Czech Republic/Hong Kong/Iran/Portugal/United Arab Emirates	5	3^f
29.	Malaysia/The Philippines/Sri Lanka	4	1^g
30.	Greece/Indonesia/Iraq/Saudi Arabia/Tanzania/Trinidad & Tobago/Uganda/Ukraine	3	1^h
31.	Afghanistan/Bolivia/Bosnia/Croatia/Estonia/Ireland/Poland/Singapore	2	2^i
32.	Albania/Bahrain/Bangladesh/Bermuda/Brunei/Costa Rica/Cyprus/Ethiopia/French Ghana/Guatemala/Kazakhstan/Kosovo/Kuwait/Laos/Libya/Madagascar/Malawi/Malta/Nepal/North Korea/Qatar/Romania/Serbia/Sierra Leone/Slovakia/The Caribbean/Uruguay/Vietnam	1	1^j
Total		3,487	431

Note: Includes data 2004–2018 only. N = 3,487

^{a}This RCT was conducted in Brazil
^{b}N = 3 were conducted in Israel, with the fourth from Spain
^{c}N = 5 were conducted in France, with one from each of New Zealand and Nigeria
^{d}This RCT was conducted in South Africa
^{e}One RCT was from Ghana and the other from Denmark
^{f}N = 2 were conducted in Portugal, with the third from Colombia
^{g}This RCT was conducted in Malaysia
^{h}This RCT was conducted in Uganda
^{i}N = 1 conducted in Afghanistan and N = 1 conducted in Bolivia
^{j}This RCT was conducted in Slovakia

8.5 GLOBAL CONTRIBUTIONS TO THE EVIDENCE ON POLICING

One of the important questions about the evidence base in policing is whether or not the research is relevant to just a small number of countries or whether it has global relevance. Braga and his colleagues (2014) identified 75% of the world's contribution to policing RCTs to have been undertaken in the United States suggesting significant limitations in the generalizability of the body of RCT evidence beyond the US context. Our GPD systematic search and review of the policing evidence base reveals a slightly different story where 50.1% ($n = 216$) of all the RCTs identified in the GPD have been conducted in the United States. Table 8.2 presents the range of countries contributing quasi experimental, systematic review and RCT studies to the GPD between 2004 and 2018.

As Table 8.2 shows, the majority (n = 1822; 52.3%) of all GPD eligible studies (quasi, RCT and systematic reviews) originate from the United States. The top 20 countries see a high prevalence of European work, namely from the United Kingdom (n = 241; 6.9%). Australia also has a high contribution to GPD with 190 (5.4%) of the studies in the GPD. Of the top 10 countries, India (n = 42; 1.2%) is the only one of non-American, European or Oceanic status. Countries from Africa, Asia, South America and the Middle East appear in the top 20, although are under-represented with less than 1% of the publications per country. Comparative research on policing comprises 7.1% of the total research. In total, 87 different countries have contributed studies to the GPD.

When we examine the global contributions to the population of randomized controlled experiments in policing, Table 8.2 shows that 216 (50.1%) of all experiments were conducted in the United States. This tells a slightly different story from what was previously reported by Braga et al. (2014) where 75% of all policing experiments were reported as stemming from the United States. There are several reasons for why we find a greater global distribution of experimental contributions to the evidence base. First, our search is more recent than the Braga et al. (2014) search. Second, our search is far more comprehensive than previous searches, with more than 89 grey literature search locations as well as 88 databases accessed to build the corpus of evidence in the GPD. Many of the grey literature sources and accessed databases are non-criminal justice databases and are not biased towards US sources, helping cast a much wider net than was undertaken by Braga and his colleagues (2014) or by Neyroud (2017). Third, our outcome criteria for inclusion in the GPD is broader than previous searches where we have included studies examining a range of outcomes, such as police physical or psychosocial wellbeing, community perceptions (including fear of crime) and efficiency outcomes of HR practices, such as shift rosters. Overall, whilst the United States still contributes about half of the worlds' RCT evidence, the GPD reveals that there are at least 32 other countries that have contributed RCTs to the evidence base. This is also a likely underestimation of the global reach of policing experimentation given the biases in the GPD to English-written documents.

8.6 DISCUSSION AND CONCLUSION

Randomized experiments, quasi-experiments and systematic reviews are critical for developing the evidence for evidence-based policing. In this paper, we explored the role of experiments in contributing to the evidence base in policing. Drawing on the Global Policing Database (GPD) with the full corpus of studies at the time of writing (June 2020), we describe the breadth and depth of high-quality scientific evidence, particularly focusing on RCTs, that form the foundation of the evidence base in policing.

Our exploration of the population of RCTs in policing offers three primary insights: first, randomized controlled trials form only about 12% of the total evidence base in policing and systematic reviews contribute about 6% and quasi-experimental designs about 82%, suggesting the need for decision makers to draw from a variety of evaluation designs – yet still strong designs – in formulating policy and practice decisions. We conclude, however, that a relatively small number of RCTs have punched above their weight in terms of policy influence.

Second, our review of the evidence from the GPD suggests a much broader group of scholars and countries contributing RCT evidence than was previously reported (Braga et al., 2014). We find that about half of the RCTs identified by the GPD come from the United States and fewer than 10% are generated by what Braga and colleagues (2014) referred to as the "salient few". This is a good news story for the RCT evidence base as it means that more countries and more scholars across the world are now contributing to the policing evidence base than previously thought. This breadth of people and places generating high-quality evidence will help generalize policing policies and practices beyond the United States and is likely to have a snowball effect in fostering the next generation of experimentalists in policing.

Finally, our study finds that most of the evidence in policing is around frontline policing practices (such as hotspots policing, problem-oriented policing, third-party policing and community policing). Other policing strategies, programmes, techniques, approaches, activities, campaigns, training, directive or organizational change involving police were found in the GPD, but mainly as quasi-experimental studies. These other types of policing interventions include investigative techniques; studies examining police organizational structure, department sizes and human resource policies; interventions which test police tools, techniques and technologies; and legislative, regulatory or policy reforms or changes affecting police. We argue, therefore, that the use of RCTs to inform policy and practice will need to be developed more broadly across the business of policing beyond frontline service delivery to facilitate policing to become more evidence based into the future.

Acknowledgement

Development of the GPD was funded by the *Australian Research Council* and the College of Policing (United Kingdom). Funding to update the GPD has been provided by grants for systematic reviews using the GPD, from sources including Arnold Ventures, the Australian Institute of Criminology and the Department of Homeland Security (United States). We also acknowledge the 156 volunteer student interns who have contributed over 7,000 hours of work on the GPD since 2015.

References

Ater, I., Givati, Y., & Rigbi, O. (2014). Organizational structure, police activity and crime. *Journal of Public Economics, 115*, 62–71. https://doi.org/10.1016/j.jpubeco.2014.04.003

Austin, S. L. (2021). Top Influential Criminologists Today. *Academic influence.* https://academicinfluence.com/rankings/people/most-influential-criminologists-today

Bennett, S., & Newman, M. (2018). *Evidencing Police Training*. Paper presented at the ANZ Society of Evidence-Based Policing Conference, Australian Institute for Police Management (AIPM).

Braga, A. A. (2007). Effects of Hot Spots Policing on Crime. *Campbell Systematic Reviews*, 3(1), 1–36. https://doi.org/10.4073/csr.2007.1

Braga, A. A., & Bond, B. J. (2008). Policing crime and disorder hot spots: A randomized controlled trial. *Criminology: An Interdisciplinary Journal*, 46(3), 577–607.

Braga, A. A., Turchan, B., Papachristos, A. V., Hureau, D. M. (2019). Hot spots policing of small geographic areas effects on crime. *Campbell Systematic Reviews*, 15(3), 1–88. https://doi.org/10.1002/cl2.1046

Braga, A. A., Welsh, B. C., Papachristos, A. V., Schnell, C., & Grossman, L. (2014). The growth of randomized experiments in policing: The vital few and the salience of mentoring. *Journal of Experimental Criminology*, 10, 1–28. https://doi.org/10.1007/s11292-013-9183-2

Blattman, C., Green, D., Ortega, D., & Tobón, S. (2018). Hotspots interventions at scale: the direct and spillover effects of policing and city services on crime in Bogotá, Columbia (No. 88). www.3ieimpact.org/sites/default/files/2019-01/IE%2088_DPW1.1044_Colombia_hotspots_policing_crime_1.pdf

Collazos, D., García, E., Mejía, D., Ortega, D., & Tobón, S. (2020). Hot spots policing in a high-crime environment: An experimental evaluation in Medellin. *Journal of Experimental Criminology*, 17(3), 473–506. https://doi.org/10.1007/s11292-019-09390-1

Eggins, E., Hine, L., Higginson, A., & Mazerolle, L. (2020b). The impact of arrest and seizure on drug crime and harms: A systematic review. *Trends & issues in crime and criminal justice*, (602), 1–16.

Eggins, E., Hine, L., Mazerolle, L., McEwan, J., Hassall, G., Roetman, S., Roetman, S., & Bevis, K. (2020c). *Mental health co-response models: a rapid review of the evaluation literature*. The University of Queensland.

Eggins, E., Mazerolle, L., Higginson, A., Hine, L., Walsh, K., Sydes, M., McEwan, J., Hassall, G., Roetman, S., Wallis, R., & Williams, J. (2020a). *Criminal justice responses to child exploitation material offending: a systematic review and evidence and gap map*. The University of Queensland.

Eggins, E., Mazerolle, L., Hine, L., McEwan, J., Hassall, G., Roetman, S., & Roetman S. (2020d). *Policing child sex offenders and offending – A rapid review of the evaluation literature: final report* (for the New Zealand Evidence Based Policing Centre). The University of Queensland.

Farrington, D. P., & Petrosino, A. (2001). The Campbell Collaboration Crime and Justice Group. *The ANNALS of the American Academy of Political and Social Science*, 578(1), 35–49. https://doi.org/10.1177%2F000271620157800103

Garner, J. H., & Visher, C. A. (2003). The Production of Criminological Experiments. *Evaluation Review*, 27(3), 316–335. https://doi.org/10.1177%2F0193841X03027003006

Gill, C., Weisburd, D., Telep, C., Vitter, Z., & Bennett, T. (2017). Protocol: Community-oriented policing to reduce crime, disorder, and fear and improve legitimacy and satisfaction with police: a systematic review. *Campbell Systematic Reviews*, 13(1), 1–30. https://doi.org/10.1002/CL2.174

Head, B. W. (2008). Three lenses of evidence-based policy. *The Australian Journal of Public Administration*, 67(1), 1–11. https://doi.org/10.1111/j.1467-8500.2007.00564.x

Heide, S., Stiller, D., Lessig, R., Lautenschläger, C., Birkholz, M., & Früchtnicht, W. (2012). Medical examination of fitness for police custody in two large German towns. *International Journal of Legal Medicine*, 126(1), 27–35. https://doi.org/10.1007/s00414-011-0557-6

Higginson, A., Eggins, E., & Mazerolle, L. (2017). Police techniques for investigating serious violent crime: A systematic review. *Trends and Issues in Crime and Criminal Justice*, (539), 1–13.

Higginson, A., Eggins, E., Mazerolle, L., & Stanko, E. (2015). *The Global Policing Database [Database and Protocol]*. www.gpd.uq.edu.au

Hinkle, J. C., Weisburd, D., Telep, C. W., & Petersen, K. (2020). Problem-oriented policing for reducing crime and disorder: An updated systematic review and meta-analysis. *Campbell Systematic Reviews*, 16(2), 1–86. https://doi.org/10.1002/cl2.1089

Kelling, G. L., Pate, T., Dieckman, D., & Brown, C. E. (1974). *The Kansas City Preventive Patrol Experiment: A Technical Report*. Police Foundation. www.policefoundation.org/publication/the-kansas-city-preventive-patrol-experiment/

Kelling, G. L., Pate, A., Ferrara, A., Utne, M., & Brown, C. E. (1981). *The Newark Foot Patrol Experiment*. Police Foundation. www.policefoundation.org/publication/the-newark-foot-patrol-experiment/

Kelling, G. L., & Wilson, J. Q. (1982). Broken Windows. *The Atlantic*, 249(3), 29–38.

Laycock, G. (2012). In support of evidence-based approaches: A response to Lum and Kennedy. *Policing: A Journal of Policy and Practice*, 6(4), 324–326. https://doi.org/10.1093/police/pas040

Lum, C., & Kennedy, L. W. (2012). In support of evidence-based approaches: a rebuttal to Gloria Laycock. *Policing: A Journal of Policy and Practice*, 6(4), 317–323. https://doi.org/10.1093/police/pas041

Lum, C., Kennedy, L. W., & Sherley, A. (2006). Are counter-terrorism strategies effective? The results of the Campbell systematic review on counter-terrorism evaluation research. *Journal of Experimental Criminology*, 2, 489–516. https://doi.org/10.1007/s11292-006-9020-y

Lum, C. M., & Koper, C. S. (2017). Evidence-based policing: Translating research into practice. *Policing and Society – An International Journal of Research and Policy*. https://doi.org/10.1080/10439463.2019.1678621

Lum, C., Koper, C. S., Wilson, D. B., Stoltz, M., Goodier, M., Eggins, M., Higginson, A., & Mazerolle, L. (2020). Body-worn cameras' effects on police officers and citizen behavior: A systematic review. *Campbell Systematic Reviews*, 16(3), 1–40. https://doi.org/10.1002/cl2.1112

Mazerolle, L., Bennett, S., Antrobus, E., & Eggins, E. (2017). The coproduction of truancy control: Results from a randomized trial of a police–schools partnership program. *Journal of Research in Crime and Delinquency*, 54(6), 791–823. https://doi.org/10.1177/0022427817705167

Mazerolle, L., Bennett, S., Eggins, E., Higginson, A., & Antrobus, E. (2018a). Legitimacy in policing: an updated Campbell Collaboration systematic review.

Mazerolle, L., Cherney, A., Eggins, E., Higginson, A., Hine, L., & Belton, E. (2020c). Protocol: Multiagency programmes with police as a partner for reducing radicalisation to violence. *Campbell Systematic Reviews, 16*(3), 1–15. https://doi.org/10.1002/cl2.1110

Mazerolle, L., Eggins, E., Bennett, S., Roetman, S., Hine, L., McEwan, J., Hassall, G., & Hockey, A. (2019a). Policing alcohol impaired driving. A rapid review of the evaluation literature.

Mazerolle, L., Eggins, E., Bennett, S., Roetman, S., Hine, L., McEwan, J., Hassall, G., & Hockey, A. (2019b). Road policing and level of centralisation: a rapid review of the evaluation literature.

Mazerolle, L., Eggins, E., Cherney, A., Hine, L., Higginson, A., & Belton, E (2020a). Police programmes that seek to increase community connectedness for reducing violent extremism behaviour, attitudes and beliefs. *Campbell Systematic Reviews, 16*(3), 1–48. https://doi.org/10.1002/cl2.1111

Mazerolle, L., Eggins, E., & Higginson, A. (2016). PROTOCOL: Third party policing for reducing crime and disorder: A systematic review. *Campbell Systematic Reviews, 12*(1), 1–77. https://doi.org/10.1002/CL2.153

Mazerolle, L., Eggins, E., Higginson, A. (2020b). Street-level drug law enforcement: An updated systematic review. *Trends and Issues in Crime and Criminal Justice*, (599), 1–20.

Mazerolle, L., Eggins, E., Sydes, M., & Hine, L (2019c). Policing domestic and family violence: A review of the evaluation literature. *Police Science, 4*(1), 18–20.

Mazerolle, L., Eggins, E., Sydes, M., Hine, L., McEwan, J., Norrie, G., & Somerville, A. (2018b). *Criminal justice responses to domestic and family violence: A rapid review of the evaluation literature*. The University of Queensland.

National Academies of Sciences, Engineering, and Medicine. (2018). *Proactive policing: Effects on crime and communities*. The National Academies Press. https://doi.org/10.17226/24928

Neyroud, P. W. (2017). Learning to Field Test in Policing: Using an analysis of completed randomised controlled trials involving the police to develop a grounded theory on the factors contributing to high levels of treatment integrity in Police Field Experiments. [Doctoral thesis, University of Cambridge]. https://doi.org/10.17863/CAM.14377

Pierce, G. L., Spaar, S., & Briggs, L. R. (1988). *The character of police work: Strategic and tactical implications*. Center for Applied Social Research, Northeastern University.

Sherman, L. W. (1998). *Evidence-based policing*. Police Foundation. www.policefoundation.org/wp-content/uploads/2015/06/Sherman-1998-Evidence-Based-Policing.pdf; www.cebma.org/wp-content/uploads/Sherman-Evidence-Based-Policing.pdf

Sherman, L. W., Gartin, P. R., & Buerger, M. E. (1989). Hot spots of predatory crime: Routine activities and the criminology of place. *Criminology, 27*(1), 27–56.

Sherman, L. W., Gottfredson, D. C., MacKenzie, D. L., Eck, J., Reuter, P., & Bushway, S. (1997). Preventing crime: What works, what doesn't, what's promising: A report to the United States Congress. *National Institute of Justice (NIJ)*. www.ncjrs.gov/App/Publications/abstract.aspx?ID=165366

Sherman, L. W., & Weisburd, D. (1995). General deterrent effects of police patrol in crime "hot spots": A randomized, controlled trial. *Justice Quarterly, 12*(4), 625–648. https://doi.org/10.1080/07418829500096221

Sherman, L., Williams, S., Ariel, B., Strang, L.R., Wain, N., Slothower, M., & Norton, A. (2014). *TTPS hotspot experiment: Murder, wounding, shooting data graphs [Unpublished manuscript].* www.enterprise.cam.ac.uk/case-studies/hot-spot-policing/

Sousa, W., Ready, J., & Ault, M. (2010). The impact of TASERs on police use-of-force decisions: Findings from a randomized field-training experiment. *Journal of Experimental Criminology, 6*(1), 35–55. https://doi.org/10.1007/s11292-010-9089-1

Telep, C. W., Garner, J. H., & Visher, C. A. (2015). The production of criminological experiments revisited: The nature and extent of federal support for experimental designs, 2001–2013. *Journal of Experimental Criminology, 11*(4), 541–563. https://doi.org/10.1007/s11292-015-9239-6

Wilson, D.B., Mazerolle, L., & Neyroud, P. (2020). Campbell Collaboration systematic reviews and the Journal of Experimental Criminology: Reflections on the last 20 years. *Journal of Experimental Criminology, 17*, 539–544. https://doi.org/10.1007/s11292-020-09433-y

Woody, W. D., Forrest, K. D., & Yendra, S. (2014). Comparing the effects of explicit and implicit false-evidence ploys on mock jurors' verdicts, sentencing recommendations, and perceptions of police interrogation. *Psychology, Crime & Law, 20*(6), 603–617. https://doi.org/10.1080/1068316X.2013.804922

9

The Potential Contribution of Subjective Causality to Policing Research

The Case of the Relationship between Procedural Justice and Police Legitimacy

Gali Perry, Tal Jonathan-Zamir, and James J. Willis

Questions of cause and effect have been occupying policing scholars and practitioners for decades. Researchers ask, for example, if specific policing strategies are effective in preventing crime, and what their outcomes are in terms of community reactions (Weisburd & Majmundar, 2018). One example of a recent, unsettled debate on causality in policing concerns the relationship between procedural justice (PJ) and police legitimacy (e.g., Nagin & Telep, 2017, 2020; Tyler, 2017). While Tom Tyler (Tyler, 2004, 2006; Tyler & Huo, 2002) and many others (e.g., Gau, 2014; Hinds & Murphy, 2007; Jackson et al., 2010; Mazerolle et al., 2013) persuasively argue that the fairness embedded in the processes by which the police exercise their authority (PJ) is the primary *cause* of police legitimacy, others maintain that while studies find a strong correlation between PJ and legitimacy, there is little evidence that this relationship is both causal and in the expected direction (Nagin & Telep, 2017, 2020; Weisburd & Majmundar, 2018).

Social scientists (including policing scholars) have traditionally relied on quantitative research methods for establishing causality (Pósch, 2020), and particularly on randomized controlled trials (RCTs; e.g., Ariel, 2018), which are considered the "gold standard" and obvious methodology for addressing the challenge (see Mazerolle et al. in this volume). However, despite the important contribution RCTs have made to the accumulated body of knowledge in policing, due to limited feasibility and other shortcomings, many questions around causality in policing remain unanswered (Ariel, 2018; Nagin & Telep, 2017).

The present chapter explores a qualitative approach to the study of causality. Instead of relying on a temporal order of events whereby the independent variable (IV) precedes the dependent variable (DV), coupled with the elimination of alternative explanations (Lewis, 1974), this approach views individuals' inner subjective evaluations of cause and effect as the basis of causality (Abell & Engel, 2019; Maxwell, 2004, 2012, 2019). This "subjective causality" approach has become common in the social sciences (Tacq, 2011). At the same time, and despite a long tradition of qualitative and ethnographic research in policing (Bittner, 1967; Muir, 1979; see also Willis & Toronjo, in this volume), an explicit focus on causality from this qualitative perspective is scarce in policing research.

Subjective causality cannot (and does not aspire to) replace quantitative analyses; it offers a complementary perspective, which helps illuminate how different actors in the criminal justice system perceive their own, internal causal processes. Put differently, the subjective causality approach examines the reasons individuals give *themselves* for feeling or acting in certain ways. As articulated by Thacher (2004, p. 180), the "*because* of motivation and justification" for why someone acted "…does not generally mean that a sociological or psychological law made it inevitable, but instead that she felt she had a compelling reason to act as she did."

This chapter continues as follows: we begin by discussing the role and importance of causality in policing research, and the research designs that have been used to study causality in policing to date, with particular emphasis on RCTs. We describe some of the main limitations of RCTs, and present "subjective causality" as a complementary approach to the study of causal mechanisms in policing. We describe its use in the social sciences, and demonstrate its potential contribution to policing using findings from recent, qualitative analyses of the relationship between PJ and police legitimacy (Jonathan-Zamir et al., 2020; Perry & Jonathan-Zamir, in progress). We conclude by discussing some implications and benefits of using subjective causality in evidence-based policing (EBP) more generally.

9.1 QUESTIONS OF CAUSALITY IN POLICING AND RANDOMIZED CONTROL TRIALS

In the quest for best evidence for best practice, identifying causal relationships is often considered the "holy grail" of EBP (Ariel, 2018). Empirical evidence of causality indicates that there is a process in which one or more factors influence another. This relationship can be measured, and then translated into effective policies, strategies, and tactics. Causal relationships are important for promoting EBP, both because empirical evidence of a causal relationship supports (or disproves) theoretical hypotheses, thus contributing to our basic understanding of "how the world works," and because these relationships provide practitioners with a "recipe" to work with, which, in turn, increases the likelihood of effective practices (Sherman, 1998). To date, questions of causality in policing have been defined and treated in quantitative/statistical terms. In his chapter on research methods for policing, Ariel (2018, p. 68) explains (also see Bunge, 2017):

In science, causality means something quite specific, and scholars are usually in agreement about three minimal conditions for declaring that a causal bond exists between the independent variables (IV) and dependent variables (DV): (1) that there is a correlation between the two variables; (2) that there is a temporal sequence whereby the IVs precede the DVs; and (3) that alternative explanations are safely removed from or controlled for in the stated mechanism.

RCTs are a specific type of experimental design that confirms to all three conditions (Ariel, 2018; Sherman, 2013). In RCTs, researchers randomly assign participants to treatment and control groups, and sometimes pre-test the levels of the DV. Random assignment and pre-test data support the assumption that the groups are similar in all relevant characteristics. Researchers then apply an intervention to the treatment group, and measure and compare the DV across the two groups. If the intervention is the cause of the outcome, we would expect to find a significant difference in the DV between the treatment group and control group. Only a small percentage of studies in policing have used RCTs; however, their popularity has been growing and they have had much influence on both research and practice (Braga et al., 2014; Neyroud, 2017). Some well-known RCTs in policing have tested, for example, the effect of hot-spots policing on crime (Sherman & Weisburd, 1995), the effect of body-worn cameras on citizens complains against the police (Ariel et al., 2015), and the effect of restorative justice on victims (Angel et al., 2014).

Nevertheless, RCTs are not without limitations (e.g., Thacher, 2019). In our brief review here, we focus on some limitations that may be counteracted by the subjective causality approach (see below). First, it is not always possible to conduct RCTs (Weisburd, 2000), as they require significant funds and the full cooperation of the designated police agency. Agencies not only have to allow researcher to access their data, but also to manipulate the way they operate. This may be extremely challenging in some policing realms (e.g., undercover work), countries, or agencies

(Neyroud, 2017). Second, experimental designs are limited in the number of outcomes they can consider, and frequently focus on a single outcome. For example, experiments in policing have often focused on the effect of a policing strategy on crime, thereby neglecting a range of other potential outcomes that are equally important, such as equity, due process, and just deserts (Thacher, 2019).

Third, some of the most interesting phenomena in policing are extremely difficult to manipulate within an experimental design (Brown et al., 2018). For example, to test the effect of citizens' perceptions of police-provided PJ on police legitimacy, the researcher would need to manipulate these views. S/he may choose to subject officers in the treatment group to PJ training, assuming that they would subsequently treat citizens with more PJ, which, in turn, would lead citizens to feel that they were indeed treated more fairly. However, the training may have only marginal effects on officers' behavior, and even if major behavioral changes occur, they may not produce variation in citizens' subjective perceptions of PJ (see Worden & McLean, 2014), thus making the intervention futile.

Finally, even when an experiment demonstrates a causal effect, the process underlying the relationship frequently remains a "black box." It is often unclear what the specific "active ingredients" causing the effect are, or why it is smaller for some participants than for others (Sampson et al., 2013). In other words, examining causality through a quantitative lens leaves us with an "input-output" understanding of the process: if police agencies apply a specific intervention on one end, they should (with a certain level of likelihood) receive a specific outcome on the other. What happens within this "machine," and what affects the likelihood of an observable effect, is left for speculation.

9.2 THE SUBJECTIVE APPROACH TO THE STUDY OF CAUSALITY

"Subjective causality" is a qualitative method for assessing causality, initially developed for ethnographic research (Abell & Engel, 2019). It resembles earlier approaches that sought to treat causality as an internal, subjective process [e.g., see "process-oriented causality" (Maxwell, 2004, 2012), and "local causality" (Miles & Huberman, 1984)], and it provides an important, complementary angle to the quantitative study of causality. It is based on the premise that human action (both external behavior and internal feelings/perceptions) is the source of causal relationships between events and their outcomes (Goldthorpe, 2001;

Hedstrom, 2005). To identify the causal relationship influencing a specific individual, the researcher must examine the narrative of the process as subjectively perceived and expressed by that individual (Abell & Engel, 2019; Pósch, 2020). This narrative may include, for example, statements about why the person felt a certain way or engaged in a particular behavior ("I felt/did X because of Y"); statements about the individual's future anticipated course of action ("If Y happens, I will feel/do X"); and statements describing an alternative course of action ("I would not have felt/done X, if Y had not happened") (for further elaboration see Abell & Engel, 2019).

Like any other research method, "subjective causality" is not without limitations. Unlike traditional, quantitative, "objective" causality, it relies on personal interpretations of past experiences or predictions regarding future ones, which are inevitably based on one's ability to introspect, recall causes and outcomes, and accurately assess future reactions (Abend et al., 2013; Maxwell, 2004). In other words, subjective causality belongs to the inner realm of perceptions, attitudes, interpretations, feelings and expectations, and is less suitable for examining the role of objective actions (as both IV and DV). As suggested by its name – it is subjective by nature. Thus, it is not meant to replace quantitative tests of causality, but provide a preliminary or complementary dimension in the quest for richer understanding of complex causal mechanisms (Kling et al., 2005; Tacq, 2011; Trafimow, 2014; Weisner, 2005).

9.2.1 "Subjective Causality" in the Social Sciences and Potential Contribution to Policing

To date, subjective causality has been used in various disciplines within the social sciences (Abell & Engel, 2019; Abend et al., 2013; Maxwell, 2004), including public health (Morse & Tylko, 1985; Morse et al., 1987), education (Goldenberg et al., 1992; Maxwell, 2004; Regan-Smith, 1992), and psychology (Weisner, 2005). For example, Regan-Smith (1992) interviewed medicine students about their academic experiences. All interviews were content analyzed, and statements concerning students' learning experiences, perceptions of teaching, achievements, and the mechanisms linking these variables were categorized into themes. She found that the vast majority of students described a subjective, causal relationship between specific teaching strategies and both positive learning experiences and high academic achievements. Moreover, students categorized their teachers according to this mechanism, differentiating between "good teachers," who use teaching strategies they believed contributed to their success, and "bad teachers," who did not.

Morse and colleagues (Morse et al., 1987) examined the risk factors associated with falling down among 100 elderly hospital patients. They conducted a mixed method study focusing on patients' movement around the hospital, subjective experience of a fall, and the process leading to it. They found that patients often perceived objects in their environment, such as furniture or IV polls, as causally linked to the fall. The researchers note that these causes were not identified in past quantitative studies. The subjective causal mechanism illuminated in this study formed the basis for a larger, quantitative study, which was subsequently used to create an instrument for measuring patients' risk of falling (Morse et al., 1989).

Apart from the two studies reviewed below, we are not aware of similar endeavors in policing research. However, this is not to say that qualitative studies in policing have not sought to examine actors' subjective motivations and insights. For example, Bittner (1967) interviewed ~100 police officers in two large cities about their actions to keep the peace among skid-row residents, and their perceived effectiveness. He found that officers subjectively considered some strategies, such as getting to know the residents and accumulating personal knowledge about them, to be more effective than others. In other words, the officers subjectively linked some of their actions with successful peace-keeping. Similarly, Muir (1979) interviewed 28 police officers in an American city in the early 1970s about their policing experiences, philosophy and preferences. He identified qualities he termed "passion" and "perspective" (p. 47) as leading to "good policing" and appropriate exercise of discretion. More recently, Willis and Mastrofski (2018) interviewed 38 patrol officers about their craft, and found that they often judge the quality of police work by focusing on processes, such as identifying the challenges within a specific situation. The researchers conclude that policing scholars should focus more on the relationship between craft and successful police work as subjectively perceived by officers.

Nevertheless, and despite the wealth of qualitative research in policing and scholars' interest in understanding actors' subjective experiences, causality has not been an explicit focus of this body of work. In other words, qualitative studies in policing have not deliberately and systematically inquired about individuals' internal subjective understandings of the potential causal relationships between occurrences and emotional/behavioral responses. By embracing this focus, subjective causality has the potential to contribute to the policing evidence base in three important ways, which directly develop from the limitations of RCTs reviewed above:

First, when conducting an experiment is not feasible (e.g., when police agencies are unwilling to cooperate with researchers), a qualitative examination of subjective causality can provide the first significant step in the direction of understanding the process of interest. Second, by allowing actors to tell their stories and express internal causal relationships as they see them, subjective causality can potentially illuminate more than a single outcome, such as the perceived effect of experiences with the police on trust in authorities, fear of crime, and social cohesion. Third, subjective causality allows us to examine the effect of internal/psychological IV, such as perceptions, emotions, attitudes and subjective experiences on specific outcomes (Pósch, 2020). These may include citizens' views of police treatment or social cohesion on their street, or police officers' perceptions of their external legitimacy. Such variables are of interest to policing scholars (e.g., Jonathan-Zamir & Harpaz, 2014; Mastrofski et al., 2016; Murphy & Cherney, 2012; Nix, 2017; Nix et al., 2018; Tankebe, 2019), but, as already noted, are almost impossible to manipulate within an experimental design. Finally, subjective causality does not only identify a (subjective) causal relationship, but it may also capture the mechanism – one's interpretation of the process by which the causes are linked to the outcomes (Abell & Engel, 2019; Miles & Huberman, 1984), thus laying the ground for a process model, or "theory of change" (Rossi et al., 2019; Weiss, 1997).

9.3 THE EXAMPLE OF THE RELATIONSHIP BETWEEN PROCEDURAL JUSTICE AND POLICE LEGITIMACY

We now turn to demonstrating the use of the subjective causality approach in policing, using an important question that has generated a timely, lively debate: do citizens' perceptions of police-provided PJ "produce" police legitimacy? (Nagin & Telep, 2017, 2020; Pósch, 2020; Weisburd et al., 2019). In our demonstration we draw from two recent, qualitative studies (Jonathan-Zamir et al., 2020; Perry & Jonathan-Zamir, in progress), but first we provide background on the concepts of PJ and police legitimacy, and review the challenge of providing empirical support for the claim that there is a causal relationship between them.

The concept of PJ was originally developed in social psychology by Thibaut and Walker (1975), who defined it as the perceived fairness of a decision-making process. They suggested that when a process is perceived as fair, the outcome (decision) would be accepted by the individual, even if unfavorable (see also Thibaut et al., 1973). Several decades later, Tom Tyler (1990, 2004) and others (e.g., Sunshine & Tyler, 2003; Tyler & Huo, 2002) proposed that this model applies to the policing context: when citizens interact with police, they care more about the way they are treated than about the outcome of the encounter. The reason for this is that treatment by the police, who represent the "state on the street" (Hinton, 2006), sends important messages about citizens' value and status, thus influencing their social identity and self-worth (Blader & Tyler, 2003; Tyler & Lind, 1992). Four features of police treatment are argued to affect citizens' overall assessment of fair treatment and are thus considered the "building blocks" of PJ: (1) dignity and respect ("was I treated with politeness and dignity, and were my rights recognized and respected?"); (2) participation/voice ("was I given the opportunity to express my views before decisions were made about my case?"); (3) neutrality ("was I treated in a neutral, unbiased manner?"); and (4) trustworthy motives ("was the officer motivated by true concern for my wellbeing, or that of others?") (Schulhofer et al., 2011; Sunshine & Tyler, 2003; Tyler, 2004, 2009; see also Jonathan-Zamir et al., 2015).

Proponents of the PJ model argue that there is a causal relationship between perceptions PJ and police legitimacy, which is defined as "the belief that the police are entitled to call upon the public to follow the law and help combat crime, and that members of the public have an obligation to engage in cooperative behaviors" (Tyler, 2004, pp. 86–87). Legitimacy, in turn, is considered a highly important attribute of police agencies, for both normative and instrumental reasons. On the normative level, in democratic societies, where citizens are policed by consent, the police should be viewed as an expression of the community rather than an external, detached force acting against it (Moore, 1992). On the more practical level, it has been argued that police legitimacy leads to numerous socially desirable outcomes, including willingness to empower, assist, and cooperate with the police, and even to obey the law in the long term (Hamm et al., 2017; Tyler & Fagan, 2008).

To date, the proposed relationship between PJ and police legitimacy, and between legitimacy and its expected outcomes, has been the subject of hundreds if not thousands of studies. In accordance with the traditional approach to causality, the overwhelming majority of these studies are quantitative, with many using panel (e.g., Gau, 2014; Hinds & Murphy, 2007; Hough et al., 2013; Nix et al., 2015; Reisig & Lloyd, 2009; Sunshine & Tyler, 2003) or longitudinal survey designs (e.g., Oliveira et al., 2020), and some using experiments (e.g., Maguire et al., 2017; Mazerolle et al., 2012; Murphy et al. 2014; Sahin et al. 2017; Sargeant et al. 2016). The vast majority of these studies, across different countries, agencies, and contexts, find the expected relationship between perceptions of PJ and police legitimacy, and between legitimacy and its expected outcomes. At the same time, the question of whether PJ *produces* legitimacy, and whether legitimacy, in turn, *produces* obedience to the law, and compliance and cooperation with the police, is still unsettled, as detailed below [e.g., see Nagin & Telep (2017) vs. Tyler (2017), and Nagin & Telep (2020)]. We should note that from this point on we focus on the first of the two steps in this relationship – the proposed effect of PJ on police legitimacy – as it is the focus of our demonstration of the subjective causality approach.

Nagin and Telep (2017, 2020) argue that despite the volume of empirical research demonstrating a relationship between PJ and legitimacy, there is no evidence that the relationship is both causal and in the expected direction. In their first critique in 2017, they argued that most studies in this area use cross-sectional surveys, and thus cannot demonstrate that PJ came before police legitimacy, and cannot eliminate alternative explanations for the correlation, such as a third common factor (e.g., individual stakes in conformity or community effects). They further argued that researchers' ability to test the relationship between PJ and legitimacy using experimental designs is limited because perceptions of PJ cannot be directly manipulated. Despite significant developments since 2017, in their 2020 essay Nagin and Telep postulate that they "still see a lack of evidence that these associations reflect a causal connection, whereby policies that are successful in increasing procedurally just treatment of citizens alter their perceptions of legitimacy" (p. 762). Moreover, they insist that their critique should not be interpreted as a call for more RCTs, but as a conception that the relationship between PJ and legitimacy reflects a complex set of personal experiences, perceptions and attitudes, that is larger than any single police–citizen encounter.

Similarly, a consensus study of the National Academies of Sciences, Engineering, and Medicine (Weisburd & Majmundar, 2018) finds no evidence that PJ *causes* police legitimacy and notes that in experiments that sought to test the outcomes of PJ, the intervention typically includes tactics from other strategies, which makes it difficult to isolate the specific effect of PJ on police legitimacy. At the same time, they conclude:

Although the application of procedural justice concepts to policing is relatively new, there are more extensive literatures on procedural justice in social psychology, in management, and with other legal authorities such as the courts. Those studies are often designed in ways that make causal inferences more compelling, and results in those areas suggest that the application of procedural justice concepts to policing has promise and that further studies are needed to examine the degree to which the success of such strategies in those other domains can be replicated in the domain of policing. (p. 317)

9.3.1 Using Subjective Causality to Examine the Relationship between Procedural Justice and Police Legitimacy

Two recent studies use the subjective causality approach to examine the relationship between perceptions of police-provided PJ and views of police legitimacy (Jonathan Zamir et al., 2020[1]; Perry & Jonathan-Zamir, in progress). Both take advantage of in-depth, semi-structured interviews conducted as a part of a larger study on protest policing (see Perry et al., 2017; Perry, 2020). The first author and one/two research assistants attended all "Occupy" protest events that took place in Tel-Aviv, Jerusalem, Haifa or Beer-Sheva (four central cities in Israel) between March and October 2012. The 20 largest events (150 protestors or more as estimated by the police) were included in the final sample. The researchers arrived at all events before the protest began, stood in central locations (e.g., entry point), and randomly approached protesters who passed them. They briefly introduced the study, and asked the protesters to participate by providing their e-mail address. An online survey was emailed to those who concurred (91% on average) up to seven days following the event. The final item in the survey asked if the protestor was willing to take part in an in-depth interview. Of 470 protesters who completed the online survey, 52 agreed, and were interviewed by the first author within 4–9 days of the event.

---

[1] It should be noted that in Jonathan-Zamir et al. (2020) the relationship between PJ and police legitimacy was not the main focus of the analysis, and thus the term "subjective causality" is not explicitly used. The relationship emerged as a theme in a grounded-theory analysis.

The interviews lasted 2–6 hours, and were conducted in a location chosen by the interviewee (e.g., their home or a coffee shop). The interviewer explained the general topic of the interview, that it would be recorded and transcribed, and that the interviewee can cease the interview at any time. The interviews were tape recorded, but the researcher also took notes documenting what came across as significant points, or information about the interviewee's behavior (such as if s/he became tearful). All recordings were transcribed and merged with the notes within a week of the interview.

In terms of the interviewing protocol, the participants were asked about their experiences with the police during the event (e.g., Did you encounter any police officers during the demonstration? If so, did they speak to you? How did you feel/react?); general perceptions of and attitudes toward the police (e.g., Do you trust the Israel Police? Do you think they treat all citizens equally?); and previous experiences and role as a protester (e.g., Was this your first protest? Would you describe your role in the event as a participant or organizer?). At no point were the interviewees directly asked about a potential causal relationship between fair police treatment and emotional/behavioral responses, as this was not the focus of the study at the time. Thus, any statements of (subjective) causality were initiated by the interviewees.

Our interview narratives allow us to address the question of whether or not there is a causal relationship between perceptions of PJ and police legitimacy, its direction, and the process underlying the relationship, without relying on the cooperation of police agencies or manipulating officers' behavior in hope to induce change in citizens' perceptions of PJ. Further, this analysis does not rely on correlations between survey items that measure PJ and items that measure police legitimacy, as is often the case in this literature (e.g., Nix et al., 2015; Sunshine & Tyler, 2003; Wolfe et al., 2016). Alternatively, in these narratives interviewees describe in their own words the effects that the nature of police treatment (PJ) has had on their subsequent views of police legitimacy.

The focus of the first analysis (Perry & Jonathan-Zamir, in progress) was on subjective perceptions of a causal relationship between what the interviewees perceived as fairness (or unfairness) in police treatment during the demonstration, and subsequent assessments of police legitimacy. Protesters' narratives were analyzed using deductive content analysis (or "directed content analysis"; Hsieh & Shannon, 2005, p. 1281): The first author and one/two research assistants read all interviews 2–3 times, line-by-line, searching for statements that indicated experiences of procedural justice/injustice; views related to police legitimacy; and a causal relationship between the two, or, in other words, "a subjective first person singular causally related statement" (Abell & Engel, 2019).

The large majority of interviewees (43; 82%) described experiences of PJ (6) or, more frequently, injustice (37). Forty-six (88%) expressed their views of police legitimacy. But most important – the majority of the interviewees (40; 77%) proactively described a subjective, causal, relationship between the two, whereby perceptions of the fairness embedded in police treatment influenced subsequent, broader evaluations of elements related to police legitimacy. No indications of a reverse relationship or a third common factor were found.[2] For example, Interviewee 4 describes lack of respect in police treatment, which led to negative emotional reactions (such as humiliation), which, in turn, undermined police legitimacy in her eyes, as expressed in fear:

What bothered me most was the way he (the officer) spoke to me – all the shouting, I felt threatened... It's not what he said, because an officer is allowed to tell me to "fly off the road" ("get the hell off the road"), I have no problem with that... But come on... why would you talk to me this way?... When this happens to you, you feel diminished, offended, humiliated... Before the demonstration I don't know, I didn't really think about the police, I generally didn't think anything bad. After the demonstration I'm very afraid of them. It is clear to me that I don't want any further contact with the police, I'm even a bit scared.

A similar process was expressed by Interviewee 36, who focused on lack of transparency with regard to use of force, and then explained why it influenced his trust in the police, referring to feelings of helplessness and loss of control:

...and then I saw five officers grabbing one of the protesters... and I keep asking him (the officer) "Why? Why are you doing this?" He never replied. What drives me crazy is when they (the police) are violent like that without any explanation. If only they would say something, give me a reason... I was in shock when they acted like that. Just shocked. How am I supposed to listen to a person who treats me like that? How am I supposed to follow their orders? It's no wonder no one trusts them anymore.

You feel helpless when they don't explain why they are doing what they're doing... How am I supposed to know what to expect? It's like they took away your power to decide what to do, how to behave, because you have no idea what the implications will be, you can't trust their reaction.

---

[2] We recognize that no indication of a reverse relationship or third common factor does not guarantee they were not part of the participants' internal mechanisms, as they may not be fully aware of all factors shaping their views.

While most interviewees (35; 88%) described a negative encounter with the police, few reported improved trust as a result of a positive encounter. Interviewee 15, for example, described dignity and respect in an encounter, which led to a sense of confidence:

...one officer... came and asked me: "What's your name? Au, [name]? So I am [name], nice to meet you. I want to ask that you do not walk on the road because of so and so and so..." When someone comes and talks to you like that, it makes all the difference. Suddenly there is a good feeling, there is confidence.

The second analysis (Jonathan-Zamir et al., 2020) used the same interviews to examine the constitute elements of a newly developed concept – "group-level PJ" (O'Brien et al., 2020), which is used to characterize situations where the police are not treating a specific individual within the context of her/his personal circumstances, but a group/community, such as in demonstrations, community meetings, press conferences, or when treating an individual as an official/unofficial representative of a group/community. Jonathan-Zamir and colleagues (2020) found that 11 interviewees (21% of those who mentioned group-level PJ) directly linked the type of group-level treatment they experienced to emotional and behavioral outcomes related to police legitimacy, such as poor expectations from the police:

Police officers treat us as terrorists. There is no other way to describe it. They don't see us as individuals, to them we are all the same, just a bunch of anarchists worthy of nothing but violence... You clearly see that they don't see you as an individual, but as part of a group that they perceive to be the enemy... to them, we are all terrorists, so we should be treated as such, and that's what you see at demonstrations... this is why we don't really expect anything from them anymore... We do things our way, do what we think is right, without expecting too much. (Inter. 4)

Interviewee 12 describes lack of communication and transparency (expressions of procedural injustice) as the specific factors undermining police legitimacy, as expressed in little willingness to cooperate with the police in the future:

Beyond anything else, I think that the police are just not communicating with "Occupy." We tried, but they wouldn't. We said, "let's make it easier for all of us, we'll let you know exactly what we plan to do, and we'll work together to maintain public order [at the demonstration]." But the message we received was – this is a one-way [street] here, you have to tell us what you plan to do, but we'll do (say) nothing. So during the demonstration, you never know what's coming – it can be completely peaceful for one moment, and in the next people are being arrested for no reason... Why would we even try to listen to them after that?

Similarly, Interviewee 19 mentioned lack of respect as the specific factor undermining police legitimacy and hope for a positive, future relationship with the police:

I think it's how they (the police) see us as activists in a protest... they think we are a bunch of spoiled, childish anarchists, everything about their behavior shows that. They think to themselves, "who are these children who have the time and money not to go to work, to be at demonstrations all day, wasting everybody's time?" ... This is why we don't stand a chance with them (the police), that's what it taught me. The way I see it, it's a waste of time with them. The way they think of us, it's a lost [case].

9.4 DISCUSSION AND CONCLUSIONS

This chapter introduces policing researchers to a unique approach to the study of causality and demonstrates the potential contribution of subjective causality to policing using the example of the relationship between police-provided PJ and police legitimacy. As reviewed above, this approach bears unique advantages, which, at the very least, can complement quantitative analyses. In the specific example of the relationship between PJ and legitimacy, this approach helps us to appreciate how individuals feel in encounters with police and, more importantly, if and how these experiences affect police legitimacy in their eyes. We did not rely on correlations between survey items, which may or may not represent causal relationships in the expected direction; we did not need to obtain the consent of any police agency, manipulate their operational procedures or access their data; and we did not need to engage in the difficult task of manipulating subjective perceptions, attitudes, or feelings. Alternatively, we took the approach that the answer to whether or not there is a causal relationship between two subjective perceptions can lie within the individual her/himself (Abell & Engel, 2019; Maxwell, 2004, 2012).

The analyses carried out by Perry and Jonathan-Zamir (in progress) and Jonathan-Zamir et al. (2020) support the proposition that there is indeed a causal relationship between PJ and police legitimacy, whereby perceptions of unfair treatment undermine police legitimacy and vice versa. Concerns that the effect may be reversed, or that there is a third, common factor affecting both PJ and legitimacy (Nagin & Telep, 2017, 2020), were not supported. Moreover, the analyses illuminate the processes by which fairness assessments affect legitimacy, at least within the context of protest policing. For example, the interviews show that the effect may be mediated by emotional responses, such as feelings of humiliation and lack of control.

Could the subjective causality approach contribute to understanding other relationships within the police legitimacy model? We expect that the answer is positive. Policing researchers may use this approach to examine, for example, if citizens' perceptions of police legitimacy are causally linked to willingness to cooperate with the police, empower them, comply with their directive and obey the law more generally. Such views may be examined both as future intentions ("because of X I intend to do Y") and as retroactive interpretations of past behavior ("I did X because of Y"). Shifting the focus to the officers, subjective causality may be used to understand, for example, the types of citizens' reactions that strengthen (or weaken) police officers' self-legitimacy (Bottoms & Tankebe, 2012).

More generally, there are several ways by which policing scholars may integrate the subjective causality approach into their work. One possibility is to treat subjective causality as a supporting methodology. Quantitative methods such as RCTs could benefit from a preliminary, qualitative assessment of the main variables of interest. This could be done, for example, by or for police agencies facing a new challenge or entering a new area. It may assist in understanding how citizens perceive a problem and its causes, and lay the foundations for a large-scale experimental study, an intervention, or both. Studies assessing subjective causality are also useful after RCTs have been completed, for the purpose of understanding why an intervention worked (or did not work), and why, when, for whom and in what context the causal mechanism applies. For example, Roach et al. (2017) sought to reduce thefts from insecure vehicles using a leaflet campaign. Their experiment showed promising results, but they nevertheless conclude by noting:

…without a follow-up qualitative study to find out from the vehicle owners in the treatment areas whether they: (a) saw the leaflet and (b) believe that it had an effect on them, we cannot be sure that the reduction in the proportion of insecure thefts from cars was indeed due to the nudge treatment. We suggest that this is a common criticism of much research of this ilk (including randomized control trials) where conclusions of effect are drawn without speaking with the seemingly "affected." (p. 37)

Another timely example is the relationship between police enforcement of the COVID-19 emergency regulations and citizens' willingness to comply with these regulations. Subjective causality can be used to understand not only if and how specific police practices affect compliance but also how this process may vary in different social/cultural contexts (e.g., Bradford et al., 2020; Murphy et al., 2020).

A different approach proposes to treat subjective causality as a research philosophy rather than an additional methodology in researchers' toolbox (Maxwell, 2004), as it offers a different answer to the question of what causality *is*. It views causality not as an objective correlation that meets a set of conditions (see above), but as a subjective view of more complex mechanisms involving internal processes, which vary across people, contexts, and situations. This perspective can help illuminate the nature of relationships we expect exist in policing, but the psychological nature of the variables has made them challenging to investigate using traditional quantitative methods. These include, for example, the relationship between community cohesion and fear of crime; social/group identity and trust in agents of the criminal justice system; authority-provided PJ and legal compliance; and perceived discrimination and willingness to cooperate with authorities.

To conclude, in this chapter we have argued for the benefits that subjective causality may bring to the field of policing, and have demonstrated its use in the context of the relationship between PJ and police legitimacy. Given the focus of EBP on causality, we propose this approach could encourage greater integration of qualitative methods into policing research, which, alongside experimental designs, should ameliorate the quality of the evidence policing research has to offer. We encourage policing researchers to continue exploring the benefits that the subjective causality approach entails, both in relation to police legitimacy, and in other areas of policing where processes connecting causes to outcomes are yet to be illuminated.

References

Abell, P., & Engel, O. (2019). Subjective Causality and Counterfactuals in the Social Sciences: Toward an Ethnographic Causality?. *Sociological Methods & Research*, 0049124119852373.

Abend, G., Petre, C., & Sauder, M. (2013). Styles of causal thought: An empirical investigation. *American Journal of Sociology*, 119(3), 602–654.

Angel, C. M., Sherman, L. W., Strang, H., Ariel, B., Bennett, S., Inkpen, N., Keane, A. & Richmond, T. S. (2014). Short-term effects of restorative justice conferences on post-traumatic stress symptoms among robbery and burglary victims: a randomized controlled trial. *Journal of Experimental Criminology*, 10(3), 291–307.

Ariel, B. (2018). "Not all evidence is created equal": on the importance of matching research questions with research methods in evidence based policing. In R. J. Mitchell & L. Huey (Eds.), *Evidence Based Policing: An Introduction* (pp 63–86). Policy Press.

Ariel, B., Farrar, W. A., & Sutherland, A. (2015). The effect of police body-worn cameras on use of force and citizens' complaints against the police: A randomized controlled trial. *Journal of Quantitative Criminology, 31*(3), 509–535.

Bittner, E. (1967). *The police on skid-row: A study of peace keeping*. Ardent Media.

Blader, S. L., & Tyler, T. R. (2003). What constitutes fairness in work settings? A four-component model of procedural justice. *Human Resource Management Review, 13*(1), 107–126.

Bottoms, A., & Tankebe, J. (2012). Beyond procedural justice: A dialogic approach to legitimacy in criminal justice. *The journal of criminal law and criminology*, 119–170.

Bradford, B., Hobson, Z., Kyprianides, A., Yesberg, J., Jackson, J., & Posch, K. (2020). *Policing the lockdown: compliance, enforcement and procedural justice*. COVID-19 Special Papers. UCL. http://eprints.lse.ac.uk/104227

Braga, A. A., Papachristos, A. V., & Hureau, D. M. (2014). The effects of hot spots policing on crime: An updated systematic review and meta-analysis. *Justice Quarterly, 31*(4), 633–663.

Brown, J., Belur, J., Tompson, L., McDowall, A., Hunter, G., & May, T. (2018). Extending the remit of evidence-based policing. *International Journal of Police Science & Management, 20*(1), 38–51.

Bunge, M. (2017). *Causality and modern science*. Routledge.

Gau, J. M. (2014). Procedural justice and police legitimacy: A test of measurement and structure. *American Journal of Criminal Justice, 39*(2), 187–205.

Goldenberg, C., Reese, L., & Gallimore, R. (1992). Effects of literacy materials from school on Latino children's home experiences and early reading achievement. *American Journal of Education, 100*(4), 497–536.

Goldthorpe, J. H. (2001). Causation, statistics, and sociology. *European Sociological Review, 17*(1), 1–20.

Hamm, J. A., Trinkner, R., & Carr, J. D. (2017). Fair process, trust, and cooperation: Moving toward an integrated framework of police legitimacy. *Criminal Justice and Behavior, 44*(9), 1183–1212.

Hedstrom, P. (2005). *Dissecting the social: On the principles of analytical sociology*. Cambridge University Press.

Hinds, L., & Murphy, K. (2007). Public satisfaction with police: Using procedural justice to improve police legitimacy. *Australian & New Zealand Journal of Criminology, 40*(1), 27–42.

Hinton, M. S. (2006). *The state on the streets: police and politics in Argentina and Brazil*. Lynne Rienner Publishers.

Hough, M., Jackson, J., & Bradford, B. (2013). Legitimacy, trust and compliance: An empirical test of procedural justice theory using the European Social Survey. In J. Tankebe & A. Liebling (Eds.), *Legitimacy and Criminal Justice: An International Exploration* (pp.326–352). Yale University Press.

Hsieh, H. F., & Shannon, S. E. (2005). Three approaches to qualitative content analysis. *Qualitative Health Research, 15*(9), 1277–1288.

Jackson, J., Tyler, T. R., Bradford, B., Taylor, D., & Shiner, M. (2010). Legitimacy and procedural justice in prisons. *Prison Service Journal, 191*, 4–10.

Jonathan-Zamir, T., & Harpaz, A. (2014). Police understanding of the foundations of their legitimacy in the eyes of the public: The case of commanding officers in the Israel National Police. *British Journal of Criminology, 54*(3), 469–489.

Jonathan-Zamir, T., Mastrofski, S. D., & Moyal, S. (2015). Measuring procedural justice in police-citizen encounters. *Justice Quarterly, 32*(5), 845–871.

Jonathan-Zamir, T., Perry, G., & Weisburd, D. (2020) Illuminating the Concept of Community (Group)-Level Procedural Justice: A Qualitative Analysis of Protestors' Group-Level Experiences with the Police. *Criminal Justice and Behavior, 48*(6), 791–809. https://doi.org/10.1177/0093854820983388

Kling, J. R., Liebman, J. B., & Katz, L. F. (2005). "Bullets don't got no name": Consequences of fear in the ghetto. In T. Weisner (Ed.), *Discovering successful pathways in children's development* (pp. 243–282). University of Chicago Press.

Lewis, D. (1974). Causation. *The Journal of Philosophy, 70*(17), 556–567.

Maguire, E. R., Lowrey, B. V., & Johnson, D. (2017). Evaluating the relative impact of positive and negative encounters with police: A randomized experiment. *Journal of Experimental Criminology, 13*(3), 367–391.

Mastrofski, S. D., Jonathan-Zamir, T., Moyal, S., & Willis, J. J. (2016). Predicting procedural justice in police–citizen encounters. *Criminal Justice and Behavior, 43*(1), 119–139.

Maxwell, J. A. (2004). Causal explanation, qualitative research, and scientific inquiry in education. *Educational Researcher, 33*(2), 3–11.

Maxwell, J. A. (2012). The importance of qualitative research for causal explanation in education. *Qualitative Inquiry, 18*(8), 655–661.

Maxwell, J. A. (2019). Evidence for what? How mixed methods expands the evidence for causation in educational research. *Qualitative Inquiry*.

Mazerolle, L., Bennett, S., Antrobus, E., & Eggins, E. (2012). Procedural justice, routine encounters and citizen perceptions of police: Main findings from the Queensland Community Engagement Trial (QCET). *Journal of Experimental Criminology, 8*(4), 343–367.

Mazerolle, L., Bennett, S., Davis, J., Sargeant, E., & Manning, M. (2013). Procedural justice and police legitimacy: A systematic review of the research evidence. *Journal of Experimental Criminology, 9*(3), 245–274.

Mazerolle, L., Eggins, E., Hine, L., & Higginson, A. (this volume). The Role of Randomized Experiments in Developing the Evidence for Evidence-Based Policing. In D. Weisburd, T. Jonathan, G. Perry & B. Hasisi, (Eds.), *The Future of Evidence-Based Policing*. Cambridge University Press.

Miles, M. B., & Huberman, A. M. (1984). Drawing valid meaning from qualitative data: Toward a shared craft. *Educational Researcher, 13*(5), 20–30.

Moore, M. H. (1992). Problem-solving and community policing. *Crime and Justice, 15*, 99–158.

Morse, J. M., Morse, R. M., & Tylko, S. J. (1989). Development of a scale to identify the fall-prone patient. *Canadian Journal on Aging/La Revue Canadienne du Vieillissement, 8*(4), 366–377.

Morse, J. M., & Tylko, S. J. (1985). *The use of qualitative methods in a study examining patient falls*. In annual meeting of the Society for Applied Anthropology, Washington, DC.

Morse, J. M., Tylko, S. J., & Dixon, H. A. (1987). Characteristics of the fall-prone patient. *The Gerontologist*, 27(4), 516–522.

Muir, W. K. (1979). *Police: streetcorner politicians*. University of Chicago Press.

Murphy, K., & Cherney, A. (2012). Understanding cooperation with police in a diverse society. *The British Journal of Criminology*, 52(1), 181–201.

Murphy, K., Mazerolle, L., & Bennett, S. (2014). Promoting trust in police: Findings from a randomised experimental field trial of procedural justice policing. *Policing and Society*, 24(4), 405–424.

Murphy, K., Williamson, H., Sargeant, E., & McCarthy, M. (2020). Why people comply with COVID-19 social distancing restrictions: Self-interest or duty?. *Australian & New Zealand Journal of Criminology*, 53(4), 477–496.

Nagin, D. S., & Telep, C. W. (2017). Procedural justice and legal compliance. *Annual Review of Law and Social Science*, 13, 5–28.

Nagin, D. S., & Telep, C. W. (2020). Procedural justice and legal compliance: A revisionist perspective. *Criminology & Public Policy*, 19(3), 761–786.

Neyroud, P. W. (2017). Learning to Field Test in Policing: Using an analysis of completed randomised controlled trials involving the police to develop a grounded theory on the factors contributing to high levels of treatment integrity in Police Field Experiments [Doctoral dissertation, University of Cambridge]. https://doi.org/10.17863/CAM.14377

Nix, J. (2017). Police perceptions of their external legitimacy in high and low crime areas of the community. *Crime & Delinquency*, 63(10), 1250–1278.

Nix, J., Wolfe, S. E., & Campbell, B. A. (2018). Command-level police officers' perceptions of the "war on cops" and de-policing. *Justice Quarterly*, 35(1), 33–54.

Nix, J., Wolfe, S. E., Rojek, J., & Kaminski, R. J. (2015). Trust in the police: The influence of procedural justice and perceived collective efficacy. *Crime & Delinquency*, 61(4), 610–640.

O'Brien, T. C., Tyler, T. R., & Meares, T. L. (2020). Building popular legitimacy with reconciliatory gestures and participation: A community-level model of authority. *Regulation & Governance*, 14(4), 821–839.

Oliveira, T. R., Jackson, J., Murphy, K., & Bradford, B. (2020). Are trustworthiness and legitimacy 'hard to win, easy to lose'? A longitudinal test of the asymmetry thesis of police-citizen contact. *Journal of Quantitative Criminology*, 1–43.

Perry, G. (2020). Promoting Protesters' Compliance: The Effect of General Perceptions of the Police versus Police Actions. *Policing: A Journal of Policy and Practice*, 15(2), 1245–1261.

Perry, G. & Jonathan-Zamir, T. (in progress). Is there a subjective, causal relationship between procedural justice and trust in the police?: A qualitative analysis of protesters' experiences with police.

Perry, G., Jonathan-Zamir, T., & Weisburd, D. (2017). The Effect of Paramilitary Protest Policing on Protestors' Trust in the Police: The Case of the "Occupy Israel" Movement. *Law & Society Review*, 51(3), 602–634.

Pósch, K. (2020). Prying open the black box of causality: a causal mediation analysis test of procedural justice policing. *Journal of Quantitative Criminology*, 1–29.

Sahin, N., Braga, A. A., Apel, R., & Brunson, R. K. (2017). The impact of procedurally-just policing on citizen perceptions of police during traffic stops: The Adana randomized controlled trial. *Journal of Quantitative Criminology*, 33(4), 701–726.

Sampson, R. J., Winship, C., & Knight, C. (2013). Translating causal claims: Principles and strategies for policy-relevant criminology. *Criminology & Public Policy*, 12, 587.

Sargeant, E., Antrobus, E., Murphy, K., Bennett, S., & Mazerolle, L. (2016). Social identity and procedural justice in police encounters with the public: Results from a randomised controlled trial. *Policing and society*, 26(7), 789–803.

Schulhofer, S. J., Tyler, T. R., & Huq, A. Z. (2011). American policing at a crossroads: Unsustainable policies and the procedural justice alternative. *Journal of Criminal Law & Criminology*, 101, 335.

Sherman, L. W. (1998). *Evidence-based policing*. Police Foundation. www .policefoundation.org/wp-content/uploads/2015/06/Sherman-1998-Evidence-Based-Policing.pdf

Sherman, L. W. (2013). The rise of evidence-based policing: Targeting, testing, and tracking. *Crime and Justice*, 42(1), 377–451.

Sherman, L. W., & Weisburd, D. (1995). General deterrent effects of police patrol in crime "hot spots": A randomized, controlled trial. *Justice Quarterly*, 12(4), 625–648.

Sunshine, J., & Tyler, T. R. (2003). The role of procedural justice and legitimacy in shaping public support for policing. *Law & Society Review*, 37(3), 513–548.

Regan-Smith, M. G. (1992). *The teaching of basic science in medical school: The students' perspective* [Unpublished dissertation, Harvard Graduate School of Education].

Reisig, M. D., & Lloyd, C. (2009). Procedural justice, police legitimacy, and helping the police fight crime: Results from a survey of Jamaican adolescents. *Police Quarterly*, 12(1), 42–62.

Roach, J., Weir, K., Phillips, P., Gaskell, K., & Walton, M. (2017). Nudging down theft from insecure vehicles. A pilot study. *International Journal of Police Science & Management*, 19(1), 31–38.

Rossi, P. H., Lipsey, M. W., & Henry, G. T. (2019). *Evaluation: A systematic approach*. Sage Publications.

Tacq, J. (2011). Causality in qualitative and quantitative research. *Quality & Quantity*, 45(2), 263–291.

Tankebe, J. (2019). In their own eyes: an empirical examination of police self-legitimacy. *International Journal of Comparative and Applied Criminal Justice*, 43(2), 99–116.

Thacher, D. (2004). Police research and the humanities. *The ANNALS of the American Academy of Political and Social Science*, 593(1), 179–191.

Thacher, D. (2019). The Aspiration of Scientific Policing. *Law & Social Inquiry*, 44(1), 273–297.

Thibaut, J. W., & Walker, L. (1975). *Procedural justice: A psychological analysis*. L. Erlbaum Associates.

Thibaut, J., Walker, L., LaTour, S., & Houlden, P. (1973). Procedural justice as fairness. *Stanford Law Review*, 26, 1271.

Trafimow, D. (2014). Considering quantitative and qualitative issues together. *Qualitative Research in Psychology, 11*(1), 15–24.

Tyler, T. R. (1990). Justice, self-interest, and the legitimacy of legal and political authority. In J. J. Mansbridge (Ed.), *Beyond self-interest* (p. 171–179). University of Chicago Press.

Tyler, T. R. (2004). Enhancing police legitimacy. *The ANNALS of the American Academy of Political and Social Science, 593*(1), 84–99.

Tyler, T. R. (2006). *Why people obey the law*. Princeton University Press.

Tyler, T. R. (2009). Legitimacy and Criminal Justice: The Benefits of Self-Regulation. *Ohio State Journal of Criminal Law, 7*(1), 307–360.

Tyler, T. (2017). Procedural justice and policing: A rush to judgment?. *Annual Review of Law and Social Science, 13*, 29–53.

Tyler, T. R., & Fagan, J. (2008). Legitimacy and cooperation: Why do people help the police fight crime in their communities. *Ohio State Journal of Criminal Law, 6*, 231.

Tyler, T. R., & Huo, Y. (2002). *Trust in the law: Encouraging public cooperation with the police and courts*. Russell Sage Foundation.

Tyler, T. R., & Lind, E. A. (1992). A relational model of authority in groups. In *Advances in experimental social psychology* (Vol. 25, pp. 115–191). Academic Press.

Weiss, C. H. (1997). How can theory-based evaluation make greater headway?. *Evaluation Review, 21*(4), 501–524.

Weisburd, D. (2000). Randomized experiments in criminal justice policy: Prospects and problems. *Crime & Delinquency, 46*(2), 181–193.

Weisburd, D., & Majmundar, M. (Eds.) (2018). *Proactive policing: Effects on crime and communities*. The National Academies Press.

Weisburd, D., Majmundar, M.K., Aden, H., Braga, A., Bueermann, J., Cook, P.J., Goff, P.A., Harmon, R.A., Haviland, A., Lum, C., & Manski, C. (2019). Proactive policing: A summary of the report of the National Academies of Sciences, Engineering, and Medicine. *Asian Journal of Criminology, 14*(2), 145–177.

Weisner, T. S. (Ed.) (2005). *Discovering successful pathways in children's development: Mixed methods in the study of childhood and family life*. University of Chicago Press.

Willis, J. J., & Mastrofski, S. D. (2018). Improving policing by integrating craft and science: what can patrol officers teach us about good police work?. *Policing and Society, 28*(1), 27–44.

Willis, J., & Toronjo, H. (this volume). A Way Ahead: Re-Envisioning the Relationship Between Evidence-Based Policing and the Police Craft. In D. Weisburd, T. Jonathan, G. Perry & B. Hasisi, (Eds.), *The Future of Evidence-Based Policing*. Cambridge University Press.

Wolfe, S. E., Nix, J., Kaminski, R., & Rojek, J. (2016). Is the effect of procedural justice on police legitimacy invariant? Testing the generality of procedural justice and competing antecedents of legitimacy. *Journal of Quantitative Criminology, 32*(2), 253–282.

Worden, R. E., & McLean, S. J. (2014). *Assessing police performance in citizen encounters: police legitimacy and management accountability*. Report to the National Institute of Justice. Albany, NY: John F. Finn Institute for Public Safety.

PART IV

CHALLENGES TO THE IMPLEMENTATION
OF EVIDENCE-BASED POLICING

10

Practitioners' Inclination to Rely on Experience

What Does This Mean for Evidence-Based Policing?

Tal Jonathan-Zamir and David Weisburd

Since Sherman's (1998) seminal address to the Police Foundation in 1998, advocates of evidence-based policing (EBP) have been determined to convince police to begin basing decisions regarding policies, strategies, and tactics on rigorous scientific evaluations, and on analytic knowledge generated within the agency (e.g., Sherman, 1998, 2015; Weisburd & Neyroud, 2011). At the same time, they were also aware of a critical obstacle to their efforts: professional experience (or "craft") plays a key role in police decision-making in the field (e.g., Bayley & Bittner, 1984; Muir, 1977; Wilson, 1978). Proponents of EBP have thus sought to convince police that basing decisions on experience rather than on science is irrational, flawed, and not likely to lead to the best outcomes (e.g., Lum, 2009; Sherman, 1984, 1998). In their efforts, however, they have treated the inclination to rely on experience as a rational choice made by professionals within the policing environment. They have paid little attention to the generality of the phenomenon or to the psychological mechanisms at its root that are not necessarily influenced by rational claims.

In this chapter, we make the following argument: Police (like other practitioners) are psychologically inclined to rely on experience (not science) when making decisions, even when they are aware of, have access to and understand research evidence, value its potential contribution to their work, and support the philosophy of EBP more generally. Thus, attempts to rationally convince police of the benefits of science and make research evidence clear and accessible are of limited value. In the first two sections of the chapter we provide support for this claim, based on receptivity-to-research studies in policing and the psychology literature discussing the roles of experience versus science in decision-making. Next, we ask what this means for implementing EBP. How should proponents of EBP go about advocating for this philosophy while recognizing police officers' inherent inclination to rely on experience? In the third and final section of the chapter we address this question and make two recommendations: scientifically sound practices should be "injected" into officers' experience, and thus when they fall back on their experience, evidence-based practices would be there; and policing scholars should treat both research evidence and professional experience as necessary components in successful policing, and begin reflecting on and investigating exactly what their roles should be.

10.1 THE SCIENCE–EXPERIENCE PARADOX IN POLICING

For over two decades now, proponents of EBP have been determined to rationally convince police practitioners of the benefits of scientific evidence over arbitrary experiences and unsystematic reasoning (e.g., Lum, 2009; Sherman, 1984, 1998, 2013, 2015; Weisburd & Neyroud, 2011). Scientific evidence and personal experience may sometimes lead to a similar course of action, but proponents of EBP argue that there are important advantages to the former decision-making process. For example, Lum (2009) reviews convincing arguments in favor of basing police strategies and tactics on scientific evidence: evidence-based practices are more likely to be effective in controlling crime, which, in addition to direct benefits in terms of crime reduction, should improve officer motivation, decrease workload, and make efforts and investments more rational; harmful practices can be banned from use; evidence-based practices are more justifiable to the public, and can thus improve the legitimacy of the agency and its actions; systematic collection and analysis of data can lead to improvements in the agency's information technology systems, which should, in turn, improve managerial practices and officers' accountability; and, finally, EBP should make the workplace more interesting for officers, as they would be required to look outward for information, ideas, and worldviews, deal with new challenges, and engage in new relationships.

As part their efforts to convince police to give research evidence a seat at the decision-making table, proponents of EBP have also worked diligently to make scientific knowledge more "user friendly" – short, clear, accessible, and relevant to real-world policing (see Lum & Koper, 2017). One example is scientific, peer-reviewed journals aimed for practitioners' use. For example, *Policing: A Journal of Policy and Practice* (edited by Peter Neyroud and William Terrill) seeks to encourage high-quality research on police policy, reform, training, education, operations, and its implications for policing on the ground. The *Cambridge Journal of Evidence-Based Policing* (edited by Lawrence Sherman) focuses on research on the three strategic principles of EBP: Targeting – identifying priorities of police intervention; Testing – examining the outcomes of police interventions; and Tracking – evaluating the effectiveness of police action (Sherman, 2013).

Another important example is the Evidence-Based Policing Matrix (Lum et al., 2011; also see Veigas & Lum, 2013), which is a freely accessible, online visual representation of all moderate to rigorous studies on police crime control interventions (updated annually). Each intervention is mapped into a three-dimensional box according to its characteristics: the type and scope of the target of the interventions, the level of specificity of the intervention, and the extent to which the intervention is proactive. The shape and color of the icon representing the intervention indicate whether the study found that it is effective/the findings were mixed/there were no significant effects/the study revealed a significant backfire effect. Thus, clusters of studies indicate as to the characteristics of effective and ineffective practices. Moreover, a simple click on an intervention icon provides a short summary of the study and its findings. In short, the Matrix provides practitioners with a readily available database of high-quality studies assessing the effectiveness of various crime control interventions, a summary of their findings and the characteristics of the intervention, as well as indication as to the more general principles characterizing effective, ineffective, and harmful police practices.

Indeed, recent studies assessing police officers' receptivity to research in different contexts and countries often show that police express both familiarity with and support for EBP, suggesting that rational arguments in favor of EBP and attempts to make research evidence clear and accessible were not overlooked (Blaskovits et al., 2020; Fleming & Rhodes, 2018; Hunter et al., 2015; Jonathan-Zamir et al., 2019; Palmer, 2011; Telep, 2017; Telep & Lum, 2014; Telep & Winegar, 2015). Interestingly however, these same studies also report what appears to be a conflicting finding: despite valuing EBP, officers show a clear preference for relying on professional experience, not research evidence, when making decisions. For example, Telep and Lum (2014) surveyed nearly 1000 officers from three police agencies in the U.S., and found that the overwhelming majority (74%–89%) agreed or strongly agreed that collaboration with researchers is important for helping an agency reduce crime. At the same time, they also found that the most common response to a question about the appropriate balance between the use of scientific research and personal experience was 25%:75%, respectively.[1] These findings were replicated in a sample of chiefs and sheriffs from Oregon (Telep & Winegar, 2015) and in a Canadian study (Blaskovits et al., 2020). They are also in line with findings from surveys, interviews, and focus groups from the UK (Fleming & Rhodes, 2018; Hunter et al., 2015; Palmer, 2011).

The same tendency was also identified outside the English-speaking world. A recent survey of high-raking field officers from the Israel Police revealed much support for EBP, coupled with a strong inclination to rely on experience when making decisions (Jonathan-Zamir et al., 2019). On the one hand, over 60% of the officers disagreed with statements such as "Policing studies are often not about the core of police work"; "Most policing studies are not relevant to my work"; and "In the world of policing, research should be viewed as a luxury rather than a necessity," while only 7–16% agreed. On the other hand, when officers were asked to rank order what they think should be considered when making decisions at the unit/organization level, the value assigned most frequently to the "personal experience of the top command" consideration was "1," indicating that in the view of most officers, this should be the primary factor affecting decision-making. Research evidence was ranked after the personal experience and common sense of the top command, and, in the view of most officers, the further from the decision-making unit the study originates – the less effect it should have on decisions. While most policing studies were carried out in the United States, Europe, and Australia, 71%/82% of the officers expressed the view that they should have the least effect on decision making at the organization/unit level.

These studies clearly illustrate the science–experience paradox in policing: on the one hand, police officers are aware of relevant research evidence, value its potential contribution to their work, are happy to cooperate with research initiatives, and support the philosophy of EBP more generally. On the other hand, they prefer to rely on experience

---

[1] An interesting question is "what would an ideal split be?" For example, it may be that had the survey been carried out 5 or 10 years earlier, the most common response would have been 0%:100% in favor of personal experience. In that case, the 25%:75% split is in fact an improvement. But what split would satisfy proponents of EBP? A 50%:50% split? Perhaps 75%:25% in favor of EBP? In this section we merely present the findings showing a clear preference for personal experience over research evidence as the basis for decision-making. We reflect on the question of the "right" balance between experience and scientific evidence in the last section of the chapter.

when making real-world decisions.[2] The explanations offered in the policing literature for this paradox were based on the assumption that officers make rational choices within the policing environment. Willis and Mastrofski (2014), for example, argue that police would "continue to rely on experience, not science, to direct their practices" because "science does not solve 'their' most pressing problem" (p. 322). Indeed, in numerous areas (such as police recruitment and training, use of force, and perceived police legitimacy), criminology research has yet to produce a body of knowledge that enables prediction with high probability and sufficient strength to generate guidance for both what police should be doing and how they should be doing it (President's Task Force, 2015; Telep, 2016; Weisburd, & Majmundar, 2018). Lum and Koper (2017) claim that police persistently argue for the value of their "craft" to avoid forces, such as technology or scientific knowledge, from limiting their discretion and autonomy. Such explanations are insightful, but overlook the generality of the phenomenon. As reviewed below, the inclination to rely on experience when making decisions is not unique to policing. It characterizes professionals from various fields, which is not surprising given that it develops from familiar psychological mechanisms.

10.2 PRACTITIONERS' INCLINATION TO BASE DECISIONS ON PROFESSIONAL EXPERIENCE[3]

There is broad agreement in the literature that practitioners display a preference for basing professional decision-making on experience and intuition, even when scientific evidence is available and its value is recognized. This tendency, which is very much in line with Kahneman's (2011) argument regarding the preference for "fast thinking" (subjective, intuitive judgments – system I), over "slow thinking" (systematic, rigorous analysis – system II), was identified in diverse fields, such as medicine

---

[2] It should be noted that receptivity-to-research studies in policing have not focused on the organizational context in which officers express their views. While some have considered the size of the agency (e.g., Rojek et al., 2012; Telep & Lum, 2014) or the influence of an innovative leader (Jonathan-Zamir et al., 2019; Telep, 2017), we do not know how specific situations or challenges affect attitudes and preferences regarding EBP. It may be, for example, that officers in an agency that is satisfied with its achievements in fighting crime and with its relationship with the community would be less open to questioning their practices ("if it ain't broke don't fix it"). On the other hand, crises or failures may make police more receptive to innovations (e.g., Weisburd & Braga, 2006), including EBP. Nevertheless, to date, such hypotheses have not been tested.
[3] The literature review in this section is adopted from Jonathan-Zamir et al. (2019).

(Freeman & Sweeney, 2001; Hay et al., 2008; Swennen et al., 2013); psychiatry (Hannes et al., 2010); nursing (Mills et al., 2009); physical therapy (Schreiber & Stern, 2005); occupational therapy (Thomas & Law, 2013); psychology (Baker et al., 2008; Stewart et al., 2012); and human resources (Highhouse, 2008; Rynes et al., 2002; Terpstra, 1996).

The psychology literature provides important insight into this phenomenon. Ruscio (2010), for example, discusses judgment errors in clinical practice and notes that "clinicians' personal experience often exerts a strong influence on their judgments even when more reliable and valid information is available" (p. 301). He explains that because personal experience produces firsthand knowledge, it is often more emotionally resonant than the colorless scientific evidence reported in the literature, and thus more vivid. Vivid information, in turn, is more easily retrieved from memory. The availability heuristic (Tversky & Kahneman, 1973) leads one to believe that an experience that is easily recalled is frequent or highly likely. Thus, the vivid personal experience, which quickly came to mind, appears particularly relevant.

Giluk and Rynes (2012) argue that the tendency to trust personal experience stems from a combination of individuals' preference for "anecdotal evidence" – evidence in the form of "stories" (p. 140), coupled with a strong need to believe in one's own stories. They explain that people use stories to make sense of the world (Mink, 1978), and specific cases tend to influence people more than abstract probabilities (Kahneman & Tversky, 1973). To illustrate, they cite research demonstrating that when presented with statistical evidence followed by a contradictory example, individuals display a bias in favor of the example (the base-rate fallacy; see Allen et al., 2006).

But Giluk and Rynes (2012) take the argument a step further, proposing that personal experience is a particular type of "story," "one of the most powerful stories of all in terms of its ability to produce resistance to contradictory research evidence" (p. 141). The first reason for this is that individuals have the need to view themselves favorably, and thus think and behave in ways that maintain their positive self-image (e.g., Allport, 1955; Epstein, 1973; Steele, 1988). Research evidence that suggests to practitioners that their knowledge is incorrect, or that their methods are flawed, challenges their self-image and thus arouses the need to defend it. Second, people have the need for consistency between their attitudes and behavior. When the two conflict, individuals experience cognitive dissonance, which, in turn, triggers the need to adjust their attitudes to match their behavior (or vice versa) (Festinger, 1957). In other words, practitioners have the need to believe in what they do. Moreover, the risk of cognitive dissonance inhibits their ability to question the effectiveness of their practice (see comprehensive review by Giluk and Rynes, 2012).

Taking a somewhat different approach, Grove and Meehl (1996) discuss impressionistic versus mechanical prediction, and list several socio-psychological factors that, in their view, help explain the frequent preference for subjective, impressionistic prediction in various clinical settings: fear that "technology" (or science) would make practitioners unnecessary to the point of unemployment; threats to their self-image (which is often closely tied to their professional self-esteem); attachment to a particular "theory" about how the world works (threats to this "theory" may arouse cognitive dissonance); concern that actuarial, "technical" methods may be dehumanizing to their individual clients (they would produce cold, detached, and un-empathic treatment); resentment to the idea that computers (or science more generally) can outdo human cognitive performance; and finally poor education, which they argue "is probably the biggest single factor responsible for resistance to actuarial prediction" (Grove & Meehl, 1996, p. 318).

Finally, Highhouse (2008) offers an explanation based on the need to feel optimistic about the outcome of a decision. He builds on Einhorn (1986), who differentiates between the intuitive and analytical approaches to human prediction. The intuitive (or experience-based) approach reflects a deterministic view of the world, in which the idea that the future is inherently probabilistic is rejected. Thus, potential errors in predicting the outcome of a decision remain abstract and ambiguous. The analytical (or research-based) approach accepts uncertainty as inevitable, and thus, error is recognized and becomes an inherent part of the prediction. In turn, ambiguity about the likelihood of an outcome allows for more optimism than a known, low probability of success (Kuhn, 1997). In other words, relying on experience-based solutions with an unknown chance of success is attractive because it allows one to be more optimistic about the outcome, compared to a research-based solution with a known probability of failure.

In sum, the psychology literature suggests that the proclivity to rely on professional experience and common sense when making decisions, even when recognizing and valuing science, is rooted in various psychological needs and cognitive biases and heuristics, which influence everyone, including highly experienced practitioners. Personal experience is vivid, easily retrieved from memory, and thus appears particularly relevant. It makes sense because it is a "story" rather than "data," and people have a strong need to believe in these stories in order to preserve their favorable self-image and avoid dissonance between what they believe and what they do. For similar reasons, they are concerned that "technical" or "statistical" solutions would take over, making them unnecessary and/or their work impersonal and detached. Due to poor education, some may not fully recognize the value of scientific methods and the limitations of personal experience. Finally, practitioners are inclined to solutions with an unknown chance of failure, because it allows them to be more optimistic about the outcomes of their decisions.

10.3 WHAT ARE THE IMPLICATIONS FOR EVIDENCE-BASED POLICING?

The receptivity-to-research studies in policing and the psychology literature reviewed above lead to several conclusions that are the starting point for our discussion. First, on the rational level, police officers often do value EBP, recognize the importance of scientific evidence to their work, and are willing to cooperate with research initiatives. At the same time, when making real-world professional decisions, they show a contradictory preference for relying on experience and intuition. And they are not alone – the tendency to trust experience over science characterizes professionals from various disciplines, which is understandable given that it develops from inherent psychological mechanisms that are not necessarily influenced by rational reasoning. Thus, we argue that police officers' inclination to base decisions on experience and intuition is not likely to change on a large scale as a result of being rationally convinced that scientific evidence is "better" and "easy to use." This insight raises important questions about how proponents of EBP should go about promoting this philosophy. Below we review what we believe are the two main implications for the future of EBP.

10.3.1 "If You Can't Beat Them, Join Them": Make Science Part of the Experience

The first question we raise is pragmatic: is it possible to "make" officers place less weight on experience and more on scientific evidence when making decisions? The literature reviewed above suggests that the proclivity to rely on experience develops, in large part, from deep-rooted psychological mechanisms that are not necessarily rational or easily susceptible to change. If we accept that the tendency to rely on experience is "a fact of life," it will likely be more useful to try to strengthen (rather than suppress), the intuition/experience based information processing system, by making the content of officers' experience and intuition more reliable and aligned with scientific evidence. This proposition is in line with Lum and Koper's (2017) argument that police "experience" or "craft" are not magical or immutable. They develop from daily tasks, policies, procedures, and organizational structures and rules. If these change – the content of one's experiences change. Thus, science can be made part of the "experience" and "intuition."

How can this be accomplished? We propose that given the psychological significance of knowledge that is acquired firsthand (Ruscio, 2010), police training and other reform initiatives should be structured around officers fully experiencing EBP, that is, gaining direct, personal experience both in the process of scientific reasoning, and in implementing policing practices that were found to be effective. Thus, when they fall back on their experience, evidence-based approaches (such as hot spots policing; see Weisburd, & Majmundar, 2018), would be the first thing that comes to mind. While police training today may involve simulations and real-world experience (e.g., Kringen & Kringen, 2017; Litmanovitz, 2016), the strategies and tactics officers are trained for are often *not* based on scientific evidence or academic knowledge, and training curricula typically do *not* include the principles of scientific inquiry (Chan et al., 2003; Hanak & Hofinger, 2005; Weisburd & Neyroud, 2011).

Our proposition is consistent with the "experience-based learning" approach (e.g., Andresen et al., 2000) and the idea of "intuitive expertise" in organizations (Hodgkinson et al., 2009). "Experience-based learning" (or "experiential learning") views experience as the basis for all learning. It is holistic, in the sense that it involves learners' intellect, feelings and senses, and invokes perceptions, awareness, and values. It builds on learners' earlier experiences to construct meaning and integrate the present experience into their understanding and values, through a process of debriefing and reflective thought (see Kolb, 2015). In the context of intuition in organizations, Hodgkinson et al. (2009, p. 287) have argued for the development of "intuitive expertise," which "enables decision makers to frame problems rapidly and identify the appropriate course of action long before they are able to articulate their reasoning as to why that course of action is appropriate." Intuitive expertise "is not attained merely through the successful completion of a formal…qualification and/or limited on the job experience; on the contrary, it requires a blending of conceptual/analytical knowledge, probably best gained in the classroom, with experiential knowledge, gained through years of exposure to challenging problems in the workplace. In other words, formal... education needs to be allied to a programme of ongoing professional development. Deliberate practice, accompanied by candid but constructive, feedback is the order of the day."

An example of this can be found in the New Haven Police Department, where recruits learned "community policing" by experiencing it. In addition to regular, lecture-based academy training, they were required to complete 40 hours of community service and take part in a community project while attending the academy. Qualitative, in-depth interviews with recruits revealed substantial community orientation and much support for community policing (Kringen & Kringen, 2017). In sum, rather than trying to suppress officers' natural psychological tendency to rely on experience by persuading them that it is not a reliable source for decisions, we propose to accept the inclination to trust experience, build on it, and make scientific reasoning, as well as scientifically sound practices, part of that experience.

The training approach we are proposing entails another important benefit. In their efforts to promote EBP, Shepherd (2001) and Weisburd and Neyroud (2011) advocate for "university policing centers" (Weisburd & Neyroud, 2011, p. 14), which follow the model of university teaching hospitals in medicine: practitioners and researchers are trained together, which allows them to gain shared understanding of both the science and practice of their field. Thus, police researchers would become familiar with their research environment and would be in a better position to identify the questions that are relevant to real-world policing, and practitioners would have better appreciation of research evidence and its potential contribution to their work. However, as noted by Weisburd and Neyroud (2011), there are many impediments to this vision, including the fact that police agencies often do not require any academic education beyond high school for employment. Police unions have also resisted attempts to introduce a bachelor's requirement in policing. Structuring police training around officers fully experiencing both the process of scientific inquiry and the implementation of policing strategies and tactics that were found to be effective, can be a realistic, intermediate approach that provides some of the benefits of university policing centers until this vision can be more fully achieved.

Beyond "injecting" evidence-based practices into officers' experience thus making them readily available, we expect that using these practices would allow officers to directly observe their benefits rather than simply accept scientists' claims. We do recognize, however, an important caveat to this proposition: police may not be able to see the outcomes of their actions, either because they are preoccupied with handling the immediate situation or because the effects may not appear instantly. Technological developments may prove to be of great value in in this regard. For example, computerized programs tracking calls for service or crime data could allow officers to follow the outcomes of their actions over time. In this sense, any intuitive assumptions they may have about the consequences would be contrasted with objective data (Litmanovitz et al., this volume). With regard to immediate outcomes, footages from body-worn cameras could assist officers in reflecting on their behavior and choices in specific encounters and evaluating their direct effects. Thus, they could assess for themselves if procedural justice, for example, produced immediate desirable responses, such as citizen satisfaction, compliance, and cooperation (Willis & Mastrofski, 2014).

10.3.2 Acknowledge the Roles of Both Science and Experience in Successful Policing

The second question to address is normative: is the proclivity to rely on experience "good" or "bad?" Should there be a place for experience *and* intuition-based decision-making in evidence-based policy? Scholars are of two minds (Rousseau & Gunia, 2016). Some view the inclination to base professional decision-making on experience as a major obstacle to the successful implementation of evidence-based policy. Ruscio (2010), for example, claims that "(t)o grant center stage to one's personal experience...can be to devalue the more informative collective experience of many other clinicians who have worked with a much larger and broader sample..." (p. 301). He explains that generalizing from personal experience violates the principles of scientific reasoning: it is unclear what the sample of one's experiences represents and how much or what type of "data" is missing due to memory limitations and biases; "conditions" of treatment were not "assigned" randomly; the reliability and validity of the outcomes as recalled from memory are questionable; and the "analysis" is vulnerable to illusory correlations, while real relationships that are subtle or counterintuitive may go unnoticed. In this context, Sherman (2013, p. 428) summarizes Meehl's (1954) comparison of actuarial and clinical methods of prediction by noting that "statistically validated predictions were always either more accurate than clinical prediction or – at worst – just as good, at a much lower cost."

In the context of policing, Lum and Koper (2017) have argued that experience can often be overvalued, and given the high levels of discretion that characterize the profession, it can impend receptivity to outside knowledge and change. This becomes particularly problematic when research evidence contradicts conventional wisdom. Similar arguments were made by other proponents of EBP (e.g., Lum 2009; Sherman, 1984, 1998).

On the other hand, some researchers have argued for the importance of "expertise-based intuition," developed through extensive practice and experience. For example, based on vast literature on human cognition, Salas et al., (2010, p. 945) clarify the distinction between two information processing systems (which often interact): an "intuitive" system, that is "fast, holistic, and does not require conscious cognitive effort" [e.g., Kahneman's (2011) system I] and a "conscious deliberative" system, that is "slower, analytic, and cognitively effortful" [e.g., Kahneman's (2011) system II]. Their review of the literature suggests that, in contrast to the above arguments, there are conditions under which the intuitive system is more likely to be accurate: among more experienced practitioners (as long as this experience was accompanied by feedback); when the present situation falls within the experience domain of the decision-maker; when the task is complex (for example, the definition of "success" is ambiguous); and when the environment is characterized by stressors, such as time pressure.

In the context of policing, Muir (1977) argued that while officers frequently use their experience, this does not mean that they do so in a haphazard, unstructured manner. He observes that police frequently employ systematic, calculated thinking in organizing previous experiences into "concepts," or "classifications" (p. 153), which help them identify the nature of a problem and how best to respond. Further, they carefully prepare "experiments" to test their "hypotheses" about the nature of the situation. For example, they may form hypotheses about the intentions of specific individuals and test them using techniques, such as creating distractions and inducing reactions.

Willis (2013) echoes early propositions by Bayley and Bittner (1984) about the importance of the policing "craft," and provides a thoughtful discussion on "what might be a good marriage" (p. 4) between this craft, which includes capabilities developed through personal experience, and the science of policing. He argues that unlike strict scientific evidence, the policing craft enables creativity and flexibility in matching responses both to the particulars of the situation, and to the skills and personal traits of the responding officer, such as level of experience and verbal facility. Additionally, police are often expected to accomplish numerous goals beyond crime control (which has traditionally been the focus of scientific inquiry), such as responsiveness to the victim, ensuring safety at the scene, preventing escalation, and more broadly – equity, legitimacy, liberty, and other public values. Science is often silent about the best way to achieve such outcomes, and thus, there is no substitute for officers' professional experience (also see Willis & Mastrofski, 2014).

We argue that given the potential benefits of both information processing systems, coupled with the intrinsic nature of the inclination to rely on experience, it would be useful for policing scholars to begin viewing scientific evidence and professional experience not as conflicting viewpoints, but as elements that have to be combined for successful policing (e.g., Sherman, 2013; Willis & Mastrofski, 2014; Willis, 2013), because this perspective would open the door for considering exactly what their roles should be. Such attempts have already begun in other fields, such as critical care medicine (Tonelli et al., 2012).

One proposition is to differentiate between levels of decision-making when thinking about the optimal information processing system. It may be that when making tactical decisions at the street level, in complex situations under varying degrees of stress and time pressure, patrol officers should be encouraged to trust their experience and intuition (which would ideally form based on education, on-the-job experiences, and feedback that have all developed on the basis of scientific evidence). Assuming the officers exercise "intuitive expertise" (Hodgkinson et al., 2009), the benefits of the fast, holistic, and relatively effortless processing system appear to outweigh its limitations in this context. At the same time, when making strategic decision at the agency or unit level, high-ranking officers should be encouraged to rely on the best available evidence, including the literature and in-house assessments (Sherman, 1998). Decision-making at this level should allow for the slower, analytic, and cognitively effortful processes.

10.4 CONCLUSIONS

No matter how rational or convincing researchers' arguments may be, they are unlikely to be successful in making police officers at large abandon their intuitive inclination to rely on experience when making professional decisions. This understanding suggests a different approach to the dissemination of EBP, one that does not go against the natural tendency to rely on experience, but works with it. There is no harm, of course, in making rational arguments in favor of EBP and seeking ways to make research evidence relevant, clear, and accessible to practitioners. But policing scholars should recognize that such efforts, which may well change general orientations toward EBP, are unlikely to make a large-scale change to the way decisions are made in the field. Acknowledging the dominant role that experience will likely continue to play in police decision-making, we propose to focus efforts on influencing police officers' experiences by making their content in line with research evidence. Thus, while police continue to rely on experience, it would be infused with scientifically sound practices and a systematic way of thinking. Further, we argue that scholars should recognize that in some situations, quick, intuition-based decision-making may be superior to the slow, analytic, information processing system. Thus, instead of framing science versus experience in terms of "good" versus "bad," proponents of EBP should seek to provide police practitioners with more nuanced, evidence-based advice on the circumstances in which each of these information processing systems would likely lead to better outcomes.

References

Allen, M., Preiss, R. W., & Gayle, B. M. (2006). Meta-analytic examination of the base-rate fallacy. *Communication Research Reports, 23*, 45–51.

Allport, G. W. (1955). *Becoming*. Yale University Press.

Andresen, L., Boud, D., & Cohen, R. (2000). Experience-based learning. In G. Foley (Ed.), *Understanding adult education and training* (second edition, pp. 225–239). Allen & Unwin.

Baker, T. B., McFall, R. M., & Shoham, V. (2008). Current status and future prospects of clinical psychology: Toward a scientifically principled approach to mental and behavioral health care. *Psychological Science in the Public Interest, 9*(2), 67–103.

Bayley, D. H., & Bittner, E. (1984). Learning the skills of policing. *Law & Contemporary Problems, 47*, 35–59.

Blaskovits, B., Bennell, C., Huey, L., Kalyal, H., Walker, T., & Javala, S. (2020). A Canadian replication of Telep and Lum's (2014) examination of police officers' receptivity to empirical research. *Policing and Society, 30*(3), 276–294. https://doi.org/10.1080/10439463.2018.1522315.

Chan, J., Devery, C. & Doran, S. (2003). *Fair cop: Learning the art of policing*. University of Toronto Press.

Einhorn, H. J. (1986). Accepting error to make less error. *Journal of Personality Assessment, 50*, 387–395.

Epstein, S. (1973). The self-concept revisited: Of a theory of a theory. *American Psychologist, 28*, 404–416.

Festinger, L. (1957). *A theory of cognitive dissonance*. Row Peterson.

Fleming, J., & Rhodes, R. (2018). Can experience be evidence? Craft knowledge and evidence-based policing. *Policy & Politics, 46*(1), 3–26.

Freeman, A. C., & Sweeney, K. (2001). Why general practitioners do not implement evidence: Qualitative study. *BMJ, 323*, 1–5.

Giluk, T. L., & Rynes, S. L. (2012). Research findings practitioners resist: Lessons for management academics from evidence-based medicine. In D. M. Rousseau (Ed.), *The Oxford hand-book of evidence-based management* (pp. 130–164). Oxford University Press.

Grove, W. M., & Meehl, P. E. (1996). Comparative efficiency of informal (subjective, impressionistic) and formal (mechanical, algorithmic) prediction procedures: The clinical–statistical controversy. *Psychology, Public Policy, and Law, 2*(2), 293.

Hanak, G., & Hofinger, V. (2005). Police science and research in the European Union. In J. Fehérváry, G. Hanak, V. Hofinger & G. Stummvoll (Eds.), *Theory and practice of police research in Europe: Contributions and presentations from CEPOL Police Research & Science Conferences 2003–2005* (pp. 51–66). European Police College.

Hannes, K., Pieters, G., Goedhuys, J., & Aertgeerts, B. (2010). Exploring barriers to the implementation of evidence-based practice in psychiatry to inform health policy: A focus group based study. *Community Mental Health Journal, 46*(5), 423–432.

Hay, M. C., Weisner, T. S., Subramanian, S., Duan, N., Niedzinski, E. J., & Kravitz, R. L. (2008). Harnessing experience: Exploring the gap between evidence-based medicine and clinical practice. *Journal of Evaluation in Clinical Practice, 14*(5), 707–713.

Highhouse, S. (2008). Stubborn reliance on intuition and subjectivity in employee selection. *Industrial and Organizational Psychology, 1*(3), 333–342.

Hodgkinson, G. P., Sadler-Smith, E., Burke, L. A., Claxton, G., & Sparrow, P. R. (2009). Intuition in organizations: Implications for strategic management. *Long Range Planning, 42*(3), 277–297.

Hunter, G., Wigzell, A., May, T. & McSweeney, T. (2015). *An evaluation of the 'What Works Centre for Crime Reduction.' Year 1: Baseline*. Institute for Criminal Policy Research.

Jonathan-Zamir, T., Weisburd, D., Dayan, M., & Zisso, M. (2019). The proclivity to rely on professional experience and evidence-based policing: Findings from a survey of high-ranking officers in the Israel Police. *Criminal Justice and Behavior, 46*(10), 1456–1474.

Kahneman D. (2011). *Thinking, fast and slow*. Macmillan.

Kahneman, D. & Tversky, A. (1973). On the psychology of prediction. *Psychological Review, 80*, 237–251.

Kolb, D. A. (2015). *Experiential learning: Experience as the source of learning and development (second edition)*. Pearson Education.

Kringen, A.L., & Kringen, J.A. (2017). Outside the academy: Learning community policing through community engagement. *Ideas in American Policing, 20* (July 2017). www.policefoundation.org/publication/outside-the-academy-learning-community-policing-through-community-engagement/

Kuhn, K. (1997). Communicating uncertainty: Framing effects on responses to vague probabilities. *Organizational Behavior and Human Decision Processes*, 71, 55–83.

Litmanovitz, Y. D. (2016). *Moving towards an evidence-base of democratic police training: The development and evaluation of a complex social intervention in the Israeli Border Police* [Unpublished Doctoral dissertation]. University of Oxford.

Litmanovitz, Y., Weisburd, D., & Hasisi, B. (this volume). Implementing Evidence-Based Policing: Findings from a Process Evaluation of the EMUN Reform in the Israel Police. In D. Weisburd, T. Jonathan, G. Perry & B. Hasisi, (Eds.), *The Future of Evidence-Based Policing*. Cambridge University Press.

Lum, C. (2009). Translating police research into practice. *Ideas in American Policing*, 11.

Lum, C., & Koper, C. S. (2017). *Evidence-based policing: Translating research into practice*. Oxford University Press.

Lum, C., Koper, C., & Telep, C. W. (2011). The evidence-based policing matrix. *Journal of Experimental Criminology*, 7, 3–26.

Meehl, P. E. (1954). *Clinical vs. statistical prediction: A theoretical analysis and a review of the evidence*. University of Minnesota Press.

Mills, J., Field, J., & Cant, R. (2009). The place of knowledge and evidence in the context of Australian general practice nursing. *Worldviews on Evidence-Based Nursing*, 6(4), 219–228.

Mink, L. O. (1978). Narrative form as a cognitive instrument. In R. H. Canary & H. Kozicki (Eds.), *The writing of history: Literary form and historical understanding* (pp. 129–149). University of Wisconsin Press.

Muir, W.K. (1977) *Police: Streetcorner politicians*. University of Chicago Press.

Palmer, I. (2011). *Is the United Kingdom Police Service receptive to evidence-based policing? Testing attitudes towards experimentation* [Unpublished master's thesis]. University of Cambridge.

President's Task Force on 21st Century Policing. (2015). *Final report*. U.S. Department of Justice.

Rojek, J., Alpert, G., & Smith, H. (2012). The utilization of research by the police. *Police Practice & Research: An International Journal*, 13, 329–341.

Rousseau, D. M., & Gunia, B. C. (2016). Evidence-based practice: The psychology of evidence-based policing implementation. *Annual Review of Psychology*, 67, 667–692.

Ruscio, J. (2010). Irrational beliefs stemming from judgment errors: Cognitive limitations, biases, and experiential learning. In D. David, S. J. Lynn, & A. Ellis (Eds.), *Rational and irrational beliefs: Research, theory, and clinical practice* (pp. 291–312). Oxford University Press.

Rynes, S. L., Colbert, A. E., & Brown, K. G. (2002). HR professionals' beliefs about effective human resource practices: Correspondence between research and practice. *Human Resources Management*, 41, 149–174.

Salas, E., Rosen, M. A., & DiazGranados, D. (2010). Expertise-based intuition and decision making in organizations. *Journal of Management*, 36(4), 941–973.

Schreiber, J., & Stern, P. (2005). A review of the literature on evidence-based practice in physical therapy. *Internet Journal of Allied Health Sciences and Practice*, 3(4), 2–10.

Shepherd, J. P. (2001). Emergency medicine and police collaboration to prevent community violence. *Annals of Emergency Medicine, 38*(4), 430–437.

Sherman, L. W. (1984). Experiments in police discretion: Scientific boon or dangerous knowledge? *Law and Contemporary Problems, 47*, 61–81.

Sherman, L. W. (1998). *Evidence-based policing.* Police Foundation. www.policefoundation.org/wp-content/uploads/2015/06/Sherman-1998-Evidence-Based-Policing.pdf

Sherman, L. W. (2013). The rise of evidence-based policing: Targeting, testing, and tracking. *Crime and Justice, 42*(1), 377–451.

Sherman, L. W. (2015). A tipping point for "totally evidenced policing": Ten ideas for building an evidence-based police agency. *International Criminal Justice Review, 25*(1), 11–29.

Steele, C. M. (1988). The psychology of self-affirmation: Sustaining the integrity of the self. In L. Berkowitz (Ed.), *Advances in experimental social psychology* (Vol. 21, pp. 261–302). Academic Press.

Stewart, R. E., Stirman, S. W., & Chambless, D. L. (2012). A qualitative investigation of practicing psychologists' attitudes toward research-informed practice: Implications for dissemination strategies. *Professional Psychology: Research and Practice, 43*(2), 100.

Swennen, M. H., van der Heijden, G. J., Boeije, H. R., van Rheenen, N., Verheul, F. J., van der Graaf, Y., & Kalkman, C. J. (2013). Doctors' perceptions and use of evidence-based medicine: A systematic review and thematic synthesis of qualitative studies. *Academic Medicine, 88*(9), 1384–1396.

Telep, C. W. (2016). Expanding the scope of evidence-based policing. *Criminology & Public Policy, 15*(1), 243–252.

Telep, C. W. (2017). Police officer receptivity to research and evidence-based policing: Examining variability within and across agencies. *Crime & Delinquency, 63*(8), 976–999.

Telep, C. W., & Lum, C. (2014). The receptivity of officers to empirical research and evidence-based policing: An examination of survey data from three agencies. *Police Quarterly, 17*(4), 359–385.

Telep, C. W., & Winegar, S. (2015). Police executive receptivity to research: A survey of chiefs and sheriffs in Oregon. *Policing: A Journal of Policy and Practice, 10*(3), 241–249.

Terpstra, D. E. (1996). The search for effective methods. *HR Focus, 73*, 16–17.

Thomas, A., & Law, M. (2013). Research utilization and evidence-based practice in occupational therapy: A scoping study. *American Journal of Occupational Therapy, 67*(4), e55–e65.

Tonelli, M. R., Curtis, J. R., Guntupalli, K. K., Rubenfeld, G. D., Arroliga, A. C., Brochard, L., Douglas, I. S., Gutterman, D. D., Hall, J. R., Kavanagh, B. P., Mancebo, J., Misak, C. J., Simpson, S. Q., Slutsky, A. S., Suffredini, A. F., Thompson, B. T., Ware, L. B., Wheeler, A. P., & Levy, M. M. (2012). An Official Multi-Society Statement: The Role of Clinical Research Results in the Practice of Critical Care Medicine. *American Journal of Respiratory and Critical Care Medicine, 185*(10), 1117–1124. https://doi.org/10.1164/rccm.201204-0638ST

Tversky, A., & Kahneman, D. (1973). Availability: A heuristic for judging frequency and probability. *Cognitive Psychology, 5*, 207–232.

Veigas, H., & Lum, C. (2013). Assessing the evidence base of a police service patrol portfolio. *Policing: A Journal of Policy and Practice, 7*(3), 248–262.

Weisburd, D., & Braga, A. A. (2006). Introduction: Understanding police innovation. In D. Weisburd and A. A. Braga (Eds.), *Police innovation: Contrasting perspectives* (pp. 1–26). Cambridge University Press.

Weisburd, D. & Majmundar, K. (Eds.) (2018). *Proactive policing: Effects on crime and communities.* National Academies Press.

Weisburd, D., & Neyroud, P. (2011). Police science: Toward a new paradigm. *New Perspectives in Policing, January.*

Willis, J. J. (2013). Improving police: What's craft got to do with it? *Ideas in American Policing, 16.*

Willis, J. J., & Mastrofski, S. D. (2014). Pulling together: Integrating craft and science. *Policing: A Journal of Policy and Practice, 8*(4), 321–329.

Wilson, J. Q. (1978). *Varieties of police behavior: The management of law and order in eight communities.* Harvard University Press.

11

Implementing Evidence-Based Policing

Findings from a Process Evaluation of the EMUN Reform in the Israel Police

Yael Litmanovitz, David Weisburd, and Badi Hasisi

Throughout the last decade, experimental and quasi-experimental research in the field of policing and crime reduction has gained ground and recognition (Mazerolle & Neyroud, 2020; Weisburd, 2003; Weisburd & Majimundar, 2018). However, Evidence-Based Policing (EBP) is about more than conducting high-quality research. It is an approach to practicing policing aimed at producing "the best results" (Sherman, 2002, p. 231) by giving scientific research "a 'seat at the table' of law enforcement decision making about tactics, strategies and policies" (Lum & Koper, 2017, p. 4). In other words, implementation of research findings into the work of police agencies is integral to EBP. Some theoretical literature has addressed how EBP might be promoted in police organizations. Scholars have explored the role of professional and organizational identity (Sherman, 2015); the exercise of agency by the police in producing and consuming scientific research (Weisburd & Neyroud, 2011; Neyroud & Weisburd this volume); and the potential for creating research products that can be easily applied by police organizations and officers in the field (Lum & Koper, 2017; Koper & Lum, 2012).

However, not many studies have allowed us to examine the implementation of EBP as an organization-wide practice. There has been little empirical examination of the factors that enable successful, quality implementation of EBP as a way of "doing" policing. How is evidence transmitted from a research report to the front lines of the police service? What actions should organizations take to promote "what works"-oriented decision-making? Which organizational systems need to be reconfigured or refocused or built up from scratch? Investigating these questions is a crucial step toward making EBP a reality.

This chapter attempts to bridge the existing gap in the literature. It focuses on the implementation of EBP as an organizational practice and aims to advance understanding of how to make it part of the business-as-usual of police organizations. It proposes essential elements for implementing EBP, which were identified through a mixed-methods evaluation of an organizational reform in the Israel Police (IP). The EMUN reform, launched in 2016, incorporated EBP approaches into the IP's operations. As we have documented elsewhere, the reform has had a significant impact on crime. There was a meaningful reduction in property crime and traffic-related offences in police stations that used the EMUN approach to deal with these offences, as compared to those that did not (Weisburd et al., 2020; Hasisi et al., 2019).

In this chapter, we present the findings of the process evaluation of the EMUN reform, looking beyond the crime-related outcomes of the reform to assess how it was implemented. These qualitative findings allow us to go beyond declaring evidence-based practice in policing is effective, by identifying catalyzers and barriers to the successful implementation of EBP. It should be noted that this chapter does not focus on how well the EMUN reform was implemented (though this was assessed as part of the study, and reported to the IP). Rather, our objective is to draw more general lessons from the findings.

The chapter begins with a review of the literature, highlighting organizational factors from policing, medicine, and social work that have been identified as enabling or disrupting the adoption of evidence-based practice. We then describe in detail the reform at the center of our study: we explain how it used a combination of evidence-based approaches to shape police work, and describe the results of the impact evaluation. Finally, we turn to the methodology and findings of the process evaluation, which examined the implementation of EMUN across four crime categories (property crime, traffic-related offences, violence, and gun crime).

Based on a thematic analysis of the data, we identify three overarching themes associated with a heightened capability to practice evidence-based policing. First, a crime analysis and program assessment system that enables officers to understand the crime data, and tests the effectiveness of policing responses. Second, organizational flexibility in allocating resources, in working across organizational boundaries, and in making professional decisions. Third, ownership and engagement with the process and outcomes of policing, which is expressed in three ways: a shift in the meaning of success, ownership of crime reduction goals across the ranks, and engagement with the reform at the local level. Our findings, which strongly resonate with the existing literature, have potentially wide-reaching implications for practicing and promoting evidence-based policing.

11.1 REVIEW: THE ROLE OF IMPLEMENTATION IN EVIDENCE-BASED POLICING AND BEYOND

In criminology, as in medicine, the mere existence of an evidence base does not ensure its smooth transfer or translation into practice (Nutley et al., 2007; Sherman, 2009; Weisburd & Hasisi, 2018). There is little dispute that effort must be invested in creating a rigorous evidence base (Chalmers et al., 1992). But for this evidence to become standard practice there needs to also be solid understanding of effective implementation approaches (Kitson et al., 1998; Rycroft-Malone, 2004; Ubbink et al., 2013).

Nutley and her colleagues explore this issue of evidence translation into public organizations in the fields of health and criminal justice (Nutley et al., 2007; Nutley et al., 2009). They propose three main models of research use: a "research-based practitioner model," in which practitioners lead the implementation; the "organizational excellence model," in which the organization is a site of experimentation and generates research; and finally the "embedded research model," in which evidence-based procedures and interventions "become embedded in systems, processes, and standards" (Nutley et al., 2009, p. 555). In this third model, research insights enter practice through the actions of managers and policy makers. This third model appears highly suited to the policing environment.

Lum and Koper (2017) provide an extensive discussion of how to implement EBP in police organizations, recognizing the fundamental adjustments that this requires. They draw on the work of Nutley and her colleagues (2007), and on their own experiences with the EBP Matrix demonstration project (Koper & Lum, 2012), to propose a framework of four organizational "systems" through which evidence-based policing can be institutionalized. The first of these is the professional development system of police organizations: training (at all levels) should include both the necessary knowledge (i.e., the theory of the concentration of crime in place, see Weisburd, 2015) and the necessary skills of relevance. The second system is the de-facto deployment of officers "in the field." In order to ensure that police work is aligned with evidence, research findings should be translated into work protocols that relate to all aspects of police work. For example, deployment of police officers in crime hotspots should be based on the Koper Curve principles. The third system concerns the crime analysis capabilities of police organizations. The analysis "products" can be powerful tools for police managers. They can be used to identify crime trends, and to measure the impact of interventions on crime, quality of life, and public trust. The fourth system is that of management in the wider sense, which includes supervision, strategic planning, and leadership.

While both Nutely et al.'s (2009) and Lum & Koper's (2017) theoretical models are valuable for designing organizational reform, there is still a gap in the empirical literature regarding what works in implementation of EBP. Empirical studies have so far focused on two issues. First, studies on the *receptivity to research* of police officers, which investigate their willingness to rely on research evidence (Jonathan-Zamir et al., 2019; Lum et al., 2012). Second, studies examining the *implementation fidelity* of particular evidence-based interventions or policing approaches; these studies are essentially concerned with the feasibility of such interventions, as they assess whether an intervention/approach, including all its core ingredients, was delivered as intended (Century et al., 2010; Neyroud et al., 2017). While both strands of research can inform understanding of evidence-based practice in police organizations, they cannot replace studies examining the implementation of EBP directly.

Turning to other fields for answers is of partial benefit, since the issue of implementing evidence-based practice at the organizational level is underdeveloped outside of policing as well. Existing research relies mostly on cross-sectional data (i.e., self-report questionnaires). The organization is rarely the focus of research but mostly studied as the context in which individual practitioners operate (Barzkar et al., 2018; Ubbink et al., 2013; but see, e.g., Draaisma et al., 2018); it is usually framed as the factor barring evidence-based practice (Gray et al., 2013; van Dijk et al., 2010).

The most prominent barriers identified in health organizations are a lack of autonomy and a lack of incentives for professionals to change existing practices toward evidence-supported ones (Williams et al., 2015). Research in social work has identified similar barriers: inadequate agency resources, an inflexible management system, and an organizational culture that stifles attempts to step outside existing practice and provides no organizational training or support in research translation (Gray et al., 2013, 2015).

Taken together, the findings point to the futility of holding street-level practitioners responsible – against the will of the wider organization – for aligning practice and evidence. The findings also serve as a reminder of the powerful role of the organizational context in the success of a reform. We now turn to describing an evidence-oriented reform promoted by the organization itself. While such top-down reforms have shortcomings (Worden & McLean, 2017), our findings show the organization can play a meaningful role in realizing EBP.

11.2 THE STUDY: AN EVALUATION OF THE EMUN REFORM IN THE ISRAEL POLICE

In 2018, the Institute of Criminology at the Hebrew University of Jerusalem was commissioned by the Israel Police (IP) to carry out an evaluation study of the EMUN reform. Initiated in 2016 by Commissioner Roni Alsheich, it included some drastic changes in organizational terms, by openly drawing on the evidence-base available in policing (Weisburd et al., 2020). A central goal of EMUN (which, in Hebrew, means "trust") was to improve public trust by increasing effectiveness and focusing on local problems.

While the Israel Police is a national organization, with a centralized, hierarchical command structure (Shitrit, 2019), in many aspects it is quite similar to other police forces in Western democracies. It must contend with the same fundamental issues: questions of effectiveness in reducing crime and increasing safety (Aviv & Weisburd, 2016), relations with minorities (Ben-Porat et al., 2012), and public debates concerning the legitimacy and (mis)use of force (Perry & Jonathan-Zamir, 2020). As such, it has been shown to provide generalizable lessons beyond this context (e.g. Jonathan-Zamir et al., 2019).

The EMUN study included two strands of research: an impact evaluation to assess the effectiveness of the reform in reducing and preventing crime, and a qualitative process evaluation to assess its implementation. The impact evaluation, which utilized a quasi-randomized design, found significant reductions in property crime and traffic-related offences. There was a meaningful reduction in these offences in the stations that used the EMUN approach, compared to those that did not (Weisburd et al., 2020; Hasisi et al., 2019). These findings provide support for the feasibility and value of evidence-based practice in policing in Israel.

The process evaluation allows us to go beyond this claim, and to understand what organizational or reform characteristics might promote EBP.

Because the EMUN reform incorporated several policing approaches that are strongly supported by experimental research, it provides an opportunity to study this issue systematically. Problem-oriented policing provides the framework for the reform (Hinkle et al., 2020), and several other approaches – hotspots policing (Braga et al., 2019), situational prevention (Bowers & Johnson, 2016), third-party policing (Mazerolle & Ransley, 2019), and community policing (Gill et al., 2014) – are embedded within it as supporting strategies.

The core operational idea of the reform is that each police station across the country (80 at the present time) identify three local crime or disorder problems as part of their yearly work plan, and focus efforts and resources on dealing with them; this is an embodiment of problem-oriented policing. In line with community-oriented policing principles, the problem had to be defined as significant not only by the stations' leaders but also by the local citizens (as determined by a representative survey of these citizens). This departs from the IP's traditional modus operandi, in which stations needed to direct their efforts at long lists of crime statistics that reflected the "national priorities"[1] (Kadosh, 2015).

As we have demonstrated elsewhere (Weisburd et al., 2020), EMUN institutionalized the four elements of the SARA model of problem-oriented policing: scanning, analysis, response, and assessment (Cordner & Biebel, 2005). Stations devoted time during the last quarter of the year to *scanning* for local problems within several broad categories: property crime, violence, gun crime, traffic-related offences, noise disturbances, etc. For their choices to be approved by the district and national command, stations were required to conduct an in-depth *analysis* of the problem. The analysis relied on crime data, augmented by local knowledge of the station's personnel. The central method for this was the creation of a crime analysis system, which was widely available and easy to use. It was introduced simultaneously with the reform and given the same name ("the EMUN system").

Place-based policing was an additional building block within the reform. Each problem that was chosen by the stations was not just a problem category (i.e., "property crime") but a specific problem occurring in a specific location (i.e., burglary of private residences in the Flowers neighborhood of South-Ville, as seen in Figure 11.1, screenshot 2).

---

[1] There is one exception to this: all the stations had to include traffic accidents in their list of yearly problems. This reflected the commissioner's and the minister's decision to address this issue.

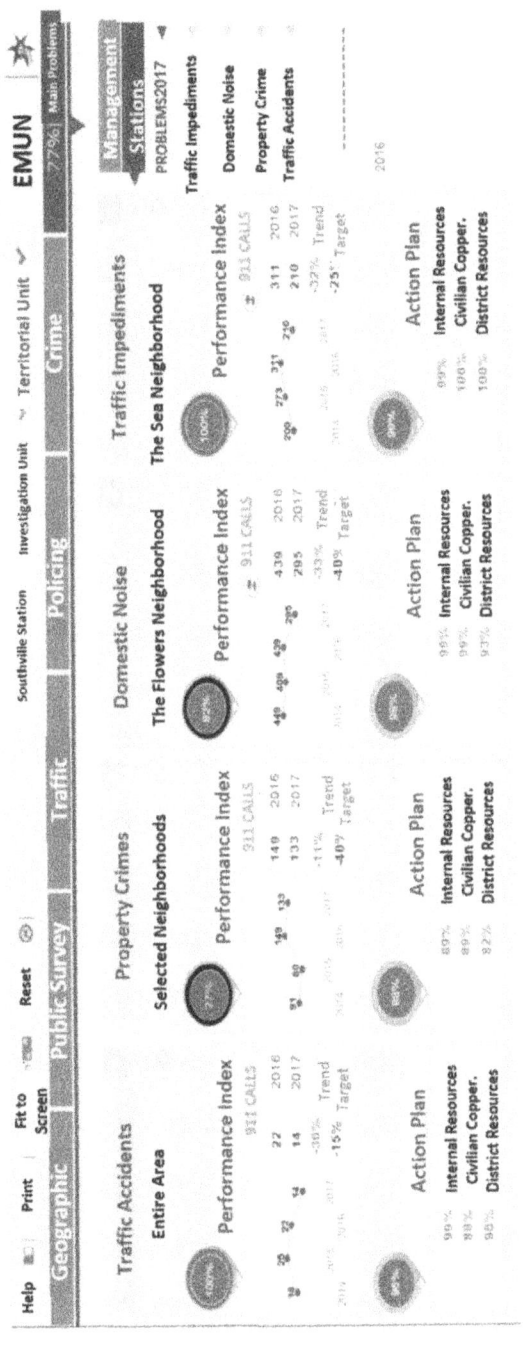

FIGURE 11.1 Screenshots of the EMUN crime analysis computer system

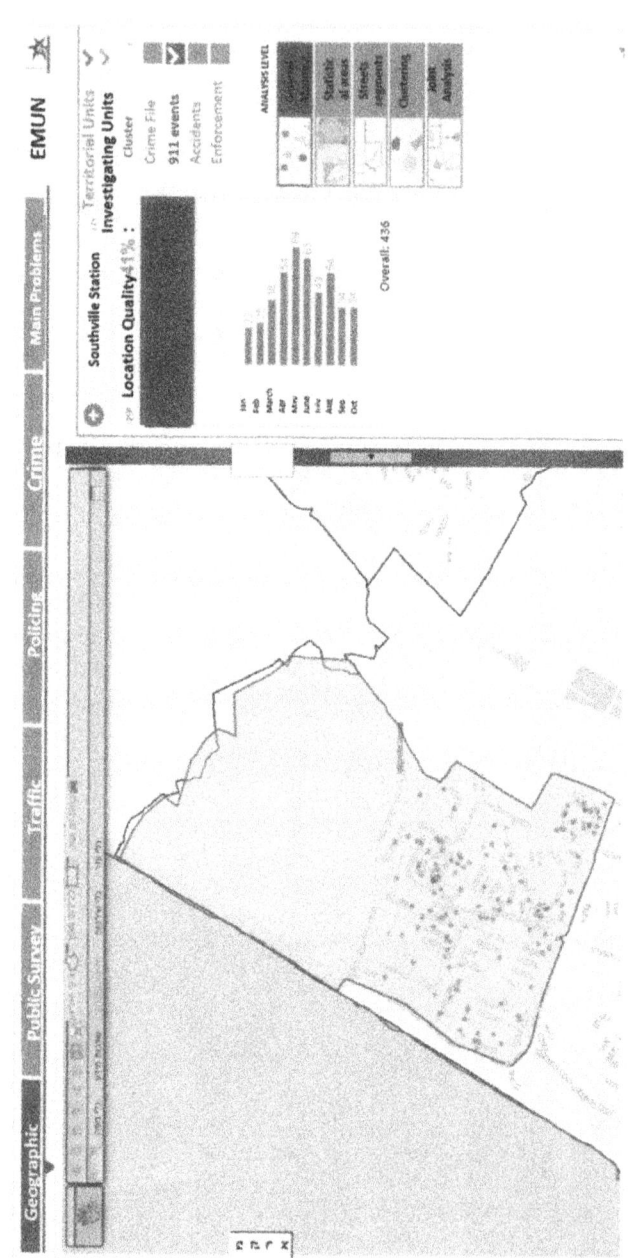

FIGURE 11.1 (Continued)

*These images are translated versions of the actual interface of the system including actual crime data and performance indicators, as would be available to an anonymized police station in the south of Israel during a specific day in May 2017.

These locations were termed *polygons*, referring to a continuous and usually convex area, ranging from a group of streets to a neighborhood or even a small municipality.

After choosing the problems, stations had to publish a yearly action plan (termed "attack plan"), which directed their *response* to the specific problem in the specific locality. While each station could design the action plan as they saw fit, based on their analysis of the problem and their available resources, two additional evidence-based approaches had to be included in the plan for it to be authorized. First, *situational prevention* techniques (Bowers & Johnson, 2016) had to account for a third of the actions listed. This was meant to embed a preventive approach to policing in all the stations' work, steering them away from the standard model of policing. In practice this included varied items: from decoy police cars situated at the entrance to neighborhoods to discourage thieves from entering, to the planned disruption of alcohol supplies at venues prone to outbreaks of violence, achieved by fining the suppliers. Second, the resources for a portion of the items listed in the action plan had to come from "external resources"; this directed stations, de facto, to a third-party policing approach (Mazerolle & Ransley, 2019), in which a station identified additional parties (e.g., business owners, civil regulators, and other governmental agencies) with a vested interest in dealing with the problem or preventing it. An example of this is collaborations with rail management authorities to tackle crime in train station parking lots.

Ongoing *assessment* of how well the problem was being dealt with was also an essential part of EMUN. The crime analysis system simultaneously served as an on-going assessment mechanism, providing live and constant feedback. The system's homepage displays the chosen problems with clear visual indications of how the station is performing (see Figure 11.1, screenshot 1: main problems screen).

To conclude, the reform embedded evidence-based approaches into the daily work of police stations. The EMUN evaluation study, which we now turn to describing, can therefore provide valuable lessons on implementing evidence-based practice in police organizations.

11.3 THE EMUN EVALUATION STUDY: AIMS, SETUP, AND METHODOLOGY

As noted above, the EMUN study is made up of two conjoined studies examining the impact of the reform alongside the quality of its implementation. We examined four distinct crime categories: property crimes, traffic-related offences, violence (a wide category that includes both relatively minor offences alongside serious violent crimes), and gun crime. These were the main "problem categories" stations could choose from when deciding which yearly problems to focus on. By studying the crime categories separately, we were able to move from a general examination of "does EMUN work" to a more nuanced understanding of which types of crimes EMUN is more suited to addressing, and what kind of implementation challenges and benefits each crime category holds.

The impact study was set up as several quasi-experiments. The experiments assessed the effects of each crime category separately by examining data from police stations that chose one of these four problem categories during 2017 and comparing them with stations that did not (see Weisburd et al., 2020 for a full description of this methodology). The study focused on fourteen intervention stations: three each for property crime and traffic-related offences, and four each for violence and gun crime. These stations were chosen randomly from the pool of relevant stations and matched to control stations using a bespoke algorithm. In the first two categories, the evaluation showed significant, large crime reduction benefits for the EMUN program (see Hasisi et al., 2019 and Weisburd et al., 2020). Regarding the violence category, the stations studied failed to clearly define this problem (i.e., to choose a specific problem in a specific location); this initial faulty implementation led to substantial difficulties in the implementation of focused strategies and in turn led to null outcomes (Hasisi et al., 2021). Finally, in the case of gun crime we were not able to carry out quasi-experimental analyses, due to the small sample size and lack of relevant comparison stations (Litmanovitz et al., 2021).

The aim of the process evaluation, which is the focus of this chapter, was to assess how well each station implemented the principles of the EBP approaches that make up EMUN. The study focused on the same stations chosen in the impact evaluation, and therefore benefits from the rigor of their selection process[2]; the stations were chosen at random but in a stratified fashion, which means they include different levels of the crime problems (low–middle–high). The 14 stations included in the process evaluation represent the diversity of stations across the organization; they are from all geographical districts, and of varying sizes in terms of manpower and the population served.

---

[2] We note that because the gun crime category was not evaluated using an experimental method, the stations in this category were not chosen randomly. The sampling was purposive and ensured representativeness in terms of geography, pattern of the phenomenon, etc.

In order to assess the quality of implementation, we examined the stations' choice of crime problem, their design of the action plan, and how well they executed this plan. Two types of data were collected and analyzed for this purpose: the documented action plans, which each station had to prepare and account for as part of the reform; and interviews with the key personnel at the intervention stations involved in designing and executing the plans (mostly station commanders, their deputies, and the stations' top officers). Between two and five officers were interviewed at each station, and these interviews were transcribed in full to aid the analysis process.[3]

The interviews were conducted and analyzed with the aid of an implementation assessment tool. The assessment tool, designed for the purpose of this study, allowed us to consider how closely the stations' actions matched a list of the essential attributes of each policing approach (Belsky et al., 2007). We chose attributes that had been previously identified in the literature as core to the approach. For example, problem-oriented policing was assessed according to six aspects underscored by the theoretical and empirical literature: quality of scanning, analysis, response, assessment, engagement, and innovation (Cordner & Biebel, 2005). In line with *thematic analysis* procedures (Braun & Clarke, 2006), the data collected were coded systematically and analyzed per problem category to classify how well the stations implemented each type of policing approach.[4] Working inductively from the data, we also identified organizational issues relevant to successful (or failed) implementation (Clarke et al., 2015).

Building on this analysis, we explored the data in order to identify the overarching themes of relevance to EBP. For this purpose, we examined the categories that were found across all four of the crime problems (which had been analyzed separately) and singled out the principal, unifying ideas that emerged from them. Methodologically, this is a continuation of the thematic analysis. In the *axial coding* phase (Corbin & Strauss, 1990) the data, which were organized into discrete categories at the initial stage of coding, are now put "back together by making connections between the categories and sub-categories" (Kendall, 1999, p. 747). Essentially, this analysis provides a bird's-eye view of the data.

---

[3] The procedures were approved by the Institute of Criminology's ethics committee.
[4] The data were coded first manually and then using word processing software. Open and axial coding were conducted by the first author (YL) and cross-checked by the third author (BH).

11.4 RESULTS: THEMES ASSOCIATED WITH QUALITY IMPLEMENTATION

The results of each process evaluation were published in detailed reports to the IP.[5] Our results indicate that across the four crime categories, all the stations included elements of the different EBP approaches EMUN was designed to feature: problem-oriented policing, a place-based approach, situational prevention tactics, and third-party policing initiatives. However, there was significant variance between the stations and across problems regarding the quality of implementation on the ground. For example, in the violence category, stations did not coherently "define problems" – a core attribute of problem-oriented policing – but rather grouped together different, unrelated phenomenon under this category. As noted above, this was a cardinal failure that led to null results. With regards to place-based policing, while in all crime categories the stations focused on a particular locality as required, some stations went past this basic level and included hotspots deployment and place-related situational prevention techniques. This variation demonstrates how evidence may be either lost in translation or – to extend the metaphor – spoken fluently in a new context.

The bird's-eye view of the data, which we now turn to, uncovered three overarching themes that enabled practitioners to integrate evidence-based tactics and approaches into police work: the ability to analyze data and reflect on it; organizational flexibility; and local ownership and engagement with the reform.

11.4.1 Theme 1: The Ability to Analyze Data and Reflect on It

Crime analysis capabilities have long been identified as necessary in order for police organizations to achieve their goals (Goldstein, 1979; Lum & Koper, 2017). The first prominent theme identified by the analysis is the vital role of the crime analysis and program assessment systems set up alongside the EMUN reform: the EMUN system. This sophisticated computer system was installed on every workstation across the organization, available to all ranks from field officers to middle managers to station commanders and up to central command. It was designed by experienced

---

[5] The reports are all available at www.gov.il/he/departments/topics/organization_and_planning_division. (in Hebrew only). The results of the property crime process evaluation are described in Weisburd et al., 2020.

in-house specialists: crime analysts, Geographic Information Systems (GIS) experts, and business intelligence engineers.

As a crime analysis system, it provided an intuitive, easy-to-use interface for analyzing crime and disorder patterns across time cycles (hours of the day, months, and years) (see Figure 11.1: screenshots of the EMUN system). The crime statistics could be viewed numerically at different geographical levels: the entire station, a neighborhood, or street segments. By clicking on the map icon, the users could view the data on a map format as part of the "geographic portal" of the system (see Figure 11.1, screenshot 2). This allowed stations to focus their efforts in the geographical areas most affected, sometimes attending to specific hotspots.

The EMUN system was utilized throughout the stations' yearly work cycle: to scan for problems and analyze them, for daily supervision and on-going assessment of the chosen "problems," and at the end of the year to determine if the stations' targets had been met. In nearly all the stations, the system was viewed and discussed as a powerful work and management tool. It was acknowledged as a valuable instrument that provided them with timely access to practical, usable crime data. For example, in the traffic-related offences study, a station commander described the EMUN system as giving him the ability "to win." In particular, he tied this to the capability of even junior commanders in the station to operate it with ease and provide in-depth crime and disorder snapshots:

Take the younger officers, … They can use the system much better than I can, and that makes me the happiest… They can do the integration, they can get the data every day, and see where they stand, and if they are failing… and they improve so quickly. (Traffic-related offences study, Station B)

Beyond this function of the system as providing accurate data on which to base decisions, the system also emerged as a tool for testing hypotheses, including preconceptions. One prominent example of this is the officers' convictions that crime "moves around the corner" – would merely be displaced, geographically, by police efforts to deal with it (Weisburd et al., 2006). This phenomenon was (and remains) a matter of controversy among participants of the study, though there is strong scientific literature that now challenges the idea that displacement is inevitable (Weisburd et al., 2006; Braga et al., 2019). As one commander described, "If I act preventively, I will transfer the problem to a different neighborhood. Because the criminals have to strike somewhere … The only way for me to succeed is to catch them" (Property crime study, Station A).

However, a second narrative emerged alongside this traditional one, one which relied on officers using the crime analysis system to check if displacement was indeed occurring; as the experimental results also show, this was not the case. In Station B of the property study, interviewees voiced the opinion that displacement was likely occurring somewhere, but not on their turf. They relied on data of their station and of their district to postulate their work yielded significant benefits that lasted over time: "We see a 16% reduction in break-ins even after we have left the polygon [i.e., completed focused work in a specific area]. It has not evaporated, our entire district is seeing a crime drop. We are getting the job done."

This showcases the crime analysis system as a decision-making aid for assessing choices and outcomes, and for re-navigating one's course of action where necessary. Considering that evidence-based practice requires professionals to sometimes make decision that go against their own prior experience (Jonathan-Zamir et al., 2019), or craft wisdom (Willis, 2013), such systems are an important function that can support EBP.

11.4.2 Theme 2: Organizational Flexibility

Institutional perspectives of police organizations have highlighted the orthodoxies that develop around a technical core of how policing is done, or how the organizational day-to-day operations should be conducted (Crank & Langworthy, 1992; Maguire & Katz, 2002). This helps explain phenomena, such as the entrenchment of the standard model of policing (Willis et al., 2007). In contrast to this, EBP requires making decisions based on what will lead to the best results.

Flexibility was the second theme identified in our analysis, and it included several aspects: flexibility in allocating resources, flexibility across organizational boundaries, and flexibility in designing the action plan. These three expressions of flexibility helped realize EBP as a framework for professional decision-making. They stand out in the interviewees' experiences as giving them a chance to make actual, meaningful choices. As a reform, EMUN gave police officers power to make professional decisions about which problems to address and how to address them. An important source of this control is the ability to allocate their own resources more freely and also request resources from the district (resources primarily in the form of manpower but also technological tools and special units). It allowed station commanders to not only (or mostly) deal with reactive policing, but with the issues they thought would make the most difference in their jurisdiction.

This was expressed mostly (but not exclusively) by officers in medium and small stations, who prior to this reform had less power to set an agenda. For example, a senior commander in the gun crime study reflected:

> In the past there were certain tools that were simply not available to me: intelligence, technology... EMUN forced the district to listen to the needs of the station. If it weren't for this, the SWAT teams would keep being sent to combat crime in the larger cities, ...where public opinion is. (Gun crime study, Station D)

Flexibility also characterizes the ability to work across the boundary between patrol and investigations divisions that traditionally exists in the IP, as was repeatedly described in the interviews. Each problem was assigned a coordinator from the senior ranks of the station, who became responsible for delivering the action plan. This created a task-force approach to dealing with problems, with the coordinator enlisting all relevant personnel to work together in implementing the response, as part of the stations' day-to-day operations.

By creating this position, EMUN changes the management and supervision structure of the organization. But it also allows the coordinator to allocate resources based on how the crime problem is best addressed, rather than being constrained by existing organizational structures. This flexibility was acknowledged as essential to success: "Now everyone is working under the head Investigations Officer and he can combat crime in this geographical unit" (Property crime study, Station B).

Flexibility in designing each local action plan is another element in this theme. As described above, stations were obliged to present an action plan with pre-set parameters limiting them to evidence-based approaches (i.e., to include situational prevention, community consultations, etc.). Beyond these parameters, commanders were granted professional autonomy to shape their responses. This led to the inclusion of highly tailored and innovative items in the action plans, alongside more traditional business-as-usual ones. For example, one of the stations in the violence category study chose to focus on youth violence in a Jewish ultra-Orthodox city. They set up a pioneering "mothers-only neighborhood watch" (in line with cultural norms of gender separation), which patrolled the hotspot parks and streets relevant to these offences, identified at-risk youths, and intervened using community-specific approaches. A significant reduction in crime was recorded in this locality (Hasisi et al., 2021) and new ties between the community and the police were established in the process – likely to benefit both the police and the community in the long run (Sampson, 2006).

11.4.3 Theme 3: Ownership of and Engagement with the Reform

Police organizations have been characterized as *loosely coupled systems* (DiMaggio & Powell, 1983), in which there may be a substantial disconnect between proclaimed goals and means and what actually occurs on the ground (Maguire, 2003; Mastrofski et al., 1987). This disconnect, which has been used to explain poor implementation fidelity in police reforms (Giacomantonio & Litmanovitz, 2017), might also bar efforts to implement EBP. A remedy for this may lie in processes that encourage the police to "own" science, as described by Neyroud & Weisburd (this volume). Ownership of the EMUN approach was the third theme identified. This was expressed through three sub-themes: a shift in the meaning of success, ownership of policing goals across the ranks, and engagement with the reform at the local level.

The first aspect of ownership arises through the changing conceptualization of success in the organization. A key to professional success since the reform's launch has been success in meeting the crime/problem targets, rather than high scores on an endless list of crime statistics. The shift in focus was enabled primarily though the computerized crime analysis and assessment system. As already noted, the EMUN system is a "live" system, which updates automatically and is available on each workstation. Evaluating success in dealing with the main problems identified at each station became a constant, central, organizational activity. Notably, this also shifts the meaning of success, as it does not simply place value on outputs like more arrests or cases brought to trial but also instead signals that prevention is an important goal of policing, in line with the principles of problem-oriented policing (Cordner & Biebel, 2005).

Station leaders began and ended each day with the problems screen of the EMUN system. They and their superiors (district and national command) could track their performance and decide if different actions should be used that may improve their ability to deal with the problem. The central command published half-yearly advice on actions that had led to the best results in each problem category in order to encourage stations to examine and revise their action plans and improve their outcomes. If performance indicators were low, the station command was encouraged by central command to assess if this was due to deficiencies in carrying out planned activities or to a problem with the plan itself, in which case the plan should be revised. Station commanders now "owned" their local problems: they were held responsible for their problem targets and this became a central aspect through which they were professionally valued.

The second aspect of ownership identified is the ownership of policing goals across organizational ranks, not only by the top ranks. This was a topic of discussion in many interviews. Commanders described different tactics for achieving this. Here too, the EMUN system served a key function. Because it was available to all officers in the station it was used to communicate the station's achievements and failings; this became a strategy to involve the frontline officers without whom successful implementation of the action plan is not possible. Commanders in several stations described how a screenshot of the problems page of the system was sent daily to all the stations' officers through WhatsApp groups, with the purpose of keeping them updated on the station's performance. One commander described how EMUN's priorities permeated throughout the ranks: "We reversed the trend! When there is an arrest in the polygon there is excitement" (Property crime study, Station A).

Most senior officers saw this process of winning heart and minds as central to the reform's success. As one deputy commander put it, "Our biggest success is that our [rank-and-file] officers are involved" (Gun crime study, Station A). There were also some testaments of patrol officers taking a proactive stance and self-directing their work to ensure tasks related to the central EMUN problems (as listed in the action plans) were being carried out. In at least one case, the reform may have led to increased stress and burnout because of officers taking on extra duties to meet the program's goals (Gun crime study, Station D). But the overall impression was that in many stations the crime and disorder problems became "our problems" and also "our success."

The third expression of this theme was engagement with the reform at a local level. This was evidenced by innovative tailoring of the evidence-based approaches to local settings and challenges. One way this was realized was in duplicating work principles introduced in EMUN beyond the three official "problems." For example, in the property crime study and the violence study, commanders "exported" ideas of place-based policing to other locations in their jurisdictions (beside the predefined polygons). This included using the GIS tools to identify additional polygons, and using situational prevention techniques based on the analysis of these geographies.

Another form of engagement is extending work principles beyond their original framing. For example, consultation with the public to identify and assess the chosen problems was one of the elements of the reform; valuing the perspective of citizens is indeed an essential principle of community policing (Skogan & Hartnett, 2019). One station chose to also conduct consultations with the station's rank-and-file police officers in addition to this. The commander set up an advisory forum of veteran officers and used their input to supplement the work plan, for example, placing mock cameras in a high-crime street in which it was not possible to set up actual cameras. The commander explained his motivation: "These are people with 25, 30 years of experience. It gives you a different perspective" (Property crime study, Station B).

A third form of engagement occurred when stations understood the core principles of the evidence-based approaches and took steps to ensure their work was fully aligned with them. The most striking example of this is the work done in one of the gun violence stations to geo-map crime events. This station serves a large Arab city which had not yet been mapped by the authorities, making it impossible to use GIS to map crime and identify hotspots. The station's leaders decided to take it upon themselves to map the city in order to identify gun crime hot areas. The station commander describes his conviction of why this was needed: "I understood the problem. We need focus, and we don't have it." Three months of intense work of the stations' top officers – including gritty leg work – supported by the IP's Technology Division, enabled the station to geo-map gun crime and focus their work on four neighborhoods. Following this, in 2018 there was a 40% reduction in gun violence in this city, which may be partially attributed to this focusing of resources. This type of engagement with the principles of EBP was not mandated by national headquarters, but rather was driven by the conviction of middle managers who adopted an evidence-based world view.

11.5 DISCUSSION

The process evaluation described in this chapter demonstrates how evidence-based approaches and procedures were weaved into the fabric of a police organization. The approaches became part of the daily operations of the IP, infused into the strategic and tactical planning, with local and national resources allocated accordingly. As a reform, EMUN is representative of Nutely et al.'s (2007) embedded research model for enhancing research use in the public sector. It should again be noted that this chapter does not aim to evaluate the implementation of EMUN or to argue that there were no difficulties in its implementation. Indeed, as described with respect to the violence category, faulty implementation possibly led to null results in the impact evaluation in this problem category.

Our analysis identified three key themes which were associated with quality implementation of EBP. The first focuses on the functions of the crime analysis and program assessment system; the second describes the value of organizational flexibility; and the third relates to the ownership and engagement with the process and outcomes of the reform. Across the chapter, we have included examples of best practice, because these allow us to elucidate the themes that we identified. All three themes strongly resonate with the existing literature on this subject. Firstly, they provide a mirror image to the factors identified in medicine and social work as barring the successful implementation of evidence-based practice in organizations, particularly with regard to inflexibility, lack of resources, and lack of incentives to change practices toward more research-based ones.

The three themes provide empirical support for three of the four organizational systems highlighted in Lum and Koper's (2017) work as most meaningful to successful implementation of EBP: deployment of officers in the field, crime analysis, and management. The second theme in particular – "the ability to analyze crime and reflect on it" – supports Lum and Koper's hypothesis that the more integrated crime analysis is into the fabric of the organization, the greater the benefits reaped. This theme demonstrates the significance of a crime analysis system that enables officers, even unaided by analysts, to understand the crime data, test the success of policing responses, as well as to test existing preconceptions they hold of "what works." The EMUN system – as a crime analysis and program assessment system – emerged as a vital element; it connected all parts of the organization like a neural system, wired to activate evidence-based practices.

The three themes also support Weisburd and Neyroud's (2011) proposal that fostering ownership of science is a prerequisite for making EBP a reality; they proposed structural change, police-academia collaborations, and training as the mechanisms through which it could be achieved (Neyroud & Weisburd, 2014). Our empirical findings demonstrate how such ownership plays out in the context of an institutionalized reform. The third theme – ownership of the reform process and its success – manifests three distinct forms of ownership: shaping a new meaning of success that is aligned with evidence-based principles; ownership of policing goals across the ranks and not only at the very top of the organizations; and engagement with the reform at the local level, which allows local police leaders to "translate" research findings into their own context while remaining true to the essence of the evidence-based intervention. Within the second theme of "organizational flexibility," the sub-theme relating to the flexibility in designing local action plans also clarifies how ownership of science can be manifested.

Taken together, these findings anchor EBP as being, at its core, about making decisions that incorporate the best available evidence. A careful examination of the themes and sub-themes substantiates they are all essentially about providing police officers (of different ranks) with the possibility of including research insights as a parameter in their professional decision-making. The examples provided through the findings section are illustrations of what it means for research evidence to "have a seat at the table" (Lum & Koper, 2017, p. 4).

Our findings are based on an extensive process evaluation that assessed four separate areas of police work and spanned a national organization, relying on appropriate sampling, data collection, and data analysis procedures. Some limitations should nonetheless be considered. First, we note the interviews were conducted retrospectively, between one and two years post-implementation. This could lead to a misrepresentation of officers' "real-time" decisions and actions. We were able to compensate for this by relying on the original action plans and records of the delivery of action items. Second, we acknowledge the national, hierarchical-leaning formation of the Israel Police might paradoxically create a context that is particularly conductive to such reforms. Further research of EBP reforms in other police forces with varying characteristics is needed to substantiate the themes identified, ideally using experimental designs. Since not all elements identified can be experimentally manipulated, studies that systematically assess the elements longitudinally are also necessary.

In conclusion, the findings of the EMUN evaluation offer a roadmap for the design and empirical investigation of reforms promoting EBP. The findings paint an optimistic picture regarding the ability of police organizations to successfully implement evidence-based practices and become co-producers of evidence in the process. The reform made evidence an integral part of the organization's core work and still provided the space for professionals to make decisions based on their craft knowledge

(Willis, 2013). This balance seems to us to be a key to the successful implementation of EBP.

References

Aviv, G., & Weisburd, D. (2016). Reducing the gap in perceptions of legitimacy of victims and non-victims: The importance of police performance. *International Review of Victimology*, 22(2), 83–104.

Barzkar, F., Baradaran, H. R., & Koohpayehzadeh, J. (2018). Knowledge, attitudes and practice of physicians toward evidence-based medicine: A systematic review. *Journal of Evidence-Based Medicine*, 11(4), 246–251.

Belsky, J., Melhuish, E. C., & Barnes, J. (Eds.) (2007). *The national evaluation of Sure Start: does area-based early intervention work?*. Policy Press.

Ben-Porat, G., Yuval, F., & Mizrahi, S. (2012). The challenge of diversity management: police reform and the Arab minority in Israel. *Policy Sciences*, 45(3), 243–263.

Bowers, K. J., & Johnson, S. D. (2016). Situational prevention. In D. Weisburd, D.P. Farrington, & C. Gill's (Eds.), *What Works in Crime Prevention and Rehabilitation* (pp. 111–135). Springer.

Braga, A. A., Turchan, B. S., Papachristos, A. V., & Hureau, D. M. (2019). Hot spots policing and crime reduction: an update of an ongoing systematic review and meta-analysis. *Journal of Experimental Criminology*, 15(3), 289–311.

Braun, V., & Clarke, V. (2006). Using thematic analysis in psychology. *Qualitative Research in Psychology*, 3(2), 77–101.

Century, J., Rudnick, M., & Freeman, C. (2010). A framework for measuring fidelity of implementation: A foundation for shared language and accumulation of knowledge. *American Journal of Evaluation*, 31(2), 199–218.

Chalmers, I., Dickersin, K., & Chalmers, T. C. (1992). Getting to grips with Archie Cochrane's agenda. *British Medical Journal*, 305(6857), 786–788.

Clarke, V., Braun, V., & Hayfield, N. (2015). Thematic analysis. In J. A. Smith's (Ed.), *Qualitative psychology: A practical guide to research methods* (pp. 222–248). Sage.

Corbin, J. M., & Strauss, A. (1990). Grounded theory research: Procedures, canons, and evaluative criteria. *Qualitative Sociology*, 13(1), 3–21.

Cordner, G., & Biebel, E. P. (2005). Problem-oriented policing in practice. *Criminology & Public Policy*, 4(2), 155–180.

Crank, J. P., & Langworthy, R. (1992). Institutional perspective on policing. *Journal of Criminal Law & Criminology*, 83, 338.

DiMaggio, P. J., & Powell, W. W. (1983). The iron cage revisited: Institutional isomorphism and collective rationality in organizational fields. *American Sociological Review*, 48(2), 147–160.

Draaisma, E., Bekhof, J., Langenhorst, V. J., & Brand, P. L. (2018). Implementing evidence-based medicine in a busy general hospital department: results and critical success factors. *BMJ Evidence-Based Medicine*, 23(5), 173–177.

Giacomantonio, C., & Litmanovitz, Y. (2017). Implementation fidelity in a loosely coupled system: The challenges of maintaining consistent 'problem theory' and 'programme theory' in a multi-force training pilot. *Policing and Society*, 27(6), 1–16.

Gill, C., Weisburd, D., Telep, C. W., Vitter, Z., & Bennett, T. (2014). Community-oriented policing to reduce crime, disorder and fear and increase satisfaction and legitimacy among citizens: A systematic review. *Journal of Experimental Criminology, 10*(4), 399–428.

Goldstein, H. (1979). Improving Policing: A Problem-Oriented Approach. *Crime & Delinquency, 25*(2), 236–258.

Gray, M., Joy, E., Plath, D., & Webb, S. A. (2013). Implementing evidence-based practice: A review of the empirical research literature. *Research on Social Work Practice, 23*(2), 157–166.

Gray, M., Joy, E., Plath, D., & Webb, S. A. (2015). What supports and impedes evidence-based practice implementation? A survey of Australian social workers. *The British Journal of Social Work, 45*(2), 667–684.

Hasisi, B., Weisburd, D., Litmanovitz, Y., Carmel, T., Tshuva, S., & Trachtenberg, T. (2019). EMUN evaluation report: Traffic disturbances and reckless driving. *Research Essence: A collection of Studies on Police and Criminology.* Department of Planning and Strategy, Israel Police (pp. 29–60).

Hasisi, B., Weisburd, D., Litmanovitz, Y., Tshuva, S., & Trachtenberg, T. (2021). EMUN evaluation report: Violence Problem Category. *Research Essence: A collection of Studies on Police and Criminology.* Department of Planning and Strategy, Israel Police (pp. 247–281).

Hinkle, J. C., Weisburd, D., Telep, C. W., & Petersen, K. (2020). Problem-oriented policing for reducing crime and disorder: An updated systematic review and meta-analysis. *Campbell Systematic Reviews, 16*(2), 1–86. https://doi.org/10.1002/cl2.1089

Jonathan-Zamir, T., Weisburd, D., Dayan, M., & Zisso, M. (2019). The proclivity to rely on professional experience and evidence-based policing: Findings from a survey of high-ranking officers in the Israel Police. *Criminal Justice and Behavior, 46*(10), 1456–1474.

Kadosh, H. (2015). Evolving systems of performance indicators in the Israel Police. *Research Essence: A collection of Studies on Police and Criminology.* Department of Planning and Strategy, Israel Police (pp. 19–26).

Kendall, J. (1999). Axial coding and the grounded theory controversy. *Western Journal of Nursing Research, 21*(6), 743–757.

Kitson, A., Harvey, G., & McCormack, B. (1998). Enabling the implementation of evidence-based practice: a conceptual framework. *BMJ Quality & Safety, 7*(3), 149–158.

Koper, C. S., & Lum, C. (2012). Incorporating research into daily police practices: The Matrix Demonstration Project. *Translational Criminology,* Fall issue, 16–17.

Litmanovitz, Y., Hasisi, B, Weisburd, D., & Tshuva, S. (2021). *Gun violence in the Arab society in Israel: Findings of the process evaluation of the EMUN reform.* Research Essence: A collection of Studies on Police and Criminology. Department of Planning and Strategy, Israel Police (pp. 226–245).

Lum, C. M., & Koper, C. S. (2017). *Evidence-based policing: Translating research into practice.* Oxford University Press.

Lum, C., Telep, C. W., Koper, C. S., & Grieco, J. (2012). Receptivity to research in policing. *Justice Research and Policy, 14*(1), 61–95.

Maguire, E. R. (2003). *Organizational structure in American police agencies: Context, complexity, and control*. SUNY Press.
Maguire, E. R., & Katz, C. M. (2002). Community policing, loose coupling, and sensemaking in American police agencies. *Justice Quarterly, 19*(3), 503–536.
Mastrofski, S. D., Ritti, R. R., & Hoffmaster, D. (1987). Organizational determinants of police discretion: The case of drinking-driving. *Journal of Criminal Justice, 15*(5), 387–402.
Mazerolle, L., & Neyroud, P. (2020). The Campbell Crime & Justice Coordinating Group: Celebrating 20 years of achievements. *Campbell Systematic Reviews, 16*(2), 1–2. https://doi.org/10.1002/cl2.1099
Mazerolle, L., & Ransley, J. (2019). Third-party policing. In D. Weisburd & A. A. Braga (Eds.), *Police innovation: Contrasting perspectives* (2nd ed.) (pp. 347–365). Cambridge University Press.
Neyroud, P. W. (2017). *Learning to Field Test in Policing: Using an analysis of completed randomised controlled trials involving the police to develop a grounded theory on the factors contributing to high levels of treatment integrity in Police Field Experiments* (Doctoral dissertation, University of Cambridge).
Neyroud, P., & Weisburd, D. (2014). Transforming the police through science: The challenge of ownership. *Policing: A Journal of Policy and Practice, 8*(4), 287–293.
Neyroud, P., & Weisburd, D. (this volume). Re-Inventing Policing: Using Science to Transform Policing. In D. Weisburd, T. Jonathan, G. Perry & B. Hasisi (Eds.), *The Future of Evidence-Based Policing*. Cambridge University Press.
Nutley, S. M., Walter, I., & Davies, H. T. (2007). *Using evidence: How research can inform public services*. Policy press.
Nutley, S., Walter, I., & Davies, H. T. (2009). Promoting evidence-based practice: Models and mechanisms from cross-sector review. *Research on Social Work Practice, 19*(5), 552–559.
Perry, G., & Jonathan-Zamir, T. (2020). Expectations, Effectiveness, Trust, and Cooperation: Public Attitudes towards the Israel Police during the COVID-19 Pandemic. *Policing: A Journal of Policy and Practice, 14*(4), 1073–1091.
Rycroft-Malone, J. (2004). The PARIHS framework – a framework for guiding the implementation of evidence-based practice. *Journal of Nursing Care Quality, 19*(4), 297–304.
Sampson, R. J. (2006). Collective efficacy theory: Lessons learned and directions for future inquiry. *Taking Stock: The Status of Criminological Theory, 15*, 149–67.
Sherman, L. W., (2002). Evidence-based policing: Social organization of information for social control. In E. Waring & D. Weisburd (Eds.), *Crime and social organization* (pp. 217–248). Transaction Publishers.
Sherman, L. W. (2009). Evidence and liberty: The promise of experimental criminology. *Criminology & Criminal Justice, 9*(1), 5–28.
Sherman, L. W. (2015). A tipping point for "totally evidenced policing" ten ideas for building an evidence-based police agency. *International Criminal Justice Review, 25*(1), 11–29.
Shitrit, S. (2019). "It all depends on the police officer..." The Israel Police and Public Trust 1948-1953. *Police & History, 1*, 50–88.

Skogan, W. G., & Hartnett, S. M. (2019). Community policing. In D. Weisburd & A. A. Braga's (Eds.), *Police innovation: Contrasting perspectives*, (2nd Ed., pp. 27–44).

Ubbink, D. T., Guyatt, G. H., & Vermeulen, H. (2013). Framework of policy recommendations for implementation of evidence-based practice: a systematic scoping review. *BMJ open, 3*(1), 1–12.

van Dijk, N., Hooft, L., & Wieringa-de Waard, M. (2010). What are the barriers to residents' practicing evidence-based medicine? A systematic review. *Academic Medicine, 85*(7), 1163–1170.

Weisburd, D. (2003). Ethical Practice and Evaluation of Interventions in Crime and Justice: The Moral Imperative for Randomized Trials. *Evaluation Review, 27*(3), 336–354.

Weisburd, D. (2015). The law of crime concentration and the criminology of place. *Criminology, 53*(2), 133–157.

Weisburd, D., & Hasisi, B. (2018). The Winding Road to Evidence-Based Policy in Corrections: A Case Study of the Israel Prison Service. *Israel Law Review, 51*(1), 111–125.

Weisburd, D., Hasisi, B., Litmanovitz, Y., Carmel, T., & Tshuva, S. (2020). Institutionalizing problem-oriented policing: An evaluation of the EMUN reform in Israel. *Criminology & Public Policy, 19*(3), 941–964.

Weisburd, D., & Majimundar, M. K. (Eds.) (2018). *Proactive policing: Effects on crime and communities*. National Academies Press.

Weisburd, D., & Neyroud, P. (2011). Police science: Toward a new paradigm. *New Perspectives in Policing*. Harvard Kennedy School Program in Criminal Justice Policy and Management & National Institute of Justice.

Weisburd, D., Wyckoff, L. A., Ready, J., Eck, J. E., Hinkle, J. C., & Gajewski, F. (2006). Does crime just move around the corner? A controlled study of spatial displacement and diffusion of crime control benefits. *Criminology, 44*(3), 549–592.

Williams, B., Perillo, S., & Brown, T. (2015). What are the factors of organisational culture in health care settings that act as barriers to the implementation of evidence-based practice? A scoping review. *Nurse Education Today, 35*(2), e34–e41. https://doi.org/10.1016/j.nedt.2014.11.012

Willis, J. J. (2013). Improving police: What's craft got to do with it. *Ideas in American Policing, 16*, 1–13.

Willis, J. J., Mastrofski, S. D., & Weisburd, D. (2007). Making sense of COMPSTAT: A theory-based analysis of organizational change in three police departments. *Law & Society Review, 41*(1), 147–188.

Worden, R. E., & McLean, S. J. (2017). *Mirage of police reform*. University of California Press.

12

Towards Implementing Evidence-Based Policing

Challenges in Latin America and Caribbean

Laura Jaitman

Evidence-Based Policing (EBP) is broadly based on the ideas of Sherman (1998), who suggested that rigorous scientific evaluations should inform and underpin decisions made by police practitioners within the workplace; these are thoroughly examined in the first part of this volume. The implication is that police actions should be linked to desired outcomes, and this connection should be based on research, analysis, evaluation, evidence and empirical information (Lum & Koper, 2017). Despite two decades of progress in EBP in the developed world, Latin America and the Caribbean (LAC) is clearly lagging in its adoption.

The region's levels of crime and violence suggest that traditional models of policing do not provide solutions to current and future violence problems. The police institution is generally seen as corrupt, unreliable and ineffective. The adoption of EBP can strengthen police accountability, lead to greater transparency and legitimacy as well as improve the relationship between the police and the community, among other benefits. However, such a change in the policing paradigm brings important challenges that should be considered when undertaking reforms towards greater use of EBP in the region.

This chapter examines the challenges of integrating EBP into routine policing in LAC and highlights avenues for future research and action to promote EBP in the region. Some of the challenges are common to developed countries while others are specific to LAC. The latter include lack of reliable data, deficiently equipped police officers, poor perception of the police and its effectiveness, unstable political institutions, absence of continuity in any process of police reform, lack of evidence specific to the region, among others. Successful EBP implementation requires committed political support for experimentation, police leadership, more reliable information systems, academic-practitioner collaboration, as well as well-developed learners' critical mindsets and improved capacity building and training of police members. These issues, analyzed in this book, gain even more relevance and urgency in LAC.

This chapter is organized as follows. Section 12.1 reviews the crime situation in LAC compared with other regions. Section 12.2 briefly highlights the main challenges of implementing EBP in the international context as stated in other chapters, that are critical in LAC. Section 12.3 examines the main challenges of implementing EBP in the region, and Section 12.4 proposes areas for future research and action to promote EBP in LAC. Finally, Section 12.5 discusses the main takeaways from LAC's experience that can be useful for the implementation of EBP in other countries or regions.

12.1 THE CONTEXT: CRIME AND VIOLENCE IN LATIN AMERICA AND THE CARIBBEAN

While Latin America and the Caribbean (LAC) is home to fewer than 9 per cent of the world's population, it accounts for 33.6 per cent of the world's homicides according to the United Nations Office on Drugs and Crime (UNODC, 2020), making it the most violent region on earth. Its annual homicide rate of 20 per 100,000 population in 2018 is more than three times the world average, six times that of North America, and nearly 23 times that of Australia and New Zealand. Not only are murder levels high, but recent trends are worrisome. While the rate of homicide is decreasing in many regions, driving down the global trend, only in LAC does it continue to increase (Figure 12.1).

Within the region there is great heterogeneity in the homicide rates: the variance across sub-regions and countries is staggering. Central America has the highest incidence of homicides (28.1 homicides per 100,000 population). South America and the Caribbean follow with a rate of 21.0 and 12.1 per 100,000 population in 2018. In terms of countries, the variance is also noticeable: at the top of the ranking are El Salvador, Jamaica and Honduras with homicide rates of around 40 or more cases per 100,000 population; while at the bottom are countries in South America with rates below 6 per 100,000 population.

Although data are less reliable in terms of comparability than those for homicides (due to reporting and registering differences), the rates of theft, robbery and assault are also worrisome. In less than a decade, robberies in

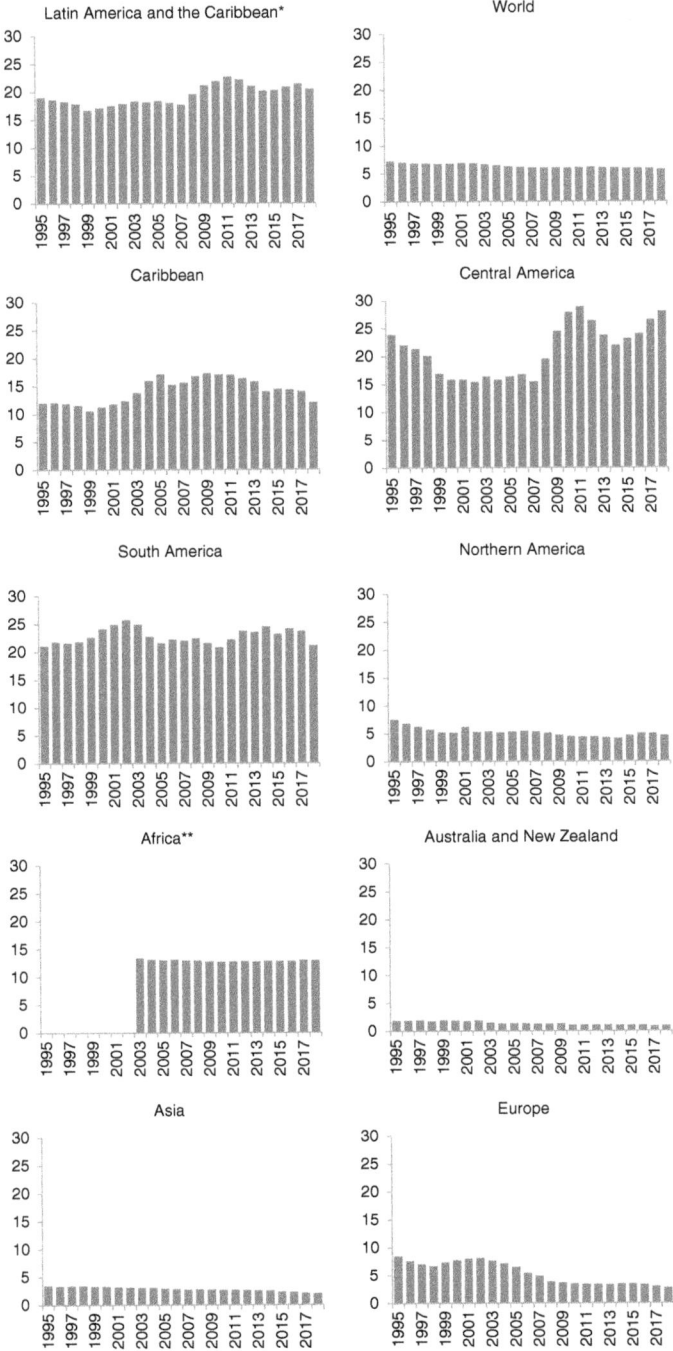

FIGURE 12.1 Intentional homicide rates per 100,000 population, 1995–2018
Source: Produced by the author based on UNODC (2020) database.
Note: *LAC figures calculated as a simple average between South America, Central America and the Caribbean. **UNODC provides homicide data of Africa (as a region) only since 2003.

many LAC countries not only have dramatically increased reaching more than 1,000 robberies per 100,000 population but also have become more violent. LAC also has high rates of violence against women.

Given this context, it is not surprising that crime and violence are the major concern in the region: almost one of every four citizens states that insecurity and crime are the main problems in their lives (23.2 per cent) even worse than the economic situation (15.3 per cent) or unemployment (15.1 per cent) (Latinobarometer, 2018).

By contrast, immigration is the leading concern at the European Union level with 38 per cent of mentions, terrorism is second with 29 per cent, followed by economic issues with 18 per cent. Crime remains the eighth largest concern, with 10 per cent of mentions (European Commission, 2018). In the case of the US, immigration is also at the top of the list for Americans asked to name the most important problem facing the nation (22 per cent), followed by dissatisfaction with the government (19 per cent) and racism (7 per cent) (Gallup, 2018). According to the Gallup survey, crime is considered the main problem by less than 3 per cent of the population.

This context of failed traditional policing strategies suggests both that the implementation of EBP has the potential of reducing crime rates and that introduction of any such change is challenging and complex.

12.2 THE CHALLENGES OF EBP IN THE INTERNATIONAL CONTEXT

With EBP research, evaluation, analysis and scientific process help guide decision-making about tactics, strategies and policies. This requires translating knowledge into digestible and usable forms and institutionalizing that knowledge in daily police tasks (Lum & Koper, 2017). EBP provides mechanisms that help police agencies select the strategies that best work to achieve the desired goal. Thus, an organization's risk of increasing harm is reduced, as is the likelihood of having no impact on crime, agitating police-community relations, or wasteful spending. Because using objective processes to select strategies is more ethically justifiable than nonscientific methods (Lum & Koper, 2017), EBP is more transparent and legitimate, potentially improving trust in the institution, citizen relations, and accountability. The authors also point out that EBP can increase satisfaction in police work because outcomes are more clearly linked to inputs and it can change the organizational and cultural forces that inhibit growth and dynamic learning.

However, the experience of different countries has shown that bringing EBP into practice can be difficult. In the international context, looking primarily at developed countries, authors found a number of implementation challenges. The first one is *institutionalization of EBP*. There is a consensus that police agencies are complex organizations conditioned and shaped by rules, incentives and procedures. As Lum and Koper (2017) argue, they are steeped in tradition and organizational and cultural frameworks. The authors claim that in order to institutionalize EBP, research knowledge must be internalized and held to account in everyday practices, cultures, systems, activities and habits of policing. Failure to institutionalize EBP results in problem-solving that is idiosyncratic and not part of a larger organizational effort (see, e.g., Read & Tilley, 2000; Weisburd & Braga, 2019). One recent exception is the EMUN reform, which sought to institutionalize problem-oriented policing across the entire national network of police stations in Israel's National Police. According to Weisburd et al. (2020), EMUN did so through a coordinated system of reforms supported by a data platform. The authors find the EMUN system created an organizational climate of evidence-based problem solving in which not only commanders but also ordinary police were exposed directly to the message of the reform and contributed to the process.

A second challenge is the still persistent *disconnect between science and policing*. In general, research is not part of the decision-making process. EBP decision-making competes with, and usually loses to, the believed merits of intuition or orders from the top. Resistance by officers to adjust their discretion based on the knowledge they deem suspicious or threatening is a crucial factor that hinders EBP. On the other hand, most police practices are not systematically evaluated, even in developed countries, and we still know too little about what works in policing and under what conditions (Weisburd & Neyroud, 2011). For instance, a CEPOL study of police research in European police agencies found that participants in nearly half the countries considered research to be "low" value (Hanak & Hofinger, 2005). This is compounded by lacking or insufficient data from which to evaluate police strategies – a key challenge for LAC that we will discuss later. Additionally, most studies are based on very simplistic methodologies and focus on implementation rather than design (Weisburd & Neyroud, 2011).

A third international challenge – very important in LAC – is *police education and training*. According to Weisburd and Neyroud (2011), the limited progress toward the creation of accredited standards of education and training for police officers has reinforced the realities of policing as a "blue-collar job" rather than a profession supported by a credible corpus of knowledge. This, in turn, has further distanced police from the importance and relevance of police science.

A culture of continuous professional development, supported by accreditation, that encourages practitioners to engage with the evidence is needed, as are rewards and recognition in policing that showcase high-quality evidence-based practice and the function of a chief scientific officer working beyond forensics to embrace all aspects of the application of science to the development and deployment of policing (Weisburd & Neyroud, 2011).

As we will discuss in the next section, these challenges are exacerbated in LAC countries by the particular context in which police agencies function, which greatly differs from that of more developed countries in at least four aspects: the outstanding levels of crime and violence; citizens' perception that the police is corrupt, unreliable and ineffective; lack of evidence; and weaker crime statistics systems.

12.3 CHALLENGES TO IMPLEMENTING EBP IN LATIN AMERICA AND CARIBBEAN

Given the crime and violence incidence levels in the Latin American and Caribbean (LAC), and the importance of the issue to the public, introducing reform is difficult in politically unstable environments. In this section we argue that the challenges that are apparent in regions with lower rates of crime and violence are exacerbated in LAC and compounded by idiosyncratic challenges; this makes the potential benefits of EBP greater but its introduction more complex. The major challenges are elaborated below.

12.3.1 Weak and Untrusted Police Institutions

The origins of today's police institutions in the region are diverse. In some countries, a new or reformed police emerged either from post-conflict situations or from transitions between authoritarian and democratic regimes.

Until the mid-1990s, the police were a central element in the maintenance of internal order and support of the Armed Forces, especially in Central American countries (Dammert, 2019). Police officers were trained almost exclusively to handle the armed insurgency and to cooperate with the military in maintaining internal order, at the expense of education and training for crime control, let alone prevention (Johnson et al., 2012). The participation of police officers in confrontations with the population and the extreme use of force necessitated the creation of new institutions with greater legitimacy and citizen recognition. However, political swings, which happened simultaneously with sharp increases in crime and violence, affected the institutional arrangements related to the police. Many LAC countries underwent transitions from various forms of authoritarianism to formal democracies: Between 1950 and 1990, there were dictatorships in 11 countries in LAC. Then, in the 2000s, 13 countries had left-wing governments under democracies which had different views on the role of the police than the military governments that were in office before.

Regardless of the route of transition, the form of the democracies that emerged in most countries tended to be shallow and fragile. Unfortunately, the process of creating new police forces failed to gain societal approval, to generate trust, to have a solid institutional anchor, or to reduce crime (see Hathazy, 2013, for examples in South America and Cruz, 2015, in Central America).

In most countries, there have been attempts in recent years to reform the police in order to enhance the institution's legitimacy and effectiveness. There have been gradual efforts to reorganize the police, purge corrupt officers and improve recruitment and training, as well as increase the vigilance and participation of civil society, including through the introduction of community policing. Politically motivated without fundamental institutional reform, these efforts have largely failed to induce longer-term and substantive changes.

There are other challenges in LAC emerging from the police force to consider. The size of the police force, as well as the skills and training of the officers, is fundamental to understanding the feasibility of implementing EBP and what is required to do so. As a response to growing insecurity, many governments increased their public spending on security, mainly on police. This translated directly into an increase in the number of police officers: LAC regional average is 422 officers per 100,000 inhabitants, similar to that of the Middle East and almost double that of developed nations like the US, Canada and Northern European countries (UNODC, 2020). However, these officers typically have neither skills and training nor the equipment necessary to perform their duties. In fact,

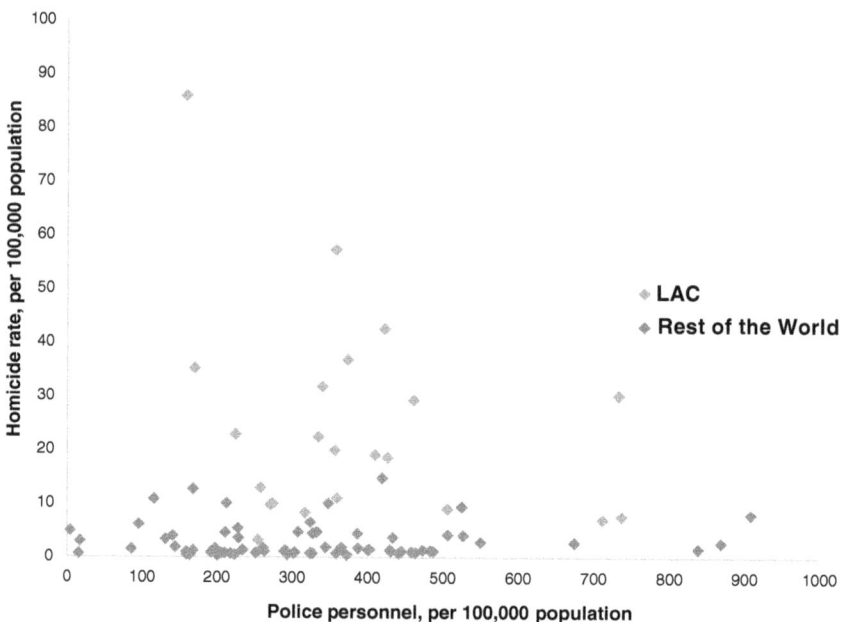

FIGURE 12.2 Police personnel and homicide rates
Source: Jaitman (2019) based on UNODC and World Bank World Development Indicators.
*Note: LAC: Latin America and the Caribbean

Figure 12.2 shows that despite the high number of police officers, the police do not seem to be very effective in the region, as indicated by the high homicide rates in LAC compared with those in regions of the world with comparable police headcount.

In most countries, there is a general consensus that preparing, equipping and training the police is necessary, and many countries have taken steps to improve the educational requirements for police (Sanguinetti et al., 2015). At the beginning of the 1990s, many police institutions' requirement for enrollment was primary school. By 2016, however, that requirement had in most cases become secondary school (Casas et al., 2018), and some countries recently introduced higher education requirements and strengthened police training.

Finally, another challenge related to the police institutions is that most police institutions in the region are not trusted by the citizenry: 64 per cent of LAC citizens have little or no confidence in the police (see Figure 12.3A). One factor in the lack of citizen confidence in the police force is the perception of corruption. We can see in Figure 12.3B that

Towards Implementing Evidence-Based Policing 243

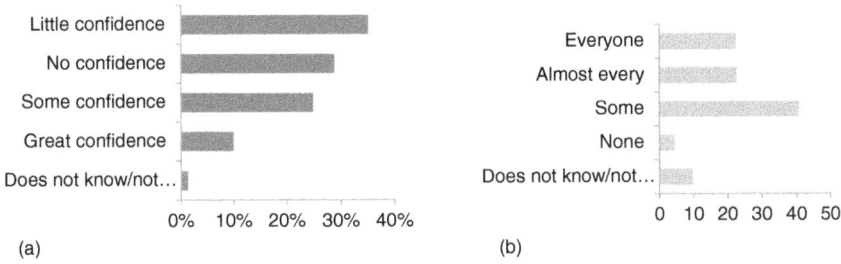

FIGURE 12.3 (a) Citizen confidence in the police in LAC, 2018; (b) Perception of Proportion of police members involved in corruption in LAC, 2018
Source: Latinobarometer (2018) – latest available dataset.

86 per cent of citizens perceive that some or all members of the police forces are corrupt.

12.3.2 Lack of Scientific Evidence

Despite the magnitude of the security problem in LAC, only a small portion of public policy interventions in citizen security is based on evidence and backed by enough information to rigorously assess their impact. This is one of the most important obstacles to EBP implementation. Without intervention assessments, police reform and security policies in general are at the mercy of biases, trends, prejudgments and/or extreme rhetoric. This factor is also recognized as an important obstacle in the international context as mentioned before.

According to Muggah and Tobón (2018), there were at least 1,300 documented citizen security programs and projects developed in LAC between the late 1990s and 2017. They are mainly concentrated in a few countries: nearly 60 per cent of them have been carried out in Colombia, Brazil, Guatemala, Nicaragua, Honduras and El Salvador. However, very few of them have been assessed. From a random sample of 304 interventions (23% of the total), only 20 (7%) were subjected to some kind of evaluation implying a control group (not necessarily a robust impact evaluation). In addition to this, if we look at the Global Policing Database (GPD) analyzed in Chapter 8 of this volume by Mazzarole and colleagues, only 1.3% of the 952 studies included in the GPD relate to LAC (Higginson et al., 2014).[1] This is also the case in other fields like

---

[1] The GPD is a searchable online bank of quality police impact evaluations that utilize a range of methods including randomized experimental or quasi-experimental designs with a comparison group that does not receive the intervention.

economics, in which the number of published crime economics papers has been increasing but those covering LAC are only 3.5% of the total crime economics papers since 1990 in economic journals.[2]

EBP starts with solid evidence from which to design effective crime reduction and crime control policies. But crime in LAC is still understudied. Some of the reasons for this are exposed in the following two sections: weak crime information systems and political concerns. Another reason is cultural – there is resistance to scientific experiments in the area of security. Indeed, this cultural obstacle is an issue in other sectors as well but greater progress has been made for example in education and social protection with initiatives such as large-scale conditional cash transfer programmes in Mexico or Brazil that were designed and expanded based on evidence from randomized trials or other solid evaluations. As discussed earlier, the resistance of officers to adjust their discretion to research and science is an issue outside the region as well.

12.3.3 Weak Crime Information Systems

In order to undertake rigorous research on citizen security programs, robust information systems are crucial. However, crime statistics in the region are fragmented, inconsistent, and aggregated only to the most macro levels, hindering the construction of times series and comparability across countries. Unfortunately, within the region, there are significant institutional differences in recording crime and in the efficiency of public agencies. This is also true within countries when different government agencies are in charge of reporting crime statistics. There are no clear guidelines about how to code information, and there are no proper standards to judge the quality of information. All of this raises a number of questions regarding validity and credibility. Furthermore, official data is not updated frequently and is generally not available to the public.

Although some countries are making progress on the statistics front – for instance, Chile, Colombia, Ecuador, Uruguay, and some states in Brazil and Mexico, and a few provinces in Argentina have made considerable progress and are moving toward having useful and interconnected information systems – crime statistics systems in the region still lag behind the ideal statistics system.

---

[2] Papers related to crime and the criminal justice system that were published in general interest or top field journals in economics that are mainly on Latin America or on a country of the region. Database of crime papers compiled by Doleac (2021).

Finally, official statistics are affected by problems of underreporting, that is, people tend to not report crimes of which they have been victims. This may stem from the distance to the institutions where crimes should be reported, low confidence in such institutions, doubts about the usefulness of reporting crimes, or fear of being victimized again. Jaitman and Anauati (2020) show that underreporting is significant in the region. They quantify the dark figure of crime defined as the gap between crimes reported in victimization surveys and crimes registered in administrative police records in Latin America and the Caribbean over 2004–2014. They find that the dark figure of gender-based violent crimes is between 92 and 95 per cent in comparison with a dark figure of between 63 and 80 per cent in developed countries. This means that in the region, around 5 out of every 100 gender-based violent crimes are found in administrative police records. The dark figure of assaults and robberies of vehicles is 65 and 52 per cent, respectively, in the region.

12.3.4 Political Concerns

Another challenge is political; security in the developing world is a sensitive topic closely related to public opinion and political concerns. The dissemination of research projects is frequently obstructed when those projects run counter to established political gains, expose corruption or simply are considered by political operators to undermine society's perception of security.

The implementation of EBP is hence also stymied by political decision-making processes, the instability of institutions and the police culture. In most cases, police initiatives become a political issue: politicians often take up crime control as a campaign banner and compete in offering anticrime programs, many of which are not based on evidence. In fact, the trajectory of police reforms or initiatives is intimately linked to national political and bureaucratic structures throughout the region. Among the challenges described in this section, political concerns is a prominent one in LAC.

This is compounded by two factors. First, the great instability of political institutions as noted earlier that makes it difficult to adopt medium- and/or long-term policies. Second, given the context of highly disjointed party systems and extremely volatile elections in the region, continuity of leadership in any process of police reform is very difficult to achieve (Casas et al., 2018). Building a political consensus before the start of any reform effort to guarantee its continuity over time is crucial for the successful implementation of any policy.

Finally, the police's institutional culture is another factor that could hinder the implementation of EBP. In general, police officers in LAC are impervious to change and resistant to incorporating new theories. Furthermore, the police are usually sceptical of those policies that involve significant changes and often view them as a distraction from the tasks perceived as necessary for effectively combatting crime. This is an obstacle to EBP implementation especially present in LAC given the other institutional challenges mentioned before.

12.4 PROMOTING EBP IN THE REGION

Persistent high crime rates and increasing discontent and distrust between the police and the citizens show that traditional policing strategies have not succeeded in Latin America and the Caribbean (LAC). This suggests that, on the one hand, the implementation of EBP has the potential of reducing crime rates and on the other, the promotion of any such change in policing is challenging and complex.

The region faces many of the International challenges to implement EBP, such as institutionalization of EBP, the disconnect between science and policing, and inadequate police education and training. These challenges are exacerbated in LAC countries by the particular context in which police agencies function, which greatly differs from that of more developed countries in several aspects: the outstanding levels of crime and violence; citizens' perception that the police is corrupt, unreliable and ineffective; lack of scientific evidence for the LAC region; and weaker crime statistics systems. In LAC there is also a main barrier that exacerbates even further all the challenges mentioned: political concerns which prevent the dissemination of knowledge that could infuse change in policing.

There is a lot of potential to improve crime and violence outcomes in the region if EBP could be widely promoted. The dissemination of both the knowledge gained from developed-country police forces and of the scant research on policing in the region are critical first steps. Many of the lessons learned from developed countries could be applied in a number of LAC settings. The few papers using quality crime data and robust research methods show that although crime levels are much higher in LAC, crime dynamics and the impact of some policies tested are comparable to those of developed countries.

For example, Jaitman and Ajzenman (2016) validate for a set of LAC cities Weisburd's "law of crime concentration at place" (Weisburd, 2015).

Using micro-geographic units of analysis (street segments), they find that crime in the region is highly concentrated in a small proportion of street segments as in cities in developed countries. Thus, many important policy recommendations from the literature of crime and place could be applied to LAC cities. The evaluation of more crime and place interventions in the region would also be highly valuable to test whether the findings in advanced economies can be generalized to other settings.

To induce a paradigm shift in the region, in light of the discussion above, many challenges must be addressed. Policing is an area where experimental and quasi-experimental methods are gradually becoming powerful research tools. However, academic-police partnerships face many challenges and experimentation can be difficult to implement and knowledge difficult to disseminate if they run against the pre-assumed results. Incentive schemes for the police commanders could help to promote champions of these types of reforms. Galiani and Jaitman (2022) study a case in which a pay-per-performance scheme was enacted to reward the police officers and commanders who allocated most of the patrol time to the agreed micro-geographic units of the city. This was one of the steps to institutionalize EBP adoption, in this case, hotspots policing. EMUN program in Israel is another example of incentivizing EBP adoption by institutionalizing EBP (in this case the program institutionalized every stage of problem-oriented-policing) (Weisburd et al., 2020). In both cases, technology for accountability tools had to be developed. Institutionalization of EBP must also be accompanied by an effort to address low levels of skills and education and to professionalize the police force.

There are examples of police and academic partnerships that were successful in applying EBP while conducting a rigorous evaluation of the policies. This facilitated that changes would be more sustainable over time. Along these lines, Galiani and Jaitman (2022) working together with the police force of Uruguay run a randomized trial to test whether the implementation of an international predictive policing software outperforms predictions made by trained local crime analysts. They find that there were no statically significant differences in crime rates when comparing randomly assigned police precincts to the software and to the local crime analysts. As a result of this evaluation, the government decided to train more local crime analysts to guide police deployment in the country as it proved to be more cost-effective than using international software.

It is important to note that the promotion of EBP and impact evaluations is an opportunity to reassess security policies in the region and identify improvements to existing policies or potential non-desirable effects that may lead to policy changes. For example, Acemoglu et al. (2020) analyzed the implications of providing high-powered incentives for the military and security services under weak institutional controls in Colombia. They find that high-powered incentives produced several perverse side effects, and had no discernible improvement in the overall security situation, while also weakening the judicial dimension of state capacity. Another example in the context of organized crime, is the kingpin strategy study carried out by Lindo and Padilla-Romo (2018). The authors analyze the effects of an approach to fighting organized crime in which law-enforcement efforts focus on capturing the leaders of criminal organizations, on community violence in the context of Mexico's drug war. The results show that kingpin captures have large and sustained effects on the homicide rate in the municipality of capture and smaller but significant effects on other municipalities where the kingpin's organization has a presence, supporting the notion that removing kingpins can have destabilizing effects throughout an organization that are accompanied by escalations in violence.

Given the severity of crime issues in the region, it is of critical importance to promote EBP through knowledge transfer and fostering academic-practitioners partnerships to overcome the main challenges to adopt EBP, mainly political concerns with experimentation and findings that can run against the status quo or the hierarchy's beliefs.

12.5 CONCLUSION

In this chapter, we made the case for the promotion of EBP in Latin America and the Caribbean (LAC), given the great potential that this could have to reduce crime in the most violent region on earth. This will not also alleviate the problem in LAC countries themselves but also directly benefit other countries given the cross-border nature of some crimes that are very prominent in the region, like organized crime.

The Chapter discussed several challenges to implementing EBP in LAC: first, the international challenges developed countries face, second challenges particular to LAC such as the citizens' weak perceptions of the police, the lack of a body of research with sound evaluations of crime control policies, and data issues which makes research and accountability more complex.

Advancing the implementation of EBP in the region is not only an opportunity to reduce crime rates and the incidence of violence in the region that registers the highest homicides rates on earth, but it is also an opportunity to draw lessons from the region that can be useful in other countries and cities both in developing and advanced regions.

Although LAC has compounded challenges to implement EBP, several of them are also important in other regions. Many developing countries face similar challenges, especially those with high crime rates and high levels of informality. In addition to this, weak institutions and lack of trust in the police is a common feature in several cities across the world due to different reasons and drivers, including in advanced economies.

Potential lessons on accountability, predictive policing, police training and incentive mechanisms from LAC explored in this Chapter could be useful in several settings from US cities (given recent movements on police reform), to Nigeria (and the Special Anti-Robbery Squad) or Hong Kong (to restore trust eroded in the last years after policing the protests), among many other countries. This Chapter can also draw lessons from LAC's failed police reforms which are relevant for other settings in which police reform and features like the militarization of the police are considered.

The chapter discussed another avenue to connect EBP in LAC to the mainstream EBP literature that focuses on other cities. Research shows that crime concentration patterns in LAC cities and US cities are similar. This means that, potentially, implementing EBP in LAC cities can also help build evidence, for example on the impact of proactive policing, that is useful for other cities in the developed world. Especially those cities with high crime rates. Also, the external validity of policies could be tested in LAC to gather information for their suitability in other contexts. Furthermore, EBP implementation in LAC could provide the opportunity to test policies and strategies that have not been tested before in other contexts due to other constraints.

Finally, as the Chapter argues and given the potential benefit of promoting EBP in LAC for other countries, it would be important to facilitate knowledge sharing across the world. In this regard, it would be extremely beneficial to promote practitioner–academic partnership between different countries or cities with shared challenges.

References

Acemoglu, D., Fergusson, L., Robinson, J., Romero, D., & Vargas, J. (2020). The Perils of High-Powered Incentives: Evidence from Colombia's False Positives. *American Economic Journal: Economic Policy*, 12(3), 1–43.

Casas, K., González, P., & Mesías, L. (2018). *Police Transformation in Latin America by 2030*. Inter-American Development Bank. Washington, DC.

Cruz, J. M. (2015). Police Misconduct and Political Legitimacy in Central America. *Journal of Latin American Studies, 47*(2), 251–283.
Dammert, L. (2019). Challenges of police reform in Latin America. In *Routledge handbook of law and society in Latin America* (pp. 259–277). Routledge.
Doleac, J. (2021). *Database of crime papers in economic journals.*
European Commission. (2018). Spring 2018 Standard Eurobarometer. https://europa.eu/eurobarometer/surveys/detail/2180
Galiani, S. & Jaitman, L. (2022). Predictive Policing in a Developing Country: Evidence from Two Randomized Controlled Trials. *Journal of Quantitative Criminology.*
Gallup. (2018). *Gallup opinion survey 2018.* https://news.gallup.com/poll/237389/
Hanak, G., & Hofinger, V. (2005). *Police Science and Research in the European Union: Report.* Vienna: Institute for the Sociology of Law and Criminology.
Hathazy, P. (2013). Fighting for a democratic police: Politics, Experts and Bureaucrats in the transformation of the police in post-authoritarian Chile and Argentina. *Comparative Sociology, 12*, 1–43.
Higginson, A., Eggins, E., Mazerolle, L., & Stanko, E. (2014). The Global Policing Database [Database and Protocol].
Jaitman, L. (2019). Frontiers in the economics of crime: lessons for Latin America and the Caribbean. *Latin American Economic Review, 28*(1), 19.
Jaitman, L. & Ajzenman, N. (2016). *Crime Concentration and Hot Spot Dynamics in Latin America.* IADB working paper.
Jaitman, L. & Anauati, V. (2020). The Dark Figure of Crime in Latin America and the Caribbean. *Journal of Economics, Race, and Policy, 3*(2).
Johnson, S., Mendelson, J., & Bliss, K. (2012). *Police Reform in Latin America. Implications for US policy.* CSIS.
Latinobarometer (2018). *2018 Report.*
Lindo, J. M., & Padilla-Romo, M. (2018). Kingpin approaches to fighting crime and community violence: Evidence from Mexico's drug war. *Journal of Health Economics, 58*, 253–268.
Lum, C. M., & Koper, C. S. (2017). *Evidence-based policing: Translating research into practice.* Oxford University Press.
Mazerolle, L., Eggins, E., Hine, L., & Higginson, A. (this volume). The Role of Randomized Experiments in Developing the Evidence for Evidence-Based Policing. In D. Weisburd, T. Jonathan, G. Perry & B. Hasisi, (Eds.), *The future of evidence-based policing.* Cambridge University Press.
Muggah, R., & Tobón, K. A. (2018). *Citizen security in Latin America: facts and figures.* Igarape Institute.
Read, T. & Tilley, N. (2000). *Not Rocket Science? Problem Solving and Crime Reduction.* Crime Reduction Research Series Paper 6. London: Home Office.
Sanguinetti, P., Ortega, D., Berniell, L., Álvarez, F., Mejía, D., Castillo, J. C., & Brassiolo, P. (2015). *Towards a safer Latin America. A new perspective to prevent and control crime.*
Sherman, L. W. (1998). *Evidence-based policing.* Police Foundation. www.policefoundation.org/wp-content/uploads/2015/06/Sherman-1998-Evidence-Based-Policing.pdf

United Nations Office on Drugs and Crime (UNODC). (2020). *Statistics Database*.
Weisburd, D. (2015). The law of crime concentration and the criminology of place. *Criminology, 53*(2), 133–157.
Weisburd, D., & Braga, A. A. (Eds.) (2019). *Police innovation: Contrasting perspectives*. Cambridge University Press.
Weisburd, D., Hasisi, B., Litmanovitz, Y., Carmel, T., & Tshuva, S. (2020). Institutionalizing problem-oriented policing: An evaluation of the EMUN reform in Israel. *Criminology & Public Policy, 19*(3), 941–964.
Weisburd, D., & Neyroud, P. (2011). *Police science: Toward a new paradigm*. New perspectives in policing.

13

Evidence-Based Policing and the Law

The American Perspective

Rachel Harmon

Policing and the law are intricately intertwined. Indeed, in a free society governed by the rule of law, the police inevitably exist as both a product and subject of legal rules. Fundamentally, police officers are government agents authorized to commit otherwise illegal acts to allow them to protect life and property, resolve conflicts over public space, and bring criminals to justice. Without a statute or judicial decision permitting it, a police stop would be false imprisonment, an arrest kidnapping, a home search breaking and entering, and a use of force anything from assault to murder. Since officers' coercive tools harm as well as help, threatening freedom, privacy, equality, and bodily integrity, the law imposes limits – often detailed limits – on police authority. Inevitably, then, the law enables and constrains policing.

Yet, as enthusiasm has grown for ensuring that policing reflects the best available evidence about what practices are effective and fair, almost nothing has been written about the relationship between evidence-based policing and the law. Social scientists and advocates of evidence-based policing usually direct their work at police executives and policymakers who might choose among policing strategies, rather than to courts and legislatures that define the scope of lawful police activity. Courts and lawyers, and perhaps even legislatures, in turn have largely overlooked the evidence-based policing movement and, often, social science research about what works in policing.

Perhaps this gap in the literature is unsurprising. If there were to be a conversation about evidence-based policing and the law, it would have to include, on one side, legal actors and scholars who might influence or be influenced by evidence about what works in policing and, on the other side, police executives and social scientists who embrace evidence-based policing and might consider its relationship to the law. But both sides mostly act as if there were nothing much to say: Courts and legal scholars often treat social science research on policing as if it were exogenous and marginally relevant. Perhaps ironically, social scientists who study policing and police executives similarly view the law as a fixed constraint on evidence-based practices.

Despite the silence, the relationship between social science evidence about policing and law is more important and complicated than it first appears. First, the law both constrains and incentivizes research on policing practices. It therefore affects what is known about what works in policing – the basis for evidence-based practices – and therefore what evidence-appreciating practitioners will do. Yet, we know little about how legal uncertainty or variability affects social scientists carry out research on policing.

Second, legal actors make empirical assessments about policing and weigh its costs and benefits in evaluating the legality of police practices and developing forward-looking legal rules that govern the police, so that the same evidence base that informs policing practices can, and sometimes does, inform the law that enables or constrains those practices. While legislatures often consider the perspective of the social sciences in formulating enactments on policing, courts are more variable, frequently drawing conclusions about what effective policing necessitates or how policing practices affect individuals and officers without consulting available research. Nevertheless, even courts sometimes – perhaps increasingly – look to research on policing to inform their decision-making. When they do so, the same evidence base that guides police executives toward more scientifically informed decisions may also strengthen law-making concerning the police, at least if it addresses the questions with which courts and legislatures are concerned.

Using legal examples from the United States to illustrate, this chapter explores the relationship between evidence-based policing and the law by considering the manners in which law may shape research on policing and research on policing may shape the law. It also makes three recommendations for researchers.

13.1 HOW LAW SHAPES EVIDENCE-BASED POLICING

13.1.1 Law as a Constraint

It is easy to see that the law functions as a substantial constraint on policing practices, even those that might be effective. In the limiting case, a legal rule simply prohibits a policing practice, making it irrelevant whether the activity is effective in reducing crime. No one need study whether the rack and the screw produce accurate confessions. These practices are widely forbidden, in the United States by the Fourteenth Amendment's prohibition on depriving individuals of life or liberty without due process of law.

While perhaps researchers do not need the law to tell them that torture offers poor promise as a criminal investigation technique, the law also constrains research on policing activities that are not obviously beyond the pale. For example, researchers do not test whether random pedestrian stops in high crime areas – without individualized suspicion of criminal activity – effectively deter gun crime. In a sense, this is surprising. Hot spots policing has clear promise as a crime control strategy (Braga et al., 2019). Randomized stops may well be less harmful than those based on suspicion, since they limit what legal scholars call "targeting harm," the harm that comes about when those subjected to police attention wonder, "Why me? Why have the police singled me out …?" (Colb, 1996, p. 1464; cf. Hasisi et al., 2012). Randomization also better ensures that harms of policing are fairly distributed (Harcourt & Meares, 2011). And given the low hit rates police often achieve in suspicion-based pedestrian stops and the absence of clear correlates for criminality, they might well be as effective in uncovering and deterring criminal activity in a target-rich environment. But, like torture, random stops are widely barred, famously in American law by *Terry v. Ohio* and its progeny, which interpreted the Fourth Amendment to demand that officers have individualized reasonable suspicion of involvement in criminal activity before they detain a member of the public (Terry v. Ohio, 1968; Illinois v. Wardlow, 2000). As a result of statutes and judicial decisions in other countries, and as a result of Fourth Amendment doctrine in the United States, departments cannot plausibly adopt such a strategy, and researchers are not likely to study it.

Of course, researchers also refrain from studying whether pepper spray is effective in zero gravity or whether violent crime can be deterred by assigning every young person a police officer to surveil them. However, the law is not simply one more practical constraint on policing practices and therefore research. The law does not necessarily make a policing activity implausible, either physically or financially. Police officers can and sometimes do violate the laws of men – unlike the laws of physics – and given the relative rarity of successful damages actions against officers or departments, the financial consequences of doing so are usually not prohibitive. Instead, police executives avoid adopting illegal policing strategies for complex normative, political, and practical reasons, to which legal remedies, such as evidentiary exclusion and civil damages awards, contribute. The effect, however, is similar: police departments do not openly adopt clearly illegal strategies, and researchers – who have normative and practical reasons of their own – do not test them.

Often, however, the law is less an on/off switch and more a matter of probability or patchwork. It can be a long time before the legal status of a newly adopted policing practice is resolved. For example, although American police departments authorizing the use of conducted energy weapons dramatically increased in the early 2000s (Reaves, 2015), the law governing these devices is still catching up. Only after agencies widely began employing conducted energy devices in the United States did federal courts in the United States meaningfully restrict common uses, such as wielding the devices to overcome passive resistance (e.g., Armstrong v. Village of Pinehurst, 2016). And even well-developed legal doctrines often leave ambiguities and open questions. Similarly, police practices may be permissible in some jurisdictions, but not in others. In the United States, for instance, most jurisdictions permit police officers to ask drivers for consent to search their vehicles without individualized reason to suspect evidence or contraband will be found, but several states and more municipalities and agencies ban suspicionless consent searches (e.g., Minnesota v. Fort, 2003).

How much does the law influence research on policing practices in cases in which the law is inconsistent or not (yet) clear? One should expect departments and researchers to be influenced by their predictions about the law: It hardly seems probable that departments or researchers will invest heavily in strategies that are highly likely to be declared illegal given existing constitutional doctrine or that states have overwhelmingly barred by legislation. Yet, departments often adopt – and researchers study – policing strategies when some jurisdictions forbid them, or when their legal status is unknown, but they are less probably illegal.

Additionally, when the law remains uncertain but shifts against a practice, one cannot expect either academics or police executives to turn on a dime. Thus, one might also expect that legal starting points could have an anchoring effect, exerting an inertial force on the kinds of practices considered worth studying and adopting, even as their legal status changes.

Consider, for example, the use of automated license plate readers (ALPRs). ALPRs automatically and rapidly capture a vehicle's license plate number and sometimes additional images of the vehicle and occupants. The systems can compare data from the images with government databases to identify stolen vehicle or find a person subject to an arrest warrant, or to track (in real time or historically) a car's movements. Police departments in the United States adopted ALPRs in the 1990s and 2000s against a highly favorable legal backdrop: According to long-standing Fourth Amendment doctrine, the government does not conduct a search within the meaning of the Fourth Amendment when it observes a person or object that has been "knowingly exposed" (United States v. Katz, 1967). The U.S. Supreme Court has interpreted that to mean that the government may – without implicating the Fourth Amendment – observe people and objects in plain view (Horton v. California, 1990) and watch a person's movements in public (United States v. Knotts, 1983). Moreover, the Supreme Court has permitted police departments to use technology to facilitate public surveillance that would be lawful, but impractical, if carried out unassisted (United States v. Knotts, 1983). Before courts decided cases concerning ALPRs, police departments reasonably concluded that that the Court's doctrine amounted to a legal permission slip for such systems.

Recently, the legal landscape for ALPRs has begun to change. While some uses of ALPRs will almost certainly remain legal, others raise new constitutional concern. The Supreme Court now distinguishes between a single observation of a person's movements in public and technologies that permit a detailed account of a person's movement over time (Carpenter v. United States, 2018). Lower courts are beginning to consider the implications of this doctrinal shift for ALPRs. For instance, the highest court in Massachusetts has concluded that, with enough cameras in enough locations, either the historic location data from an ALPR system or sufficiently precise real-time location of individuals could constitute a search within the meaning of the Fourth Amendment, and therefore require individualized suspicion and perhaps a warrant (Commonwealth v. McCarthy, 2020). Concern about the use of ALPR data has also led some states to regulate police use of ALPRs by statute (e.g., Cal. Civ. Code § 1798.90.51, .52, .54, .55, 2019). Yet over the same period in which the law started to become less favorable, license plate reader employment by law enforcement agencies expanded dramatically in the United States, and researchers have advocated more study of their effectiveness in crime control (e.g., Lum et al., 2019a).

This kind of legal uncertainty might influence research on policing and policing practice by multiple mechanisms. If police executives respond to legal uncertainty as well as outright bans, then when the law suggests a practice may not be legal or may be restricted in the future, that law will discourage some agencies from adopting it. The practice, even if currently lawful, may become less common, though perhaps unevenly so. As agencies avoid a practice, researchers may have less opportunity and interest in studying it. Moreover, researchers interested in informing police practices may also respond directly, even if slowly, to uncertain legal environments: They may avoid studying activities that could soon be barred, because their research would become largely irrelevant to police departments, if and when that happened. Any change in research will, in turn, further modulate strategies adopted in the name of evidence-based policing; only those studied will be supported by research. Even if a controversial policing practice is eventually authorized by statute or upheld in courts, agencies looking to social science evidence may still be less likely to adopt it, because – at that point – less research would be available to support it. Thus, legal uncertainty may chill both police uptake of contested police activities and research into them, not just immediately, but over time. One might expect legal inconsistency across jurisdictions to have a similar dampening effect.

Not all laws restrict police practices: some statutes or cases *mandate* police conduct. These too could potentially dampen research and thus evidence on policing. If states overwhelmingly mandate body-worn cameras, will researchers be as interested in how they affect citizen complaints, uses of force, and community trust? (Lum et al., 2019b). Certainly, researchers initially studied the impact of rights warnings on interrogations after the U.S. Supreme Court decided Miranda v. Arizona (1966), mandating warnings and other protections during custodial interrogations. That research continued while the constitutionality of the opinion remained heavily contested. But, to a significant extent, researchers lost interest once the legal status of the opinion became more resolved (Dickerson v. United States, 2000), and while legal scholars revive empirical debates on major anniversaries of the U.S. Supreme Court's decision in *Miranda* (e.g., Cassell & Fowles, 2017), social scientists have largely moved on to other questions about interrogation (e.g., Snook, et al., 2020), even as the warnings and waiver scheme required by *Miranda* remain the law, and research could inform that law's development, as well as how warnings are carried out and rights-waivers obtained.

Still, neither legal uncertainty nor inconsistency will necessarily inhibit research and the practices supported by it. One can imagine confounding forces: legal controversies bring media attention, which could increase interest in studying a practice, for example. Until we know more about how departments and researchers react to legal evolution, it will be hard to predict the impact that legal uncertainty has on research or, in turn, evidence-based policing practices. Luckily, the law governing police practices changes often, offering frequent opportunities for researchers to explore the answers.

13.1.2 Law as an Incentive

Unlike legislatures, which often defend statutes as grounded in science, courts facing challenges to police conduct often focus exclusively on precedent, text, and history. Still, who wins in court is frequently determined at least in part by judicial assessment of empirical questions concerning policing. Consequently, parties that wish to challenge policing practices and departments that wish to defend them both leverage available research and occasionally solicit research about those practices in arguing cases. Researchers in turn study police practices that often end up in court. In this way, the law motivates some kinds of research on policing rather than others.

For instance, in the United States, intentional racial discrimination in selecting targets for police scrutiny usually violates the Equal Protection Clause and often state and federal statutes as well. But proving discrimination is difficult and frequently turns on empirical estimates of disparate treatment. Parties build class action cases by turning to experts to prove that racial disparities are (or are not) likely caused by discrimination. Over time, litigation on racial discrimination has led – both directly and indirectly – to a well-developed literature on racial disparities in police traffic and pedestrian stops, a subject of frequent litigation (Weisburd & Majmundar, 2018). One might think that this body of research would have arisen in any case, but that is unlikely. Contrast research on racial discrimination in arrests and the use of force. Despite the political salience and practical import of discrimination in these policing contexts, the social science literature regarding that discrimination has developed far more slowly (Geller et al., 2020; Hollis & Jennings, 2018; Mitchell & Caudy, 2015).

The law, at least in the United States, suggests a partial explanation: stronger legal and practical barriers exist to challenging discrimination in arrests and in force. For example, many class action suits challenging discriminatory police practices seek equitable relief in the form of injunctions against or court-ordered changes in policing practices rather than monetary damages. But in City of Los Angeles v. Lyons (1983), the

Supreme Court held that plaintiffs seeking equitable relief must show a real or immediate threat that they will unavoidably have their rights again violated. This is hard to establish with respect to illegal arrests or uses of force. In *Lyons* itself, the plaintiff alleged that Los Angeles officers carried out chokeholds against criminal suspects whose resistance justified only less extreme force, but the Court barred the suit, suggesting that Lyons could avoid future chokeholds by simply refraining from committing a crime or from resisting arrest. Not so victims of color alleging that officers targeted them in pedestrian or traffic stops without reasonable suspicion; such an allegation carries with it the claim that the plaintiffs were doing nothing wrong. Although individual damages actions do not face this barrier, well-financed class action litigation concerning discrimination in arrests and force is rarer because of *Lyons*. Thus, courts less often look to research, lawyers less often commission it, and researchers have less incentive to conduct it. Here, too, research about policing, which in turn means the evidence base for research-informed policing, follows the law.

In criminal cases in the United States, defendants frequently seek to exclude evidence by arguing that it is the product of an illegal search, seizure, or interrogation technique. In this context as well, legal doctrine can encourage research agendas. For example, in Delaware v. Prouse (1979), the Supreme Court struck down a random vehicle stop to check a drivers' license and registration because it concluded – in the absence of empirical evidence – that the spot check program was not a "sufficiently productive" means of serving the government's interest (p. 659–660). By contrast, the Supreme Court upheld border patrol checkpoints used in United States v. Martinez-Fuerte (1976) in part because statistical evidence supported their effectiveness. Departments interested in suspicionless stop programs, such as checkpoints, would be well cautioned to choose strategies for which there is research support. Researchers seeking to expand evidence-based policing can do so doubly by evaluating such strategies: finding a strategy effective could encourage departments to adopt a productive activity, and the research that supports engaging in the activity will also strengthen the department's legal position if it needs to defend the practice in court.

In an important sense, however, *Prouse*, is an outlier. Although Fourth Amendment doctrine often requires courts to make judgments about the consequences of policing practices, they usually take a more deferential approach in the absence of evidence. Courts are especially permissive with respect to officer arguments about what behaviors indicate criminal activity. For example, in *Illinois v. Wardlow* (2000), the Supreme Court concluded that a suspect's "unprovoked flight" upon seeing an officer combined with the suspect's presence in a "high crime area" constituted reasonable suspicion that the person was involved with criminal activity (p. 124). The Court acknowledged that no evidence supporting its conclusion: "In reviewing the propriety of an officer's conduct, courts do not have available empirical studies dealing with inferences drawn from suspicious behavior, and we cannot reasonably demand scientific certainty from judges or law enforcement officers where none exists. Thus, the determination of reasonable suspicion must be based on commonsense judgments and inferences about human behavior." (pp. 124–125). Instead of looking at social science research, it noted that its own decisions had previously treated nervous or evasive conduct as pertinent to reasonable suspicion (p. 124). If the Court had instead demanded support for the officer's claim that unprovoked flight indicates criminal activity, presumably far fewer officers would stop suspects whose only "suspicious" activity is fleeing the police, at until researchers evaluated the question, perhaps a difficult one to study.

As legal scholars frequently decry, American courts at all levels fail to demand that empirical claims made by officers and departments in criminal cases meet even minimal standards of reliability and validity. Since *Wardlow*, for example, lower courts have effectively set a lower threshold of individualized, behavioral suspicion for stops that occur in "high crime areas," because the location contributes to the suspiciousness of otherwise innocent activity. But they rarely require any objective or empirical data justifying an officer's testimony that the area in which a stop occurred is justifiably labeled "high crime" (Ferguson, 2008).

Both in setting rules based on unverified empirical conclusions and in permitting departments and officers to make unverified claims, courts do evidence-based policing no favors. They may permit or encourage policing practices that are not be worth their harms, and they fail to incentivize departments to look for research, and researchers to conduct studies, that would enable better decision-making both by courts and by departments. Or, to say it another way, when courts depend solely on officer experience and judicial intuition to support essentially empirical conclusions about the harmfulness, fairness, or effectiveness of police practices, they not only fail to make evidence-based decisions, but they also miss an opportunity to promote research about policing practices and the use of that research by departments. In this way, courts encourage intuition-based policing instead of the evidence-informed kind.

13.1.3 Law as an Aid

A final way in which law shapes the course of research on policing is by making it easier to conduct. Research on what works in policing is limited by available data, something the law frequently influences. For instance, nearly half of states in the United States have statutes concerning racial profiling by police departments. Some of those laws mandate extensive data collection, which in turn can be used to assess disparities and determine the kinds of policing that produce them (e.g., Neb. Rev. Stat. § 20-504; N.C. Gen. Stat. § 114-10.01, 2013).

Similarly, lawsuits challenging police conduct often reach settlements that mandate data collection and access that in turn can facilitate research. For example, in March 1999, the Center for Constitutional Rights filed a class action lawsuit challenging the New York Police Department (NYPD) Street Crime Unit's stop and frisk practices (Daniels v. City of New York, 2001). That lawsuit settled, and the settlement required the NYPD to make its UF-250s, the forms on which officers recorded stops and frisks, available to the Center for Constitutional Rights (Stipulation of Settlement, Daniels v. City of New York, 2003). Those forms helped the Center for Constitutional Rights bring a subsequent class action lawsuit against the City of New York, challenging its stop, question, and frisk program. In that suit, the district court relied on expert analysis of the UF-250 database in concluding that the NYPD's practices violated the Fourth Amendment prohibition against unreasonable searches and seizures and the Equal Protection Clause (Floyd v. City of New York, 2013a), and the data have since been used to generate further research, even after the lawsuit resolved itself (e.g., Legewie & Fagan, 2019). The research growing out of the New York data has been important in drawing conclusions about whether proactive policing through stop, question, and frisk contributes to racial disparities (Weisburd & Majmundar, 2018), an important consideration for any agency contemplating adopting the strategy. As this example suggests, just as legislation can generate data on policing that can facilitate research that influences agency practices, litigation can do the same.

13.2 HOW EVIDENCE ABOUT POLICING SHAPES THE LAW

Courts rarely acknowledge the role they play in shaping research about policing. Instead, they see the existence or absence of research as an external fact. Similarly, police executives and social scientists tend to treat the law as a fixed, exogenous force on both research and policing. But this view is equally mistaken. The mechanisms by which law may influence social science research also suggest the converse, that social science research sometimes shapes the law that governs police activities: Legislatures often look to experts and available research to guide them, and while courts frequently make unsupported empirical statements about how policing is carried out or what is required for effective policing, they also sometimes look to social science evidence about policing when formulating legal rules or when evaluating officer conduct. With some assistance, they might do so more.

13.2.1 Balancing Interests and Fourth Amendment Law

Inevitably, as courts, legislatures, and policymakers evaluate policing practices, they must consider both the effectiveness of those practices and their impact on individuals and communities. Often, commentators emphasize the tradeoffs policymakers make; practices that yield public safety benefits may also infringe on privacy, undermine equality, or sacrifice freedom. But the relationship between the effectiveness of police practices and their intrusiveness is not so simple. For example, procedural justice research (controversially) suggests that beliefs about the legitimacy of police practices, which in turn may be affected how those practices are carried out, may influence compliance with the law and therefore the effectiveness of policing at preventing crime (Walters & Bolger, 2019). Even contested practices, such as hot spots policing (Weisburd, 2016), or heavily contested practices, such as racial profiling in airport screening (Hasisi et al., 2012), may be conducted in ways that either exacerbate or minimize harm. Thus, policing policymaking involves complex consideration of the benefits and harms of policing practices and how they interact.

In the United States, the Fourth Amendment is the single most important legal rule governing police behavior. Its doctrines illustrate how empirical questions about the *effectiveness* of a policing activity can be central to evaluating its *lawfulness*, which determination in turn affects whether it is a practice that agencies may consider. Courts assess Fourth Amendment reasonableness in two alternative ways, both of which depend on factual assessments about policing. First, in many circumstances, the Fourth Amendment requires individualized suspicion and a warrant (or exception to the warrant requirement) before the government may initiate a search or seizure. Determining whether an officer had reasonable suspicion or probable cause – the two common measures of suspicion – almost inevitably turns on whether a court believes the observed behavior is sufficiently associated with criminal activity, a matter that the court views as nontechnical and intuitive, despite its obvious empirical nature. Second, since the late 1960s, when warrants and probable cause make little sense as a method for assessing and protecting individual rights, courts evaluate whether a practice is reasonable within the meaning of the Fourth Amendment by weighing the government's interest in carrying out the intrusive activity against the effects of the intrusion on the individual (e.g., Maryland v. King, 2013; Terry v. Ohio, 1968). Both sides of this doctrinal scale depend on empirical questions – the same kinds of questions that guide evidence-based practices: How harmful is the policing practice in question? How well does it promote public safety or order? How does it compare to plausible alternatives? Thus, in principle, the research that supports evidence-based policing can also inform and influence the law that governs police practices.

However, it is not clear how much courts are moved by research. Courts often overlook social science evidence in drawing empirical conclusions. And even when a court invokes social science evidence about policing in an opinion, it is difficult to tell the degree to which this evidence *causes* the Court's decision. Courts might cite evidence for rhetorical effect while making decisions for other reasons.

Yet, there are reasons to think evidence may matter. Absent conclusions about the consequences of policing practices, a judge's priors and preferences will often be too indeterminate to resolve some Fourth Amendment questions. In that circumstance, the judge might turn to research to fill the gap. Moreover, even if a judge prefers to draw an empirical conclusion based on intuition, judges defend their reasoning in opinions. If they overlook research, another judge might turn to social science evidence in a concurrence or dissent, undermining the persuasive value of the first judge's views, perhaps influencing the course of the case. This possibility provides at least some incentive to consider research on both sides of the issue. All things considered, social science research relevant to constitutional analysis probably makes decisions consistent with that evidence more likely than they would otherwise be.

Of course, evidence is unlikely to have an effect if courts never see it. Courts, including the Supreme Court, rarely consider whether social science evidence is available to inform the factual assessments they make about policing (cf. Harmon & Manns, 2017). In California v. Acevedo (1991), for instance, the Supreme Court concluded that existing rules governing warrantless searches of cars "have impeded effective law enforcement" and "led to confusion for law enforcement officers," citing only its own cases to support those propositions (pp. 574, 577). In Illinois v. Gates (1983), the Court instructed lower courts to be more permissive in weighing anonymous tips because the existing, more restrictive rule "poorly serves the most basic function of any government: to provide for the security of the individual and of his property," and "cannot avoid seriously impeding the task of law enforcement," since anonymous tips "frequently contribute to the solution of otherwise perfect crimes" pp. 237–238). And in Berkemer v. McCarty (1984), the Court contended "that [t]he vast majority of roadside detentions last only a few minutes," that "[a] motorist's expectations ... are that he will be obliged to spend a short period of time answering questions and waiting while the officer checks his license and registration," that "exposure to public view both reduces the ability of an unscrupulous policeman to use illegitimate means to elicit self-incriminating statements and diminishes the motorist's fear, that if he does not cooperate, he will be subjected to abuse" (pp. 437–438). In none of these cases did the Court look to external evidence to determine whether its factual assertions were supported.

No doubt lower courts lack incentive to look at research in part because appellate courts do not fault their unsupported conclusions. But they also lack capacity. In the United States, constitutional doctrines that most regulate criminal investigation are developed largely in the context of criminal cases, through motions to suppress evidence that is illegally obtained by law enforcement. Over-burdened criminal defense attorneys and government prosecutors rarely have the resources to develop fully the empirical basis for their legal claims. Courts with high caseloads have few mechanisms for obtaining evidence and incorporating it into its decisions (Harmon, 2012). Only a few criminal cases reach the Supreme Court each year, and while in these, briefs by amicus curiae – outside groups that serve as "friends of the court" – help collect and present evidence, those briefs may distort facts as well as elucidate them (Larsen, 2014).

Legal scholars have repeatedly called on courts to incorporate more often relevant social science data when developing doctrines concerning the police (e.g., Meares & Harcourt, 2000) and when evaluating the testimony of individual officers (e.g., Ferguson, 2008). The U.S. Supreme Court may be listening, at least a little. Its use of social science research in constitutional law cases has increased significantly and consistently since the Warren Court, at least as measured by the percentage of cases citing articles in social science journals and the mean number of social science articles cited (Epstein et al., pp. 1027–1028). Still, courts have difficulty collecting and weighing such evidence. Perhaps researchers could improve legal decision-making by translating evidence concerning the police for courts as well as for law enforcement agencies.

Of course, social scientists cannot translate research for courts unless they conduct it. Some questions central to developing legal rules concerning the police seem largely overlooked by researchers. For example, the Supreme Court frequently permits or restricts policing practices based on its assessment about what endangers officers and how legal rules will affect efforts to protect them. In Terry v. Ohio (1968), for example, the Supreme Court developed a rule permitting officers to frisk suspects during pedestrian stops reasoning that the rule was both necessary and sufficient to protect officer safety. In Arizona v. Gant (2009), by contrast, the Supreme Court rejected automatic searches incident to arrests during traffic stops because it concluded the rule was unnecessary to keep officers safe. And, for decades, the Supreme Court has permitted intrusive officer conduct during traffic stops because it has concluded that even traffic stops for minor offenses are especially dangerous for officers (e.g., Maryland v. Wilson, 1997; Michigan v. Long, 1983; Pennsylvania v. Mimms, 1977). Yet, little research has analyzed officer safety in legally relevant contexts. According to a 2018 study on the matter, the Court has been wrong in its assessment of traffic stops (Woods, 2018). Without research, how could courts know? If further research bears out this study, it will mean that several Supreme Court cases that permit intrusive police activities to protect officers are built on a faulty empirical premise, one that could have been identified earlier.

Courts, like police executives, consider the effects of policing practices in assessing them, and like chiefs, but unlike legislatures, courts cannot help but decide policing questions. A legislature may postpone any action until more research is available. But criminal cases and civil suits cannot be avoided. If research is unavailable or inaccessible to courts, judicial decisions will suffer accordingly. Given the force of precedent, those decisions may last, even after research undermines them. In such circumstances, even if policing practices are informed by evidence, the rules that govern them will not be.

13.2.2 Preventing Constitutional Violations

This analysis has focused primarily on courts deciding criminal procedure cases because rules of criminal procedure often dominate the law of the policing, at least in the United States, but there are several other contexts in which social science evidence about policing can influence the law. For example, in the United States, chiefs, supervisors, and departments may be liable under federal civil rights law for failing to train or supervise officers adequately if doing so causes constitutional violations (City of Canton v. Harris, 1989). A failure to provide training or supervision that does not actually change behavior could hardly be said to cause conduct inconsistent with that training. Thus, at present, plaintiffs should have difficulty establishing liability for failure to provide implicit bias or de-escalation training or failure to implement an early intervention system, despite widespread calls for these reforms (cf. Engel et al. 2020). Without adequate research, not only departments will find it difficult to train and supervise officers effectively to protect civil rights, but plaintiffs will also find it difficult to use civil suits to encourage them to do so.

When civil rights suits against police departments succeed or settle, courts often seek to prevent future rights violating by mandating departmental reforms in remedial orders (e.g., Floyd v. City of New York, 2013b) or by approving reforms specified in consent decrees negotiated by parties (e.g., United States v. Baltimore Police Dep't, 2017). In the United States, where there are no national standards guiding policing, these rulings – especially those resulting from lawsuits initiated by the Department of Justice – are the closest things we have to government-endorsed best practices. Yet, frequently, parties have sought – and courts have ordered – reforms not yet proven effective at preventing civil rights violations, such as body-worn cameras, community-oriented policing, and civilian review (cf. Engel et al., 2020; Lum et al., 2019b). Given how little research is available about what prevents constitutional violations (Weisburd & Majmundar, 2018), courts and parties would seem to have little choice. The result is that even a police department that otherwise turns to research may be forced by courts to adopt unsupported reforms, at least until courts are persuaded that effective alternatives exist.

As these examples suggest, little research exists for either police departments or for courts about which officer or departmental practices make constitutional violations more or less likely. Such research can be difficult in part because it is difficult to operationalize legal violations by the police (Harmon, 2017). But the absence of such research doubly stymies evidence-based policing: It leads courts to impose reforms that may be well ineffectual, and it leaves other departments looking to court orders for best practices unaware that they are unsupported by evidence. If researchers develop better evidence about the implications of policing practices on legal violations, they will provide both a stronger research basis for reform and for law guiding it.

13.3 CONCLUSION

As this discussion suggests, research on policing both informs and is informed by the law, and evidence-based policing is inherently bound up with the legal rules that govern it. Accordingly, researchers who seek to improve the scientific basis of both policing and the law should keep three lessons in mind.

First, just as police executives cannot ignore the harms of policing or its community effects in evaluating whether a police practice "works," those executives cannot ignore the potential legal consequences of a practice. Nor can they avoid adopting judicially or legislatively ordered reforms. Yet existing research rarely helps illuminate whether police practices increase or reduce legal violations. Researchers should therefore turn more attention to questions about whether specific policing practices lead officers to break the law more often and how well particular reforms work to prevent legal violations by officers.

Second, courts frequently evaluate empirical questions concerning the police – such as the effects of different legal rules on police effectiveness, on the harm police impose, or on police safety – that have been left largely unstudied by researchers. Courts therefore have little basis for formulating the law governing the police, law which could constrain departments' ability to adopt practices that research supports. Strengthening research on the questions that courts inevitably must consider in evaluating police activity could improve the quality of legal rules that govern the police.

Finally, just as researchers work to translate knowledge about police practices into comprehensible lessons for everyday policing, researchers should consider translating research on law enforcement interventions for a different audience, the lawyers who litigate and judges who decide legal constraints on policing. By doing so, researchers may advance the cause of producing public safety fairly, effectively, and minimally harmfully in a new way, by contributing to evidence-based law governing the police.

References

Braga, A. A., Turchan, B. S., Papachristos, A. V., & Hureau, D. M. (2019). Hot spots policing and crime reduction: An update of an ongoing systematic review and meta-analysis. *Journal of Experimental Criminology*, 15(3), 289–311. https://doi.org/10.1007/s11292-019-09372-3

Cassell, P. G., & Fowles, R. (2017). Still handcuffing the cops: A review of fifty years of empirical evidence of Miranda's harmful effects on law enforcement. *Boston University Law Review, 97*(3), 685–848.

Colb, S. F. (1996). Innocence, privacy, and targeting in fourth amendment jurisprudence. *Columbia Law Review, 96*(6), 1456–1525.

Engel, R. S., McManus, H. D., & Isaza, G. T. (2020). Moving beyond "best practice": experiences in police reform and a call for evidence to reduce officer-involved shootings. *The ANNALS of the American Academy of Political and Social Science, 687*(1), 146–165. https://doi.org/10.1177/0002716219889328

Epstein, L., Friedman, B., & Stone, G. R. (2015). Testing the constitution. *New York University Law Review, 90*(4), 1001–1040. https://doi.org/10.1177/0002716219889328

Ferguson, A. G. (2008). The high-crime area question: Requiring verifiable and quantifiable evidence for fourth amendment reasonable suspicion analysis. *American University Law Review, 57*(6), 1587–1644.

Geller, A., Goff, P. A., Lloyd, T., Haviland, A., Obermark, D., & Glaser, J. (2020). Measuring racial disparities in police use of force: methods matter. *Journal of Quantitative Criminology*, 1–31. https://doi.org/10.1007/s10940-020-09471-9

Harcourt, B. E., & Meares, T. L. (2011). Randomization and the fourth amendment. *University of Chicago Law Review, 78*(3), 809–877.

Harmon, R. A. (2012). The problem of policing. *Michigan Law Review, 110*(5), 761–817.

Harmon, R. A. (2017). Evaluating and improving structural reform in police departments. *Criminology & Public Policy, 16*(2), 617–628. https://doi.org/10.1111/1745-91

Harmon, R. A., & Manns, A. (2017). Proactive policing and the legacy of Terry. *Ohio State Journal Criminal Law, 15*(1), 49–72.

Hasisi, B., Margalioth, Y., & Orgad, L. (2012). Ethnic profiling in airport screening: lessons from Israel, 1968–2010. *American Law and Economics Review, 14*(2), 517–560. https://doi.org/10.1093/aler/ahs009

Hollis, M. E. & Jennings, W. G. (2018). Racial disparities in police use-of-force: a state-of-the-art review. *Policing: An International Journal, 41*(2), 178–193. https://doi.org/10.1108/PIJPSM-09-2017-0112

Larsen, A. O. (2014). The trouble with amicus facts. *Virginia Law Review, 100*(8), 1757–1818.

Legewie, J., & Fagan, J. (2019). Aggressive policing and the educational performance of minority youth. *American Sociological Review, 84*(2), 220–247. https://doi.org/10.1177/0003122419826020

Lum, C., Koper, C. S., Willis, J., Happeny, S., Vovak, H., & Nichols, J. (2019a). The rapid diffusion of license plate readers in US law enforcement agencies. *Policing: An International Journal, 42*(3), 376–393. https://doi.org/10.1108/PIJPSM-04-2018-0054

Lum, C., Stoltz, M., Koper, C.S., & Scherer, J.A. (2019b). Research on body-worn cameras: What we know, what we need to know. *Criminology & Public Policy, 18*(1), 93–118. https://doi.org/10.1111/1745-9133.12412

Meares, T. L., & Harcourt, B. E. (2000). Forward: Transparent adjudication and social science research in constitutional criminal procedure. *Journal of Criminal Law and Criminology*, 90(3), 733–798.

Mitchell, O., & Caudy, M. S. (2015). Examining racial disparities in drug arrests. *Justice Quarterly*, 32(2), 288–313.

Reaves, B. A. (2015). *Local police departments, 2013: Equipment and technology.* Bureau of Justice Statistics.

Snook, B., Barron, T., Fallon, L., Kassin, S. M., Kleinman, S., Leo, R. A., Meissner, C. A., Morello, L., Nirider, L.H., Redlich, A. D., & Trainum, J. L. (2020). Urgent issues and prospects in reforming interrogation practices in the United States and Canada. *Legal and Criminological Psychology*, 26, 1–24. https://doi.org/10.1111/lcrp.12178

Walters, G. D., & Bolger, P. C. (2019). Procedural justice perceptions, legitimacy beliefs, and compliance with the law: A meta-analysis. *Journal of Experimental Criminology*, 15(3), 341–372. https://doi.org/10.1007/s11292-018-9338-2

Weisburd, D. (2016). Does hot spots policing inevitably lead to unfair and abusive police practices, or can we maximize both fairness and effectiveness in the new proactive policing. *University of Chicago Legal Forum*, 2016(1), 661–689.

Weisburd, D., & Majmandur, M. (Eds.) (2018). *Proactive policing: Effects on crime and communities.* National Academies of Science, Engineering, and Medicine. https://doi.org/10.17226/24928

Woods, J. B. (2018). Policing, danger narratives, and routine traffic stops. *Michigan Law Review*, 117(4), 635–712.

Cases Cited

Arizona v. Gant, 556 U.S. 332 (2009).
Armstrong v. Village of Pinehurst, 810 F.3d 892 (4th Cir. 2016).
Berkemer v. McCarty, 468 U.S. 420 (1984).
California v. Acevedo, 500 U.S. 565 (1991).
Carpenter v. United States, 138 S.Ct. 2206 (2018).
City of Canton v. Harris, 489 U.S. 378 (1989).
City of Los Angeles v. Lyons, 461 U.S. 95 (1983).
Commonwealth v. McCarthy, 484 Mass. 493 (2020).
Daniels v. City of New York, 198 F.R.D. 409 (S.D.N.Y. 2001).
Delaware v. Prouse, 440 U.S. 648 (1979).
Dickerson v. United States, 500 U.S. 428 (2000).
Floyd v. City of New York, 959 F. Supp. 2d 540 (S.D.N.Y. 2013a).
Floyd v. City of New York, 959 F. Supp. 2d 668 (S.D.N.Y. 2013b).
Horton v. California, 496 U.S. 128 (1990).
Illinois v. Gates, 462 U.S. 213 (1983).
Illinois v. Wardlow, 528 U.S. 119 (2000).
Maryland v. King, 569 U.S. 435 (2013).
Maryland v. Wilson, 519 U.S. 408 (1997).
Michigan v. Long, 463 U.S. 1032 (1983).
Minnesota v. Fort, 660 N.W. 2d 415 (Minn. 2003).
Miranda v. Arizona, 384 U.S. 436 (1966).

Pennsylvania v. Mimms, 434 U.S. 106 (1977).
Stipulation of Settlement, Daniels v. City of New York, No. 99-CV – 1695 (S.D.N.Y. Sept. 24, 2003).
Terry v. Ohio, 392 U.S. 1 (1968).
United States v. Baltimore Police Dep't, 249 F.Supp. 816 (2017).
United States v. Katz, 389 U.S. 347 (1967).
United States v. Knotts, 460 U.S. 276 (1983).
United States v. Martinez-Fuerte, 428 U.S. 543 (1976).

Statutes Cited

Cal. Civ. Code §1798.90.51-55 (West 2019).
N.C. Gen. Stat. §114-10.01 (2013).
Neb. Rev. Stat. §20-504 (West 2019).

PART V

THE PRACTITIONER'S PERSPECTIVE

14

The Role of the "Super Evidence Cop" in Evidence-Based Policing

The Israeli Case

Simon Perry and Michael Wolfowicz

Even if an idea can be proven effective, it does not mean it will necessarily be adopted (Gladwell, 2000). This has certainly been the case for evidence-based policy and practice across a wide range of fields, from education to medicine, and policing has been no different (Sherman, 1998). Like other fields, the road to EBP is complicated (Weisburd & Hasisi, 2018). Even though EBP can offer significant enhancements to police's core objectives, its introduction has often been met with significant opposition. This is due, at least in part, to its perceived conflict with policing cultures that assign considerable value to personal experience (Jonathan-Zamir et al., 2019; Lum, et al., 2012; Grint, et al., 2017; O'Neill, et al., 2007; Sherman, 1984, 1998).

To overcome the barriers and more effectively facilitate and ensure the translation of research into practice, Sherman (1998) suggested the role of the "evidence cop." This figure would be responsible for overseeing the implementation of EBP through compliance. However, the degree to which this figure can be successful in achieving this ambitious objective is likely to vary considerably. The evidence cop, whether a sworn officer or an outside academic, is likely to be looked upon with suspicion, and may not be vested with the authority necessary for carrying out their compliance-related function.

It has been shown that even a chief of police is not free from the constraints and barriers of police organizational culture and structure. Therefore, the chief must be highly motivated, committed, and command sufficient influence and authority for him/her to succeed in bringing about the type of organizational changes that are needed to effectively implement EBP (Neyroud & Weisburd, 2014; Telep & Weisburd, 2014).

Yet, motivation also appears to be an insufficient condition for guaranteeing the successful implementation of EBP. Neyroud and Weisburd (2014) contend that in order to promote EBP, the police as an organization must take ownership over the science of EBP. This means that a) the police must "value" science and its potential contributions to practice and comply to the norms and procedures of science; b) the police must have knowledge about the scientific enterprise; and c) the police must take a leadership role in the science of EBP which requires involvement and activity. In our opinion, since the police is a rigid hierarchical organization, the organization's ownership of EBP necessitates that the head of the organization/the commissioner take upon themselves ownership of EBP.

Like elsewhere, Israel has seen police chiefs who have championed and attempted to implement EBP, yet their success has varied considerably. Identifying which factors may be related to different outcomes may provide guidance for others, both in terms of what areas should be focused on, and which should be avoided.

Our analysis takes a historical perspective, focusing in on the background of two distinct attempts at strategic reform in the Israel Police (IP), one in the mid-1990s, and another in the last few years. While the recent reforms have received attention, the earlier attempt is less well documented. It is here that our analysis benefits from the first-hand knowledge of the first author who was a senior figure in the IP throughout this period.

We focus on the characteristics and tactics of the two leaders with respect to EBP and draw on existing evidence regarding the effectiveness and success of their reforms. The specific knowledge and overall approach of the police chief at the time had direct impact on determining the strategy of EBP implementation. The two periods varied from one another in the way the reforms were implemented and this became the decisive factor in determining whether EBP would be successful. In both periods the commissioners championed and attempted to implement EBP. Yet, while the first entrusted the implementation of EBP to "evidence cops," the second commissioner took upon himself ownership of EBP and became what we propose be referred to as the "super evidence cop." In line with the qualitative difference between evidence-based policing and "total evidence-based policing," (Sherman, 2015), we believe that our analysis demonstrates a similar significant difference between what Sherman referred to as the "evidence cop" and what we propose as the role of the "super evidence cop."

The next section describes the role of the evidence cop and presents the concept of the "super evidence cop." The following section briefly describes the IP and explains why it is possible to learn from the experience of the IP and apply it to other Western police agencies. The fourth section presents the two test cases of Commissioners Hefetz and Alsheich's EBP reforms. Lastly, the final section discusses the differences between the change processes that Hefetz carried out through the use of evidence cops, as opposed to the essential benefits of the change process carried out by Alsheich, who took upon himself the role of the super evidence cop.

14.1 THE EVIDENCE COP AND THE CONCEPT OF THE SUPER EVIDENCE COP

Evidence-based policing is more than just a method or group of strategies. Rather, it represents an organizational philosophy that policing practices should be based on scientific evidence about "what works best" (Sherman, 1998, p. 2). Accordingly, an EBP approach is one in which a policing organization draws upon, and generates scientific research that informs decision making, at both the strategic and tactical levels (Sherman, 1984, 1998). Inherent in this statement are two possible identities that EBP can take on, and the differences are not superficial. They represent different approaches, one externally and the other internally focused, and the difference between science-led policing and police-led science (Sherman, 2011). Police-led science means that the police take ownership over science to implement EBP. This model is actually more in line with evidence-based policy and practice from other fields and is more likely to be successful in overcoming barriers to implementation (Sherman, 2013). Similarly, Neyroud and Weisburd (2014) explain that giving police ownership over the science helps to perpetuate EBP, and this leads to its successful adoption.

Policing organizations are most likely to move toward "total EBP" as a result of one or more "tipping points" – conditions that are conducive to leading to such a change. Arguably, the most effective tipping point comes when a senior police figure, ideally the chief, engages in a deliberate and active policy of creating the foundations and conditions needed for total integration into the police force, including for after their departure. Institutionalization can be said to have been achieved when "an entire system of technology, policies, procedures, training, and resources" is able to be "sustained through the police hierarchal structure, through formal accountability, and informally through the organizational culture."

(Santos & Santos, 2019, p. 12). Institutionalization is a factor which is too often overlooked. This can be promoted through greater cooperation with academia, both in terms of research as well as the education, and training of officers, thus promoting sustainability (Sherman, 2015). Additionally, by introducing functions of crime analysis as part of the daily routines rank-and-file, EBP can take hold at all levels (Piza et al., 2020). Of course, all of this is only possible under the direction of a strong and stable leadership, and importantly, a leadership with a clear vision (Santos & Santos, 2019).

There are three types of individuals who may play a pivotal role in moving a police organization toward EBP: embedded criminologists, police pracademics, and crime analysts (Piza et al., 2020). All these actors could potentially serve as what Sherman (1998) referred to as an evidence cop. As such, to facilitate the adoption of EBP, a police organization would require an "evidence cop." This individual would be responsible for keeping abreast of new EBP research and transmitting it to those responsible for policy and practice decision making (Sherman, 1998, 2002; Walsh, 2006). This individual would ideally be someone who commands extensive experience, perhaps even measured by years, which is highly valued in police culture and could possibly help to overcome some of the potential reluctance (Willis, et al., 2010). Evidence cops are more likely to be successful when they have some level of responsibility and authority over the area of the organization that is most likely to be impacted by the implementation of EBP (Rojek, et al., 2015). Almost all accounts of both successful and less successful attempts to implement EBP highlight the central role of evidence cops (Sherman, 2013).

However, others have identified that the likelihood that EBP will be adopted is more commonly dependent on the existence of an EBP advocate or champion. Indeed, without an EBP advocate there will not be any evidence cops or pracademics since they are the result of initial steps toward EBP.

The advantages of being a chief of police are clear and include the ability to overcome many of the cultural-related roadblocks, as well as having the authority to make changes to official policy (Goldstein, 2003). When the chief himself takes ownership over science and is the driving force behind EBP, the likelihood of the organization successfully implementing EBP increases greatly. For example, in South Australia, the commitment of Commissioner Hyde, who initiated a reform in 2002, has been credited for its success (Mazerolle, et al., 2013). The most successful accounts of EBP always include a police organization's chief overseeing the implementation and institutionalization of EBP (Santos & Santos, 2019; Braga, 2016; Huey & Mitchell 2016; Neyroud, 2017; Sherman, 2013).

Often, pro-EBP police chiefs will identify existing staff who can serve as assistants in the implementation of EBP. For example, in the Port St Lucie, Florida Police Department (PSLPD), there was "a Sergeant, who was then promoted to Lieutenant, had earned a master's degree in criminology and criminal justice and truly understood theory and its application to policing" (Boba, 2010). This individual was seen as key to the department's implementation of EBP and its ability to persist through the transfer of leadership in the following years (See also Boba, 2011; Santos, 2013; Santos & Santos, 2012).

The mere existence of an evidence cop is by no means a guarantee of the successfully implementation of EBP. Similarly, a motivated and EBP-oriented police chief also does not guarantee success. However, when these elements converge, there is an increased likelihood that a tipping point will be reached, and a policing organization will move toward a full EBP orientation and approach (Sherman, 2015). We believe that the Israeli case is demonstrative of this hypothesis. As we describe below, the 1990s saw the arrival of a highly motivated police chief who steered the Israel Police toward EBP in many areas. However, his reforms did not establish deep roots in the organization and for the most part were undone by his successors, highlighting the failure of his attempts to institutionalize the change. Some two decades later, an outsider, who studied police theories and innovations in a criminology graduate program, was appointed as the IP commissioner and in fact became himself the evidence cop, a combination we call the "super evidence cop." He made sweeping reforms that were continued by the new command, and signs of successful institutionalization are apparent.

In this chapter, we will try to demonstrate how the fact that the evidence cop is the commissioner himself, acting as a "super evidence cop," who takes ownership of the science, significantly improves his ability to lead organizational change toward EBP. This is different from the situation where the commissioner attempted to introduce change through the transfer of ownership of science to "evidence cops" he appointed.

14.2 THE ISRAEL POLICE (IP)

The Israel Police (IP) was established with the creation of the modern State of Israel in 1948. While many organizational, philosophical, and strategic changes have taken place over the years, the IP has retained its strong, centralized, quasi-military orientation and character. Much of this structure's origins are owed to the model of the colonial British Mandate Police that existed in pre-state Israel for about 30 years (Jonathan-Zamir & Harpaz, 2018; Perry & Jonathan-Zamir, 2015). The IP is headed by the commissioner, whose appointment is based on the recommendation of the Minister of Public Security. Unlike most other western countries, the IP is a single organization which is responsible for policing the entire country. This is carried out through its seven districts, each of which are divided into two to four sub-districts (depending on the size of the district), which are composed of several local police stations. Approximately 30,000 sworn officers make up the force's two main sub-organizations. About two-thirds make up the "regular" police force, often termed the "Blue Police." The rest comprise the "Border Guard," a quasi-military body serving primarily as the operational and professional arm of the police for matters of internal security and the combating of terrorism.

Despite the differences (mostly structural) between the IP and police agencies in other Western democracies, there are important similarities (Perry & Jonathan-Zamir, 2015). When it comes to EBP, the IP is like other policing organizations around the world in terms of the organizational, institutional, and cultural barriers toward EBP. A recent study found that the IP is similar to other countries in that its senior officers are often split between support and respect for the ideas of evidence based policing, and a proclivity toward basing decisions on personal experience (Jonathan-Zamir, et al., 2019). As we describe below, the experience of evidence-based policing in the IP has traversed the familiar rocky road (May, et al., 2017; Weisburd & Hasisi, 2018). These similarities, we believe, allow for a careful application of the conclusions from the Israeli experience presented in this chapter to police agencies in other Western democracies.

14.3 THE TWO CASE STUDIES OF STRATEGIC REFORM IN THE ISRAEL POLICE (IP)

14.3.1 Case #1 – Two of Hefetz's Reforms: Community Policing and the "YACHBAL"

The 1990s in Israel were somewhat of a tumultuous period, with the First Intifada continuing until September 1993, a massive wave of immigration from the former Soviet Union, and unfavorable attitudes toward the police and police violence in particular. It was against this backdrop that in 1994 Assaf Hefetz was appointed as the 12th commissioner of the IP.

When Hefetz assumed command of the police, he commissioned an evaluation from David Weisburd of the Institute of Criminology at Hebrew University of Jerusalem (Weisburd et al., 1997). Hefetz sought to institutionalize community policing, which was envisioned to include a significant organizational change (Weisburd, et al., 2002). Hefetz's assigned Brigadier General Dr. Dani Gimshi to take the leading role in these community policing efforts. Not only had Gimshi been a long-time figure in the police and proponent of community policing, but he was also quite familiar with EBP. Gimshi held a degree in Criminology and had just returned from studies in Harvard in 1994. During his tenure, he would go on to receive his doctorate in Criminology from the Hebrew University of Jerusalem in 1997 and would later establish the Hebrew academic journal "Police and Society" (Weisburd et al., 2002). In fact, Gimshi fulfilled the classic role of the evidence cop. The new unit headed by Gimshi had the objective of implementing community policing by the year 2003 (Weisburd et al., 2002). While Hefetz appointed Gimshi to implement community policing, he himself did not take ownership of the science, but left it to the Chief Scientist of the Ministry of Homeland Security, an external entity with limited influence over the IP organization.

Hefetz, who had at the time successfully integrated community policing and problem-oriented policing (Goldstein 1990) as a way of dealing with drug crime (Hefetz, 1996; Weisburd et al., 2002), continued with attempts to integrate EBP. Soon after assuming command of the IP, he initiated the creation of thinking tanks. These selected teams, made up of officers some of which acting as evidence cops with expertise in different areas, were instructed to identify new and upcoming threats as well as possible solutions for dealing with them. One of the groups dealt with international and other forms of severe crime, and included the first author, a pracademic with extensive intelligence and operational experience. This group identified the growing threat posed by Russian organized crime, and those who were increasingly taken advantage of Israel's "Law of Return," under which descendants of Jewish grandparents had the right to citizenship. Israel was an especially attractive destination for organized crime figures given its 1978 law prohibiting extradition of its citizens (Abramovsky, 1995, 1996). Additionally, to encourage immigration, Israel asked few questions about the origins of the money that these immigrants deposited in Israeli banks (Siegel, 2003). For all these reasons, the Russian organized crime groups took advantage of this opportunity to create a base in Israel for their growing activity in Israel and in the western world. Their area of criminal activity included financial crimes, money laundering, prostitution, drug trafficking, and illegal gambling (Keane & Bell, 2013; Amir, 1998, 2001). This thinking tank identified one of the police's most significant gaps as existing in the area of information and intelligence gathering, and which was hampered by cultural and language barriers.

To combat this growing problem, Hefetz created the "YACHBAL" (the National Unit for Severe Organized and International Crime) in 1997. This new unit was tasked with handling organized crime, internal security, and politically sensitive investigations/cases. The unit's character was essentially that of an intelligence division, coopting personnel and resources from existing national investigation units. The YACHBAL developed advanced human and signal intelligence, as well as surveillance and operational capabilities (Israel Police, 2007). It also successfully established strong cooperation with policing agencies overseas. The YACHBAL was soon able to identify key figures and organizations operating in Israel, and began targeting them through investigations and increased scrutiny. Due to these increased police activity, it was not long before many Russian organized crime bosses ceased their travel to and from Israel. Additionally, several Israeli passports were eventually revoked, after having been shown that they were fraudulently obtained. This unit was also successful in carrying out successful key investigations in the areas of Israeli criminal organizations and internal security. It has also carried out politically sensitive investigations and made some high-profile arrests. In a short time, the unit made a name for itself in the general public, but more importantly within the criminal world, and became a significant deterrent.

The changes Hefetz led through evidence cops, such as Gimshi and the first author of this chapter, despite being significant, in many cases provoked opposition to the messenger (the evidence cop) as well as to the message/reform. This opposition, in turn, prevented these innovative reforms from being fully integrated into the organizational culture. In 1998, Hafetz's term ended, and he was replaced by Yehuda Wilk. At the time of the changeover of leadership, Gimshi (1999) would refer to Hefetz's reforms as the most far-reaching changes carried out in the IP until that point. However, whatever successes had been achieved in implementing EBP over Hefetz's four-year term were short lived. As Weisburd et al. (2002) describe the change in leadership was marked by an end to community policing, with a move away from the original model and toward one that "focused not on the philosophy of community policing, but rather on how the objectives of community policing could be achieved and measured" (Weisburd et al., 2002, p. 87).

Although Yehuda Wilk was committed to the vision behind the establishment of the YACHBAL, this was not the case for much of the police command and Wilks's successors. This opposition manifested itself in the outbreak of the Trade Bank affair. A middle management employee of the Trade Bank stole 270 million NIS over a five-year period to pay off her brother's and father's illegal gambling debts to criminal organizations. The three were tried and convicted, yet none of the heads of the criminal organizations who received the 270 million NIS were tried and convicted in this case. This is due to the failure of the YACHBAL to take the lead in the ensuing investigation against the criminal organizations involved. In actual fact, district commanders insisted on conducting an investigation against the criminals in their district. The investigation, instead of being led and coordinated nationally, was dealt with by the central units of the various local districts. This division of responsibility let to a poor outcome, where none of the heads of the various criminal organizations were arrested and no money was retrieved. This negligence in pursuing the various criminal organizations responsible for extorting an astounding sum of 270 million resulted in a war between the various organizations and financed their acquisition of "soldiers" and weapons. This reality subsequently resulted in the outbreak of bloody street wars that claimed lives of innocent bystanders, as well as an escalation in the level of criminal violence in Israel, defined as crossing a red line which continues to impact on the level of violence until this day.

14.3.2 Case #2 – Alsheich's "EMUN" (Trust) Reform

In 2015, Israel's Minister of Public Security Gilad Erdan was widely criticized when he announced that Roni Alsheich would be the new commissioner of the Israel Police. Unlike his predecessors, Alsheich had not been a senior police officer. Rather, he had been the deputy director of Israel's Security Agency (ISA), which can be compared to the British MI-5 in terms of mandate and function. Alsheich had been selected for the purpose of carrying out significant reforms at a time when police–community relations were strained (Saunders et al., 2014).

Upon assuming command of the IP, Alsheich wasted little time in working on the development and implementation of the "EMUN" strategy; a Hebrew term that can mean "trust," "faith," and "belief." Alsheich was quite intentional in his approach, which drew heavily on his academic background. Alsheich had studied Criminology at the Hebrew University of Jerusalem, which included courses on evidence-based policing (taught by this chapter's first author). At the time of his studies, Alsheich was between positions in the ISA, just prior to his promotion to deputy director. As Alsheich (2020) acknowledges in his recent Hebrew language book "Police Commissioner at the Forefront in Defense of Values," his time in the program provided the foundations for his approach:

> The second element that was extremely helpful was the Hebrew University, where I previously studied everything, I know about criminology ... I asked for the most up-to-date studies on police innovations .... I was sent a "short" presentation of several hundred slides, which was exceptionally beneficial and enabled me to highlight and focus on key criminological anchors which are policing practices that have gained research validity in the literature... (p.28)

The degree to which Alsheich's studies influenced his ideas and subsequent approach went beyond mere familiarization with EBP, as he continues:

> ... It is not possible that anyone who had the opportunity to attend the Institute of Criminology at the Hebrew University, would not have an appreciation of research, especially quantitative studies ... It was clear to me that I had to strive for evidence-based policing, as part of my responsibility to perform my duties professionally (p.66).

Alsheich perceived striving for evidence-based policing, as part of his responsibility. For him, introducing EBP was essential to his policing strategy and he believed that he needed to take ownership over the science of EBP. Alsheich wasted little time in establishing cooperation with academia. He even instituted the use of academic terminology as official police terminology, enabling a common, shared language. Similar to the former chief of the Metro police in the UK, Peter Neyroud (2017), Alsheich established an academic advisory board, led by the renowned Prof. David Weisburd from the Hebrew University and included the head of the Institute of Criminology, Prof. Hasisi, the first author of this chapter, and other leading researchers from across the country. As stated, he was not satisfied only with the implementation of the EBP in the field but also instructed the Research Department in the Strategic Planning Division of the Police to lead research and collaboration with university scholars.

The EMUN strategy focused on four primary policing practices: 1) Problem-Oriented Policing, 2) Situational Crime Prevention, 3) Place-Based Methods, and 4) Community Policing, all while emphasizing the central importance of de-centralization. The reform was based on ideas as follows: 1) Law abiding citizens are the central "customer" of the police and their crime problems are the central focus of the police; 2) The police will treat citizens with fairness, courtesy, and respect; 3) The police are unable to successfully carry out their functions without a high degree of public legitimacy; 4) Policing will be divided into three central functions: providing police services to the citizens according to their needs and in accordance with the needs of the community in which they live in (low policing), sophisticated enforcement of complex crimes (high policing), and effective treatment of all offenses that harm quality of life (Israel Police, 2017).

De-centralization was envisioned as being key to the success of EMUN (Weisburd et al., 2020). Under this model, EMUN focused on changes at the station level, where stations and their officers were tasked with engaging in problem-oriented policing (Laufman-Gavri & Hasisi, 2017). As detailed by Weisburd et al. (2020), the tool that facilitated this was a domestically developed version of COMPSTAT and given the same name as the reform- EMUN. This new approach was computerized in a way considered to be very advanced, providing an automated, user friendly system. Importantly, the system was implemented in a way that provided access to all sworn officers, effectively enabling all of them to engage in at least some of the functions of crime analysts (Weisburd et al., 2020).

EMUN encouraged the application of the reforms and its strategies through compliance, by assigning EBP objective and targets to the officer at station level. It simultaneously resulted in ongoing processes of police-led research. For example, in one locale, the station commanders identified agriculture crimes, including damage and theft, as representing a key local issue. In fact, in this district, these were also the most frequent types of crime. Having identified the nature of the crime problem, the station put together a targeted strategy making use of extensive data (Cassey, 2019).

Alsheich's mandate (2015–2018) was characterized by additional examples of police-led research and cooperation between the police and academia. The EMUN program assessment revealed immediate and short-term successes. First and foremost, there was a significant drop in crime nationwide. In fact, 2018 had the lowest crime rate in almost a decade (Israel Police, 2019a). Moreover, while trust and legitimacy in the police had reached a new low by 2016, the years of 2017 and 2018 saw significant improvements. Also, among the Arab minority communities, improvements were found across virtually every category pertaining to police legitimacy and perceived police performance (Israel Police, 2019b). The initial evaluation of a pilot experiment using body-worn cameras was also carried out and found to lead to significant improvements in citizens' perceptions of police–citizen encounters (Hollenberg, 2017).

It is important to emphasize that Alsheich, over a short period of time, introduced significant changes in almost all areas of police activity: policing methods, priority changes, transferring responsibility, and authority to field units/police stations, introducing technological means, computing processes, improving promotion tracks, training, and even in changing some of the police jargon. Undoubtedly, such fundamental changes in a hierarchical organization, such as the police necessitated making changes in the organizational culture and overcoming natural opposition.

14.4 DISCUSSION

As mentioned above, even the chief of police is not free from constraints and obstacles when attempting to introduce changes into the organizational culture, structure, strategies, and tactics. Therefore, bringing about the type of organizational change that is needed to effectively implement EBP requires that the chief of police take ownership of the science and demonstrate extraordinary commitment, influence, and immense leadership ability.

Evidence cops, whether a police officer, pracademic, crime analyst or embedded criminologist, have a higher chance of succeeding when they exhibit high levels of responsibility and authority over the part of the organization that is introducing EBP. Yet, when the change is broader and deeper, and more pervasively affects parts of the organization or even the entire organization, the evidence cop will likely encounter opposition from others with higher or equivalent ranks. This opposition often results from feelings of competition, suspicion, jealousy, non-acceptance of authority, fear of change, etc. Unfortunately, those colleagues, whose support for the success of the EBP is required, are at times more threatened by the messenger (evidence cop) than by the EBP message itself.

The advantage of the chief of police being the messenger, the "evidence cop," or what we suggest calling the "super evidence cop," is that the entire organization is required to focus on and to be committed to the EBP message. When the chief of police himself is the science and EBP advocate, he has the authority necessary to ensure that the entire organization adopts the changes and carries out compliance-related functions, subsequently overcoming many of the cultural and organizational-related barriers. Moreover, in situations where the chief himself is the driving force leading EBP, the prospect of successful implementation increases significantly. In such cases, the likelihood that the reform will diffuse in the organization and endure after he/she is gone increases significantly as well.

There are several similarities between Hefetz and Alsheich when it comes to their reforms. First and foremost, both were the primary champions of EBP. That is, rather than being tasked with implementing reforms decided upon at the ministerial or governmental level, it was the appreciation for EBP of the two chiefs themselves that led to its implementation. In terms of specific EBP strategies, both chiefs had personal familiarity with community policing and problem-oriented policing, as well as ways by which these strategies could be used in a complementary way. Indeed, for both, these strategies were central to their reforms and overall approaches. While there are certainly many similarities, clear differences are apparent. These dissimilarities may serve to explain why Hefetz's reforms were less successful and did not survive as well the change of the guard in comparison to Alsheich's reforms.

First, with respect to the types of figures involved and their specific functions, Hefetz handed over authority for the reforms to an evidence cop "pracademic" such as Dani Gimshi and left ownership of the community policing science to an external entity (the Chief Scientist of the Ministry of Public Security). In police organizations, it is often the case that new senior commanders will undo or reverse their predecessors' initiatives while attempting to make a name for themselves. This is why in order for EBP to survive such transitions, a degree of commitment must be instilled in the wider leadership structure (Mastrofski, 2015).

In the case of the YACHBAL, we witness how the establishment process, its original mandate and functioning, represent a clear application of problem-oriented policing led by evidence cops. Despite considerable successes, this innovation failed to produce change in the perceptions and culture of the organization. Upon the departure of Hefetz and Wilk as chiefs of police, the YACHBAL was exposed to growing opposition within the organization from the district commanders. The district commanders and the commanders of the district units responsible for serious crime did not cooperate nor agree to transfer the responsibility of major criminals in their districts to the national unit in cases where the crime crossed districts or became international. As has been noted time and time again, in order for EBP to succeed, structures need to be put in place that protect against competing demands that may disrupt the work and mandate of officers and units involved (Goldstein, 2003). Clearly, that was not the case in the YACHBAL creation process by the evidence cops.

The Trade Bank affair is demonstrative of how such competing interests can derail successes and potential successes.

As opposed to the above, a recent survey conducted by Jonathan-Zamir et al., (2019) found that Alsheich's pro-EBP culture diffused in the organization and had lasting effects on the senior command. It should be emphasized that this survey describes the actual situation rather than presenting a causal effect. In the case of EMUN, Alsheich took ownership over the science of EBP which meant that he incorporated into the organization the "value" of science and its potential contributions to practice. He assigned EBP objectives and targets to officers at the station level and demanded involvement and ongoing activity. In addition, he instructed the Research Department to lead the science and IP research in collaborations with university scholars to acquire knowledge. Alsheich's leadership role in science resulted in ongoing processes of police-led research while adapting norms and procedures of science. As detailed by Weisburd et al. (2020), specific attention was paid to institutionalization and engendering a cultural shift. Of course, Alsheich was able to take advantage of additional years of research in EBP, which emphasized certain factors as the key to success (Santos & Santos, 2019). It is the opinion of Weisburd et al. (2020) that the EMUN analysis platform played a vital role in the institutionalization and dissemination of the approach. Yet, the EMUN approach certainly would not have been successful if the head of the organization himself had not appointed officers to fulfill specific roles, tasks, and functions and achieve specific objectives. A process evaluation of EMUN found it to have successfully penetrated all levels of the organization, and to signify a cultural shift (Weisburd et al., 2020). Alsheich's cooperation with the academia supported and enhanced this cultural shift.

A tender was put out in 2017 inviting Israeli academic institutions to develop and deliver an academic program to officers. The tender was granted to the Hebrew University of Jerusalem, whose Institute of Criminology now operates a dedicated program for sworn officers to undertake both undergraduate and graduate programs in Criminology. The officers who take part in the programs are also exposed to the type of state-of-the-art evidence-based policing that first inspired Alsheich himself. This program, similar to programs at Cambridge University, United Kingdom, has the potential to support a bottom-up, self-sustaining process of EBP, as well as to develop a new generation of evidence cops (Sherman, 2013). The successful penetration to all levels of the organization coupled with the academic program for officers, ensures an ongoing diffusion of EBP in the IP. Maybe one of these officers will one day be appointed to be the commissioner and a new super evidence cop.

As police commissioner, Hefetz's vision and commitment is well reflected by his post-service activities, which included his joint efforts with academics for the benefit of the police (Sizer, 2017). However, unlike Alsheich, he was less successful in institutionalizing his reforms or vision. This reality left them vulnerable, with high a likelihood that they would be reversed or abandoned (Lum & Koper, 2017; Tilley & Scott, 2012). By comparison, Alsheich's reforms have been found in multiple evaluations (as mentioned above) to provide evidence of a high level of successful institutionalization. The fact that most of these studies were carried out and based on data from after his mandate expired (and was not renewed due to political pressures) lends further support to such an evaluation. Having achieved successful results in improving crime and crime-related outcomes, and in institutionalizing EBP both culturally and operationally, we believe it is befitting to refer to Alsheich as a super evidence cop.

14.5 CONCLUSIONS

The road to evidence-based policing is often a rocky one (McKenna, 2018), and the Israeli experience has been no different (Weisburd & Hasisi, 2018). The ups and downs are often the result of poor implementation, and more often than not, failure to effectively institutionalize reforms. The fact that the EMUN strategy has managed to survive the departure of its initiator indicates that its emphasis on institutionalization and generating an organizational shift may have paid off. Like in any society, cultural shifts take time and are more likely to occur when implemented consistently and methodically. While this is known to be extremely difficult in policing organizations, it appears that Alsheich was able to achieve considerable success. The reason why Alsheich was able to implement such substantial EBP reforms in the police force when Hefetz and many commissioners around the world were less successful, lies, in our opinion, in the fact that Alsheich himself took over science and led the process as the super evidence cop. Alsheich's pro-EBP culture, diffused in the organization and has had a lasting effect, which can be explained by the fact that Alsheich (unlike evidence cops) proactively instituted changes in the culture and practices of his force and brought about the conditions needed for a total move to EBP.

While some have written about the importance of a "natural," trained successor to ensure the consistency and continuity of EBP implementation, this is not always possible. In fact, the IP only approved a new commissioner in 2021, with interim commissioners having managed the organization for over two years. While such a situation may be uncommon, it serves as further evidence of the immense importance of establishing academic programs that promote the creation of pracademics. Hopefully one day a student who recognizes the promise and importance of EBP may once again become the chief of the police, and as such become the new super evidence cop.

References

Abramovsky, A. (1995). Partners against crime: joint prosecutions of Israeli organized crime figures by US and Israeli authorities. *Fordham International Law Journal, 19*, 1903–1919.

Abramovsky, A. (1996). Prosecuting the Russian Mafia: Recent Russian Legislation and Increased Bilateral Cooperation May Provide the Means. *Virginia Journal of International Law, 37*, 191–222.

Alsheich, R. (2020). Police Commissioner at the Forefront in Defense of Values. Tchelet.

Amir, M. (1998). Organized crime in Israel. In R. R. Friedmann (Ed.), *Crime and Criminal Justice in Israel: Assessing the Knowledge Base toward the Twenty-First Century* (pp. 121–138). State University of New York Press.

Amir M. (2001). Is there organized crime in Israel? *Shaarei Mishpat JUT, 2*(3), 231–337.

Asa-el, A. (2018, October 26). *Top cop Alsheikh 'neither quit nor was fired'*. Retrieved from The Jerusalem Post: www.jpost.com/jerusalem-report/top-cop-goes-home-570061

Boba, R. (2010). A practice-based evidence approach in Florida. *Police Practice and Research: An International Journal, 11*(2), 122–128.

Boba, R. (2011). *Institutionalization of problem solving, analysis, and accountability in the Port St. Lucie, FL Police Department.* Office of Community Oriented Policing Services, U.S. Department of Justice. https://cops.usdoj.gov/RIC/Publications/cops-w0613-pub.pdf

Braga, A. A. (2016). The value of 'pracademics' in enhancing crime analysis in police departments. *Policing: a journal of policy and practice, 10*(3), 308–314.

Cassey, Y. (2019). *Policing strategies in the rural area and the police dealings with agricultural crime. The main thing in research 2019 collection of articles on police issues.* Israel Police.

Gimshi, D. (1999). *Community policing in Israel and in the world.* Israel Police.

Gladwell, M. (2000). *The tipping point: How little things can make a big difference.* Little, Brown and Company.

Goldstein, H. (1990). *Excellence in problem-oriented policing.* McGraw-Hill.

Goldstein, H. (2003). On further developing problem-oriented policing: The most critical need, the major impediments, and a proposal. *Crime Prevention Studies, 15*, 13–48.

Grint, K., Holt, C. & Neyroud, P. (2017). Cultural change and lodestones in the British police. *International Journal of Emergency Services, 6*(3), 166–76.

Hefetz, A. (1996). Toward community policing. Mashabei Enosh, 105–106, 22–24.

Hollenberg, A. (2017). Body cameras in the Israel Police. In M. Ziso (Ed.), *The essence of research* (pp. 87–104). The Israel Police, Planning and Organization Department, Strategic Division. (in Hebrew) www.policemuseum.org.il/wp-content/uploads/2020/05/2017-העיקר-במחקר.pdf

Huey, L., & Mitchell, R. J. (2016). Unearthing hidden keys: Why pracademics are an invaluable (if underutilized) resource in policing research. *Policing: A Journal of Policy and Practice, 10*(3), 300–307. https://doi.org/10.1093/police/paw029

Israel Police. (2007). *Annual Accountability Report, 2007*. Government Publication Bureau of Israel. (in Hebrew)

Israel Police. (2017). *Annual statistics of the Israel police*. The Israel Police, Planning and Organization Department, Strategic Division. www.gov.il/BlobFolder/reports/police_statistical_abstract_2017/he/shanton_2017.pdf

Israel Police. (2019a). *Annual statistics of the Israel police*. The Israel Police, Planning and Organization Department, Strategic Division.

Israel Police. (2019b). *Survey of the standing of the Israel police*. The Israel Police, Planning and Organization Department, Strategic Division. www.gov.il/BlobFolder/generalpage/2018_police_freedom_of_information/he/סקרים.pdf

Jonathan-Zamir, T., & Harpaz, A. (2018). Predicting support for procedurally just treatment: The case of the Israel National Police. *Criminal Justice and Behavior, 45*(6), 840–862. https://doi.org/10.1177/0093854818763230

Jonathan-Zamir, T., Weisburd, D., Dayan, M., & Zisso, M. (2019). The proclivity to rely on professional experience and evidence-based policing: Findings from a survey of high-ranking officers in the Israel Police. *Criminal Justice and Behavior, 46*(10), 1456–1474. https://doi.org/10.1177/0093854819842903

Keane, J., & Bell, P. (2013). Confidence in the police: Balancing public image with community safety–A comparative review of the literature. *International Journal of Law, Crime and Justice, 41*(3), 233–246. https://doi.org/10.1016/j.ijlcj.2013.06.003

Laufman-Gavri, L., & Hasisi, B. (2017, November 15). *"Let my station go": Reforming police practices in Israel* [Conference presentation]. The American Society of Criminology, Philadelphia, PA.

Lum, C. M., & Koper, C. S. (2017). *Evidence-based policing: Translating research into practice*. Oxford University Press.

Lum, C., Telep, C. W., Koper, C. S., & Grieco, J. (2012). Receptivity to research in policing. *Justice Research and Policy, 14*(1), 61–95. https://doi.org/10.3818/JRP.14.1.2012.61

Mastrofski, S.D. (2015). Police CEOs: Agents of change? *The Police Chief, 82*(11), 52–54.

May, T., Hunter, G., & Hough, M. (2017). The Long and Winding Road: Embedding Evidence-based Policing Principles. In J. Knutsson & L. Tompson (Eds.), *Advances in Evidence-Based Policing* (pp. 139–156). Routledge.

Mazerolle, L., Darroch, S., & White, G. (2013). Leadership in problem-oriented policing. *Policing: An International Journal of Police Strategies and Management, 36*(3), 543–560.

McKenna, P. F. (2018). Evidence-based policing in Canada. *Canadian Public Administration*, 61(1), 135–140.

Neyroud, P. (2017). Policing with science: a new evidence-based professionalism for policing. *European Police Science & Research Bulletin, Special Conference Issue No. 2*, 39–44. http://91.82.159.234/index.php/bulletin/article/view/201

Neyroud, P., & Weisburd, D. (2014). Transforming the police through science: The challenge of ownership. *Policing: A Journal of Policy and Practice*, 8 (4), 287–292.

O'Neill, M. E., Marks, M., & Singh, A. (2007). *Police occupational culture: New debates and directions* (Vol. 8). Emerald Group Publishing.

Perry, S., & Jonathan-Zamir, T. (2015). Lessons from Empirical Research on Policing in Israel. in T. Jonathan-Zamir, D. Weisburd, & B. Hasisi (Eds.), *Policing in Israel: Studying Crime Control, Community and Counterterrorism* (pp. 237–251). CRC Press.

Piza, E. L., Szkola, J., & Blount-Hill, K. L. (2020). How can embedded criminologists, police pracademics, and crime analysts help increase police-led program evaluations? A survey of authors cited in the evidence-based policing matrix. *Policing: A Journal of Policy and Practice*, 1–15.

Rojek, J., Martin, P., & Alpert, G. P. (2015). The literature and research on police–research partnerships in the USA. In J. Rojek, P. Martin & G. P. Alpert (Eds.), *Developing and maintaining police-researcher partnerships to facilitate research use* (pp. 27–44). Springer. https://doi.org/10.1007/978-1-4939-2056-3

Santos, R. B. (2013). Implementation of a police organizational model for crime reduction. *Policing: An International Journal of Police Strategies and Management*, 36(2), 295–311. https://doi.org/10.1108/13639511311329714

Santos, R. B., & Santos, R. G. (2012). The role of leadership in implementing a police organizational model for crime reduction and accountability. *Policing: A Journal of Policy and Practice*, 6(4), 344–353.

Santos, R. G., & Santos, R. B. (2019). A four-phase process for translating research into police practice. *Police Practice and Research*, 20(6), 585–602.

Saunders, J.M. et al. (2014). *Effective policing for 21st-century Israel*. RAND. www.rand.org/content/dam/rand/pubs/research_reports/RR200/RR287z1/RAND_RR287z1.hebrew.pdf

Sherman, L. W. (1984). Experiments in Police Discretion: Scientific Boon or Dangerous Knowledge. *Law & Contemporary Problems*, 47(4), 61–82.

Sherman, L. W. (1998). *Evidence-based policing*. Police Foundation. www.policefoundation.org/wp-content/uploads/2015/06/Sherman-1998-Evidence-Based-Policing.pdf

Sherman, L. W. (2002). Evidence-based policing: Social organization of information for social control. In E. J. Waring & D. Weisburd (Eds.), *Crime and Social Organization* (2nd ed., pp. 217–248), Transaction Publishers.

Sherman, L. (2011). Police and Crime Control. In M. Tonry (Ed.), *The Oxford Handbook of Crime and Criminal Justice* (pp. 509–537). Oxford University Press. https://doi.org/10.1093/oxfordhb/9780195395082.013.0017

Sherman, L. W. (2013). The rise of evidence-based policing: Targeting, testing, and tracking. *Crime and Justice*, 42(1), 377–451.

Sherman, L. W. (2015). A tipping point for "totally evidenced policing" ten ideas for building an evidence-based police agency. *International Criminal Justice Review, 25*(1), 11–29.
Siegel, D. (2003). The transnational Russian mafia. In D. Siegel, H. Van de Bunt & D. Zaitch (Eds.), *Global organized crime* (pp. 51–62). Springer.
Sizer, S. (2017). 11. The Jewish Temple: Past, Present and Future. In S. Paas (Ed.), *Israelism and the Place of Christ: Christocentric Interpretation of Biblical Prophecy* (pp. 233–245). LIT Verlag.
Telep, C. W., & Weisburd, D. (2014). Generating knowledge: a case study of the National Policing Improvement Agency program on systematic reviews in policing. *Journal of Experimental Criminology, 10*(4), 371–398. https://doi.org/10.1007/s11292-014-9206-7
Tilley, N., & Scott, M. S. (2012). The past, present and future of POP. *Policing: A Journal of Policy and Practice, 6*(2), 122–132.
Walsh, B. (2006). Evidence-based policing for crime prevention, In D. Weisburd & A. A. Braga (Eds.), *Prospects and Problems in Police Innovation: Contrasting Perspectives* (pp. 305–321). Cambridge University Press.
Weisburd, D., Amir, M., Barak, I., Tennenbaum, A. & Shalev, O. (1997). Committee report – community policing in Israel – opportunities and risks. Mishtara Vechevra, 1, 109–30.
Weisburd, D., & Hasisi, B. (2018). The winding road to evidence-based policy in corrections: A Case Study of the Israel Prison Service. *Israel Law Review, 51*(1), 111–125. https://doi.org/10.1017/S0021223717000218
Weisburd, D., Hasisi, B., Litmanovitz, Y., Carmel, T., & Tshuva, S. (2020). Institutionalizing problem-oriented policing: An evaluation of the EMUN reform in Israel. *Criminology & Public Policy, 19*(3), 941–964.
Weisburd, D., Shalev, O., & Amir, M. (2002). Community policing in Israel: Resistance and change. *Policing: An International Journal of Police Strategies & Management, 25*(1), 80–109.
Willis, J. J., Mastrofski, S. D., & Kochel, T. R. (2010). *Maximizing the benefits of reform: Integrating Compstat and community policing in America*. US Department of Justice. www.cops.usdoj.gov/files/RIC/Publications/e051131361_FirstLine-Supervsn-Compstat_508.pdf.

15

Looking Back on the Challenges to Evidence-Based Policing

A Chief's Perspective

Darrel Stephens

> The Kansas City, Missouri Police Department in cooperation with the Police Foundation is studying the relationship between preventive patrol and the incidence of crime. *The results are not in, but the practice of preventive patrol is long established and should continue* (emphasis added).
> (National Advisory Commission on Criminal Justice and Goals, 1973)

The phrase "evidence-based policing" was coined and defined by Professor Lawrence Sherman in 1998 in a National Policing Institute Ideas in American Policing paper (Sherman, 1998). Sherman called on the police to base their strategies and programs on the best scientific evidence available. Clearly, a sensible idea that should be easily embraced by the police. He did not ask them to adopt a specific strategy like community-oriented policing (Skogan, 2006), problem-oriented policing (Goldstein, 1979, 1990), Compstat (Weisburd et al., 2006), or intelligence-led policing (Ratcliffe, 2016); he was asking them to use the best available evidence on whatever approach they decided was appropriate for policing their community. But the road to evidence-based decisions has been filled with potholes and detours.

One reason was captured in the statement above 25 years earlier in the 1973 Police report by the National Advisory Commission on Criminal Justice Standards and Goals. In a reference to the Kansas City PD and National Police Foundation research on the impact of random preventive patrol (Kelling et al., 1974), the Commission rejected the research before the findings had been published on the basis that random patrol was a long-established practice. The statement underscores the uneasy relationship between the police, research, and researchers.

Looking Back on the Challenges to Evidence-Based Policing 293

The relationship had improved by 1998 but continues to be a challenge today as many in policing look for the best available scientific evidence to guide their decisions.

My introduction to research and researchers came in the early 1970s as a police officer in the Kansas City, MO Police Department (KCPD). With funding from the National Police Foundation, in 1971 the KCPD became a living laboratory for research and innovation in policing. Chief Clarence Kelley created a task force in each of the patrol divisions to explore ways to enhance police services and effectively use 300 additional police officers who had been approved for the department. From the deliberations of those task forces came the much-heralded research on random preventive patrol (Kelling et al., 1974), response time analysis (Kansas City Police Department, 1977), domestic violence (Wilt et al., 1977), and a study to examine the effects of the establishment of a street crime intelligence center and testing the deployment of special patrol units by location or focusing on repeat offenders (Pate et al., 1976).

The National Police Foundation research in Kansas City, San Diego, and several other cities was the first broad based effort to try to understand the effectiveness of police strategies. The National Institute of Justice funded the response time analysis research in Kansas City (Kansas City Police Department, 1977), the Rand Corporation's national examination of the criminal investigation process (Greenwood et al., 1975), and the Police Executive Research Forum's (PERF) replication of the response time study (Spelman & Brown, 1981). Although the findings of much of this work were ignored by most in policing, they provided an evidence base for continued research, experimentation, and innovation.

This chapter will focus on evidence-based policing from the perspective of one who has served as a police chief in four different cities, implemented problem-oriented policing in three agencies, and engaged in numerous research initiatives with a view toward improving police effectiveness. It will also discuss the risks and rewards of a police chief conducting research in a real-world laboratory. Finally, it will provide a perspective on how evidence and the lack of evidence influences police chief's policing decisions.

I began my career in 1968 in Kansas City, MO where I had the opportunity to participate in some of the earliest experiments in policing. That experience, coupled with a 10-month fellowship at the National Institute of Justice, had enormous influence on my career goals and understanding of the importance of evidence in guiding police operational decisions.

15.1 POLICE OPERATIONS INFLUENCED BY EVIDENCE

The research of the early 1970s raised serious questions about the overall effectiveness of policing strategy at the time. The Kansas City Preventive Patrol experiment concluded that random patrol had no impact on crime (Kelling et al., 1974). The response time analysis study found that rapid response to calls had little effect on arrests or citizen satisfaction (Kansas City Police Department, 1977). And research on the criminal investigations process determined that most crimes were solved by information obtained by the initial responding patrol officer – not so much from the work of the follow-up detective (Greenwood et al., 1975). This research and other studies were the foundation for the way in which policing has changed over the past fifty years. I will discuss many of the changes and how the "evidence" has influenced both the evolution of policing and my thinking in the context of my personal experiences.

15.1.1 Kansas City PD

In 1970, the National Police Foundation (NPF) was created by the Ford Foundation in response to the various national commission reports on policing in the late 1960s (Kerner Commission, 1968; President's Commission on Law Enforcement and Administration of Justice, 1967) and provided $30 million to assist police departments in making operational changes (NPF, 2020). Chief Clarence Kelley approached the NPF with a request to assist the KCPD in making the most effective use of 300 newly authorized police officers for the department. With NPF support, task forces representing all ranks were established in each of the three patrol divisions and the Special Operations Division (SOD). Their mandate was to examine their current operations, propose ideas to improve effectiveness, and make the best use of the 300 additional police officers the department would hire over the next two years. The task forces had NPF consultants assigned to assist in their work.

I was a member of the Special Operations Division Police Foundation Task Force that was created to develop and evaluate methods of improving the effectiveness of the Division's Tactical Unit that worked exclusively in high crime areas on patterns and trends. The Task Force designed a project to test whether it was more effective to focus the Tactical Unit resources on high crime locations based on crime patterns or to focus on the most active offenders – the strategies came to be called location-oriented patrol (LOP) and perpetrator-oriented patrol (POP). These tactics were supported by a Street Crime Intelligence Center (SCIC) that I was responsible for creating and directing.

The SCIC operated 24/7 and served two key purposes. The first was to track and analyze robbery and burglary patterns and trends to direct the unit's location-oriented patrol strategy. The second was to identify the most active offenders, develop background on them, disseminate information about them to police in the metropolitan area, and support the Tactical Unit squads that were focused on the perpetrator-oriented patrol. The SCIC started by identifying the 100 most active burglary and robbery offenders although we quickly learned these offenders did not necessarily specialize. They took advantage of any opportunity to make money.

After the 100 offenders were identified, the consultants suggested they be randomly assigned to four cells – a control group, a group where information was disseminated to both patrol and the tactical unit, a group that just went to patrol, and a group that just went to the tactical unit. The idea was to test effects of disseminating information on active criminals to the tactical unit and patrol officers, against not disseminating it at all. Loose leaf notebooks with the photos and information on each of the offenders were provided to all officers in the department and to surrounding agencies. They were asked to notify the SCIC when they encountered the subjects or arrested them.

That conversation on randomly assigning offenders to the various groups, and many others during that time, with people like James Q. Wilson, Tom Sweeney, George Kelling, Bob Wasserman, Tony Pate, Dick Ward, Mary Ann Wycoff, Herman Goldstein, and others who were involved with the research in Kansas City (or visiting the department because of it), was my introduction to the challenges of research in policing. Like many police officers then, and now, I was pretty sure that what we were doing worked – we just needed more officers, so visibility could be increased, more crimes could be investigated, and more people arrested. It was the researchers and outside consultants that raised questions about the assumptions we made on our effectiveness.

Working on the NPF project provided another opportunity to expand my knowledge of police research. NIJ asked the KCPD to provide an officer who could serve as a "Fellow" to share what was taking place in Kansas City and to contribute to their work. The experience provided an opportunity to be exposed to a wide range of research as well as researchers. It also provided a view of policing across America.

FIGURE 15.1 Directed patrol: A concept in community-specific, crime-specific, service-specific policing

At the completion of the NIJ Fellowship I was assigned to the Operations Resource Unit[1] (ORU), where a team was assembled in July 1974 with the mission of taking what we had learned from our (and others) research to develop a concept of how Kansas City would be policed. That team produced a report detailing the concept that carried the title: Directed Patrol: A Concept in Community Specific, Crime Specific, Service Specific Policing (see Figure 15.1). "Community-specific policing" was pretty close to the "community-oriented policing" terminology that would not capture widespread attention for well over another decade. The concept was piloted in one of the patrol divisions. Three sector teams (a sector contained five–six patrol beats) were established for each shift, which had the responsibility for handling calls for service, identifying crime and service problems, and tailoring responses to address them. They were supported by a crime analyst assigned to the division.

---

[1] The ORU was established as an in-house consulting and support group to patrol commanders in the implementation of the various task force recommendations. It was a 15-person unit comprising police officers, social scientists, and psychologists.

The sector supervisors were given the authority to allocate their officers to ensure calls were handled and dedicate other officers to addressing the problems. The fundamental idea was to better manage the call workload, and the role of patrol officers by directing their energy toward specific crime and service problems in their geographic area of responsibility.

Directed Patrol was informed by the best available evidence at the time. We had learned from the preventive patrol research (Kelling et al., 1974) that we could remove officers from their patrol areas for a period of time without significant risk. The Response Time Analysis (Kansas City Police Department, 1977) research provided the basis for implementing call management procedures that helped create blocks of time for officers to work on specific problems or engage in high-quality preliminary investigations. The research on criminal investigations identified the importance of patrol officers engaging in thorough initial investigations.

Directed Patrol was implemented with the support of the federally funded ICAP (Integrated Criminal Apprehension Program), which aimed to improve police effectiveness through enhancing the role of the patrol officer. Crime analysis support, follow-up investigations, shedding responsibility for non-police activities, such as funeral escorts and repeat alarm calls, and telephone reporting were all apart of ICAP as it evolved to include about 50 cities.

15.1.2 Lawrence, KS and Largo, FL

I left the KCPD in July 1976 to become the assistant police chief in Lawrence, KS and from there to Largo, FL in December 1979 as the chief. Both agencies had significant challenges with union relationships. In Lawrence, the union engaged in a work speed up as a way of putting pressure on the City to negotiate a memorandum of agreement to meet their demands. In Largo the former chief was forced to retire following a resounding vote of no confidence by the union. Both departments also had significant administrative and organizational issues that had to be addressed in order to implement a new patrol strategy.

During that 6.5-year period, my primary focus was on implementing and refining the Directed Patrol concept. The key elements of Directed Patrol included

- Geographic Accountability
- Officers Assigned and Scheduled Based on Workload
- Focus on Specific Crime and Service Problems
- Patrol Officer Follow-up Investigations

- Call Management Practices
  o Telephone Reporting
  o Call Priorities
  o Patrol Beat Integrity
- Crime Analysis Support.

Although important research continued through the 1970s and began to focus on areas, such as foot patrol (Police Foundation, 1981), fear of crime (Pate & Skogan, 1985), domestic violence (Sherman & Berk, 1984a, b), and women in policing (Milton, 1972), many of the elements of the Directed Patrol were not supported by empirical evidence (Bowers & Hirsch, 1987; Police Foundation, 1981). In the search for ideas that would help improve police effectiveness, it made sense for officers to use the time devoted to random patrol to address crime and service problems in their area of responsibility. Managing patrol time properly provided the opportunity for officers to be more thorough in their preliminary and follow-up investigations. They could take the time in domestic violence cases to dig a little deeper and perhaps contribute to preventing future violence. Maintaining patrol beat integrity and ensuring officers worked the same area each day provided the opportunity for them to understand the problems and develop relationships with people and businesses in their area.

15.1.3 Newport News, VA

Newport News was a troubled police department that was firmly entrenched in an aggressive 1960s style of policing. It was a community of about 160,000 (35% African American) and the police department had about 350 employees. There were significant relationship problems with the African American community. The department had pockets of dishonest officers and the use of physical and deadly force was out of control. It was a shipbuilding city with the shipyard employing over 35,000 people who worked around the clock in the downtown area next to the James River. The department had extremely poor relationships with shipyard employees because of a long bitter strike that included a riot near the end in which police were accused of brutality in dealing with the strikers. The city also had a strong presence of military personnel – particularly the Navy. They were assigned to the aircraft carriers and submarines that were in the yard for refueling,[2] overhauls or nearing the

---

[2] Refueling a nuclear carrier or submarine could take up to a year.

completion of construction. The department's reputation was not particularly good with the military either. Unlike Lawrence and Largo where the unions turned out to be allies in the effort to improve the department, Newport News did not engage in collective bargaining. There was a union, but the leadership was combative and had little interest in collaborating on dealing with the many issues facing the department.

Like all organizations, the Newport News PD (NNPD) was filled with good people who wanted to do the right thing and be proud of what they contributed to policing the community. The department was dominated by a small number of people at every level of the organization, who had created a culture where community "respect" was defined by how much the police were feared. The majority of officers did not buy into that idea, but they went along to get along. From their perspective, it seemed the people most successful in the department subscribed to the fear culture.

Nevertheless, the NNPD was the first in the country to successfully implement problem-oriented policing in the patrol force with officers and supervisors managing their workload in a way that allowed time for them to engage in problem solving (Eck & Spellman, 1987). Evidence-based policing requires that street level officers understand and be a part of the research and change process. It requires an organization that is capable of adapting to new ideas and approaches to policing. Those organizations have to be created – an environment and culture that engages officers, values their input and provides an opportunity to be a part of framing the way the community is policed (Lum & Koper, 2017).

The first challenge was to gain some semblance of control. There were seven or eight fiefdoms in the department that operated pretty much independently of each other. The command level did not see much value in working together and in some cases, they just didn't like each other. One thing that many of them did agree on was they didn't have much use for a police chief from the outside from a smaller suburban police department that had fewer years of experience than all of them. In order to begin exerting some control over the department, it was necessary to build a supportive management team and create a structure that reinforced accountability. The patrol area of the department, for example, had five shifts – each commanded by a captain – working 4/10 shifts that rotated each week. Each of these captains had a different idea about what was important and how to police a community. One captain thought the world would be a better place if the police eradicated drunk driving. That was the focus of his entire shift – even to the extent of not dealing with some calls for service. The community had no idea what to expect from the police department because every patrol captain has different priorities. There was very little concern on the department's part with citizen expectations.

I began to look for people in the department that could play a role in implementing the significant changes that needed to take place. Everything that was done sent messages to both the department and community, so it was critically important to ensure the messages were clear that the approach to policing in Newport News was going to change. We began our work with reorganizing the department in a way that established clear lines of accountability. To do that, we had to move away from the five patrol shifts, implement fixed shifts, and, I believed, re-establish a 5/8 shift schedule. To develop a new patrol schedule, we created a task force of officers that worked on that issue. Another group focused on the organizational structure itself while a third group was dedicated to reviewing the department's policy and procedures with the priority given to policies on use of force, pursuit, citizen complaints, and internal affairs investigations.[3]

As with all collaborative efforts, there were a number of compromises – we went to a four day eight-and-a-half-hour fixed shift schedule for example – but this work achieved a couple of important things for the department. First, it sent the message that we were going to approach our work in a very different manner, and officers did not have to be a part of a clique to be heard and engaged in setting a direction for the department. Second, we were able to identify a number of very talented people who were more than willing to step up and help create a new future for the department. The new organizational structure broke up the fiefdoms and created the opportunity for accountability. Rather than 5 separate shifts that policed the entire city, we created two district commands that included patrol beats, so officers were responsible for specific geographic areas. The patrol districts reported to a commander who had overall citywide responsibility – this was not particularly innovative, but it did begin to set the tone for accountability. The new structure also added a level in the department that was given to the major's rank and a training director that was at the same level.

The appointment of the majors and the training director formed the basis to create a new management team in the department. It also

---

[3] It was interesting to learn the department had a several hundred-page manuals, but there were very few copies and none of those were available to officers.

provided another opportunity to send a strong message that things were going to be different in the department and in the way we policed the community. Unlike Largo – none of these positions were filled from the outside, and the selection process was one that I managed myself through a large number of internal and external conversations about who might be the right people for these jobs. Through these conversations, I was able to supplement my own observations with the view of people inside and outside of the department. One question that I asked many times in the department was "who do you think are the best three or four individuals that we have at the lieutenant and captain ranks in the department and why?" After narrowing down a list of people that I thought could do the job, I began to ask people in other city departments and in the community about them. That process helped me make appointments that I knew going in would have significant internal and external support and credibility. All three of the majors came from the rank of lieutenant, and the training director had been a very well respected and articulate vice detective, who also held a degree in education and had been a teacher before becoming a police officer. Except for the captains who were passed over, the choices were very well received inside and outside the department. This was the nucleus of a management team that could do the work necessary to move the department forward.

The next step was to establish a direction for the department and a fundamental set of values. Direction and focus for the department came through a collaborative effort to establish goals and objectives. The process included officers on the street developing objectives for their patrol areas that were related to the crime and service problems. The department also went through a process of developing a set of values to guide how we operated. At the time there were few examples in policing, but Houston under the leadership of Lee Brown provided a model that was tailored to Newport News.

There were two other significant initiatives the department undertook that helped move it from an ineffective organization in turmoil to one that emerged as a national model for problem-oriented policing. One of those initiatives was to seek accreditation through the Commission on Accreditation for Law Enforcement Agencies. When the department was accredited in 1986, it was the 14th department in the nation to have successfully completed that rigorous process. It helped develop a sense of pride in the department as well as playing a key role in ensuring the department's policy and procedures were current, addressed all of the areas they should, and communicated clear expectations for employees.

The second initiative was joining with the National Institute of Justice (NIJ) and the Police Executive Research Forum (PERF) to build on the work of Herman Goldstein in the implementation of Problem-Oriented Policing (POP) (Goldstein, 1979, 1990). As with all of the work that we did in Newport News, the POP initiative engaged a wide range of people in the department in the project to implement an approach to problem-oriented policing that involved patrol officers on the street. What was different for the department was the involvement of PERF staff like John Eck and Bill Spellman along with the exposure of officers to Herman Goldstein and others who worked on the project. Many police officers had the opportunity to interact with and learn from experts in policing from the United States and England much in the same way that I had as a young police officer in Kansas City working on the Police Foundation projects. In conjunction with PERF staff, the department developed a problem-solving process – scanning, analysis, response, assessment (SARA) – street officers could use to guide their efforts. This process has been refined over the past 20 years to serve as a guide to police problem-solving efforts around the world (Eck & Spelman, 1987).

The project also demonstrated that police officers could effectively involve themselves in problem solving as part of their patrol responsibilities. They took on a wide range of problems, from burglaries in a public housing complex that not only reduced the crime problems but eventually led to rebuilding the entire complex, to successfully solving large-scale larceny theft from auto problem, to numerous smaller-scale problems. In an examination of repeat calls for service, officers learned they had responded to calls over 500 times at a 7–11 convenience store in the previous 12 months. The analysis revealed several problems at the location. In partnership with the store, several solutions were implemented that reduced calls to less than 150, and crime was also reduced at the store and in the area (Eck & Spelman, 1987) (see Figure 15.2).

The experience with POP in Newport News made an important "evidence-based" contribution to demonstrating that police officers could successfully engage in problem solving along with their other responsibilities. Equally important was the transition from a troubled police department to an agency that implemented one of the most innovative approaches to policing at the time.

Looking Back on the Challenges to Evidence-Based Policing

FIGURE 15.2 Problem solving: Problem-oriented policing in Newport News

15.1.4 Police Executive Research Forum (PERF)

PERF was created in 1976 by the National Police Foundation as a membership organization dedicated to research, and spirited debate on important policy issues.[4] The first Executive Director, Gary Hayes, passed away from cancer in 1985. I was encouraged to seek the position by PERF research director John Eck and NIJ project monitor Bill Saulsbury. I served as Executive Director from 1986 through 1992. During that time, PERF engaged in a wide range of research initiatives, national legislative policy issues, such as gun control, and technical assistance and training. The primary focus of our work was on advancing POP, which was supported to a great extent by the Bureau of Justice Assistance (BJA).

In one BJA supported project, PERF partnered with four agencies (San Diego, Atlanta, Tulsa, and Philadelphia) to implement problem-oriented policing with an emphasis on neighborhood drug problems. All of the

[4] See www.policeforum.org/about-us

agencies were successful to some extent, but San Diego became one of the premier POP agencies in the world. In a partnership with PERF, the annual POP Conference was launched in 1990. The Herman Goldstein Problem Solving award was introduced in 1993 to recognize excellence in problem solving. The conference was attended by 800 plus people in the late 1990s, and was an important forum for promoting POP. Although PERF and the San Diego PD stopped supporting the conferences, a group of former PERF staff members and others have continued them. The conference attracts 300 to 400 participants each year, and the Goldstein awards are highly coveted by the officers and departments engaged in problem solving.

As the research continued in the 1980s and 1990s, the evidence for focusing on specific problems increased. Sherman and Weisburd's "hot spot" policing research in Minneapolis was important to understanding the concentration of crime and calls for service in a small number of locations (Sherman & Weisburd, 1995). These hot spots were the kind of problems that patrol officers could focus on in their beats. The 2004 report by the National Research Council reaffirmed earlier research that traditional police tactics failed to reduce crime. The Council found that police could have an impact on crime when they focused on specific problems or places and supplemented enforcement tactics with regulator and abatement activities (Bayley & Nixon, 2010). The research fueled my desire to return to active policing, and that opportunity presented itself in St. Petersburg, Florida in December 1992.

15.1.5 St. Petersburg, FL

The St. Petersburg Police Department (SPPD) was an agency in turmoil. The chief I replaced had been fired after 18 months in the position for racial insensitivity. Three interim chiefs filled the position for ten months between the firing and when I reported for work. There were many challenges: African American community trust was low, racial tension internally was high, the union was hostile toward the department administration, and there was political unrest over the police and other local government issues. Within a month after I took over the position, the former chief announced he was running for mayor and leading an effort to change the form of government from a council/manager to a strong mayor. The former chief lost the mayor's election by less than a one percent margin, but the form of government ballot measure won by a few hundred votes. The divisiveness in the department increased during the election because many officers actively worked on the former chief's campaign.

Despite the turmoil, there were many positive things about the department. The officers were well trained, and the agency had a history of innovation – particularly in the use of technology. Under the former chief, they had implemented community policing with an emphasis on problem solving. They created a centralized Community Policing Division that was staffed by 50 officers. Each of the patrol beats had a community officer assigned, but they mostly worked as small teams of five or six officers, and did not take ownership of the beat. Although these officers were dedicated to their work, the officers working patrol resented the special unit largely because all of the community officers were taken from patrol and their call workload increased.

My initial emphasis was to focus the energy of the department on the work of policing the community rather than the internal and external political intrigue. I felt it was important to decentralize the community policing division, and restructure patrol with a foundation of geographic accountability, community engagement, and problem solving. Like many agencies, patrol responsibility was oriented toward time (watch or shift) rather than the geography. Patrol officers were primarily responsible for handling calls on their shift, not specific problems.

The new deployment plan emphasized geography rather than time. Teams were created that had 24-hour responsibility for a geographic area. The teams were supervised by a sergeant and included two community officers that worked flexible schedules. Although the community officers took the lead on relationship building with the neighborhoods and problem solving, officers on the team worked on the problems during their shift.

The work was supported by grants from the COPS Office. In addition to adding 25 officers to the department, we were able to obtain funding to support the acquisition of laptops and a wireless network that allowed reports to be filed from the car. The time saved on report writing was redirected to problem-solving efforts on the street.

There was no formal evaluation of the community policing and problem-solving work in St. Petersburg. The SARA model was employed, so each problem had at least a rudimentary assessment to gauge the impact of the response. In addition, the department conducted community surveys annually that included questions about interactions with the police, fear, and victimization. The surveys also asked if residents knew the officers that worked in their neighborhood. The surveys suggested that community policing and problem solving had a positive impact. The community reported that their neighborhoods were becoming safer, and the most serious crime problems declined between 1991 and 1994. Over 80% of residents that had contact with a police officer reported they were treated fairly and with dignity. Residents that were aware of police problem solving increased by 10 points to 54% in 1994 compared with 1991, and 24% reported they had participated in problem solving. Twenty-one percent reported they knew their community officer in 1994 – up from 4% in 1991 (Stephens, 1994).

St. Petersburg also became a laboratory for research. Three studies made important national contributions to our understanding of police practice. The first was an observational study conducted by Steve Mastrofski, Roger Parks, Al Reiss, and Robert Worden in 1997 (Mastrofski, et.al. 1999). The research was conducted in St. Petersburg and Indianapolis, and has contributed considerable insight into understanding the work of both patrol and community policing officers on the street. It helped the department manage officer activity more effectively because it provided evidence on what officers were doing with their time when not handling a call for service.

The second study was on the use of force. St. Petersburg was one of six cities involved in the research that was part of a broad initiative of understanding police use of force following the Rodney King incident in Los Angeles. The research was very helpful in providing a picture of when force was used, the type and the impact of its use (Garner & Maxwell, 1999). The third study focused on integrity. Initially officers participated in a survey developed by Karl Klockers to gauge how they would react to integrity related scenarios. It reinforced the department's disciplinary philosophy, as the majority of the officers believed the process resulted in fair treatment. Based on the analysis of the data, St. Petersburg was one of three agencies selected for further study (Klockers et al., 2006).

Participation in this research provided the department with important information on our operations and officer's perspectives on integrity and discipline. Given the toxic environment in the department, it would have been easy to say to researchers that it was not a good time to participate. There was a risk that some might want to undermine the efforts. But that was not the case. In many ways, involvement in the research helped improve the department and the officers' perspective. It was a source of pride to most that their department was a part of these national efforts to improve policing.

15.1.6 Charlotte-Mecklenburg Police Department (CMPD)

The CMPD presented some different leadership challenges. It was and continues to be a very good police department. Members of the department from the officer on the street to the command levels, and both sworn and non-sworn employees, are exceptional. The City of Charlotte and the Mecklenburg County police consolidated in October 1993. By the time I became Chief in September 1999, all of the significant consolidation issues had been resolved. I followed Dennis Nowicki who served as the first Chief of the consolidated department for five years. Under his leadership, a countywide strategy was developed to guide the department toward full implementation of community problem-oriented policing. He was able to acquire significant federal COPS funding to begin the development of a wireless network to serve officers and detectives' problem-solving information needs. He launched a fast-paced effort to bring two police departments together and create one that would operate under a philosophy of working in partnership with the community to solve problems and prevent crime.

In all of the previous positions of chief that I had held, there were substantial organizational problems that required immediate attention. In September 1999, the most important challenges the CMPD faced were continuing the implementation of community problem-oriented policing, completing the technology work that was underway, and developing tools to support our policing philosophy while keeping up with the enormous growth. One of the department's strengths was two chiefs in succession with similar views on the way the community should be policed. Adjustments were made along the way to reflect the changing community and the policing environment, but the fundamental problem-solving focus with an emphasis on crime prevention remained the same. In addition to patrol officers engaging in problem solving, we emphasized several areas we believe complimented our efforts:

- **Crime Prevention Through Environmental Design (CPTED).** We provided CPTED training to our community officers, members of the community, including businesses representatives and the school system. CPTED is a problem-solving method that holds the proper design of buildings and public spaces can reduce crime and fear (e.g., Cozens & Love, 2015).
- **Technology.** With support from federal grants and the city budget, the department was able to create a strong base of technology that helped officers more efficiently use their time and provide information to support problem analysis.

- **Crime Analysis.** Analytical support was provided to officers to assist with the identification of problems and their analysis. The identification of hot spots was a key part of the problem identification of the process. Analysts were responsible for identifying crime hot spots in the patrol divisions. In addition, officers received a list each month of the locations in their patrol beat where police had responded to five or more calls for service. They were expected to determine the reasons for the repeat calls and address them.
- **Detective Problem Solving.** Engaging investigators in community and problem-oriented policing has always been difficult. They are focused on solving crime and developing a case for prosecution. Preventing crime to them was incapacitation through incarceration. Nevertheless, the department encouraged the investigative units to apply the SARA model to their work, and support patrol officers that were working on crime problems in their areas. Although success was limited, there were a number of notable initiatives in the property crime arena using problem solving that demonstrated that detectives could do this work while managing their caseloads.
- **Problem-Based Learning.** In traditional police training officers learn from instructor lectures and reading. They demonstrate their retention of the information through written tests. In problem-based learning, trainees apply knowledge as they learn it, and are expected to solve problems with the newly acquired knowledge (e.g., Savery, 2006). Working with the North Carolina Standards and Training staff, the CMPD was able to incorporate problem-based leaning in a number of areas in the basic academy. We also introduced problem-based learning in the three-month field training program. In addition, officers in field training had to identify a problem in their area and, using the SARA model, attempt to solve the problem. They had to present their work to their chain of command at the conclusion.
- **Wrongful Convictions.** The research on wrongful convictions at the time provided strong evidence that some police practices contributed to innocent people being convicted and sent to prison (Batts et al., 2014). In response, the department implemented changes to eyewitness identification protocol, initiated videotaping interrogations, and enhanced policy on storing biological evidence.

With the department's growth and natural turnover, by 2008 over 50% of the employees had operated under this basic philosophy their entire time. Even with the consistent focus it was a challenge to create a department and community where community problem-oriented policing was fully embraced by everyone.

One of the lessons from the experience in Charlotte-Mecklenburg is how important it is to stay focused over a period of time. Change sometimes appears as if it is made quickly, but I have come to believe that real change in the substance of how we police is a generational process. Few large police departments have maintained a consistent focus over a period of time, with a bottom-line philosophy that provides a foundation for addressing most issues they face. All police departments patrol the community, respond to calls and investigate crimes, but the priorities and focus quite often change with the chief. Given the tenure of chiefs in large cities, it is very difficult to maintain focus.

There is evidence that the CMPD made enormous progress in creating a culture of problem-oriented policing in the fourteen years when it was emphasized by two consecutive chiefs:

The Charlotte Mecklenburg Police Department's successful institutionalization of problem-oriented policing has demonstrated that a department can change the way it conducts police business.

The CMPD had gone well beyond the documented previous organizational change efforts of other departments to obtain a favorable culture. Research findings from the CMPD demonstrate that the department implemented various policy and procedural changes that emphasized problem-oriented policing and obtained cultural buy in. The department revised its promotions, training, performance evaluations, mission statement, technology systems, and rewards systems to reflect problem-oriented policing. Further, the department has continued to emphasize the practice in future departmental plans by incorporating problem-oriented policing into its communications plan and by revising its technology systems. The strength of the favorable culture in the CMPD confirms that these policy and procedural changes are related to the successful institutionalization of problem-oriented policing. Success also was shown in the relationships with the policy and procedural changes and the CMPD captains' and rank and file's knowledge, attitudes, and behaviors. (Ikerd & Walker, 2010, p. 35)

9/11 presented a significant challenge requiring all large cities in America to develop the capacity to prevent and respond to acts of terrorism (Bayley & Weisburd, 2009; IACP, 2005). Not only did 9/11 create an important new priority for the police, but the tragedy itself also contributed to three other issues that affected policing in Charlotte and nationally. The first was the economic blow to the travel and tourism industry at a time when economic growth was slowing. That rippled through the entire economy as every business connected with the travel industry suffered – along with the significant tax revenue reductions. Many cities, including Charlotte, had to make immediate cutbacks to maintain a balanced budget.

The second issue for local police was the attack on Afghanistan followed by Iraq. The war made it important for the police to be even more vigilant in the effort to prevent terrorism, and it reduced staffing levels through the activation of police officers that were also members of the military reserves. The third issue that 9/11 presented for local policing was the loss of federal funding support for community policing. Federal support was shifted away from policing to homeland security with very narrow restrictions on where and how the money would be spent – mostly equipment and training (Wells, 2003).

These were all important challenges for the CMPD and required they be addressed in a way that did not abandon our policing philosophy. A national tragedy that causes a significant investment of resources in a new priority while reducing the resource base does not eliminate community expectations that other services be maintained (Jonathan-Zamir et al., 2014). To the extent possible, the police must absorb the new responsibilities while minimizing the impact on the community. There was little evidence available to guide the response to taking on a significant new responsibility with reduced resources. The police did what they are doing today in dealing with COVID-19 and the loss of community confidence with reduced resources – they make adjustments based on what seems to be the best approach to address the issues (Perry & Jonathan-Zamir, 2020).

15.2 CONCLUSION

Policing practice has made enormous improvements since 1968 when I began my career as a police officer in Kansas City, Missouri. The launch pad for those improvements was the President's Commission on Law Enforcement and the Administration of Justice. In their 1967 report *The Challenge of Crime in a Free Society* they emphasize the importance of research, and the National Institute of Justice (NIJ) was created in response. NIJ has been a critically important institution in supporting research to provide empirical evidence to guide operational decisions. The opportunity to be involved with research as a young police officer and the NIJ fellowship influenced both my commitment and involvement in using research to improve the way we policed our community. As a Chief in four police departments for over twenty years evidence-based decisions were an integral part of my approach to the job. There are a few things that might be helpful in encouraging broader adoption of evidence-based policing going forward. They include:

- **Engaging Officers.** The most successful efforts to conduct research or implement new programs and policy engage officers in the process. Officers should be involved from the outset and have their perspectives included in the design phase for research or in the introduction of new policies and programs.
- **Engaging the Community.** The world of policing today requires a great deal more transparency and engagement with the community. Research and policy making has involved the community in only a limited way in the past – that has to change going forward. An example from Charlotte, the CMPD had a telephone reporting program that was the subject of criticism at times from members of the City Council when someone would complain. The community was surveyed about the practice to gain their input on the policy. The survey provided information on the policy and the cost of sending officers to take reports. Although they indicated a strong preference for an officer being present, after learning the cost the overwhelming majority felt telephone reporting was the best alternative. The survey provided sufficient evidence to continue a more efficient/ effective policy.
- **Research Results** – Reports/Journal Articles. Reports and journal articles on the outcome of research are frequently written in a style that is not friendly to practitioners. Moreover, the time delay from research to reporting often minimizes the value of the work. Police chiefs, the public, and policy makers are not willing to wait two or three years before doing something. The impact of evidence-based policing has been limited because most practitioners will not read academic reports and articles. Reports must be written with a view toward a non-academic audience (Lum & Koper, 2017).
- **Research Risks/Rewards.** Participating in research comes with some risks for the chief. The public generally understands medical research – side effects with medications, risk with treatments or surgery, but they do not have the same level of tolerance for taking risks in public safety. Research documenting the failure of a strategy puts the chief and department in an awkward position and must be explained (Weisburd & Neyroud, 2011).

All of these issues should be considered when working with police agencies to conduct research.

Finally, for evidence-based policing to become an integral part of policing, researchers need to have a much wider focus than crime (Lum & Koper, 2017; Weisburd & Neyroud, 2011; Neyroud & Weisburd, in this volume). A substantial part of the police workload does not involve crime. There are many operational issues as well that have not been the subject of much research for many years. Some examples of the evidence-based knowledge gaps (National Research Council, 2004):

- **Training.** Police make a substantial investment in recruit and in-service training. And, in every crisis there are calls for more training for police officers. Although this is beginning to change, there are significant gaps in our knowledge on the best methods for officers to learn, and the effectiveness of various types of training. Does crisis intervention training or bias training make a difference?
- **Recruiting/Hiring.** Police make a substantial investment in the recruiting and hiring process with virtually no evidence on the most efficient and effective process.
- **Criminal Investigations.** The work of detectives has not received the attention it should. What are the best investigative methods? How should detectives be assigned? How many are needed and what is the optimum case load?
- **Operational Issues.** Although the work of patrol officers has been the subject of a lot of research – most has been directed at their impact on crime. Deployment methods, shift scheduling, and one/two officer cars are important issues that have received little attention.
- **Accountability.** Discipline processes and civilian oversight are widely discussed as part of police reform, but the various approaches that are taken are not informed by research. What are the most effective strategies for ensuring officers are both held accountable when appropriate and supported when they have operated in accordance with the law and policy?

This is beginning to change – Cynthia Lum and colleagues at the Center for Evidence-Based Crime Policy[5] have begun doing research on the impact of technology, proactive policing, dispatcher decision making, mass shootings, traffic stops, and the important and timely topic of the impact of COVID-19 on policing (Lum & Coper 2017). This type of research will be welcomed by practitioners and will be helpful in the years ahead as communities attempt to reimagine what policing should look like.

[5] https://cebcp.org/

References

Batts, A., deLone, M., & Stephens, D. (2014). *Policing and wrongful convictions*. National Institute of Justice. Washington, DC.

Bayley, D., & Nixon, C. (2010). *The changing environment for policing, 1985–2008*. National Institute of Justice. Washington, DC.

Bayley, D. H., & Weisburd, D. (2009). Cops and spooks: The role of police in counterterrorism. In D. Weisburd, T. Feucht, I. Hakimi, M. Lois, & S. Perry (Eds.), *To protect and to serve: Policing in an age of terrorism* (pp. 81–99). Springer.

Bowers, W., & Hirsch, J. (1987). The impact of foot patrol staffing on crime and disorder in Boston: An unmet promise. *American Journal of Policing, 6*(1), 17–44.

Cozens, P., & Love, T. (2015). A review and current status of crime prevention through environmental design (CPTED). *Journal of Planning Literature, 30*(4), 393–412.

Eck, J. E., & Spelman, W. (1987). *Problem-solving: Problem-oriented policing in Newport News*. Police Executive Research Forum.

Garner, J., & Maxwell, C. (1999). *Measuring the use of force by and against the police in six jurisdictions: An overview of national and local data*. National Institute of Justice. Washington DC.

Goldstein, H. (1979). Improving policing: A problem-oriented approach. *Crime & Delinquency, 25*(2), 236–258.

Goldstein, H. (1990). *Problem-oriented policing*. McGraw-Hill.

Greenwood, P. W., Chaiken, J., Petersilia, M., & Prusoff, L. (1975). *Criminal investigation process, III: Observations and analysis*. RAND Corporation.

Ikerd, T., & Walker, S. (2010). *Making police reforms endure: The keys for success*. Office of Community Oriented Policing. Washington, DC.

International Association of Chiefs of Police. (2005). *Post 9/11 policing: The crime-control-homeland security paradigm – Taking command of new realities*. International Association of Chiefs of Police.

Jonathan-Zamir, T., Weisburd, D., & Hasisi, B. (2014). *Policing terrorism, crime control, and police-community relations: Learning from the Israeli experience*. Springer

Kansas City Police Department. (1977). *Response time analysis*. Kansas City Police Department.

Kelling, G. L., Pate, A., Dieckman, D., & Brown, C. E. (1974). *The Kansas City preventive patrol experiment: Technical report*. Police Foundation.

Kerner Commission. (1968). Report of the National Advisory Commission on Civil Disorders.

Klockers, K., Ivkovic, S., & Haberfeld, M. (2006). *Enhancing police integrity*. Springer.

Lum, C., & Koper, C. (2017). *Evidence based policing: Translating research into practice*. Oxford University Press.

Mastrofski, S., Parks, R., Reiss, A., & Worden, R. 1999. *Policing neighborhoods: A Report from St. Petersburg*. National Institute of Justice. Washington, DC.

Milton, C. (1972). *Women in policing*. Police Foundation.

National Advisory Commission on Criminal Justice and Goals. (1973). *Report on Police*. Government Printing Office. Washington DC.

National Police Foundation. (2020). History. www.policefoundation.org/about-the-police-foundation/history/.

National Research Council. (2004). *Fairness and effectiveness in policing: The evidence*. National Academies Press.

Neyroud, P., & Weisburd, D. (this volume). Re-Inventing Policing: Using Science to Transform Policing. In D. Weisburd, T. Jonathan, G. Perry & B. Hasisi, (Eds.), *The future of evidence-based policing*. Cambridge University Press.

Pate, A., Bowers, R., & Parks, R. (1976). *Three approaches to criminal apprehension in Kansas City: An evaluation Report*. Police Foundation.

Pate, A., & Skogan, W. (1985). *Coordinated community policing: The Newark experience. Technical report*. Police Foundation.

Perry, G., & Jonathan-Zamir, T. (2020). Expectations, effectiveness, trust, and cooperation: Public attitudes toward the Israel Police during the COVID-19 pandemic. *Policing: A Journal of Policy and Practice*, 14(4), 1073–1091.

Police Foundation. (1981). *The Newark foot patrol experiment*. Police Foundation.

President's Commission on Law Enforcement and Administration of Justice. (1967). *The challenge of crime in a free society*. Washington, DC: U.S. Government Printing Office.

Ratcliffe, J. H. (2016). *Intelligence-led policing*. Routledge.

Savery, J. R. (2006). Overview of problem-based learning: Definitions and distinctions. *Interdisciplinary Journal of Problem-Based Learning*, 1, 9–20. https://doi.org/10.7771/1541-5015.1002

Sherman, L. (1998). *Evidence based policing*. Police Foundation.

Sherman, L., & Berk, R. (1984a). *Specific deterrent effects of arrest for domestic assault Minneapolis*. National Institute of Justice.

Sherman, L., & Berk, R. (1984b). Specific deterrent effects of arrest for domestic assault. *American Sociological Review*, 49(2), 261–272.

Sherman, L., & Weisburd D. (1995). General Deterrent Effects of Police Patrol in Crime "Hot Spots": A Randomized, Controlled Trial. *Justice Quarterly*, 12(4):625–648.

Skogan, W. G. (2006). *Police and community in Chicago: A tale of three cities*. Oxford University Press.

Spelman, W., & Brown, D. K. (1981). *Calling the police: A replication of the citizen reporting component of the Kansas City response time analysis*. Police Executive Research Forum.

Stephens, D. (1994). *St. Petersburg Community Survey Results*. St. Petersburg Police Department.

Weisburd, D., Mastrofski, S.D., Willis, J.J., & Greenspan, R. (2006). Changing so that everything can remain the same: Compstat and American policing. In D. Weisburd & A.A. Braga (Eds.), *Police innovation: Contrasting perspectives* (pp. 284–304). Cambridge University Press.

Weisburd, D., & Neyroud, P. (2011). *Police science: Toward a new paradigm*. New perspectives in policing. Harvard Executive Session on Policing and Public Safety. National Institute of Justice, US Department of Justice.

Wells, B. W. (2003, September). Bush's war on cops. *Washington Monthly* www.washingtonmonthly.com/features/2003/0309.wallace-wells.html.

Wilt, G. M., Bannon, J. D., Breedlove, R. K., Kennish, J. W., Sandker, D. M., & Sawtell, R. K. (1977). *Domestic violence and the police: Studies in Detroit and Kansas City*. Police Foundation.

16

Support for Evidence-Based Policing at the National Level

More Help Than Harm?

James H. Burch, II

In this chapter, we will focus on how evidence-based policing has been supported from the national level in the United States, from the author's perspective having served in a senior leadership role in the federal government's agencies designed to improve local criminal justice responses through grants, training, and assistance and currently serving as the President of a national U.S.-based policing research organization and think tank. While there is much to reflect on at the agency level, in the world of research, and in places like the United Kingdom, Canada, and Australia with regard to the growth and evolution of evidence-based policing, this chapter will focus on U.S. national efforts, a system that this author is familiar with and currently provides leadership in. It is recognized that the U.S. system is different from most others (though other democratic nations have some similarities); however, it is thought that a discussion of the U.S. system offers a unique perspective into both the challenges and the advantages of implementing evidence-based policing that can be relevant outside of the United States. Our exploration of the national landscape is framed initially around the concept of "national forces" that Professor Lawrence Sherman has referred to in talking about the rise of evidence-based policing and comparing it to a similar movement within the medical profession (Sherman, 1998). We will review how national forces, such as the federal government and national and local organizations, have helped encourage this transformation (or not) along with some of the challenges and barriers to the adoption of evidence-based policing.

We will close this chapter by offering recommendations for how we can better address these challenges from the national perspective by supporting and encouraging bottom-up adoption and confronting other obstacles standing in the way. These recommendations may be useful in gaining support for top-down approaches used in places that have such a framework, such as the United Kingdom and other nations.

Professor Lawrence Sherman's (1998) *Ideas in American Policing* essay, "Evidence-Based Policing," gave rise to a new term and approach to police and justice decision-making, borrowing from the medical practice field, which had done the same, less than a decade earlier (Zimmerman, 2013). Sherman had followed the progression of scientific medicine or evidence-based medicine closely and in 1998 made the case for doing the same in policing. Sherman's essay defined and described the idea while also addressing how it might be "institutionalized," describing "certain national forces that can help start the ball rolling. This can be seen, for example, in national rankings of big-city police agencies, as well as national mandates for improving police data systems to provide getter evidence." Sherman acknowledged that "national forces" alone would not succeed in moving policing to an evidence-based mode, citing the need for internal "evidence cops" as well as "strong external pressure," taking note of the history of evidence-based medicine which "strongly suggests that professionals will only make such changes under external coercion."

Curious is the idea that despite how much we hear about medical studies and trials (particularly in the era of COVID-19), the medical field has not seen the miraculous adoption of evidence-based practice that one might assume. In fact, there is ample evidence to suggest that medicine has struggled with the adoption as well. Sherman pointed out this struggle in his essay and as recently as 2016, studies stated that although medical practitioners reported that they believe in the value of evidence-based practice, their own implementation of evidence-based practice is relatively low, concluding that "it is not enough to disseminate evidence-based guidelines and expect clinicians to readily implement them. For many clinicians, EBP requires behavior change from practice steeped in tradition and organizational culture of "this is the way we do it here" to practice that is supported by science" (Melnyk et al., 2016).

Sherman's mention of "national forces" is without clear explanation or assignment of responsibility for advancing the concept of evidence-based policing. Literature describing the evolution of evidence-based medicine seems to point to multiple such "forces" that may have been directly or indirectly responsible for the growth in awareness of the topic in that field, including precipitating factors, such as the evolution of medical education in the United States and Canada, the evolution of epidemiology as a practice (which shares fundamental concepts around quantification, surveillance and control with evidence-based medicine), and adoption of the term by the American College of Physicians, as well as a significant increase of the phrase "evidence-based medicine" since 2001 (Zimmerman, 2013). Others have pointed to education as the place to look for examples of how "national forces" can play an important role in a decentralized and independent profession, such as policing. Weisburd and Neyroud (2011) argue that "evidence-based science has grown exponentially in education. We see no reason why such growth would not be possible in policing. We would argue that if police chose to invest in the evidence-based science movement, they would enhance the value and reputation of the profession in the public sphere" (Weisburd & Neyroud, 2011).

16.1 "NATIONAL FORCES" IN THE ADVANCEMENT OF EVIDENCE-BASED POLICING

Which organizations with a national reach could lead this effort for policing? Although many Americans may prefer that the federal government have less involvement in our daily lives and in local decision-making, we must acknowledge its national reach and resources to both lead and support this transformation of policing.

The U.S. Department of Justice (DOJ) is the primary department within the Executive Branch of government that is responsible for reducing crime and providing more effective justice. While the DOJ's history of working to improve the justice system dates back to the 1960s, it wasn't until 1979 that the National Institute of Justice (NIJ) was established. In the 1990s when Sherman coined the phrase, "evidence-based policing," the NIJ was steeped in the "What works?" focus and the implementation of the 1994 Crime Bill, emphasizing the evaluation of new programs. Similar to its counterparts in the DOJ's Office of Justice Programs (OJP), and including the Bureau of Justice Assistance, the NIJ conducts its work by requesting and then administering grant funding from Congress to support system improvement, research, and evaluation in local communities across the United States.

Outside of government but receiving substantial funding support at the federal level, are a number of international and national associations and think tanks. Among the largest and oldest is the International Association of Chiefs of Police (IACP, 2020), which boasts "more than 31,000 members in over 165 countries" and "is a recognized leader within the profession." Since 1893, the association has been serving communities globally by speaking out on behalf of law enforcement and advancing leadership and professionalism in policing worldwide." While no other national organizations in this space can rival the IACP's membership and reach, there are other influential organizations that have overlapping missions and scopes, including the Police Executive Research Forum (PERF), the National Sheriffs' Association, the Major Cities Chiefs Association, and Major County Sheriffs of America. Smaller national organizations dedicated to advancing policing include the National Policing Institute*, a national independent policing research organization; the National Organization of Black Law Enforcement Executives (NOBLE); the American Society of Evidence-Based Policing (ASEBP); and others. Among these organizations, the IACP, PERF, National Policing Institute, and the ASEBP maintain a stated focus on their websites regarding policing research and the advancement of evidence-based policing.

To understand how challenging it can be to implement a consistent change at once in the United States even with the existence of such national groups, we need to examine its unique structure of the policing system in the U.S. The structure and powers of government in the U.S. emanates from the powers given by the U.S. Constitution as ratified by the states. The states have and continue to retain "local control" through legislatures of locally elected officials who make state laws. Although many observe the U.S. system to be led by the federal government and its legislative and executive branches, the U.S. system was designed to assert and retain state's rights and local control, including local control over matters, such as crime and policing. Local governments (counties and cities) not must only comply with state law but may also develop their own ordinances so long as such ordinances do not conflict with state laws. Federal laws and regulations can only preempt state laws when such authority is provided by the Constitution and the Bill of Rights, though this is often tested by a federal system that is eager to regulate and by issues that don't always cleanly fall within the federal government's granted authority. This is relevant because policing in the United States emanates primarily from state law and direction versus federal, because crime control and safety is deemed a responsibility of the states. States have granted authorities for local

---

* The National Policing Institute, formerly known as the "Police Foundation," was established in 1970.

law enforcement at the sublevels of counties, cities, and even special districts, such as universities, transit systems, and parks, and for special services, such as the service of warrants for arrest. As a result, state laws and local ordinances differ widely and there are more than 18,000 state and local law enforcement agencies that can enforce these laws. Federal laws are overlaid and enforced by dozens of federal law enforcement agencies and organizations as notorious as the Federal Bureau of Investigation and as little known as the Government Publishing Office's Police Department, which primarily provides security related to government printing of documents, including U.S. passports, etc. But other than creating confusion in our minds, how does this matter? It matters because it makes consistent implementation of policies, laws regulating criminal behavior, and even best practice extraordinarily difficult.

To accomplish change at the national level requires all states and the federal government (not to mention here Tribal Nations, which are autonomous) to agree on the change and for local leaders to cooperate in doing so because we refrain from creating laws and policies that place burden on lower levels of government without providing the funding or some other incentive to do so. Any state or locality that believes that a higher level of government has overstepped its authority and encroached on its authority may pursue the matter before a judge in an appropriate state or federal court of law. At the opposite end of this spectrum are monarchies and other forms of government where the national government may have authorities, rights, and abilities to make change seemingly with the stroke of a pen. While there may be many benefits to this form of government, it shall never be known to have aided in the implementation of evidence-based policing. Only by offering grants and other funding to local governments and agencies can the federal government have direct influence because general crime control (setting aside civil rights matters, terrorism, illegal commerce, etc.) is a state matter, not a federal matter. The federal government can expand its influence by using its powerful ability to project its voice across the nation and through other informal yet powerful means. Many in the United States often look admirably on the seemingly straightforward framework that exists in places like the United Kingdom and on the processes and mechanisms used for change, such as the United Kingdom's former National Policing Improvement Agency (NPIA), the Chief's Council, etc. Some working in places like the United Kingdom and other European and Nordic regions have been known to casually comment "we don't know how you get anything done" in the United States. Well, as they say, "it's complicated."

16.2 EXAMPLES OF "NATIONAL FORCES" WORKING TO ADVANCE EVIDENCE-BASED POLICING

After examining the national landscape, it is fair to ask whether sufficient progress has been made to advance evidence-based policing[1]. It is important to state that Sherman (2013) himself noted "Examples of the growth of evidence-based policing abound. There is certainly a correlation over time between the rise of evidence and a decline in serious crime, in both the United States and the United Kingdom" (p. 380).

One can appropriately argue that the work of these organizations supporting a greater reliance on science in policing began decades before Sherman published his 1998 essay. However, the focus on evidence-based policing as a new policing philosophy, approach, and professional culture (beyond many ambitious and notable "what works" initiatives) did not begin to enjoy sustained federal support until the mid-2000s, following a period of significant distraction and refocus on preventing and responding to terrorism during the early decade.

In 2009, as the nation struggled to come back from a major economic recession, a large injection of federal funding was headed to communities across the country as part of the American Reinvestment and Recovery Act (ARRA). According to the U.S. Department of Justice's Office of Public Affairs (2017), by July 2009, $1 billion in federal funding had been awarded to 1,046 law enforcement agencies to provide support for retaining and hiring officers and reducing and preventing crime. Headed by Laurie O. Robinson, then Principal Deputy Assistant Attorney General of the OJP, the ARRA grants established by the Department of Justice intentionally made evidence-based policing a major focus, following the Act's primary emphasis on jobs and economic recovery. I not only served as one of the primary architects of this vision, "designing-in" evidence to ensure that we didn't just create jobs and stimulate the economy, but also furthered the policing profession, and the way in public safety is delivered. As a result, evidence-based policing activities were re-energized and given a major boost by what would amount to more than a tripling of typical federal funding for law enforcement through the ARRA. Later, in 2011, Robinson (who was then the Senate-Confirmed Assistant Attorney General at the DOJ) established the first Science Advisory Board for DOJ's OJP Programs. Robinson's (Office of Justice Programs, 2011) remarks at the event made

---

[1] The topic of what policing itself has done to advance or engage in evidence-based policing is the subject of another chapter

it perfectly clear what the Department's new priorities were in regard to policing and justice:

I returned with a list of 10 goals for OJP from my work in the Obama transition. Two relate to science. First, I pledged to instill a focus on data-driven, evidence-based approaches to reducing crime.

Second, I wanted to restore the integrity of, and respect for, science. I was concerned that this was – perhaps – not, shall we say, at the top of the list in the prior eight years.

And as I began work in late January of 2009, I had four specific priorities relating to the science work:

- First, to strengthen NIJ and BJS and to ensure their independence.
- Second, to ensure we had strong scientists to head these two agencies.
- Third, to try to increase the funding for both.
- And fourth, to increase attention to science across OJP, including on the program side.

But it's certainly not enough to discuss issues like these in the isolation of OJP. We are blessed with an Attorney General in Eric Holder who cares about science. He actually talks about it a great deal and meets fairly regularly with researchers. One reflection of his interest is that he will be coming here to meet with you at 11:00 a.m.!

The Attorney General is committed to a budget that reflects support for science. OJP's science programs receive that support in the President's budget request for FY 2011. There's a three-percent set-aside for social science in the request. This is one of my top priorities, and the President, the Attorney General, the Office of Management and Budget, and the House and Senate have all backed it. We'll have to see how this turns out, but it would produce $55 million in social science investments.

During this period, many new initiatives aimed at advancing evidence-based policing were launched, including the Smart Policing Initiative (SPI), a grant program that sought "to build on offender-based and place-based policing by replicating evidence-based practices or to encourage exploration of new, unique solutions to public safety problems" (Medaris & Huntoon, 2009). Since its launch in 2009, the SPI program has supported the application and discovery of evidence-based policing in more than 65 law enforcement agencies and the results have been shared with hundreds more. As Acting Director of the Bureau of Justice Assistance (BJA) (a sister agency to the NIJ), I can recall talking with Dr. Cynthia Lum of George Mason University about the adoption of evidence-based policing as the professional policing norm. Dr. Lum's view at the time was that BJA could do more to encourage and incentivize this transition by supporting efforts to integrate evidence-based policing into all aspects of policing, from patrol to investigations to hiring and promotions. It was with this feedback in mind that the idea of offering grant funds to support researcher–practitioner partnerships to replicate evidence-based efforts and explore innovative adaptations.

Also, in 2009, the OJP launched the Evidence Integration Initiative (E2I). "The primary goal of E2I is to better integrate evidence into the programs, policy decisions and practices of the Department of Justice and the broader criminal justice community. Two integrated resources – CrimeSolutions.gov and the OJP Diagnostic Center – are the cornerstones of E2I" (Office of Justice Programs Diagnostic Center, n.d.). While CrimeSolutions.gov continues to operate, the OJP Diagnostic Center does not appear to exist today, based on a review of the OJP.gov website. CrimeSolutions.gov continues DOJ's tradition of focusing primarily on "what works" in policing and justice by creating a "centralized resource to inform practitioners and policymakers about what works in criminal justice, juvenile justice, and crime victim services. The site assigns 'evidence ratings' – effective, promising, or no effects – to indicate whether there is evidence from research that a program achieves its goals" (Department of Justice, 2011).

In 2014, the NIJ established an annual award of 10, three-year scholarships for research-minded law enforcement officers. NIJ's Law Enforcement Advancing Data and Science (LEADS) Scholars are pioneers of the evidence-based policing movement, and present and publish frequently about their research and findings on topics, such as the effectiveness of police technology, stress in the workforce, how to increase the success rate of women in police academies, and more. The program was designed to strengthen the use of research and evidence-based policing and to support the growth of a new generation of police leaders (National Institute of Justice, 2020). An examination of research grant data found that during this time, the National Institute of Justice stepped up the rigor of its work and produced an increase in scientific experiments in justice and policing (Telep et al., 2015).

Substantial support was provided for a variety of other initiatives aimed at advancing evidence-based policing and the strengthening of the role of science in policing and criminal justice. As explained in a paper submitted to the National Academy of Sciences,

> OJP has instituted a broad strategic approach for integrating evidence in its programmatic and policymaking activities. Its efforts have received support from both Attorney General Holder, who has used his position to call for evidence-based practices in criminal justice and has appointed a Science Advisory Board to guide science into OJP's programs, and President Barack Obama, who with

the approval of Congress has set aside two percent of OJP's budget for research, statistical, and evaluation activities. Under their leadership, evidence now occupies a central position in federal criminal justice planning. The vision of President Johnson's Crime Commission—of a justice system informed by knowledge—is coming into clearer focus. (Leary & Abt, 2014)

In December 2014, then President Obama announced an Executive Order creating the Task Force on twenty-first Century Policing (2014) designed to "examine, among other issues, how to strengthen public trust and foster strong relationships between local law enforcement and the communities that they protect, while also promoting effective crime reduction" (Office of the Press Secretary, 2014). In May of 2015, the Task Force released its report after many months of public hearings and testimony from community and law enforcement leaders, researchers, and national organizations' leadership. Evidence-based policing appears throughout the report and the testimony offered as the report was being developed. Following the Report's release, an assessment of the evidence related to the recommendations in the report was developed and published in order to produce an "Evidence-based Blueprint for 21st Century Policing" (Lum et al., 2016).

16.3 NON-FEDERAL RESOURCES AND ACTIONS ADVANCING EVIDENCE-BASED POLICING

The federal government was not alone in its pursuit of evidence-based policing during this period. According to the IACP (n.d.), dozens of publications were developed by the national associations and organizations explaining evidence-based policing. The IACP launched a Center for Police Research & Policy in cooperation with the University of Cincinnati and later launched the Police Research Advancement Section, noting that its mission is to "advance police-related research and evidence-based policies and practices by facilitating and supporting practitioner-researcher partnerships" (IACP, n.d.).

The National Policing Institute, a national and independent non-profit research organization created in 1970, also developed and disseminated multiple new resources and tools to promote evidence-based policing. Examples include a mobile application, "The Evidence-Based Policing App," developed jointly with the Center for Evidence-Based Crime Policy at George Mason University and the IACP, working with state police chief associations to create evidence-based policing resources, and providing initial funding and other support to create and launch the American Society of

Evidence-Based Policing. The National Policing Institute has at times been selected to serve as the "research partner" for other policing organizations, such as the Commission on Accreditation for Law Enforcement Agencies (CALEA), the Major Cities Chiefs, the Major County Sheriffs of America, and the California Chiefs of Police Association.

The ASEBP was launched in 2015 largely by a group of police practitioners who are also academics and researchers. ASEBP membership is open to officers, professional organizations, research institutions, community groups, and any other organization working in or having an interest in making a positive impact in the criminal justice field through using the best available research evidence. The ASEBP consists of a strong professional network across the United States and through its connections to affiliated groups in Canada, the United Kingdom, Australia, and beyond, through its online blog, social media and translational briefs, and national conference. The organization has made a positive impact in the adoption of evidence-based policing in a very short time.

Other national organizations, such as the PERF (which has long had a research interest and focus), the Major Cities Chiefs Association, and others, have not opposed evidence-based policing and in many ways are supportive of the transition but advancing evidence-based policing itself and the adoption of it has not been an explicit focus based on a review of organizational web pages.

Other organizations have also taken major steps to advance the state of evidence-based policing and its use. George Mason University launched the Center for Evidence-Based Crime Policy (CEBCP) in 2008. The CEBCP team has grown from two professors and two students in 2008 to an organization of more than 50 team members, senior fellows, faculty affiliates, research assistants, and interns. While the primary goals are to generate new knowledge and translate it to the field, the CEBCP has been a major force in advancing evidence-based policing through its Evidence-Based Policing Matrix, its annual Evidence-Based Policing Symposium which attracts hundreds of practitioners and researchers annually, its Congressional briefings, and millions of visitors to its website, social media channels, and mailing list recipients (Center for Evidence-Based Crime Policy, 2020). The leaders and staff of the Center not only support their own work and programming but also play a critical role in the work of the national organizations in terms of their efforts to support the growth of evidence-based policing. The Center's Evidence-Based Policing Matrix is perhaps one of the most innovative and widely used tools to identify evidence-based policing strategies and approaches as has provided inspiration to many other organizations engaged in evidence-based policing advancement. The Evidence-Based Policing Matrix is a research-to-practice translation tool that organizes evaluations of police strategies and tactics in a visual way.

The Matrix categorizes and visualizes evaluated police tactics according to three common dimensions of crime prevention—the nature of the target, the extent to which the strategy is proactive or reactive, and the specificity or generality of the strategy. This visualization reveals clusters of studies within intersecting dimensions, or "realms of effectiveness". These realms provide insights into the nature and commonalities of effective (or ineffective) police strategies and can be used by police agencies to develop tactics and strategies or assess their tactical portfolio against the evidence. (Center for Evidence-Based Crime Policy, n.d.)

Lastly, multiple state agencies and organizations have taken up the charge to advance the use of evidence-based policing in the United States. The New York State Division of Criminal Justice Services (DCJS), which administers federal funding and provides training and technical assistance to police organizations in New York State made evidence-based policing a top priority. Its Director, Michael C. Green, was awarded the Distinguished Achievement Award by the Center for Evidence-Based Crime Policy in recognition of his prioritization of evidence-based policing. In his acceptance remarks, the Director confirmed his focus, which permeates all of the Division's work:

Seven years ago, I accepted the position working for Governor Cuomo as the head of the New York State Division of Criminal Justice Services. This appointment provided a tremendous opportunity to encourage the use of evidence-based practices across the criminal justice system in New York. At DCJS, we believe we have an obligation to only implement and support work that has been proven to be, or is highly likely to be, impactful based on evidence. The stakes are too high not to. For some, it is a matter of life and death. For families and communities, it is a matter of despair or hope. We can and do make a difference! (Green, n.d.)

Other very notable efforts include a resource in Oregon known as the "Knowledge Bank." Oregon's 2014 Justice Reinvestment Act (HB 3194) strongly promotes the use of evidence-based practices and cost-effective programs. The statute charges the newly created Center for Policing Excellence (or CPE, an initiative of the Oregon Department of Public Safety Standards and Training) with fostering interaction between law enforcement researchers and practitioners. The law also holds the Oregon Criminal Justice Commission (CJC) responsible for tasks related to sharing information and encouraging the use of best practices throughout the state's criminal justice system. In 2015, the CPE and CJC collaborated to design and develop the Oregon Knowledge Bank as a resource to fulfill these mandates. The site provides users the ability to submit, share, and search for public safety programs from around Oregon, summaries of topics and research articles relevant to the needs of Oregon agencies and the communities they serve, and profiles of Oregon public safety agencies (Oregon Knowledge Bank, n.d.).

One of the largest state chiefs of police associations, the California Police Chiefs Association (n.d.), with early collaborative support from the National Policing Institute, established an internal resource for members on evidence-based policing, including a web page and downloadable resource guide explaining key research terms and providing resources for additional information. The growing number of prominent and influential organizations and agencies that have national presence is encouraging and promising for the advancement of evidence-based policing.

16.4 OPPOSING FORCES AND BARRIERS TO THE ADVANCEMENT OF EVIDENCE-BASED POLICING

Considering the growth in national support for evidence-based policing, particularly in the last decade, it is somewhat remarkable that it has not become more widely adopted and adhered to. It is surprisingly easy to find examples of agencies adopting, implementing, expanding, and even celebrating the use of strategies and programs that have been found to be ineffective – examples of agencies and city leaders demanding interventions shown to have no effect or even high likelihood of backfired effects – and if you look at federal grant program applications from any recent year, you can find dozens of proposals strongly advocating for funding to implement interventions that have little to no research support and zero intention of evaluating their efforts. The grant selection process used for some federal grant programs may also undermine greater advancement of evidence-based policing by favoring fairness in distribution of funds across regions, community types, and concerns, and often by rewarding well-written proposals as opposed to the quality of the content or idea. This problematic outcome is sometimes supported or even preferred due to several factors in my experience, including the following:

- The view of many that all taxpayer-funded programs provide entitlements vs. competitive opportunities, and therefore, the application should not be judged competitively and the decision should be based on need alone.

- Concerns from Congressional committee staff and offices that following a strict "evidence-based only" funding model will eliminate or make it very hard for some constituent organizations to be selected, particularly those in rural areas and the less organizationally or administratively sophisticated.
- Concerns that small, well-meaning but unsophisticated organizations in high-need areas but focused on providing services vs. reducing or preventing crime would not receive support may not be able to continue operations and are important for achieving diversification in the allocation of funding within a geographic area.

I can recall many conversations with well-intended yet under-informed Congressional staff who questioned the "heavy" focus on evidence-based policing as too limiting or even irrelevant to communities that they felt were entirely unique and would be disadvantaged by having to submit evidence-based concepts, which the staff often viewed as requiring the strict replication of an already proven program. By allowing these non-evidence-based proposals to be funded through a program labeled as supporting evidence-based policing, we create more harm than good because funding such proposals suggests that evidence base has no real meaning or that it can be defined in any way one chooses. We would be better off funding proposals that acknowledge what they are proposing is not evidence based or simply not funding these proposals at all. Of course, another significant problem is the prevalent and persistent view that evidence-based approaches are limited to specific programs that must be replicated without adaptation.

What could explain the disconnect between the reality described here and our goal of becoming a science-informed profession? One explanation is that we (collectively) prefer to talk about evidence-based practices but prefer not to implement them. In other words, we are all talk. An article in IACP's Police Chief Magazine suggested:

Adoption of EBP has been slow due to many factors. First, EBP research is often written for academics by academics, using theoretical and statistical language that alienates police executives and patrol officers alike. In addition, research evidence is most commonly accessed through research journal paywalls, making it prohibitively expensive. Also, research agendas are usually designed without input from police chiefs, producing research evidence that is of interest to the academic audience but that may not be actionable in the field. (IACP, n.d)

Others have complained that evidence-based policing is about research or that it is a program, or a set of programs and the fact remains that there is still wide interest in failed programs and that there is no accountability for not using evidence or even considering it. Imagine if doctors and nurses responded this way towards medical evidence. Or your next airline's pilots deciding that the language used to describe how weather systems impact flight is alienating because its "statistical," or the NASA flight engineers discarding planetary science or trajectory analysis because it didn't have enough input from them. Sound ludicrous? That's because it is.

Could there be political motivations that interfere with the promotion and adoption of evidence-based policing and science generally? In examining documents submitted by the DOJ to the White House as part of its annual budget development process, we can see changes in terminology over the years. An analysis of budget planning and performance documents available on the U.S. Department of Justice's website (Department of Justice, n.d.), which are prepared by the Department as many as 12–18 months prior to the year in which the proposed budget is enacted, shows an interesting trend in how often the phrase "evidence-based" is used. In fiscal years (FY) 2014–2016, "evidence-based" is mentioned between 14 and 17 times in each plan, in the context of the overall budget strategy, program descriptions, and performance reports. Later, in FY2017, the first year that the Trump Administration was able to influence the plan, the words "evidence-based" appear only four times, followed by no mentions at all in the FY2018 or FY2019 plan, and only two mentions in FY2020 and FY2021 plans. In addition, the OJP Science Advisory Board was disbanded and initiatives such as E2I and Diagnostic Center were defunded or deprioritized (Butts, 2018). By the end of the Trump Administration in January 2021, the world would come to remember the Administration as many things, none of which involved embracing science and science-informed policy. In fact, the Administration seemed determine to thwart and politicize science when it wasn't convenient or aligned with the Administration's (or the President's) own desires. Reflecting back on some of the proposals mentioned during the Trump Administration, it was the same complex, decentralized framework of government in the United States that likely prevented autocratic, unproductive, and harmful approaches from becoming the law of the land.

Some consider the phrase "evidence-based policing" itself to be rhetoric and others have thought that it is used selectively, taking advantage of less than a clear definition to argue against programs or in support of others based on preferences. Others (typically in the political realm) believe that the phrase represents the substitution of academic (liberal) thinking for (more conservative) practitioner instinct and experience. Indeed, even today as many organizations call for police reform, they advocate for the implementation of strategies and programs that meet their advocacy agendas that they claim are evidence based but in actuality have little research to support them overall or in the manner they are being advocated (Engel et al., 2020). As recently as February 2019, the Chester County (SC) Sheriffs' Office continues to rely on a program modeled after Scared Straight, a "Dark Ages" throwback approach that now serves as the poster child for ineffective justice programs, even getting its own show on the A&E Network for being such a noteworthy failure (Alexander and Kimball, 2019).

Very likely, we (the collective "we") and our organizations – whether police, government generally, academia, or national or local organizations – have probably allowed evidence-based policing as a topic or phrase to be used to support favored programs, abandon others, point fingers, and to be critical for the general purpose of demonstrating wisdom or self-importance.

16.5 WHAT MORE CAN WE DO TO ADVANCE EVIDENCE-BASED POLICING?

Our challenges are big and small. They include a lot of misunderstanding, unwillingness to be guided, a decentralized and very diverse profession, political concerns, and lack of a real commitment to make science and evidence a core aspect of professional policing. In some places, such as the United Kingdom and in other national system frameworks, such as Israel, a top-down response can have a substantial impact on policing not just in those countries but worldwide. Take the example of the National Policing Improvement Agency (NPIA), which Telep and Weisburd (2014) found that the NPIA, through its support for systematic reviews, has had a major impact on our ability to embrace science in policing (Telep & Weisburd, 2014). But in the United States, until we can rely more consistently on top-down and bottom-up response, we will need to focus on bottom-up solutions as the primary driver in overcoming these barriers.

To truly be bottom up, it is vital that we translate what evidence-based policing means to everyday policing decisions. As pointed out previously, there is vast misunderstanding of what evidence-based policing means and how it is applied. One way to overcome this is to establish a set of principles that can be applied to everyday policing in ways that allow evidence-based policing to be implemented. I see this as a "doctrine" of sorts. "Doctrine" is sometimes associated with various religions of the world but in this case the word refers to what the Cambridge Business English Dictionary defines as "a principle or set of principles that are followed by a particular group or in a particular situation" (n.d.). More closely aligned but still apart is doctrine related to politics and policy, particularly foreign policy where we have examples such as the Monroe Doctrine, the Carter Doctrine, and the Bush Doctrine. In military, doctrine is used to set or establish procedures to be used in certain types of operations and war.

The Professional Policing Doctrine, if articulated well and widely adopted, could establish the principles for democratic policing while integrating evidence-based policing principles. Such doctrine should be anchored by a Hippocratic Oath, such as the one proposed by a Connecticut Police Sergeant who is also a police scholar, who argues that the Oath should resemble medicine's Hippocratic Oath. Johnson (2020) argues:

I see a need to incorporate four key themes noticeably absent from the Code of Ethics: evidence-based policing, crime prevention, the sanctity of life, and professional identity. In the years since the Code of Ethics' inception, a vast body of scientific evidence has emerged regarding what works in policing and, perhaps more important, what does not. This is not an abstract intellectual issue as our effectiveness has direct implications on the very lives of those we serve. Ignoring this evidence base in favor of tradition or personal opinion is more than irresponsible; unscientific policing is unethical policing.[2]

The Hippocratic Oath can influence The Professional Policing Doctrine by anchoring us in values and ethics, while the core elements of the Doctrine guide us in "how to think" (as opposed to what to think). As explained in an article published by the Modern War Institute at West Point, doctrine provides fundamental principles that have been learned and tested through experience and that are meant to offer an authoritative starting point in addressing new problems. The principles are meant to foster creativity and problem solving, and to form a common language across groups (Spencer, 2016). While military doctrine is perhaps too detailed or prescriptive to suit the local and agency-specific contexts and preferences that exist in American policing, as well as the myriad of problems faced, other doctrines may be less focused on specific tactics.

---

[2] www.police1.com/chiefs-sheriffs/articles/why-it-is-time-for-a-hippocratic-oath-for-policing-syoFeXGcpvhST8hu/

An example of the kind of doctrine contemplated here might be the SARA (Scanning, Analysis, Response, and Assessment) Model of problem solving. While the SARA Model has been applied to a wide variety of problems and issues faced by patrol and managers alike (and demonstrates that such doctrine can be learned and applied in policing), it may be wholly insufficient to be "the" Professional Policing Doctrine. While defining Professional Policing Doctrine is not the goal of this chapter, we could expect that a well-defined Professional Policing Doctrine for executives and other decision-makers may include the following types of principles:

- Community inclusion – viewing the community as a partner.
- Prevent harm above all else.
- Honor the sanctity of life.
- Leverage technology responsibly for the pursuit of safety.
- Commit to lifelong learning.
- Encourage and embrace the co-production of public safety.
- Actively respect and defend civil rights and liberties.
- Ensure transparency and open processes.
- Promote and ensure accountability for all.
- Use the best available research to identify the strategies and tactics that may solve or prevent a problem.
- Assess, research, and apply resources on known and predictable concentrations of harm from crime and disorder.
- Continuously test and assess policing strategies and tactics to determine what works best.
- Refine strategies and tactics and continuously monitor for efficacy and acceptance.

For those at the patrol level, carrying out the decisions of police managers and responding to problems in the community, the Professional Policing Doctrine (for patrol response) may include the following types of principles:

- Seek to understand and respect the communities' views and needs.
- Perform actions that support the prevention of future harms.
- Protect the sanctity of all life.
- Use technology and tools at disposal to find solutions to problems.
- Engage in analysis and research to understand problems and the best available evidence regarding the prevention of similar problems.
- Involve the community in prevention and problem solving.
- Actively respect and defending civil rights and liberties.
- Explain actions taken to promote procedural fairness and justice.

- Remain accountable for decisions and actions.
- Address problems by focusing on known harms (different from laws/violations).
- Monitor what works (and what does not) when addressing community problems.
- Change approaches when data and information suggest that a problem isn't being addressed effectively.

The above principles are drawn from various versions of traditional and modern Hippocratic Oaths ("Hippocratic Oath 2.0", 2018), seminal literature such as President's Task Force on twenty-first Century Policing, and Sherman's (2013) notions of the Cambridge Assignment Management system and the "Triple T strategy of policing: targeting, testing, and tracking." It is conceivable that there could be Professional Policing Doctrine established for each primary function within policing, to ensure that evidence-based policing is engrained and supported in functions, such as human resources, training, internal affairs, criminal investigations, crime analysis, and public affairs. The key is to translate what it means to be evidence based at nearly every decision point and to then teach that as "the way we do business." This then addresses much of the ambiguity in telling officers and managers to "use science" or replicate what works.

Should a Professional Policing Doctrine be defined and adopted, the further professionalization of policing and adoption of evidence-based policing can be more certain.

Whether a Professional Policing Doctrine is established or not, there is more we can collectively do to encourage a more evidence-based profession. Many of these ideas are more likely to be top down and "across" (peer accountability) strategies, including the following:

- Doing more to reach elected officials and political stakeholders who often encourage or direct policing responses or are in a position to influence them. Educating them about the role that science can and should play in a policing profession may create a more conducive environment for such.
- Advocating for an "overhaul" of basic and in-service training to emphasize the role that science should play and teaching Professional Policing Doctrine.
- Encourage and support practitioner, policymaker, and community involvement in the development of research agendas to gain greater buy-in and support for research.

Support for Evidence-Based Policing at the National Level 333

- Hold each other accountable for misuses and counter-effective approaches that jeopardize evidence-based policing by being anything but evidence based.
- Leverage the "diffusion of innovation" to encourage evidence-based practice and the growth of police science by pointing to and celebrating those leaders, agencies, communities, and officers who are relying on evidence-based policing to protect their communities.

In this chapter, I have focused on the national picture and environment for advancing evidence-based policing. Using Sherman's notion of "national forces," I have reviewed what such forces may look like in the United States, including federal and non-federal government entities. We have also talked through the barriers to evidence-based policing from a national perspective, including misunderstanding of the concept, a lack of clarity around how it should be applied, political differences and influences, and grappling with a highly decentralized and diverse professional landscape, at least here in the United States as compared to the United Kingdom and similar "unified" governments. Making recommendations to address these challenges, I have exposed the idea of a Professional Policing Doctrine as a way of integrating the concepts of evidence-based policing (relying substantially on the medical model's Hippocratic Oath and Sherman's "Triple T" concepts to break down what evidence-based police decision-making may look like). Last, we have also highlighted some top down and "across" approaches that I hope can slow or stop the divergence of everyday policing from professional, evidence-based policing.

Whatever paths we choose to take, we must acknowledge that it will require courage, perseverance, and a willingness to comfortably say, "We don't know, but we are willing to try and learn." Clearly, there have been many positive developments at the national level as it relates to evidence-based policing, both inside and outside of government, and we know that change will take time. We can also be encouraged that new generations may embrace science more that past generations and as these generations come into positions of greater power and influence, they may well be more capable of forcing the changes that current and past generations have seemingly struggled with. At the same, our evidence base continues to expand rapidly, particularly with the new investments in reform since the murder of George Floyd. Therefore, we must remain steadfast, and we must remain hopeful.

References

Alexander, A. & Kimball, T. (2019, February 27). Sheriff says 'Scared Straight' program helps troubled kids. Experts say it's child abuse. *WBTV*. Retrieved August 05, 2020, from www.wbtv.com/2019/02/26/sheriff-says-scared-straight-program-helps-troubled-kids-experts-say-its-child-abuse-2/

Butts, J. (2018, December 5). No More Science Advisory Board at OJP. https://jeffreybutts.net/2018/12/05/sabending/

California Police Chiefs Association (n.d.). Evidence based policing. Retrieved July 29, 2020, from www.ojp.gov/ncjrs/virtual-library/abstracts/consuming-and-applying-research-evidence-based-policing

Center for Evidence-Based Crime Policy. (n.d.). *Evidence-Based Policing Matrix*. Retrieved July 29, 2020, from https://cebcp.org/evidence-based-policing/the-matrix/

Center for Evidence-Based Crime Policy. (2020). *2020 Annual Report and State of the Center* (Rep.).

Department of Justice. (n.d.). Budget and performance. Retrieved August 01, 2020, from www.justice.gov/doj/budget-and-performance

Department of Justice. (2011, June 22). Department of Justice launches Crimesolutions.Gov website. www.justice.gov/opa/pr/department-justice-launches-crimesolutionsgov-website

Doctrine: Definition in the Cambridge English Dictionary. (n.d.). Retrieved July 29, 2020, from https://dictionary.cambridge.org/us/dictionary/english/doctrine

Engel, R. S., Mcmanus, H. D., & Isaza, G. T. (2020). Moving beyond "Best Practice": Experiences in police reform and a call for evidence to reduce officer-involved shootings. *The ANNALS of the American Academy of Political and Social Science, 687*(1), 146–165. https://doi:10.1177/0002716219889328

Green, M. C. (n.d.). Retrieved July 28, 2020, from https://cebcp.org/distinguished-achievement-award/michael-green/

Hippocratic Oath 2.0 – Principles of the New Hippocratic Oath. (2018, July 18). Retrieved July 31, 2020, from https://medicalfuturist.com/why-an-upgraded-hippocratic-oath-is-needed-in-the-digital-era/

IACP. (2020, July 26). About IACP. www.theiacp.org/about-iacp

International Association of Chiefs of Police (n.d.). The brief: Expanding evidence-based policing. *Police Chief*. www.policechiefmagazine.org/the-brief-expanding-evidence-based-policing/?ref=87f11e5be35ead762fa32ac8a22136d5

Johnson, J. P. (2020, April 08). A hippocratic oath for policing. Retrieved July 30, 2020, from www.police1.com/chiefs-sheriffs/articles/why-it-is-time-for-a-hippocratic-oath-for-policing-syoFeXGcpvhST8hu/

Leary, M., & Abt, T. (2014). The federal role in promoting evidence- Based violence prevention practices. In National Research Council. *The Evidence for Violence Prevention Across the Lifespan and Around the World: Workshop Summary* (pp. 61–67). National Academy of Sciences.

Lum, C. M., Koper, C. S., Gill, C., Hibdon, J., Telep, C., & Robinson, L. (2016). *An Evidence-assessment of the Recommendations of the President's Task Force on 21st Century Policing: Implementation and Research Priorities*. International Association of Chiefs of Police.

Medaris M., & Huntoon, A. (2009). *Smart policing initiative.* Bureau of Justice Assistance. www.ojp.gov/sites/g/files/xyckuh241/files/media/document/smart_policing_fact_sheet.pdf

Melnyk, B. M., Gallagher-Ford, L., Thomas, B. K., Troseth, M., Wyngarden, K., & Szalacha, L. (2016). A study of chief nurse executives indicates low prioritization of evidence-based practice and shortcomings in hospital performance metrics across the United States. *Worldviews on Evidence-Based Nursing, 13*(1), 6–14. https://doi.org/10.1111/wvn.12133

National Institute of Justice (NIJ). (March 04, 2020). *NIJ's Law Enforcement Advancing Data and Science Scholars Program for Law Enforcement Officers.* Retrieved August 01, 2020, from https://nij.ojp.gov/funding/nij-and-iacps-law-enforcement-advancing-data-and-science-leads-scholarships-law-enforcement

Office of Justice Programs Diagnostic Center. (n.d.). Evidence-Based Solutions ... What Really Works in the Fight Against Crime. Retrieved August 01, 2020, from www.leg.state.nv.us/App/InterimCommittee/REL/Document/3995

Office of Justice Programs. (2011, January 28). Remarks of Laurie Robinson, Assistant Attorney General Office of Justice Programs, Science Advisory Board Inaugural Meeting. www.ojp.gov/sites/g/files/xyckuh241/files/archives/speeches/2011/11_0128lrobinson.htm

Office of Public Affairs, U.S. Department of Justice. (2017, April 07). The Recovery Act: Results In Action. Retrieved July 26, 2020, from www.justice.gov/archives/opa/blog/recovery-act-results-action

Office of the Press Secretary (2014, December 18). *Fact Sheet: Task Force on 21st Century Policing.* https://obamawhitehouse.archives.gov/the-press-office/2014/12/18/fact-sheet-task-force-21st-century-policing

Oregon Knowledge Bank – A Local Public Safety Resource. (n.d.). www.oregonkb.com/about/

Sherman, L. W. (1998). *Evidence-based policing.* Police Foundation. www.policefoundation.org/wp-content/uploads/2015/06/Sherman-1998-Evidence-Based-Policing.pdf

Sherman, L. W. (2013). The rise of evidence-based policing: Targeting, testing, and tracking. *Crime and Justice, 42*(1), 377–451. https://doi:10.1086/670819

Spencer, J. (2016, March 21). What is Army Doctrine? [Web blog post]. https://mwi.usma.edu/what-is-army-doctrine/

Telep, C. W., Garner, J. H. & Visher, C. A. (2015). The production of criminological experiments revisited: The nature and extent of federal support for experimental designs, 2001–2013. *Journal of Experimental Criminology, 11*, 541–563. https://doi.org/10.1007/s11292-015-9239-6

Telep, C. W., & Weisburd, D. (2014). Generating knowledge: a case study of the National Policing Improvement Agency program on systematic reviews in policing. *Journal of Experimental Criminology, 10*(4), 371–398. https://doi.org/10.1007/s11292-014-9206-7

Weisburd, D., & Neyroud, P. (2011). Police science: Toward a new paradigm. *New Perspectives in Policing, National Institute of Justice, January,* 1–23.

Zimmerman, A. L. (2013). Evidence-based medicine: A short history of a modern medical movement. *AMA Journal of Ethics, 15*(1), 71–76. https://doi.org/10.1001/virtualmentor.2013.15.1.mhst1-1301

17

Conclusions

Police Science and the Future of Evidence-Based Policing

David Weisburd, Tal Jonathan-Zamir, Gali Perry, and Badi Hasisi

In the advancement of Evidence-Based Policing (EBP), scholars have largely focused on police practitioners (e.g., Lum, 2009; Lum & Koper, 2017; Sherman, 1998). They have asked, for example, how we can get the police to respect science, to take "ownership" of science, to recognize that their work would be better if they would use scientific evidence to make decisions, and to change their work routines accordingly. This is not surprising, as the resistance of practitioners and policy makers to evidence-based practice has been a key underlying problem for advancing evidence-based policy more generally. John Maynard Keynes, the noted economist, argued almost a century ago that "… there is nothing a government hates more than to be well-informed; for it makes the process of arriving at decisions much more complicated and difficult" (cited in Skidelsky, 1992, p. 630).

Our argument in the present chapter does not challenge this approach. Indeed, we view understanding how to diffuse and implement evidence-based practice as a key problem for advancing EBP, and this point is made throughout the chapters in this volume. But we think that in emphasizing how to influence practice, proponents of EBP have often ignored what *scientists* must do to advance EBP. For EBP to become a dominant paradigm, it is not simply the practitioners who will have to change; scientists and the production of evidence will also have to move in new directions. One way to think about our argument is to imagine a world in which police were ready to have scientific evidence determine the practices and programs that they implement. In this world, police leaders use science for example to reform management practices, crime prevention approaches, and police control systems. In this utopian vision, the police are fully open to EBP and seek to implement it across the broad array of police tasks and problems. But what kind of policing would this create given the present state of the science of policing? Is the science of policing ready for this world?

One of the key problems in policing that would seem naturally amenable to scientific investigation is police training. But in fact, there is little scientific evidence to aid practitioners in how to carry out training, or what types of training are most effective. The National Research Council concluded in 2004 that "for many decades it has been assumed that more and better police training leads to improved police performance," but that "few studies evaluate the impact of training programs on actual performance on the job" (Skogan & Frydl, 2004, p. 141). More than a decade later, Skogan and colleagues (2015) reached a very similar conclusion, arguing that "(w)e know virtually nothing about the short- or long-term effects associated with police training of any type" (p. 320). Similarly, in reviewing the evidence base for the President's Task Force on Twenty-First Century Policing recommendations on training, Lum and colleagues (2016, p. 38) concluded that "(a)dditional research is needed in every area of training discussed in the Task Force recommendations. In most cases, we know little about the impact of these training programs on officer knowledge, attitudes, and behavior." Our point is that even if the police were fully open to EBP in the area of training, scientists would have little to tell them.

Even in the area of police effectiveness, where there have perhaps been the most intensive efforts by scientists to advance EBP, police practitioners are often left in the dark regarding which strategies to employ and how to employ them. Perhaps the most robust scientific evidence base for a proactive policing approach is provided by evaluations of hot spots policing. Two National Academies of Sciences committees have concluded that hot spots policing is effective (Skogan & Frydel, 2004; Weisburd & Majmundar, 2018). Braga et al.'s (2019) most recent Campbell Collaboration systematic review of hot spots policing identified 65 quasi-experimental and experimental evaluations, with 62 of 78 tests of hot spots policing interventions showing crime prevention impacts. And there is evidence that the majority of large police agencies have implemented hot spots policing in some form (Weisburd & Majmundar, 2018). But as Weisburd and Telep (2014) note, the evidence base is still lacking in providing practitioners with essential knowledge for implementing this approach successfully. There is a vast array of hot spots strategies that have not been rigorously tested. Most importantly, we know little about which hot spots policing strategies are most effective in what contexts. Clearly, the effectiveness of strategies will depend on the specific types of crimes and places that are the focus of police attention. But we still do not have enough studies to provide detailed answers to these types of questions. Such detail is critical if EBP is to be fully implemented in the real world of policing. We cannot expect practitioners to implement EBP if the evidence base is not sufficient to provide the guidance that is required for real-world interventions.

As our comments suggest, advancement of the science of EBP needs to be a key focus in the future of EBP. Were our utopian policing world to come now, we would be poorly prepared to provide the science that is necessary. Indeed, without key advances in EBP science, it would likely lead to a dystopian world rather and a utopian one, where EBP was quickly abandoned. In this concluding chapter, we argue that policing scholars should strive to develop a better science of policing, one that would be "worthy" of broad implementation by police practitioners. Based on the contributions in our volume, we identify six key areas where this improvement is required:

1) Developing "second generation" studies of strategies and programs.
2) Expanding the quality and breadth of scientific methods in EBP.
3) Developing comparative research for advancing EBP.
4) Recognizing the importance of a science of street level behavior.
5) Expanding knowledge surrounding implementation science.
6) Adding normative questions to the science of EBP.

While these topics are not exhaustive, we think that the chapters in our volume have collectively suggested new directions and new ways of conceptualizing EBP. Below we detail these, but first, in the following section we place our emphasis on science in policing in a more general context. We are not the first to grapple with the development of a science for practice, and as a more general framework for our discussion, we take advantage of a useful debate that took place about 10 years ago in the field of social work (see review by Jindra, 2018). Social work scholars from both the United States (e.g., Brekke, 2012) and European, German-speaking countries (e.g., Sommerfeld, 2014) discussed whether social work should define itself as an independent scientific discipline, and what would be required from social work in order to qualify as one. Their discussions are informative for advancing our debate on the future of science in policing.

17.1 WHAT ARE THE KEY INGREDIENTS OF A SCIENCE OF PRACTICE?

Brekke (2012, p. 456) defines "science" as "a combination of theory and systematic empirical method, rooted in ontological and epistemological context, and applied to a defined set of phenomena." He argues that a "science" of a particular profession (such as social work or policing) requires three core ingredients: 1) An expression of the critical *domains of knowledge* relevant to the profession – the areas of the profession that scientists should be dedicated to investigating and understanding. This articulation both helps identify the questions researchers in the field should strive to answer and reflects the values and ethics of the profession. 2) A definition of the *core set of constructs*, or underlying assumptions, that frame the approach to the scientific study of these domains. For example, in relation to social work, Brekke (2012, p. 460) argues that they are "biopsychological, person in environment, and service systems for change." 3) An articulation of the *characteristics of the scientific approach* – what is valued by the profession in terms of research methods and theories. Again using the example of social work, Brekke (2012) argues that they include *complexity* in understanding the world, *synthesis* of various theories, and *pluralism* in research methods and approaches.

Taking a somewhat different approach, Sommerfeld (2014) focuses his discussion on "applied sciences," or, in the context of professions – what he calls "action sciences." As an example he contrasts medicine and sociology: as scientific disciplines, both do not operate on the practical level. At the same time, unlike sociology, medicine as an action science is interested in practical, real-world problems that occur in medical work practice. These problems are transformed into scientific questions, which, in turn, are investigated using scientific methods within the social system of "science." Sommerfeld argues that both science and practice benefit from this coupling: science plays an important role in turning a field of practice into a profession. The profession, in turn, provides science with actual problems emerging from practice, which encourage innovation and development. Moreover, these problems define a unique field of scientific inquiry.

In turn, relying on work in the area of the philosophy of science (Bunge, 1985; Patry & Perrez, 1982 as cited in Sommerfeld, 2014), Sommerfeld (2014) further explains that action sciences provide three types of scientific knowledge, while basic sciences only provide the first two: 1) *Knowledge of facts*, as developed from research; 2) *Nomological knowledge* – verified theories that explain the relationships between the facts; and 3)

Technological knowledge – verified theories relevant to the practical, real-world problems that characterize action sciences, such as what needs to be done in order to solve problem X in the real world. Put differently, "they are theories on the relations between ends and means. They are theories of rational target-oriented action ..." (p. 590). Importantly, Sommerfeld (2014) emphasizes that this type of knowledge needs to be considered in relation to values and professional codes of ethics – what does the science of the profession aim to do? Who does it seek to help? He argues, for example, that the overall goal of social work research and practice is to improve "the integration and participation of vulnerable individuals and groups and even whole populations," or, in other words, "contribute to the development of a 'good life'" (pp. 590–591).

As these comments suggest, the development of a police science in support of EBP is mirrored in other disciplines. We think it is important to explicitly recognize that our goal is the development of a science of policing. In that science we are interested in practical, real-world problems, and in the development and advancement of rigorous scientific methods. We need to recognize the complexities of the problems encountered, and the importance of pluralistic scientific methods to explore them and provide real-world solutions. And we begin with an assumption that the integration of police science and practice will enhance both. Finally, we think that EBP researchers should own the idea that advancing the science of EBP will improve policing, and through that benefit society more generally.

17.2 ADVANCING SCIENCE IN EVIDENCE-BASED POLICING

As noted above, the chapters of the present volume allowed us to identify six areas we think are important for the advancement of the science of policing. While scientists have addressed each of these to some degree, we think that on the whole they have not gained sufficient attention in EBP to date. Our point overall is that the future of EBP lies in advancing the science of policing, and to do that EBP will have to be much more concerned with these domains.

17.2.1 Developing "Second Generation" Studies of Police Practices and Strategies

We noted earlier how the scientific research in EBP has provided what might be termed "first generation studies" in the area of hot spots policing. In other words, these studies lead to the basic understanding that hot spots policing "works." We used this as an example because of the relatively large number of experimental and strong quasi-experimental evaluations in this area. At the same time, while these studies tell a positive story about crime prevention, they do not provide information that is the key to what can be called "second-" (Weisburd & Telep, 2014) or "next-generation" studies (Gottfredson et al., 2015) – studies that provide specific guidance on the types of programs that are effective, for whom, and in what circumstances.

In our volume this perspective is reinforced across a broad range of intervention areas in policing – whether in regard to the narrative review of the National Academies of Sciences, Engineering, and Medicine (NAS; see Chapter 6), Telep's and Weisburd's review of systematic reviews in policing (Chapter 5), or through the Global Policing Database (Chapter 8). Gill emphasizes this as well in her review of what is known about the impacts of community policing and related area studies (see Chapter 7). Existing studies provide a strong body of evidence that police can prevent crime and improve community outcomes, but they do not provide the kind of detailed information that would allow police to fit strategies to very specific populations and circumstances.

This suggests the key importance of "second generation" studies for advancing EBP – studies that go beyond the general principle and provide context-specific guidance. But moving in this direction would require a tremendous expansion in the number of primary studies in policing. This is not a new problem and has been raised numerous times by scholars (e.g., see Lipsey, 2003; Lösel & Schmucker, 2005). But the chapters in this volume emphasize the importance of creating this evidence base on "what works." While we have come very far in EBP, we have a great deal of work ahead of us.

It is likely that such work will not be carried out without a tremendous infusion of research funds into EBP. We think that scientists and police executives need to work to convince policy makers of the key importance of making this investment if we are to truly create a science that can support practical and wide spread application of EBP in police agencies. Of course, scientists themselves will have to value such an evidence base. One barrier to advancing the science of EBP is that academia does not view many practical policing problems as warranting scientific attention in universities. In turn, the study of such problems may not facilitate academic advancement or publication in high impact scientific journals (Weisburd & Neyroud, 2011). At the same time, it is important to note the emergence of scientific journals in policing like *Policing: A Journal* of *Policy and Practice* published by Oxford University Press, and the *Cambridge Journal of Evidence-Based Policing* published by Springer, which encourage the expansion of scientific work into the everyday world of policing.

Given the importance of crime prevention and rehabilitation in society, an argument in favor of expanding the evidence base on "what works" in policing should be possible to make successfully. Like evidence-based medicine, EBP can have very significant impact on the safety and security of modern societies. At this juncture, we have a paucity of primary studies. Telep and Weisburd (Chapter 5) identified 708 independent studies in their reviews of systematic reviews. One could argue here that this is positive news, especially when just a few decades ago there were few rigorous studies in policing. But even here, one has to ask whether 708 studies could possibly cover even a fraction of the entire range of policing practices. Therefore, we are left with a positive assessment of what EBP has achieved. But a successful future in EBP will require that we advocate for a major increase in evaluations conducted across the field.

17.2.2 Expanding the Quality and Breadth of Scientific Methods in Evidence-Based Policing

A science of policing requires a robust body of knowledge, built through a careful, thorough process of testing hypotheses and reaching empirical findings. As suggested by Sherman in 1998, and again in his paper "The Rise of Evidence-Based Policing: Targeting, Testing, and Tracking" (2013), this scientific approach was primarily designed to address the "what works" question that is considered to be at the heart of EBP. While an evidence-based agenda does not necessarily dictate specific research methods, it has dictated the criteria by which these methods are evaluated: the strength of evidence (Ariel, 2018; Sherman, 2013). In other words, the relevance and potential contribution of specific research methods to EBP has traditionally been measured according to their accuracy in prediction – their ability to produce a reliable forecast of future events (Sherman, 2013).

This focus on "what works," alongside the emphasis on the strength of evidence, has made particular methods, and specifically Randomized Control Trials (RCTs), the approach most closely associated with EBP (Ariel, 2018; Braga et al., 2014). Indeed, for many, EBP and randomized trials are synonymous, and this coupling, which seems to exclude a broad array of other research methods common in the social sciences, is often at the core of criticism of EBP (e.g., Greene, 2014; Laycock, 2012; Sparrow, 2016). We agree that there is no substitute for randomized trials in drawing causal conclusions about what works (Farrington & Welsh, 2006; Weisburd, 2003). Randomized experiments provide the most believable statistical conclusions for advancing such knowledge. Through randomization of treatment and control conditions, randomized experiments can rule out, in theory, the threats to validity that plague other research methods. Because the relationship between treatment and all possible confounders is made random through random allocation, such confounders can be ignored in drawing conclusions. This makes RCTs a key part of the toolbox of EBP.

But RCTs are not the only method for gaining knowledge, and there are many questions critical to the advancement of the science of EBP that need to be addressed with other research methods. For example, the views of the police and the public on specific issues are best assessed through surveys, not RCTs. Understanding reasons or processes behind an event or a phenomenon may be best addressed through in-depth interviews with relevant figures. And there are some questions that while best answered through randomized trials, cannot (for a variety of reasons) be assessed using such methods. For example, it would be unethical and socially unacceptable to conduct an experiment testing the effects of police use of force on public support for the police, while manipulating the "amount" of force. Some variables simply cannot be manipulated within an experimental design. Moreover, randomized trials are not efficient for defining what programs or practices should be tested from a broad array of "untested" practices. It is often necessary to use less focused approaches to begin to identify what is useful to examine using randomized trials. The randomized trial (when implemented with fidelity) provides the best approach to answering specific questions. But this benefit is gained by investing significant resources in examining a narrow set of questions.

EBP scholars have long lamented the dearth of randomized trials in EBP (Braga et al., 2014; Garner & Visher, 2003; Neyroud, 2017). In Chapter 8 in our volume, we add up-to-date knowledge on that reality. By analyzing the Global Policing Database (GPD) corpus of high-quality evaluation studies in policing, Mazerolle and colleagues describe the breadth and depth of the evidence base in policing. Their findings suggest that despite the centrality of RCTs in EBP, their proportion within the population of policing studies remains relatively small. The GPD includes studies only when they meet a minimum standard of evidentiary quality, defined as designs containing a quantitative impact evaluation of policing interventions that, at a minimum, include a valid comparison group. They find that just 12% of this evidence base is randomized trials. It is clear that the randomized trial should be carried out with much great frequency in the development of EBP.

At the same time, randomized trials should be carried out in ways that maximize their utility, and that recognize that they should be targeted in their application. We propose that randomized trials should be seen as a tool to come to solid conclusions regarding programs or practices for which we have evidence that they are promising. That evidence can be based on strong observational basic science, or on observational statistical, or quasi-experimental studies. Our point is that initial evidence based on other methods can provide us with means for focusing experiments where they will have most likelihood of success and greatest impact. One way to view this is to see experiments as the final arbiter regarding what programs or practices should be implemented broadly. But such experiments would build on knowledge produced by other methods. We are not saying in this regard that experiments should not be used where they are easily applied to examine new questions, or that other methods such as surveys, in-depth interviews, or systematic observations should only be used as "primers" to RCTs. We do argue, however, that overall, experiments will be most useful as part of a progression of research studies. In this context, the GPD findings can be seen as encouraging if we begin to use them to focus in on programs and practices which should now be assessed in randomized trials. Of course we recognize, as noted above, that there may be some questions for which randomized trials simply cannot be carried out. In such cases, we should strive to develop non-experimental methods that provide the most believable evidence for making decisions about policy and practice.

In this regard, it is also important to recognize that randomized trials, and in many cases the strongest non-experimental designs, are often built on developing strong methods in data collection and organization. In Chapter 12, Jaitman points out the lack of RCTs and quasi-experimental designs in policing research in Latin America and Caribbean, and suggests that this deficiency is mostly due to weak crime data collection, affected by underreporting, institutional differences in recording crime, and lack of validity of the recorded information. In turn, a number of the chapters in our volume point to the development of scientific methods in the area of citizen surveys and related methods. Both Gill (Chapter 7) and Telep and Weisburd (Chapter 5) point, for example, to the importance of expanding the types of data we collect to fully inform EBP. As Telep and Weisburd (Chapter 5) note, the next generation of systematic reviews should widen the scope of outcomes to examine citizen and community reactions to policing, which would provide practitioners with more complete evidence for choosing and implementing practices in the field.

Similarly, addressing the complex relations between proactive policing, community support, and crime prevention, Gill (Chapter 7) discusses the lack of empirical support for the effect of policing on community outcomes (Weisburd & Majmundar, 2018). She proposes that this gap steams from two main shortcomings in the breadth of scientific methods in EBP: First, focusing on the effect leading to the outcome neglects the processes, or mechanisms, by which this relationship may operate. Second, as suggested in the NAS report, these processes may remain difficult to identify due to short follow up periods (Weisburd & Majmundar, 2018). Instead of a simple input–output relationship that can be measured using short-term experimental evaluations, Gill suggests looking at community factors as "change-levers" (Wilson, 2019) in policing.

Thus, in relation to some research questions, the go-to methodological tools traditionally associated with EBP may not be enough. Specifically, this may be the case when examining the process – rather than the outcome – of an effect, and when the variables within this process include internal, subjective measurements of a community or an individual (Brown et al., 2018). When researchers are called upon to answer such questions, additional innovative methodological tools may be required. Such a tool is proposed by Perry, Jonathan-Zamir, and Willis (chapter 9). Perry and colleagues suggest integrating the qualitative method of "subjective causality," long used in the social sciences, to the study of specific, challenging inquiries in policing (Tacq, 2011). Instead of relying on random allocation and a temporal order of events to establish causality (Lewis, 1974), this approach views individuals' inner subjective evaluations of cause and effect as the basis of causality (Abell & Engel, 2019; Maxwell, 2004, 2012, 2019). By so doing, subjective causality allows for deeper understanding of the mechanisms often investigated using quantitative methods. This method allows researchers to open the "black box" and thus understand why and under what conditions an effect will take place (Thacher, 2004). Importantly, subjective causality is not meant to replace the "strong evidence" approach that is central to EBP, but to complement the toolkit of EBP by expanding the array of "appropriate" research methods.

17.2.3 Developing Comparative Research

A comparative perspective in studying crime and the responses of the criminal justice system is commonly recognized as an important focus of research in criminology (Nelken, 2009; Tonry, 2015). This approach allows us to understand how different contexts (such as Western versus non-Western settings) may affect crime rates, and how the implementation of crime prevention policies and strategies are similar/different across various social and political settings.

This should also be an important area of research in the future of EBP. For example, do evidence-based practices work differently in different national or cultural contexts? Are some strategies more effective in the United States, while others show better results in Western European countries, South American contexts, or Asian contexts? A comparative perspective can help us place national policies and practices in cross-national contexts for the purpose of understanding what differences they make in the implementation of policing strategies. In turn, this would allow researchers to examine the extent and conditions under which police agencies successfully import ideas from elsewhere, and the kinds of obstacles that may impede successful implementation.

Our book includes several chapters that examine EBP in different countries and social, cultural, and organizational settings. It thus provides a wide array of case studies that show different expressions of ideas and principles in EBP. The chapter by Jaitman (Chapter 12) shows that Latin America and Caribbean suffer from high rates of violence, which may lead us to expect great interest in EBP. At the same time, the realities of these nations suggest that the implementation of EBP faces many institutional, cultural, political, and skill-related barriers. Some of the main obstacles include the lack of reliable data, instability of political institutions, and lack of trust in the police. Contrary to Latin America and Caribbean, the chapter by Litmanovitz and colleagues (Chapter 11) describes the successful implementation of an evidence-based reform in the Israel Police (the "EMUN" reform) and shows that its success was due in good part to the strong computerized system that allowed the police to analyze data and reflect on it. The success of the reform was also found to be associated with organizational flexibility and with the ability to engage with the reform at the level of the local police stations.

Relying on the Global Policing Database (GPD), Mazerolle and colleagues (Chapter 8) found that half of the RCTs in policing originate from the United States. The authors conclude that expansion in the places

Police Science and the Future of Evidence-Based Policing   347

generating high-quality evidence will help generalize policing policies and practices beyond the United States.

The chapter by Perry and Wolfowicz (Chapter 14) is based on a comparative analysis in which two Israeli police commissioners (Hefetz and Alsheich) tried to lead EBP reforms in the Israel Police. While the term comparative research is often narrowly defined in terms of cross-national or regional studies, we think a broader perspective that recognizes the need to compare regimes or administrations, as well as geographic contexts, is useful. The chapter seeks to answer the question of what made one commissioner more successful than the other in advancing EBP. Their answer lies in the fact that Alsheich was the "evidence cop" described by Sherman (1998), or rather what they term the "super evidence cop." Their comparison of two case studies shows how valuable this type of comparative perspective is in advancing the science of EBP.

Following this expansion of the idea of comparative research, Neyroud and Weisburd (Chapter 3) propose a new paradigm that changes the relationship between science and policing. Their work was aided by looking across different disciplines for guidance in advancing EBP. Their inspiration comes primarily from comparing policing to medical practices, but the example we raised earlier comparing policing to social work also emphasizes the extent to which this approach can be expanded to other disciplines. We think there is much to be learned by comparative work between national or regional contexts, within national contexts across time, and across disciplinary approaches.

17.2.4 Recognizing the Importance of a Science of Street-Level Behavior

EBP has traditionally focused on strategies (as opposed to individual, street-level behavior). This focus was made explicit, for example, in the NAS report summarized in Chapter 6 (see also Weisburd & Majmundar, 2018): "In this report, the term 'proactive policing' is used to refer to all policing *strategies* [emphasis added] that have as one of their goals the prevention or reduction of crime and disorder and that are not reactive ..." (p. 30). At the same time, the chapters in our volume also point to the importance of investigating street-level discretion of individual officers.

For example, building on early policing scholarship, Willis and Toronjo (Chapter 4) argue that the quality of policing is determined, to a large extent, by how well individual patrol officers respond to specific occurrences (Mastrofski, 1988), many of which have little to do with crime or law enforcement, such as traffic accidents, disputes, or mild disturbances of the peace (Black, 1971). Such situations raise questions not about the strategies that work best in controlling crime, and even not about how police legitimacy could be promoted at the city level. In many day-to-day police–citizen encounters, the questions police officers find most acute may include: "how can I identify the important cues that will help me understand the problem?"; "what and how should I ask about the situation?"; "how can I deescalate the situation?"; and "how should the law be applied in these particular circumstances?". To date, the science of EBP has little to say about these questions. Willis and Toronjo further argue that the first place to look for answers to such questions are the police officers themselves. Following work by Bayley and Bittner (1984), Mastrofski (1988), and others, they argue for the importance of the police "craft," or hands-on experience that has taught police officers, for example, how to diagnose a problem, understand situational cues, use coercion and language effectively, and interpret particular situations through the eyes of the law.

To date, little room has been given to this type of knowledge in EBP. Officers' experience is typically perceived as unsystematic, subjective, and inferior to science in making accurate predictions (Lum, 2009; Sherman, 1998, 2013). While we agree that the experiences and interpretations of any particular officer are context-specific and subjective by nature, we think that the "craft" knowledge developed from police officers' accumulated experiences is invaluable, and policing scholars must find ways to systematically capture this knowledge and use it to produce scientific evidence. This could be done, for example, through systematic field observations followed by short debriefing sessions, in-person or group interviews with police officers, focus groups, surveys, vignettes, and role plays. Officers' views about what works best in deescalating particular situations, for example, could then be tested using the more traditional methods of EBP, such as RCTs. But the bottom line is that in order to move forward, EBP cannot continue to ignore questions relevant to individual, street-level discretion, nor the experience-based knowledge developed by those actually doing police work.

This approach was well demonstrated by Litmanovitz, Weisburd, and Hasisi (Chapter 11). As noted above, in this chapter the authors describe a process evaluation of the EMUN reform in the Israel Police. Their goal was not to assess the success of the reform in reducing crime (analyses they report elsewhere; see Hasisi et al., 2019; Weisburd et al., 2020), but rather the factors that promoted/inhibited the successful implementation of the reform, for the purpose of coming to more general conclusions about facilitators/barriers to the implementation of evidence-based programs in policing. This analysis is based, to a large degree, on interviews with key figures in the police stations where the reform was implemented, including station commanders, their deputies, and other leading commanding officers. These interviews allowed the researchers to identify three keys to the successful implementation of the reform: the ability to analyze data, work with it, think about its meaning, and use it to test officers' intuitive "hypotheses"; organizational flexibility in allocating resources, in the boundaries between different police units, and in shaping responses to the problems identified in the district; and taking "ownership" of the reform. It would not have been possible to generate this type of knowledge, which, in our view, has a critical place in EBP, without speaking to the commanding officers leading the reform in the "real world."

The importance of giving attention to officers' experience in EBP is also reinforced by the arguments made by Jonathan-Zamir and Weisburd (Chapter 10). Based on a review of receptivity-to-research studies in policing (e.g., Telep & Lum, 2014; Telep & Winegar, 2015), as well as the psychology literature more generally (e.g., Giluk & Rynes, 2012; Ruscio, 2010), they conclude that on a large scale, police officers will likely continue to rely on their experience and intuition, not on research evidence, when making decisions. This is because the tendency to rely on personal experience is not unique to policing and develops from deep-rooted psychological mechanisms that are not necessarily accessible or easily influenced by rational arguments. Thus, Jonathan-Zamir and Weisburd propose to "inject" scientifically sound practices into officers' experience, but also to give room to officers' experience in EBP. Relying on Salas et al. (2010) and others, they argue that in some situations, the "intuitive" decision-making system performs better than the slower, analytic system. Thus, instead of treating science and professional experience as two opposing perspectives, Jonathan-Zamir and Weisburd argue that they both have a role in successful policing, and the task of researchers is to investigate exactly what their roles should be. They propose, for example, to differentiate between strategic, macro-level decisions (where scientific evidence should dominate) and tactical street-level decisions (where experience and intuition should play a more dominant role). Whatever approaches are taken, it is time to integrate the reality of street level policing into the scientific knowledge base of EBP.

17.2.5 Expanding the Knowledge of Implementation Science

There is a growing evidence that some police strategies, such as hot spots policing, focused deterrence, and problem-oriented policing, show promising results in reducing crime and disorder, and other strategies, such as community policing, increase the trust of the public in the police (Weisburd & Majmundar, 2018). Yet, the benefit of reducing crime and increasing trust can be achieved only when these strategies are implemented properly with high fidelity, and when police officers and agencies are receptive to science. But our volume shows that even if high fidelity and receptivity to research can be achieved, other challenges need to be addressed (Lum & Koper, 2017). The chapter by Stephens (Chapter 15) provides insight into such challenges, providing an historical perspective of a practitioner who witnessed some of the leading police reforms in the United States over the last half century. For example, in his chapter, Stephen's elaborates on the successful implementation of problem-oriented policing (in the Newport News Police Department), in which police officers were given discretion to manage their workload in a way that allowed time for them to engage in problem solving. This is only an example of a basic requirement for police reform to succeed. Police organizations should be able to adopt new ideas and create an appropriate organizational environment in order to facilitate the implementation of the reform.

But episodic reform in specific agencies does not provide the leadership or resources that are often necessary to fully implement EBP. Emphasizing this, in Chapter 16 James Burch advocates for federal leadership in advancing evidence-based science. His experience as head of the agency that provides the largest amount of funding for local policing in the US, suggests the key importance of such agencies focusing on EBP, and the positive results that can be gained when they do. Burch argues that there is much confusion in what EBP is, and that providing a clearly articulated set of principles for EBP is key to its advancement. Neyroud and Weisburd (Chapter 3) also emphasize the importance of national leadership, even in countries that already have more centralized control of police agencies. In turn, it is important to note that when Sherman first raised the issue of EBP (see Sherman, 1998), he saw the commitment of national organizations as key to its success.

However, having national organizations that can play a leadership role in EBP does not necessarily lead to successful and broad implementation of evidence-based science in police agencies. One topic that was raised in a number of chapters in our book is the key role of police

Police Science and the Future of Evidence-Based Policing 351

leadership in advancing EBP. Neyroud & Weisburd (Chapter 3) call for police executives that "...value science and see it as a crucial part of their own, their staff and their agencies' development and essential to the agencies' efficiency, effectiveness and legitimacy with the public." Perry and Wolfowicz (Chapter 14) and Stephens (Chapter 15) point to the "evidence cop," first identified by Sherman (1998), as key to implementing EBP. Perry and Wolfowicz rephrase it as the "super evidence cop," since they want to emphasize that such police executives not only know about evidence and seek to implement EBP, but they take ownership of science (see Weisburd & Neyroud, 2011) with its broad implications for developing knowledge, supporting and funding scientific work, and integrating scientific norms and values into police agencies. Darryl Stephens's chapter provides us with an auto-biography of the "super evidence cop." Throughout his career, science, evidence, and collaboration with academics were the core of his practice. In this sense, our volume not only points to why police leadership is so important from an academic perspective, but also provides a first-hand description of what it means in practice.

17.2.6 Adding Normative Dimensions to the Science of Evidence-Based Policing

EBP has, to a great extent, been focused on "objective" measurement of outcomes. The question of "what works" is ordinarily not placed in the realm of moral or ethical debates. A key area where EBP has raised ethical concerns is in regard to "cures that harm" (McCord, 2003). EBP has argued, as has evidence-based science more generally (Chalmers, 2003), that a key role of rigorous evaluation of programs and practices is to identify whether they might potentially cause harm – often whether they increase crime or criminality. In part, policing scholars have avoided broader ethical and moral concerns because, as Harmon (Chapter 13) notes, police departments do not adopt illegal policies (though practices may be challenged in the courts, and be subsequently found to be illegal – e.g., "Stop, Question and Frisk" in New York City, see *Floyd v. City of New York,* 2013a; 2013b). The legal boundaries of policing as defined by the law and the courts have replaced, to some degree, the responsibility of scholars. But as Harmon notes, the courts have generally not considered the science of policing in drawing conclusions about policing strategies, and provide little guidance for the advancement of EBP more generally.

One of the key conclusions of the NAS report on proactive policing discussed in Chapter 6 is that EBP has often ignored community impacts of strategies. We noted earlier the importance of collecting such data, but we think that such data are important not just for identifying what works but also for assessing possible negative outcomes of policing strategies. Policing, by its nature, imposes restrictions on the freedom of citizens in democratic societies. Police have the authority to stop people in specific circumstances, and they are authorized to use force in some circumstances. They have the power to arrest people who they define as violating the law. While the negative consequences of such powers have often been ignored, we think that they need to become a key part of the science of EBP. More generally, ethical and moral dimensions of policing need to become a key focus of EBP.

For this reason, Neyroud and Weisburd add in Chapter 3 the category of the "Ethical and moral context of policing" to the science-based paradigm they originally proposed in 2011 (Weisburd & Neyroud, 2011). They write:

> … science also has something key to say about what the ethical questions surrounding what the police should do, and how they should do it. Coming back to the example of medicine, medical ethics is a key component of evidence-based medical science. We think that it is time for the police to look to develop a model of policing ethics and moral responsibility akin to the large-scale concern for this issue in medicine. If this had been part of the scientific model of policing, the police today and police scholars would be in a much stronger position to respond to challenges surrounding the policing task. Many of the most important challenges to policing today relate to the lack of moral boundaries in policing in relationship to use of force, arrests and other law enforcement activities. These concerns are not about police effectiveness but about fairness, discrimination, and more generally the moral boundaries of police conduct.

Ethics should become an important concern for the advancement of the science of EBP, just as it is an important concern in medical science. This means not only that ethics should become an area of focus for scientists but that scientists should also collect the necessary data for assessing what impacts policing is having on individuals, communities, and society. In Chapter 2, Sherman shows how moral concerns can lead EBP to redefine how targets are chosen and how effectiveness is measured. Drawing from public health responses to the COVID-19 pandemic, which "tiered" prevention responses to risk levels, he argues for a "tiered" policing system to prevent serious violence. In this case, the most intrusive crime prevention approaches, such as stop and search, would only be applied to the highest risk places. While such strategies can be effective, collateral damage can be reduced if they are largely restricted to hot spots (see also Weisburd, 2016). Sherman argues in Chapter 2 that

Police Science and the Future of Evidence-Based Policing 353

"police legitimacy in democracies could be enhanced by *confining most highly-intrusive policing, such as stop and search, to 'highest-tier' areas for serious violent victimizations,* possibly limited to 5% of all places in a city" [emphasis in original]. In this sense, Sherman is calling for scientists to consider the possible negative impacts of policing strategies in defining how EBP should be developed. Moral and ethical dimensions of policing are implicitly introduced in his call for a tiered policing system.

In Chapter 4, Willis and Toronjo argue that everyday policing involves making moral decisions that affect the people that they interact with. Police officers have significant discretion in how they handle interactions with the public. Albert J. Reiss Jr. noted the power of the police to affect the "fate of people" (Reiss, 1971: p. 121). More generally, scholars need to more directly include such moral questions and dilemmas in their attempts to develop a police science that is guiding the broad array of policing activities. Willis and Toronjo argue for "designing and testing different approaches for normative improvement, such as developing and evaluating a training program designed to improve not just practical but moral outcomes." Recognizing the moral and ethical context of street-level policing needs to be a key part of police science in the future. Returning to Sommerfeld's comments on the development of an action-based science in social work, in the end EBP should "contribute to the development of a 'good life'" (pp. 590–591).

17.3 CONCLUSIONS

We titled this volume *The Future of Evidence-Based Policing*, because in it we sought to take stock of where the field of EBP has been and where it is heading. In this concluding chapter we addressed the latter question, and make the argument that the future of EBP as a meaningful paradigm with substantial influence on police practice lies in a stronger science of policing.

While a key reason for resistance to EBP lies in the resistance of practitioners to implementing this approach, we think that greater recognition of what scientists need to do to advance EBP is one of the important contributions of our volume. EBP will not be able to become fully implemented in the police world until a stronger science of policing is developed. Scholars have already pointed to the need for increasing the evidence base for EBP, and our volume has reinforced this concern. If EBP is to provide guidance regarding what crime prevention approaches police should use, scholars are going to have to develop a "second generation of studies" that provide greater granularity in what strategies should be used in what circumstances. But we think that our book has pointed to a broader array of questions that need to be addressed in future research to develop a better science of policing. These include expanding the research methods we use for advancing EBP, the need for more comparative research, more research on street-level decision making, staking out new directions in implementation science, and explicitly including moral and ethical questions as scientific concerns in EBP. The future of EBP needs to place these six dimensions at the forefront of the development of the science of policing.

References

Abell, P., & Engel, O. (2019). Subjective causality and counterfactuals in the social sciences: Toward an ethnographic causality?. *Sociological Methods & Research*, 0049124119852373.

Ariel, B. (2018). "Not all evidence is created equal": on the importance of matching research questions with research methods in evidence based policing. *Evidence Based Policing: An Introduction*, 63.

Bayley, D. H., & Bittner E. (1984). Learning the skills of policing. *Law and Contemporary Problems*, 47, 35–59.

Black, D. (1971). The social organization of arrest. *Stanford Law Review*, 23, 1087–1111.

Braga, A. A., Turchan, B. S., Papachristos, A. V., & Hureau, D. M. (2019). Hot spots policing and crime reduction: An update of an ongoing systematic review and meta-analysis. *Journal of Experimental Criminology*, 15(3), 289–311.

Braga, A. A., Welsh, B. C., Papachristos, A. V., Schnell, C., & Grossman, L. (2014). The growth of randomized experiments in policing: The vital few and the salience of mentoring. *Journal of Experimental Criminology*, 10, 1–28.

Brekke, J. S. (2012). Shaping a science of social work. *Research on Social Work Practice*, 22(5), 455–464.

Brown, J., Belur, J., Tompson, L., McDowall, A., Hunter, G., & May, T. (2018). Extending the remit of evidence-based policing. *International Journal of Police Science & Management*, 20(1), 38–51.

Bunge, M. (1985). *Treatise on basic philosophy: Volume 7 (Part II)*. D. Reidel Publishing Company.

Burch, J. H. (this volume). Support for evidence-based policing at the national level – More help than harm? In D. Weisburd, T. Jonathan, G. Perry & B. Hasisi, (Eds.), *The Future of Evidence-Based Policing*. Cambridge University Press.

Chalmers, I. (2003). Trying to do more good than harm in policy and practice: the role of rigorous, transparent, up-to-date evaluations. *The ANNALS of the American Academy of Political and Social Science*, 589(1), 22–40.

Farrington, D. P., & Welsh, B. C. (2006). A half century of randomized experiments on crime and justice. *Crime and Justice*, 34(1), 55–132.

Floyd v. City of New York, 959 F. Supp. 2d 540 (S.D.N.Y. 2013a).

Floyd v. City of New York, 959 F. Supp. 2d 668 (S.D.N.Y. 2013b).
Garner, J. H., & Visher, C. A. (2003). The production of criminological experiments. *Evaluation Review, 27*(3), 316–335.
Gill, C. (this volume). Rethinking the role of the community in proactive policing. In D. Weisburd, T. Jonathan, G. Perry & B. Hasisi, (Eds.), *The Future of Evidence-Based Policing*. Cambridge University Press.
Giluk, T. L., & Rynes, S. L. (2012). Research findings practitioners resist: Lessons for management academics from evidence-based medicine. In D. M. Rousseau (Ed.), *The Oxford hand-book of evidence-based management* (pp. 130–164). Oxford University Press.
Gottfredson, D. C., Cook, T. D., Gardner, F. E., Gorman-Smith, D., Howe, G. W., Sandler, I. N., & Zafft, K. M. (2015). Standards of evidence for efficacy, effectiveness, and scale-up research in prevention science: Next generation. *Prevention Science, 16*(7), 893–926.
Greene, J.R. (2014). New directions in policing: Balancing prediction and meaning in research, *Justice Quarterly, 31*(2), 193–228.
Harmon, R. (this volume). Evidence-based policing and the law: The American Perspective. In D. Weisburd, T. Jonathan, G. Perry & B. Hasisi, (Eds.), *The Future of Evidence-Based Policing*. Cambridge University Press.
Hasisi, B., Weisburd, D., Litmanovitz, Y., Carmel, T., Tshuva, S., & Trachtenberg, T. (2019). EMUN evaluation report: Traffic disturbances and reckless driving. *Research Essence: A Collection of Studies on Police and Criminology, 29*–60.
Jaitman, L. (this volume). Towards implementing evidence-based policing: Challenges in Latin America and Caribbean. In D. Weisburd, T. Jonathan, G. Perry & B. Hasisi, (Eds.), *The Future of Evidence-Based Policing*. Cambridge University Press.
Jindra, I. W. (2018). The emerging 'science of social work' in the United States and German-speaking countries: A comparison. *International Social Work, 61*(6), 930–942.
Jonathan-Zamir, T., & Weisburd, D. (this volume). Practitioners' inclination to rely on experience: What does this mean for evidence-based policing? In D. Weisburd, T. Jonathan, G. Perry & B. Hasisi, (Eds.), *The Future of Evidence-Based Policing*. Cambridge University Press.
Laycock, G. (2012). In support of evidence-based approaches: A response to Lum and Kennedy. *Policing: A Journal of Policy and Practice, 6*(4), 324–326.
Lewis, D. (1974). Causation. *The Journal of Philosophy, 70*(17), 556–567.
Lipsey, M. W. (2003). Those confounded moderators in meta-analysis: Good, bad, and ugly. *The ANNALS of the American Academy of Political and Social Science, 587*(1), 69–81.
Litmanovitz, Y., Weisburd, D., & Hasisi, B. (this volume). Implementing evidence-based policing: Findings from a process evaluation of the EMUN Reform in the Israel Police. In D. Weisburd, T. Jonathan, G. Perry & B. Hasisi, (Eds.), *The Future of Evidence-Based Policing*. Cambridge University Press.
Lösel, F., & Schmucker, M. (2005). The effectiveness of treatment for sexual offenders: A comprehensive meta-analysis. *Journal of Experimental Criminology, 1*(1), 117–146.

Lum, C. (2009). Translating police research into practice. *Ideas in American Policing, 11.*

Lum, C., & Koper, C. S. (2017). *Evidence-based policing: Translating research into practice.* Oxford University Press.

Lum, C., Koper, C.S., Gill, C., Telep, C., & Robinson, L. (2016). *An evidence-assessment of the recommendations of the president's task force on 21st century policing: Implementation and research priorities.* Center for Evidence-Based Crime Policy, George Mason University. International Association of Chiefs of Police. http://cebcp.org/wp-content/evidence-based-policing/IACP-GMU-Evidence-Assessment-Task-Force-FINAL.pdf.

Mastrofski, S.D. (1988). Community policing as reform. In J. R. Greene & S. D. Mastrofski (Eds.), *Community policing: Rhetoric or reality?* (pp. 47–67). Praeger.

Maxwell, J. A. (2004). Causal explanation, qualitative research, and scientific inquiry in education. *Educational Researcher, 33*(2), 3–11.

Maxwell, J. A. (2012). The importance of qualitative research for causal explanation in education. *Qualitative Inquiry, 18*(8), 655–661.

Maxwell, J. A. (2019). Evidence for what? How mixed methods expands the evidence for causation in educational research. *Qualitative Inquiry.*

Mazerolle, L., Eggins, E., Hine, L., & Higginson, A. (this volume). The role of randomized experiments in developing the evidence for evidence-based policing. In D. Weisburd, T. Jonathan, G. Perry & B. Hasisi, (Eds.), *The Future of Evidence-Based Policing.* Cambridge University Press.

McCord, J. (2003). Cures that harm: Unanticipated outcomes of crime prevention programs. *The ANNALS of the American Academy of Political and Social Science, 587*(1), 16–30.

Nelken. D. (2009). Comparative Criminal Justice: Beyond Ethnocentrism and Relativism. *European Journal of Criminology, 6*(4), 291–311.

Neyroud, P. W. (2017). *Learning to Field Test in Policing: Using an analysis of completed randomised controlled trials involving the police to develop a grounded theory on the factors contributing to high levels of treatment integrity in Police Field Experiments.* [Doctoral thesis, University of Cambridge]. https://doi.org/10.17863/CAM.14377.

Neyroud, P., & Weisburd, D. (this volume). Re-inventing policing: Using science to transform policing. In D. Weisburd, T. Jonathan, G. Perry & B. Hasisi, (Eds.), *The Future of Evidence-Based Policing.* Cambridge University Press.

Perry, G., Jonathan-Zamir, T., & Willis, J. (this volume). The potential contribution of subjective causality to policing research: The case of the relationship between procedural justice and police legitimacy. In D. Weisburd, T. Jonathan, G. Perry & B. Hasisi, (Eds.), *The Future of Evidence-Based Policing.* Cambridge University Press.

Perry, S., & Wolfowitz, M. (this volume). The role of the "Super Evidence Cop" in evidence-based policing: The Israeli Case. In D. Weisburd, T. Jonathan, G. Perry & B. Hasisi, (Eds.), *The Future of Evidence-Based Policing.* Cambridge University Press.

Reiss, A. J. (1971). *The police and the public.* Yale University Press.

Ruscio, J. (2010). Irrational beliefs stemming from judgment errors: Cognitive limitations, biases, and experiential learning. In D. David, S. J. Lynn, & A. Ellis (Eds.), *Rational and irrational beliefs: Research, theory, and clinical practice* (pp. 291–312). Oxford University Press.

Salas, E., Rosen, M. A., & DiazGranados, D. (2010). Expertise-based intuition and decision making in organizations. *Journal of Management, 36*(4), 941–973.

Sherman, L. W. (1998). *Evidence-based policing*. Police Foundation. www.policefoundation.org/wp-content/uploads/2015/06/Sherman-1998-Evidence-Based-Policing.pdf

Sherman, L. (2013). The rise of evidence-based policing: targeting, testing, and tracking. *Crime and Justice in America, 1975–2025, 42.1*(2013), 377–451.

Sherman, L. W. (this volume). Three tiers for evidence-based policing: Targeting "minimalist" policing with a risk-adjusted disparity index. In D. Weisburd, T. Jonathan, G. Perry, & B. Hasisi, (Eds.), *The future of evidence-based policing*. Cambridge University Press.

Skidelsky, R. (1992). *John Maynard Keynes: A biography. Vol. 2: The economist as saviour, 1920–1937*. Macmillan

Skogan, W. G., & Frydl, K. (Eds.) (2004). *Fairness and effectiveness in policing: The evidence*. Committee to Review Research on Police Policy and Practices. The National Academies Press.

Skogan, W. G., Van Craen, M., & Hennessy, C. (2015). Training police for procedural justice. *Journal of Experimental Criminology, 11*(3), 319–334.

Sommerfeld, P. (2014). Social work as an action science: A perspective from Europe. *Research on Social Work Practice, 24*(5), 586–600.

Sparrow, M. (2016). *Handcuffed: What holds policing back and the keys to reform*. Brooking Institution Press.

Stephens, D. (this volume). Looking Back on the Challenges to Evidence-Based Policing: A Chief's Perspective. In D. Weisburd, T. Jonathan, G. Perry & B. Hasisi, (Eds.), *The future of evidence-based policing*. Cambridge University Press.

Tacq, J. (2011). Causality in qualitative and quantitative research. *Quality & Quantity, 45*(2), 263–291.

Telep, C. W., & Lum, C. (2014). The receptivity of officers to empirical research and evidence-based policing: An examination of survey data from three agencies. *Police Quarterly, 17*(4), 359–385.

Telep, C. W., & Weisburd, D. (this volume). A review of systematic reviews in policing. In D. Weisburd, T. Jonathan, G. Perry, & B. Hasisi, (Eds.), *The future of evidence-based policing*. Cambridge University Press.

Telep, C. W., & Winegar, S. (2015). Police executive receptivity to research: A survey of chiefs and sheriffs in Oregon. *Policing: A Journal of Policy and Practice, 10*(3), 241–249.

Thacher, D. (2004). Police research and the humanities. *The ANNALS of the American Academy of Political and Social Science, 593*(1), 179–191.

Tonry, M. (2015). Is cross-national and comparative research on the criminal justice system useful? *European Journal of Criminology, 12*(4), 505–516.

Weisburd, D. (2003). Ethical practice and evaluation of interventions in crime and justice: The moral imperative for randomized trials. *Evaluation Review*, 27(3), 336–354.

Weisburd, D. (2016). Does hot spots policing inevitably lead to unfair and abusive police practices, or can we maximize both fairness and effectiveness in the new proactive policing. *University of Chicago Legal Forum*, 661–690.

Weisburd, D., Braga, A. A., & Majmundar, M. (this volume). What do we know about Proactive Policing's effects on Crime and Community?: Drawing conclusions from a National Academies of Sciences, Engineering, and Medicine Report. In D. Weisburd, T. Jonathan, G. Perry, & B. Hasisi, (Eds.), *The Future of Evidence-Based Policing*. Cambridge University Press.

Weisburd, D., Hasisi, B., Litmanovitz, Y., Carmel, T., & Tshuva, S. (2020). Institutionalizing problem-oriented policing: An evaluation of the EMUN reform in Israel. *Criminology & Public Policy*, 19(3), 941–964.

Weisburd, D., & Majmundar, M. K. (Eds.) (2018). *Proactive policing: Effects on crime and communities*. Committee on proactive policing: Effects on crime, communities, and civil liberties. Committee on law and justice, division of behavioral and social sciences and education. The National Academies Press.

Weisburd, D., & Neyroud, P. (2011). Police science: Toward a new paradigm. *New Perspectives in Policing, January*, 1–23.

Weisburd, D., & Telep, C. W. (2014). Hot spots policing: What we know and what we need to know. *Journal of Contemporary Criminal Justice*, 30(2), 200–220.

Willis, J. J., & Toronjo, H. (this volume). A way ahead: Re-envisioning the relationship between evidence-based policing and the Police Craft. In D. Weisburd, T. Jonathan, G. Perry, & B. Hasisi, (Eds.), *The Future of Evidence-Based Policing*. Cambridge University Press.

Wilson, D. B. (2019). Developing a theory of effective juvenile delinquency programming through an examination of change-levers rather than program types: Preliminary evidence from a large juvenile delinquency meta-analysis [PDF slides]. www.bocsar.nsw.gov.au/Pages/bocsar_seminar_series/2019-Conference-Slides.aspx

Index

basic research, 98, 138
broken windows, 27, 73, 110, 111, 116, 118, 129, 134–136, 158

Campbell, 88–91, 100, 148, 150, 154, 156, 157, 337
Caribbean, 10, 162, 235–237, 240, 242, 245, 246, 248, 344, 346
change levers, 136, 138–141
communities, 6, 38, 39, 57, 107, 108, 110, 115, 118, 126, 131, 132, 141, 159, 262, 283, 312, 317, 318, 320, 323, 325–327, 331, 333, 352
community policing, 8, 87, 93, 95, 118
comparative research, 163
Compstat, 45, 54, 292
crime analysis, 45, 46, 49, 73, 212, 214, 216, 217, 222, 224, 226, 229, 276, 332
crime data, 203, 212, 216, 223, 229, 246, 344
crime information systems, 244
crime prevention, 113, 134, 282, 307
crime prevention through environmental design (CPTED), 307
crime statistics, 135, 216, 223, 226, 240, 244, 246

decision-making, 1, 2, 56, 57, 68–71, 73, 77, 128, 140, 177, 193, 194, 196, 197, 203, 205, 206, 224, 230, 239, 245, 252, 253, 260, 265, 316, 333, 349
defund the police, 6, 24

de-funding, 22–24, 55
democratic policing, 19, 21, 22, 28, 39, 90, 132, 133, 330
deterrence, 35, 38, 87–89, 93–95, 99, 110–112, 114, 115, 119–121, 130, 133, 350
domestic violence, 64, 87, 90, 95, 154, 293, 298

EMUN, 10, 45, 54, 211, 212, 215–217, 219, 220, 222–230, 239, 247, 281–283, 286, 287, 346, 348
ethics, 57, 59, 221, 330, 339, 340, 352
evidence-based medicine, 4, 72, 316, 342
evidence-based policing (EBP), 1–11, 19, 20, 22, 28, 34, 38, 39, 44, 47, 52, 57, 58, 64–66, 68–74, 77, 85, 86, 97, 99, 101, 107, 116, 120, 128, 132, 135, 139, 147, 148, 164, 170, 171, 185, 193–197, 200–202, 204, 205, 211–215, 220–222, 224, 226, 228–230, 235, 236, 238–241, 243–249, 252, 253, 257–260, 263, 266, 267, 273–280, 282–287, 292, 293, 311, 312, 315–330, 332, 333, 336–338, 340–343, 345–353
evidence-based policing matrix, 195, 324
evidence cop, 7, 11, 50, 273–277, 279, 280, 284, 285, 287, 288, 347, 351
experiment, 65, 149, 161
expertise, 71, 73, 74, 107, 135, 136, 201, 205, 279

Index

fast thinking, 197
Fourth Amendment, 254, 256, 259, 261–263
frontline officers, 227

global policing database (GPD), 10, 90, 147, 148, 151, 152, 154, 155, 157–161, 163–165, 243, 341, 343, 344, 346

hot spots policing, 46, 57, 110, 112, 114, 119, 254

implementation, 1, 7, 8, 10, 11, 38, 44, 53, 91, 139, 158, 193, 202, 203, 211–215, 219–222, 226, 227, 229–231, 235, 236, 238, 239, 243, 245–249, 273–277, 281, 282, 284, 285, 287, 296, 302, 307, 316, 317, 319, 329, 336, 338, 346, 348, 350, 354
innovation, 8, 31, 45–47, 50, 53, 114, 149, 221, 285, 293, 305, 333, 339
institutions, 11, 20, 24, 51, 52, 132, 235, 240–242, 245, 249, 286, 324, 346
interviews, 10, 24, 73, 76, 170, 174, 179, 180, 182, 183, 196, 202, 221, 225, 227, 230, 343, 344, 348, 349
intrusion, 20, 28, 29, 31, 34, 36, 37, 39, 58, 263
intuition, 4, 10, 32, 197, 200, 201, 203–206, 239, 260, 263, 349
investigative techniques, 159–161, 165
Israel Police, 7, 10, 11, 50, 180, 196, 211, 212, 215, 230, 273, 274, 277, 278, 280, 281, 283, 346–348

Latin America, 10, 235–237, 240, 242, 244–246, 248, 344, 346
leadership, 22, 46, 51, 52, 55, 56, 58, 136, 140, 157, 158, 214, 236, 245, 274, 276, 277, 280, 284–286, 299, 301, 307, 315, 318, 323, 350

medical model, 64, 147, 333
meta-analysis, 98, 135, 154
methodology, 91, 140, 170, 184, 185, 212, 220

narrative review, 107, 341
NAS, 107–110, 112, 114–116, 119–121, 126–130, 132, 133, 136, 341, 345, 347, 351
National Academies of Sciences, Engineering, and Medicine, 66, 107, 150, 341
national forces, 315, 316, 333

organizations, 6, 11, 201, 211–214, 219, 222, 224, 226, 229, 230, 239, 248, 275, 278, 280, 281, 285, 287, 299, 315, 317–320, 323–327, 329, 350
ownership of science, 48, 229, 277, 351

paradigm, 8, 9, 11, 44, 54, 55, 58, 65, 68, 235, 247, 336, 347, 352, 353
participatory action research, 138
partnership, 50, 68, 135, 159, 249, 302, 304, 307
patrol, 9, 64, 66, 67, 69, 70, 72, 87, 90, 93, 95, 98, 109, 131, 149, 150, 175, 205, 225, 227, 247, 259, 292–302, 304–309, 312, 321, 327, 331, 347
police accountability, 235
police craft, 64
police culture, 245, 276
police effectiveness, 19, 57, 121, 131–133, 135, 141, 267, 292, 293, 297, 298, 337, 352
Police Executive Research Forum (PERF), 52, 111, 293, 302, 303, 318
police leadership, 351
police legitimacy, 3, 10, 19, 20, 38, 88, 115, 116, 118, 120, 128, 130, 131, 133, 170, 171, 173, 176–185, 197, 283, 348, 353
police organizations, 161
police performance, 66, 68, 71, 283, 337
police policy, 11, 116, 149, 182, 195
police practices, 2, 3, 11, 21, 28, 45, 46, 50, 52, 73, 74, 109, 116, 120, 148, 158, 184, 195, 239, 252, 253, 255, 257, 258, 260, 262, 263, 267, 308
police reform, 21, 24, 48, 64, 67, 100, 235, 243, 245, 249, 312, 329, 350
police science, 44, 49, 51, 55, 58, 336
police technologies, 100
police training, 8, 65, 154, 201, 202, 242, 249, 308, 337
police-led science, 275
policing system, 9, 19, 318, 352
political concerns, 244–246, 248, 315, 329
pracademics, 6, 276, 288
practitioner, 2, 53, 67, 134, 149, 213, 235, 236, 249, 322, 323, 329, 332, 350
predictive policing, 110, 111, 115, 247, 249
proactive policing, 2, 9, 19, 26, 39, 66, 73, 107–109, 111, 112, 114, 116, 119–121, 126–134, 136, 138–140, 249, 261, 312, 337, 345, 347, 351

problem-based learning, 308
problem-oriented policing, 8, 45, 46, 86, 88, 89, 94, 111, 119–121, 126, 129–131, 133, 134, 136, 138, 139, 154, 161, 165, 216, 221, 222, 226, 239, 283, 285, 292, 293, 299, 301–303, 307–309, 350
procedural justice (PJ), 114, 117, 170, 173, 176–183, 185
process tracing, 140
professional policing, 11, 315, 330–333
protest, 19, 38, 179, 180, 183
public trust, 37, 38, 214, 215, 323

qualitative research, 170, 175
quasi-experiments, 147, 160, 164, 220

RAD Index, 35, 36
randomized controlled trial (RCT), 10, 147, 150, 154, 156, 160–164
receptivity to research, 195, 214, 350
repeat offender programs, 110, 111

scanning, analysis, response, assessment (SARA), 110, 216, 221, 302, 305, 308, 331
science of policing, 4, 5, 11, 45, 204, 336–338, 340, 342, 351, 353

science-experience paradox, 10, 196
science-led policing, 275
scientific research, 68, 196, 211, 275, 340
second generation studies, 101
slow thinking, 197
standard model of policing, 109, 120, 219, 224
stop and search, 19, 20, 26, 31, 37, 55, 352
stop, question and frisk (SQF), 26, 27, 36–38, 111, 115, 117, 119
street-level behavior, 347
subjective causality, 170, 174, 179
systematic reviews, 85, 87, 88

third party policing, 90, 110, 111, 116, 119, 121, 165
tiered policing, 21, 353
transformation, 44, 55, 58, 315, 317

values, 74–78, 136, 141, 201, 205, 299, 301, 330, 339, 340, 351
victimization, 21, 25, 32, 34, 36, 50, 245, 305
violent crime, 9, 19, 27, 35–37, 115, 154, 254

what works?, 317